W9-BIP-531

CHILDREN WITH EXCEPTIONAL NEEDS:
A Survey of Special Education

CHILDREN WITH EXCEPTIONAL NEEDS

A Survey of Special Education

M. STEPHEN LILLY, *editor*
University of Illinois

HOLT, RINEHART AND WINSTON

*New York   Chicago   San Francisco   Dallas
Montreal   Toronto   London   Sydney*

Photo research by Yvette M. DeWindt.

Library of Congress Cataloging in Publication Data
Main entry under title:
Children with exceptional needs.

   Includes bibliographical references and indexes.
   1. Exceptional children—Education. I. Lilly,
M. Stephen, 1944–
LC3965.C47   371.9   78-26579

ISBN 0-03-021911-6

To *Marilyn*
   Matt
   Mark
   Rachel
   Stephen

With whom I expect to renew acquaintance as soon as I finish reading page proofs.

CONTRIBUTING AUTHORS

M. STEPHEN LILLY, Ed.D., is associate professor and chairman, Department of Special Education, University of Illinois at Urbana-Champaign. He received his doctor of education degree from George Peabody College for Teachers in 1969. Prior to assuming his current position, Dr. Lilly held faculty appointments at the University of Oregon and University of Minnesota, Duluth, as well as being a research coordinator in the Division of Research, Bureau of Education for the Handicapped, U. S. Office of Education. While at the University of Oregon, he was research coordinator for the Northwest Regional Special Education Instructional Materials Center. Dr. Lilly has been on the Research Committee and Publications Committee of the Council for Exceptional Children, and is an Associate Editor of *Exceptional Children*. He has been a major proponent of less reliance on traditional special education categories, and has several publications in this area. His current professional interests include policy development in special education, special education in the regular classroom, and listening as an alternative input mode for adolescent poor readers.

VERNA HART, Ed.D., is associate professor of special education at the University of Pittsburgh where she is preparing teachers to work with young handicapped children as well as with older children functioning at a pre-academic level. Before going to Pittsburgh, she spent five years at Peabody College where she coordinated the program for training teachers of multihandicapped children. She has held offices in The American Association for Education of the Severely and Profoundly Handicapped, The Council for Exceptional Children's Division for Early Childhood, and currently is secretary-treasurer of both the Association for Educators of the Visually Handicapped, and the Association for the Education of Deaf-Blind. She is a member of the Editorial Board of the *Journal for Visual Impairment and Blindness* and a reviewer for the *AAESPH Review*. Her recent research efforts include a study of drug use during pregnancy followed by an examination of the child at birth. She is working on evaluating motor development as her part of a six-university consortium developing an assessment instrument for all types of handicapped children functioning below two years of age. With teaching background and experience with all types of handicapped children, she obtained her doctorate from Wayne State University. She has authored many publications, including *Beginning with the Handicapped*.

JOHN T. HATTEN, Ph.D., is professor of communicative disorders at the University of Minnesota, Duluth. He received his degree at the University of Wisconsin where he conducted early research into the supervisory process in speech pathology. He holds the certificate of clinical competence in speech pathology from the American Speech and Hearing Association and had a number of years of experience as a public school speech clinician prior to entering university teaching. Publications include *Diagnosis and Evaluation in Speech Pathology*, co-authored with Lon L. Emerick; *Emerging Language*, co-authored with two clinicians working in the Duluth Public Schools; and *Natural Language*, co-authored with his wife, Pequetti.

DONALD F. MOORES, Ph.D., is head of the Division of Special Education at The Pennsylvania State University, where he is also professor of education of exceptional children and of speech pathology and audiology. He holds masters degrees in education of the deaf from Gallaudet College and California State University at Northridge. He received a Ph.D. in special education from the University of Illinois with an emphasis in psycholinguistics and learning theory. Professor Moores has five years of classroom experience as a teacher of the deaf. He was a professor of special education at the University of Minnesota from 1967 to 1977. He was director of the Research and Development Center in Education of Handicapped Children at the same institution from 1971 to 1977 before joining The Pennsylvania State University faculty in 1978. He has conducted research in the area of deafness in early childhood education, language acquisition of the deaf children of deaf parents, reading programs, language assessment, and technical vocational education. Professor Moores is the author of *Educating the Deaf: Psychology, Principles, and Practices* as well as numerous research monographs and chapters on educating the deaf.

DOROTHY SISK, Ed.D., is director of the Office of the Gifted and Talented, Bureau of Education for the Handicapped, U.S. Office of Education, Washington, D.C. Before this, she was professor at the University of South Florida, Tampa, in the area of teacher training for the gifted; president of the Association of the Gifted; international consultant in the area of the gifted; and a member of the executive board of the World Council for the Gifted and Talented. She received her doctor of education degree in special education from UCLA and her masters in education and psychology from California State College. Dr. Sisk is presently on the editorial board of the *Gifted Child Quarterly* and the *Journal of Talents and Gifts*. She is also vice-chairperson of the World Council of the Gifted and Talented, and is directing a national task force on the gifted and talented. She is the author of numerous articles and chapters on education of the gifted.

MAJORIE E. WARD, Ph.D., is presently on the faculty for exceptional children at The Ohio State University in the Low Incidence Program for Visually Handicapped. She taught English in a junior high school for two years, then was employed as an itinerant teacher of visually handicapped students for the Allegheny County Schools surrounding Pittsburgh, before moving on to initiate an itinerant program for visually handicapped for Dauphin County around Harrisburg, Pennsylvania. After completing her doctorate at the University of Pittsburgh, Dr. Ward joined the faculty at The Pennsylvania State University where she gained extensive experience in course development for computer-assisted instruction and was major author of a CAI course on education of visually handicapped designed for regular education personnel. She co-directed the Penn State Dean's Project and developed the special education supervision certificate program. Dr. Ward is a past president of the CEC Division for Visually Handicapped.

BARBARA L. WILCOX, Ph.D., is assistant professor of special education at the University of Illinois at Urbana-Champaign. Prior to assuming her current position, Dr. Wilcox was on the special education faculty at Temple University in Philadelphia. She holds a doctorate in Psychology from the University of Illinois. She initiated the teacher education program in the area of severely and profoundly handicapped at the University of Illinois and has worked to establish integrated educational services for severely handicapped students in local public schools. She has been a hearing officer and consultant to various special education parent groups. Dr. Wilcox is an associate editor of the *Review of the American Association for the Education of Severely/ Profoundly Handicapped,* a field editor for *Teaching Exceptional Children,* and a reviewer for several other professional journals.

PREFACE

Special education is a dynamic, rapidly changing field. Special and regular educators alike cannot operate in a vacuum. Special educators must be concerned not only about their school or school district, but also about issues confronting them in the field of special education as a whole. Regular educators must attend to the complex of educational and political decisions that are affecting their profession and their daily work situations. This book is devoted to an examination of special education in the 1980s, and explores both the historical context and present trends in special education. It is the editor's opinion that we are entering an era in which teachers and administrators must accomplish more than "doing their job well" on a day-to-day basis. Educators must be advocates for sound policymaking and quality program development. In keeping with this opinion, we have focused heavily on current and future trends in special education, as well as the social and political context in which special educators work.

Readers of this book who are familiar with the professional biases of the editor may be surprised to find that a number of the chapters carry traditional categorical titles. Clearly, we must become less dependent on traditional categories of exceptionality in special education. However, this does not mean that all labels used in special education should be discarded. The editor's writings on labels and categories in special education have focused primarily on the inadequacy of designations such as educable mental retardation, learning disabilities, and behavior disorders. This concern is adequately reflected in chapters 3 and 4. Other categorical descriptors such as visual impairment and hearing impairment are most appropriate, however, and are retained in the organization of the book. In short, the attempt is to deemphasize the categories in cases in which they are of questionable utility, and to maintain the categories when they are of obvious educational relevance.

Chapters 1 and 2 of the book cover the history of special education in the twentieth century in the United States, with chapter 2 devoted primarily to an exposition of issues that have developed during the 1970s and which will form the basis for special education development in the 1980s. Chapters 3 through 11 cover specific areas of special education. Two chapters focus on mild learning and behavior problems, and two chapters are devoted to severely and profoundly handicapped populations. The areas of crippling conditions, speech and language impairments, visual impairments, hearing impairments and special gifts and talents are covered in separate chapters. Finally, chapter 12 deals with two major professional issues in special education: funding and personnel preparation. While the primary emphasis is on children of school age, attention is also given to preschool and vocational programs.

In preparing this text, the editor was faced with deciding whether to attempt to write the entire book, or to use outside contributors in specific areas of expertise. In essence, this decision demands a balancing between positive and negative features of each approach. In this case, the decision was made to solicit contributions from experts in various areas of special education. In short, it is felt that the field is too complex to be adequately grasped or described by any individual. The editor has attempted to maintain continuity between chapters, and to avoid the "piecemeal" appearance which is a constant concern in preparing (and reading!) contributed texts. The first two chapters were read by all contributors prior to preparing their chapters, to help assure a common conceptual framework. Individual authors were encouraged to present their points of view, and editing has been done for the purpose of increasing clarity and continuity, not to produce a homogeneity of viewpoints. In general, it is felt that the richness and variety of ideas in a contributed text far outweigh possible drawbacks of such an approach. Further, all chapters are presented by individuals with bona fide professional expertise in the topics being addressed.

No attempt will be made here to limit the audience for our book. The editor and authors have endeavored to make the work substantive enough for use as a graduate textbook, and yet readable enough to be used by undergraduates and others with limited background in special education. We see it as appropriate for both regular educators who want to become familiar with all aspects of special education, and special educators who need to understand the total context in which they work. The book has been field tested with graduate and undergraduate students at the University of Illinois, and with in-service teachers in Prescott, Arizona. All of these groups included both special and regular educators, and feedback indicated that all groups considered the book both readable and informative. We will continue to assume the general utility of our work until more extensive user feedback provides a sounder basis for prediction.

Special thanks are due to Sam Ashcroft, Lloyd Dunn, Bob Henderson, and Ann Nevin, all of whom reviewed early chapter drafts and gave invaluable suggestions. Also, the corps of secretaries who prepared the manuscript, led by June Chambliss and including Shirley Lockard and Kathy Brake, were accurate, untiring, and patient beyond belief. Finally, an inestimable debt of gratitude is owed to my wife, Marilyn, and our children, Matt, Mark, Rachel, and Stephen, for their patience and encouragement. Sometimes, having people you love express their pride in what you're doing is all that is necessary to overcome frustration and get the job done.

M. Stephen Lilly
Champaign, Illinois
January 1979

CONTENTS

DETAILED CONTENTS

CHAPTER 1

SPECIAL EDUCATION
Historical and traditional perspectives

M. STEPHEN LILLY

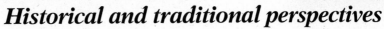

Of all of the social experiments attempted in history, one of the most challenging and perplexing has been the commitment to "education for all" which has been undertaken by the individual states in our country and by a number of other countries. Education as a right, or even privilege, of all citizens is a very recent phenomenon in the United States. Until the late 1800s, only a small percentage of the population enjoyed the benefits of formal education even at the elementary level.

A commitment to general education introduces enormous challenges, since our effort must be measured in terms not only of the *quantity* of schooling provided, but of its quality and appropriateness as well. Concern for quality has been a part of our education system since its inception, and special education has developed as an important means of striving to assure that education of the masses does not result in schooling geared only to the "average" student. Special education has been designed to ensure adequate attention to those whose school learning is either hindered by handicapping conditions, or sufficiently above or below school standards to require programs in addition to or instead of regular classroom instruction so as to maximize student growth and development.

In this book, special education will be presented and described in terms of both the children served and the array of educational services offered. Too often in the past, special education has been conceptualized solely on the basis of "handicapping conditions" of children, and decisions concerning service delivery have been predicated on the nature of the "handicap." Such an approach to providing special education has not proven to be effective in assuring that children's special school needs are met, for reasons to be discussed in detail in chapter 2. Emerging special education systems place primary emphasis on the *functional* problems of students in the educational setting, and special education services are designed to address and solve these problems directly. Handicapping conditions are not ignored in this approach, but are considered in combination with other factors insofar as they affect the child's educational needs and the services required to meet those needs. While a functional approach to defining special education services is often not reflected in actual practice, it is a future-oriented approach and will serve as a basic organizer in much of our discussion.

In endeavoring to understand the field of special education and the children it serves, it is important to recognize that special education is not a well-developed science with precise technologies of teaching, awaiting only the investment of resources necessary to deliver services to all children with special needs. On the contrary, special education is a field of continuing development and is characterized by ongoing refinement of knowledge and constant searching for new and better approaches to meeting the individual needs of children. While a state of continual development and change is perplexing to some, it is challenging to most, and constant striving for excellence by many special educators results in a vibrant, responsive professional body. This book is another chapter in the saga of special education, an attempt to chronicle the most recent and most promising developments in the field. We will begin with a look at where we have been and where we are going in the general field of special education, and will proceed from there to treatment of more specific topical areas in the field. The remainder of this chapter will present a historical sketch of special education, and an overview of handicapping conditions as traditionally defined.

SPECIAL EDUCATION—PAST TO PRESENT

The purpose of this section is to provide a brief review of selected aspects of the relatively recent history of special education, and to aid in a better understanding of special education today. The review is broken into four time periods:

1800–1900—Special education treatment begins; residential schooling is stressed.
1900–1925—Many residential schools become custodial in nature; "new" handicaps are discovered.
1925–1960—All types of special education service undergo continuous, steady expansion.

1960–1970—Controversy begins to develop concerning nature and role of special education; federal influence increases.

This section does not provide a complete history or cover all areas of special education; historical perspectives are given in subsequent chapters. For the reader with a special interest in historical information, a more comprehensive history of special education is available in Hewett (1977).

1800–1900

Special education was begun in the United States in the early 1800s and for about a century afterward nearly all special education consisted of residential programs for persons with visual or hearing impairment, or who were moderately or severely mentally retarded, or severely emotionally disturbed. The initial goal of many residential school programs, particularly for the mentally retarded, was an optimistic one: to provide corrective education (primarily "sensory training") that would ameliorate the handicapping condition and allow large numbers of handicapped individuals to return to the community (Wolfensberger, 1969). Commitment to these residential centers was often mandatory, and in many cases was demanded by court order. In the latter half of the nineteenth century, residential schools for the sensorially handicapped and the severely retarded and disturbed expanded rapidly and comprised the primary mode of service delivery in special education. During this period, little systematic attention was given to persons whose problems were milder in nature and less obvious in appearance.

During the second half of the last century, a new era of educational history began to emerge that would have profound impact on the size and nature of the special education system. Over a period of a relatively few years beginning around 1850, states changed their public education laws from *permissive* to *mandatory*, thus requiring parents to send their children to school until a certain age. While public education had been available since the early 1800s, it had been up to the parents to send or not to send their children to school. Most parents, particularly those of limited means, chose to keep their children at home so that they could contribute in some way to the family's survival and well-being.

Compulsory attendance laws gradually reshaped the face of American education, from a system designed to meet the needs of children of the upper class to a multifaceted system addressing the varied academic, social, and vocational needs of a population as diverse as that of the United States. Naturally, the adjustment of the education system to this turn of events was slow and difficult, as is evidenced by the fact that to this day vestiges of education for the elite are found in many school curricula. Compulsory attendance laws introduced a new clientele, for whom public schools were required to program educational experiences, and this movement represented the initial impetus for much of special education as we know it today.

1900–1925

By the early 1900s, the importance of education to American society was becoming firmly entrenched, and universal education *for those able to benefit from it* was becoming an accepted rule. In terms of special education, the nature of the residential facilities for the mentally retarded and emotionally disturbed which had been developing since the 1850s was beginning to change. The high hopes for cure of mental retardation through sensory training were being tempered by the harsh reality that it wasn't working. The vast majority of persons who had been sent to these residential centers for treatment and cure either had died in the institution, or were still there and not making adequate progress toward normalcy. The residential institutions gradually became more custodial than educational, and residents were admitted with the expectation that they would live out the remainder of their lives in the sheltered surroundings of the institutions. In short, the residential centers for the mentally retarded, which were begun with such high hopes and good intentions, were rapidly becoming the vehicles for protecting the handicapped from society and society from the handicapped.

Perhaps the most important and far-reaching event of the early 1900s with respect to special education was the development in France and eventual translation into English of intelligence tests. Upon request of the French government, Theodore Simon and Alfred Binet began work on tests to predict school achievement, and out of this work were published, in 1905, individual tests of intelligence. These tests were quickly translated into English, and the early 1900s saw a flurry of work on revision and standardization of individual tests. The Binet-Simon test was first translated by Henry Goddard in 1908, and the most famous and lasting outcome of this research is the Stanford-Binet Intelligence Test, first published in 1916 and used to this day in revised form.

Interest in intelligence tests was heightened in the early 1900s because of the increasing effects of compulsory attendance in terms of numbers of children attending school. Many children were coming to school not because of interest or parental pressure, but because they were forced to attend. The curriculum of the schools was not geared to these students, but rather to the children of the elite who were bound for higher education. Naturally, when these schools and children met, problems ensued, problems often couched in questions such as: "What's wrong with these students that prevents them from learning what is offered in the classroom?" Intelligence tests provided an answer to that question by defining a new group of "handicapped individuals," called "morons" at the time and "mildly mentally retarded" today. These children had not been identified as handicapped before, because they deviated most significantly from societal norms in terms of school achievement and behavior, and thus were not necessarily recognized as deviant outside the school setting. This identification of the "mildly retarded" and subsequent development of expanded special education services was an extremely significant happening in special education, since it represented the first definition of mild handicapping conditions. More importantly, the basis for school problems was firmly established as existing in the individual, not the interaction between the individual and his school environment, an assumption that still permeates the categorical structure of special education services today.

The development of intelligence tests had an extreme effect on society's view of deviance in the early 1900s, an effect which was primarily negative. The prevailing notion of psychologists involved in development and refinement of intelligence tests was that intelligence is a fixed and undeniable individual trait that has a pervading influence on a person's life. Intelligence was seen as hereditary, and low intelligence was associated with a wide array of societal ills such as crime, sexual promiscuity, and poverty. Widely respected psychologists such as G. Stanley Hall, Henry Goddard, Lewis Terman, Edward L. Thorndike, and Sir Cyril Burt all voiced support for the notion that intelligence is hereditary, and the outcome was a strong movement toward "eugenics," or selective breeding and prohibition of breeding for the purpose of improving the human genetic stock. Respected professional groups developed with names such as Committee on Inheritance of Mental Traits, Committee on the Heredity of the Feebleminded, Human Betterment Foundation, and Committee to Study and Report on the Best Practical Means of Cutting Off the Defective Germ-Plasm in the American Population (Karier, 1973).

One natural outcome of the emphasis on hereditary aspects of intelligence was the development of laws and regulations encouraging (often requiring) sterilization of persons judged to be incompetent. Sterilization was an accepted social phenomenon during the early 1900s. Karier (1973) estimates that between 1907 and 1928, over 8,500 persons were sterilized in twenty-one states. Sterilization was used not only for the mentally retarded, but for those with other impairments as well as social and criminal offenders with offenses ranging from sexual promiscuity and prostitution to chicken stealing.

In summary, the first twenty years of the present century must be viewed as both positive and negative in the history of special education. On one hand, significant advances in public acceptance of the importance of universal schooling brought about an increased attention to the educational problems of children who had not previously been considered in need of special education. This awareness laid the groundwork for a significant expansion of the realm of special education and planted the seeds for much of its value as we know it today. On the other hand, some of the very forces which brought about this awareness carried their own negative influences. Because of the heavy emphasis on intelligence in identification of children having school problems, a *child-based* identification system was established for special education which assumed that the cause of educational problems was in the child, a system which persists to this day. Further, because of improper assumptions concerning the heredity of intelligence and the pervasive effects of intelligence on many aspects of social behavior, treatment and control systems were established which stressed separation of the handicapped from the normal population, a tendency which has proven difficult to overcome. It is difficult to maintain that the early 1900s was a pleasant time to live for a person with low-measured intelligence or a handicapping condition; this era exemplifies the fact that increased attention to a situation can in fact be a two-edged sword.

1925–1960

The period from 1925 to 1960 will be covered in a single section, since it can be seen primarily as a period of expansion, sometimes rapid and sometimes slow moving, for special education. Almost all special education of this period was centered in either residential institutions, special day schools which enrolled only special education students, or special classes in regular school buildings. Some special educators, particularly in areas such as visual impairment, developed itinerant teacher and resource room programs that allowed children to spend part or all of the day in the regular classroom while receiving supportive help from a specialist. However, this was the exception rather than the rule.

Growth of special education during these thirty-five years was slow and steady until the early 1950s, which saw a rapid expansion of select areas of special education. The most significant happenings during this period are discussed below.

1. In the 1920s and, to a greater extent, the 1930s, a new area of special education came into its own, public school education of children with "mild emotional disturbance," or behavior disorders. Until this time, programs in the area of emotional disturbance had been primarily residential, for children and adults with severe emotional problems. Treatment had been primarily psychiatric in nature, and residential centers for the emotionally disturbed had seen a trend toward "development of segregated, depersonalized, often cruel custodial care" (Long, Morse, & Newman, 1976, p. 361). The increased emphasis in the 1930s on school-based services for children (mostly boys) with problems of acting-out or, occasionally, withdrawal behavior resulted in development of a large number of special class programs for children who were judged to be too disruptive for the regular classroom setting, but who did not score low enough on intelligence tests to be called mildly retarded.

2. In the area of mental retardation, the period from 1925 to 1960 saw dramatic expansion of special classes for the mildly retarded, who came to be called "educable mentally retarded" (EMR). The growth in EMR special classes was slow but stable until 1950. Then, during the decade between 1950 and 1960, the area figuratively exploded in terms of numbers of classes established and numbers of children served. Kirk (1964) estimated that EMR special class enrollment increased tenfold between

the early 1920s and late 1950s, and the majority of the growth occurred during the last ten years of that period of time. During the 1950s, teacher preparation programs were established at colleges and universities across the country to train teachers of the educable mentally retarded, but expansion of school services happened at such a phenomenal rate that the supply of trained teachers could not meet the demand. Another spin-off of the rapid growth of EMR programs was that schools often did not have available space for special classes, which ended up housed everywhere from storage rooms to boiler rooms. Since the setting for special classes was often far from ideal, and the teachers were more often than not prepared for their jobs through "crash" training efforts, the quality of the programs was subject to wide variation.

3. During the 1940s, and to an increasing extent during the 1950s, special educators began to research the effectiveness of special classes for the "educable mentally retarded" and "mildly emotionally disturbed." Numerous studies were reported in the literature comparing academic and social progress of children in special classes and children with similar characteristics who did not receive special education services. The results of these studies were, in general, not encouraging for advocates of special class services. In the area of educable mental retardation, it was generally found that students in special classes did not learn more academically than their regular class peers; in some cases, their academic growth was actually slower. The situation was slightly better in terms of social adjustment, though not enough better to make an unequivocal case for continued expansion of special class services. Kirk (1964), in reviewing the studies on EMR special class placement, warned that research findings could not justify the conclusion that special class placement is superior to regular education for EMR students.

While there were fewer studies in the area of behavior disorders, some more encouraging in their results, the comments of Rubin, Simson, and Betwee (1966) in summarizing their comparatively well-designed study of the efficacy of special classes for the "emotionally handicapped" is indicative of other findings:

> The results, themselves, are not dramatic nor do they contribute to an overwhelming confirmation of the initial hypothesis—that special class programming is generally beneficial to emotionally handicapped children as a specific method of intervention and correction.

These efficacy studies, while often ambiguous in outcome and subject to criticism on theoretical and methodological grounds, were important in helping to establish the climate for change in special education from 1960 to the present.

4. With reference to education of moderately and severely retarded individuals from 1925 to 1960, there was little debate: for almost the entire period of time, it was assumed that these children were not the responsi-

bility of the public schools. Almost all public school systems during this period of time had "minimum entry requirements," and the standard requirements were that a child needed to be toilet trained, ambulatory, and have understandable oral language before he could attend the public schools. Furthermore, in addition to being barred from school, children who did not meet these requirements generally received no public assistance in seeking alternate forms of education. The most common form of educational service provided to the moderately and severely retarded during this period consisted of special day schools run by private agencies, most often local chapters of the National Association for Retarded Children, a parents' group. These schools were often established in church basements or converted garages, and were staffed by teachers and aides who more often than not worked for wages which made the job more volunteer than occupational. The primary focus of most of these schools was on teaching self-help and socialization skills, and academic subjects were generally not covered since it was commonly assumed that these children would not be able to learn functional academic skills. It was not until the late 1950s that public school services for moderately retarded children became a subject of discussion and debate (Goldberg v. Cruickshank, 1958), and it was well into 1970s before most local school systems began to consider serving severely and profoundly retarded individuals.

5. Another area of special education which began to receive increased emphasis during the 1950s was education of gifted and talented children. This field has been of continuing interest to a small number of dedicated and persistent individuals since the early 1900s (not surprisingly, some of the early advocates of eugenics were also strong advocates of special programs for the gifted), but it took the impetus of the race for superiority in space exploration between the United States and Russia to establish education of the gifted and talented as a matter of high priority on the national agenda. Even then, public support for programs for the gifted waned as other items competed for national and state attention, and the dramatic increase in programs for the gifted that occurred during the late 1950s and early 1960s gave way to a steady but nonescalating maintenance of programs in a few school districts, often with limited or no state and federal support. Until very recently, the argument could not be made that education of gifted and talented youngsters is a matter of national priority. Even its recent resurgence (to be discussed in a subsequent section) has not been accompanied by a significant investment of money necessary to mount comprehensive and effective programs.

6. While the major activities that served as harbingers of change in special education occurred in the areas described above during the 1950s, it should also be mentioned that development of programs for the visually impaired, hearing impaired, speech impaired, and crippled maintained a steady growth rate over the entire period. With regard to programs for students with vision and hearing problems, the period from 1925 to 1960 saw an increase in the number of states offering residential school ser-

vices, but at the same time a proportionately greater increase in special class and resource services in the public schools. While parents were often encouraged to send children to the residential schools for their education, they were less often ordered to do so by court authorities. Educational services for orthopedically handicapped children also increased during this period, with almost all such services being provided in special classes or special schools, the latter often being privately operated facilities. During this period, crippling conditions were seen to be educational handicaps in and of themselves, and it was not unusual to find classrooms of children with orthopedic handicaps whose ranges of age and ability were extraordinarily broad. Also, during this period, services for speech-impaired children continued to expand, *becoming the single largest area of special education.* Almost all speech services for school-age children were offered on a tutorial basis in the public schools, and involved removal of children from the regular classroom for only short periods, two or three times a week. At this time, speech clinicians were by and large not trained to work with speech and language problems of moderately and severely handicapped individuals, and were not often involved in education of these children.

7. A significant happening of the 1950s was the establishment of university programs of research and teacher preparation in special education. In the late 1940s and early 1950s, advanced graduate programs were begun by Samuel Kirk at the University of Illinois, Lloyd Dunn at Peabody College in Nashville, William Cruickshank at Syracuse University, and others. These university programs, nearly all of which began in the area of mental retardation, were important not only because they began to produce trained personnel for special education teaching positions, but also because of their early capability for and emphasis on research. The relative newness of special education at that time demanded that nearly all questions be asked in a research framework. The emergence of university programs with research capabilities helped to assure that inefficient or ineffective practices were called into question and not allowed to establish themselves as an unalterable part of the educational status quo. The number of universities involved in special education had expanded to more than six hundred in 1978, but the capability for research, which has proven so invaluable in developing special education programs and practices, is still confined to a relatively small number of major programs.

8. Perhaps the most significant seeds for special education growth that were planted in the 1950s were in the federal and state governments, since these were to grow into major movements from 1960 to the present time. While a few state governments such as New Jersey, New York, and Massachusetts had enacted mandatory special education legislation in the early 1900s, the majority of the states enacted permissive legislation that *allowed* but did not *require* local school districts to provide special education services under the states' compulsory attendance laws. Where mandates did exist in legislation, they were often confined to the area of

educable mental retardation (Weintraub, Abeson, & Braddock, 1975). While very few states adopted mandatory special education legislation during the 1950s, the state involvement in special education planning and finance increased dramatically during this period, laying the groundwork for later shifts to mandatory legislation. Federal government involvement in special education also began in the late 1950s, with small investments of money and program assistance, and expansion of the federal role is one of the most dramatic stories to be told of the 1960s and 1970s.

It can be said that the period from 1925 to 1960 saw significant expansion in all areas of special education, but particularly in the area of "mild mental retardation." The period was one of learning for special educators, who were often "doing things for the first time." Development of programs during this period was based primarily on the special class model, with special school and residential school placement being common for more obviously and/or severely handicapped individuals. Perhaps most importantly, this period saw the beginning of an intensive quest in special education for the most effective means of serving children. Through research efforts involving university faculty and public school personnel, we began to ask searching questions concerning the efficiency and effectiveness of the common models for special education. In short, special education became an experimental venture and the stage was set for the coming events of the 1960s and 1970s.

1960–1970

While the 1950s was a time of significant increase in the number of children served in the areas of educable mental retardation and emotional disturbance, the 1960s (particularly from 1966–1970) witnessed growth in all areas of special education as well as critical examination of many commonly accepted special education practices. The following are the most noteworthy events and issues of the 1960s.

1. Perhaps the most far-reaching set of events of this decade surrounded the emergence of the federal government as a major factor in both finance and policymaking in special education. This expanded role can be traced directly to the interest of President John F. Kennedy in the area of mental retardation. President Kennedy had been closely involved as a U. S. senator in passage of Public Law 85–926 in 1958, which authorized grants to colleges, universities, and state education agencies to prepare teachers of the mentally retarded. In 1963, under the leadership of then-President Kennedy, Public Law 88–164 was passed, which expanded the teacher-training authorization to "mentally retarded, hard of hearing, deaf, speech impaired, visually handicapped, seriously emotionally disturbed, crippled, or other health-impaired children who by reason thereof require special education" (Burke, 1976, p. 144). In addition, P.L. 88–164 mandated a program of research and demonstration in the education of the handicapped, to be administered separate from general education re-

search funds in the U. S. Office of Education.

To administer P.L. 88-164, President Kennedy created in 1963, by executive order, the Division of Handicapped Children and Youth as a unit within the U. S. Office of Education. This was the first time that special education had its own identity within the federal government, and the move was greeted with considerable enthusiasm by leaders in the field. Eighteen months later, however, the division was disbanded and its responsibilities spread among several units within the Office of Education. This state of affairs was not to continue for long; in 1966, passage of P.L. 89-313 created the Bureau of Education for the Handicapped (BEH) within the U. S. Office of Education, as well as the National Advisory Committee on Handicapped Children. In addition, P.L. 89-313 expanded the role of the federal government by authorizing direct formula grants to states for initiation, expansion, and improvement of special education programs (Martin, 1976).

Establishment of BEH as a legislated entity within the U. S. Office of Education was seen as ensuring a consistent and unified voice for special education within the federal bureaucracy. The Bureau has provided a mechanism for steadily expanding the federal investment in special education over the last decade. Martin (1976) points out that special education funds at the federal level increased tenfold from 1966 to 1976, adding that federal programs during the 1960s "were expressions of the national conscience striving to serve state and local consciences" (p. 133).

Federal programs for special education during the 1960s were of three types. First, grants were provided to colleges, universities, and state agencies for preparation of special education teachers in the various categories of handicapping conditions. These funds provided support in the form of fellowships and assistantships for students pursuing special education degrees and certification, and were often used to meet other program costs such as faculty salaries and program development expenses. While many training programs at colleges and universities were begun with almost total reliance on federal dollars, most such programs have gradually acquired state and local funds to cover most or all of faculty salaries and related expenses. Federal funds for preparation of special education teachers continue to be available to the present time with over $45 million being spent for this purpose in 1978. Special education personnel preparation is discussed in more detail in chapter 12.

A second type of federal support during the 1960s consisted of grants for research and demonstration projects on education of the handicapped. This program, administered through the Division of Research of BEH, awarded grants and contracts on a competitive basis to individuals and organizations for research and demonstration activities. Most of the landmark special education research projects of the 1960s were funded through the BEH Division of Research, as were pioneering developments in the field such as alternate reading systems for the blind, and speech-training aids for the deaf. Many curricular materials in various areas of special education have been developed under this authority, and demonstration centers in areas such as learning disabilities, deaf-blind, and severely/profoundly handicapped have been established. BEH continues to fund field-initiated projects and student research projects, as well as soliciting research and demonstration on specific topics of interest through requests for proposals.

The third type of federal support for special education during the 1960s, which has exhibited the greatest rate of growth in the 1970s, is direct aid to states for initiation, expansion, and improvement of special education services. While the federal money which flows directly to states and local school systems has increased dramatically since 1966, so has the federal monitoring of state and local special education activities, as will be discussed in chapter 2.

In summary, the role of the federal government in special education has gone from next-to-nothing in 1958 to unprecedented levels at the present time. The seeds for this growth in the federal role were sewn in the 1960s, and it is probably the most significant happening of that decade for special education.

2. Related to the growth of the role of the federal government in special education is another significant happening of the 1960s, establishment of a new category of exceptionality. While services for children labeled EMR had undergone significant expansion through the early 1960s, it was clear to many special and regular educators that the categories of exceptionality enumerated in P.L. 88-164 and cited above were not sufficient. The problem was that a group of children existed who (a) did not score low enough on tests of intelligence to be called mentally retarded, (b) did not exhibit behavioral aberrance necessary to be called emotionally disturbed, but (c) were in need of special education services due to poor performance in their schoolwork. In effect, while professional educators and parents could agree they needed special help, these children "fell between the cracks" of the then-existing categories of exceptionality. Further, since practically all state and federal funding systems were predicated on the list of "handicaps" established in P.L. 88-164, or a reasonably similar list, it was often impossible to provide special education to these children and expect any financial assistance from the state or federal level.

In the late 1960s, a few states began to add the category "learning disabilities" (LD) to the list of exceptionalities to be served by special education, and by 1969, twelve states had legislation specifically containing provisions for LD services (Gearhart, 1973). Textbooks began to appear in the area, and professionals in the field began to declare LD as an area of primary interest and concern. During the latter part of the 1960s, BEH provided some funds for training of teachers in the area of learning disabilities under the category of "other health impaired" as contained in P.L. 88-164. The area of learning disabilities received national recognition in 1970, when it was added to the language of the federal statutes as a part of P.L. 91-230.

Courtesy of The Muscular Dystrophy Association.

The brief history of the field of learning disabilities, from the mid-1960s to the present, has been a series of controversies concerning definition, provision of services, and labeling practices. This controversy is dealt with in detail in chapter 3. At this point, it is sufficient to realize the emergence of the area of learning disabilities has had a profound effect on education of children with mild learning and behavior problems, and has served as a catalyst for reexamination of the areas of educable mental retardation and behavior disorders (or "mild emotional disturbance") as well.

3. Another significant development of the 1960s was an increase in the number of states mandating special education services for handicapped children. As mentioned earlier, most state laws for the 1950s and earlier *permitted* local districts to provide special education services and provided state funds to districts which elected to do so. With permissive legislation, it was altogether possible for a school district to offer no special

education services, regardless of the needs of children in the district. During the 1960s, a number of states adopted mandatory special education laws which require school districts to provide special education in certain described circumstances. It cannot be assumed that a mandatory special education law results in delivery of services to all children with special needs, for two reasons: (a) there are various types of mandates (as is discussed in chapter 12); and (b) it is possible for a mandate to exist in state law and be ignored at the local level, either because it is not taken seriously or because adequate enforcement mechanisms do not exist to ensure compliance. Thus, the state mandates introduced in the 1960s did not immediately assure appropriate special education for all who needed it. However, the move to mandatory state legislation began to establish special education as a *right* of children, rather than a privilege bestowed by a benevolent society. Mandatory legislation began to make it possible for parents and advocate groups to be aggressive in seeking needed services for children without risking the wrath of those who provided the money. Evelyn Deno (1970) has described early efforts to obtain financial support for special education as feeding on "wellsprings of sympathy" (p. 229), and it has not been uncommon for legislators and other benefactors to approach special education as a charity, for which there is a social but not a legal obligation. While appeal to sympathy is an effective means of assuring that pocketbooks will be opened and money will flow, the major drawback to such an approach is that recipients of charity are expected to be grateful, and not "bite the hand that feeds." Establishment of special education as a right of children has made possible a more aggressive search for the most comprehensive and effective system of special education, and state laws mandating special education were an early force in bringing about the acceptance of such a commitment.

4. Another significant movement of the 1960s was increased public school services for moderately handicapped children who had previously been educated either in institutions or in private day schools, which as pointed out earlier were often run by parent groups. The debate of the late 1950s concerning the public school responsibility for students who were thought not capable of learning traditional academic subjects resulted in significant expansion of public school services for children whose handicaps are obvious and significant. While the 1960s saw an increase in public school special classes and day schools for the moderately handicapped, there remained a large number of severely and profoundly handicapped individuals who were excluded from even these classes and for whom public support for education was not available. It is significant to note, however, that the scope of public school responsibility for handicapped children continued to expand during this period.

5. While special education continued to expand during the 1960s, there were also significant controversies brewing which became matters of general discussion among professionals in the field. The two most significant controversial issues of the 1960s were the problems surrounding use of

disability labels as a basis for planning and delivery of special education services, and the efficacy of special classes in producing positive educational results with children. The controversy surrounding traditional categories used to define children in need of special education services is dealt dealt with in detail in chapter 2, and is described here only in terms of the beginnings of the controversy during the 1960s. Four major factors were instrumental in evoking a critical reexamination of categorical labels for children in special education, a reexamination which was confined primarily to areas referred to as "mild handicaps" such as educable mental retardation, behavior disorders, and in the latter part of the 1960s, learning disabilities. First, intelligence tests, which were used as the primary determiner of mental retardation, were coming under increasing attack during this period, with charges that they were racially and socioeconomically biased and did not provide a valid indication of the intelligence of poor and minority-group children. Second, and clearly related to the first point, it was becoming increasingly obvious that special classes for the educable mentally retarded contained disproportionate numbers of poor and minority-group children (Franks, 1971). Socially conscious special educators such as Johnson (1969) began to question whether special education was providing an excuse for school systems which were experiencing failures of instruction, by pinpointing the problem "within the child." A third factor which contributed to the discussion of the negative effects of special education categories was the increasingly verbal concern voiced by special educators that the categories provided only an administrative means of collecting support funds from the state, and were not useful in planning instruction for children. Reger, Schroeder, and Uschold (1968) exemplify the concern of many special educators in stating that "grouping children on the basis of medically derived disability labels has no practical utility in the schools" (p. 19). Finally, the fourth factor which served as an impetus to the labeling controversy was establishment of learning disabilities as a distinct and separate category of exceptionality, an action taken by several states in the late 1960s and formalized in federal legislation in 1970. At the time the area of learning disabilities came into existence, many special educators did not see the area as a new category of exceptionality, but as an organizing concept around which much of special education could build. Indeed, it was a common expectation that the emergence of an emphasis on "learning disabilities" would lead to an eventual restructuring of the administrative and instructional bases of special education. These developments did not come to pass, and learning disabilities became a category of exceptionality as distinct and separate as any other. However, the discussion generated during the emergence of the area of learning disabilities became another force toward the reassessment of the use of categorical labels with children. This reexamination blossomed into a full-scale debate in the 1970s.

The second area of controversy which grew during the 1960s surrounded the efficacy of various types of administrative arrangements for delivery of special education services to children. The focus of most of the discussion during this period was on the advisability of special class placement for children labeled educable mentally retarded or behavior disordered, although the range of the discussion was to broaden considerably during the 1970s. As early as 1960, Burton Blatt wrote that "it has yet to be demonstrated that the special class offers a better school experience for retarded children than does regular class placement" (p. 54). The controversy continued through the 1960s, and in 1968 Dunn published a landmark article entitled, "Special Education for the Mildly Retarded: Is Much of It Justifiable?" In this article, Dunn questioned the "open arms" attitude with which special educators were willing to accept the instructional problems of general education, and recommended the abolition of most special classes for the mildly retarded. In this article, Dunn stated:

> In my view, much of our past and present practices are morally and educationally wrong. We have been living at the mercy of general educators who have referred their problem children to us. And we have been generally ill prepared and ineffective in educating these children. Let us stop being pressured into continuing and expanding a special education program that we know now to be undesirable for many of the children we are dedicated to serve (p. 5).

As with the labeling issue, the controversy concerning administrative arrangements for special education services expanded to include much more than EMR special classes in the 1970s, but the seeds of the controversy were sewn during the late 1960s.

6. A final point to be made with regard to significant happenings of the 1960s in special education concerns an area of endeavor that started on a small scale during that period and became a major concern of the special education community during the 1970s—the area of education litigation. As special education came to be considered a right rather than a privilege of children during the 1960s, it also became apparent that a viable mechanism for assuring the rights of children is through court suits seeking redress of grievances. An early special education-related court action occurred in Washington, D. C., in 1968, and resulted in abolition of a tracking system within the District of Columbia public schools which, in the words of Judge Skelley Wright (1968), discriminated against and "stigmatized the disadvantaged child of whatever race relegated to its lower track" (p. 210). While this court decision did not directly relate to a special education program, its implications for EMR special classes containing disproportionate numbers of poor and minority children were clear. Soon thereafter, lawsuits were filed charging discrimination in testing and subsequent placement of children in special education, and the era of special education and the courts began.

In summary, the decade between 1960 and 1970 saw significant developments in the field of special education, developments which were destined to have major impact on the future of *both* special and regular education. As we discuss the exciting and expansive happenings in special education in the 1970s, it will be readily discernible that seemingly revolutionary events are but logical extensions of prior developments in the field.

Before launching into an analysis of the major movements in special education in the 1970s, a task that will involve discussion of positive and negative aspects of traditional categories of exceptionality in special education, it is necessary first to review those categories of exceptionality. Thus, the final section of this chapter briefly analyzes the areas of exceptionality that were the bases for nearly all special education planning and service delivery through the mid-1970s. This analysis is not intended to provide a thorough understanding of the categories of exceptionality, a task reserved for chapters 3–11, but rather is designed to provide information necessary to gain a sound perspective on the information presented in chapter 2.

CATEGORIES OF EXCEPTIONALITY—A TRADITIONAL OVERVIEW

As indicated thus far, special education has been conceptualized from its inception as a system to serve "exceptional children," and the basic framework within which special education problems have been identified has always been "child-based." A typical definition of exceptional children is offered by Kirk (1972):

> An exceptional child is a child who deviates from the average or normal child (1) in mental characteristics, (2) in sensory abilities, (3) in neuromuscular or physical characteristics, (4) in social or emotional behavior, (5) in communication abilities, or (6) in multiple handicaps to such an extent that he requires a modification of school practices, or special education services, in order to develop to his maximum capacity (p. 4).

Traditional estimates of the number of exceptional children of school age generally range from 10 percent to 15 percent of the school population, and in nearly all states, it is necessary to diagnose and classify a child as exceptional before a school district can seek state support for special education services. The concept of child-based exceptionality has been used in establishing state and federal support systems for special education, and has served as the basis for teacher preparation and certification as well. Thus, it has become common to speak of "exceptional children," rather than "exceptional educational needs."

By the early 1970s, the following categories of exceptionality (with some slight variation from state-to-state and author-to-author) were used to classify exceptional children:

1. Mental Retardation
   a. Educable
   b. Trainable

    c. Custodial
2. Emotional Disturbance
    a. Behavior Disorders
    b. Severe Emotional Disturbance
3. Learning Disabilities
4. Visual Impairments
    a. Blind
    b. Partially Sighted
5. Hearing Impairments
    a. Deaf
    b. Hard-of-hearing
6. Speech Impairments
7. Orthopedic Handicaps and Special Health Conditions
8. Giftedness

Mental Retardation

Mental retardation has been defined by the American Association on Mental Deficiency (Grossman, 1973) as follows:

> Mental retardation refers to significantly subaverage general intellectual functioning existing concurrently with deficits in adaptive behavior, and manifested during the developmental period (p. 11).

This definition focuses on multiple conditions which must be met before a person is labeled mentally retarded. For the most part, however, the intelligence quotient (IQ) as determined by a standardized, individual test of intelligence has been used as the primary determiner of mental retardation. Individual states and school districts have set arbitrary IQ cutoffs below which children can be called mentally retarded for the purpose of providing special education, cutoffs ranging from 70 to 85. Thus, operational definitions of mental retardation vary from state to state, but are nearly always based on IQ scores as the major determinant. Further, a child might be called mentally retarded in one state but not in another, depending on the specific IQ cutoff points which have been established.

The distinctions between educable (EMR), trainable (TMR), and custodial (CMR) mental retardation are implied in the terms themselves. EMR children have been defined as "those pupils who experienced so much difficulty progressing through general education because they developed intellectually at only about one half to three quarters the rate of average children (IQ 50–75) that they required special education services" (Dunn, 1973, p. 127). It was generally agreed by experts in the field of mental retardation that EMR children would develop functional (fourth to sixth grade) academic skills during their school careers, and would lead independent lives after their school careers, usually working in semiskilled or unskilled occupations. These children were called "educable" because of the assumption that they could learn functional academic skills, thus being capable of "education" in the traditional sense of the word.

TMR children were commonly defined as scoring between 25 and 50 on intelligence tests, an IQ range presumed to mean that a TMR child developed at the rate of one fourth to one half that of a normal child. Extrapolating from IQ scores, the assumption was made that TMR children would not learn functional academic skills, but could learn limited sight words, self-help skills, and basic social skills. Because of these assumptions, children labeled TMR were generally not taught academic subjects. Instead, they were prepared for a life of sheltered living and work situations.

CMR children, generally defined as having IQ's below 25, were not presumed to be able to learn useful academic, social, or self-help skills, and were generally not educated until the 1970s. The common recommendation to parents of CMR children was to institutionalize them, an action often recommended as being in the best interest of both the child and the family.

Obviously, this classification system for mental retardation was heavily dependent on IQ scores, and the very classification used tended to set predetermined limits for children. If classified TMR, the child was presented with a curriculum designed for TMR children, which meant that academic skills were not taught since TMR children could not learn functional academics. Thus, it was not surprising that TMR children did not learn to read, thereby confirming the definition. In 1961, the American Association on Mental Deficiency proposed a new classification scheme for mental retardation with four levels, mild (previously EMR), moderate (previously TMR), severe, and profound. As with the AAMD definition of mental retardation, this classification scheme received considerable professional attention but was rarely translated into policy at the local, state, or federal level.

Emotional Disturbance

By and large, emotional disturbance has been defined in terms of behavior which is both persistent and not compatible with cultural norms. For example, Kirk (1972) defined a "behavior disorder" as "deviation from age-appropriate behavior which significantly interferes with (1) the child's own growth and development and/or (2) the lives of others" (p. 389). In recent years, there has been a tendency among professionals in the field to speak of "behavior disorders" rather than "emotional disturbance." For example, Graubard (1973) offers the following definition of this term:

> Behavioral disabilities are defined as a variety of excessive, chronic, deviant behaviors ranging from impulsive and aggressive to depressive and withdrawal acts (1) which violate the perceiver's expectations of appropriateness and (2) which the perceiver wishes to see stopped (p. 246).

Emotional disturbance, or behavior disorder, has generally been dealt with as a single set of behavioral manifestations. However, it has become increasingly clear that a distinction is needed between children with behavioral problems of a relatively mild nature, i.e., children who have been or are in regular classrooms for all or part of the school day, and children with severe emotional problems which result in markedly abnormal behavior. The former group of children is the group for whom the term "behavioral disorders" has come into common use. The typical patterns of behavior for these children are: (1) "conduct" problems (such as hitting or boisterous behavior in the classroom); (2) "personality" problems (such as lack of social interaction, fearfulness, and depression); and (3) "immaturity" problems (such as lack of interest, dislike for school, and inattentiveness) (Quay, Morse, & Cutler, 1966). The latter group of children, typically called "seriously emotionally disturbed," generally exhibit uncharacteristic behaviors in the extreme, and are often termed psychotic, childhood schizophrenic, or autistic.

Learning Disabilities

The most commonly accepted definition of learning disabilities is the one proposed by the National Advisory Committee on Handicapped Children (1968) and since adopted with only minor variations in nearly all state legislation:

> Children with special learning disabilities exhibit a disorder in one or more of the basic psychological processes involved in understanding or in using spoken or written language. These may be manifested in disorders of listening, thinking, talking, reading, writing, spelling, or arithmetic. They include conditions which have been referred to as perceptual handicaps, brain injury, minimal brain dysfunction, dyslexia, developmental aphasia, etc. They do not include learning problems which are due primarily to visual, hearing, or motor handicaps, to mental retardation, emotional disturbance, or to environmental disadvantage (p. 34).

While this definition is widely accepted and acted upon, the definition of learning disabilities has been a major source of professional discussion and controversy. Vaughan and Hodges (1973) were able to locate thirty-eight separate definitions of the term "learning disability," and Cruickshank (1972) identified more than forty approximate synonyms for the term. Gearhart (1973) cited four generalizations which tend to link various definitions of learning disabilities:

1. Most definitions refer to a discrepancy between a child's ability to learn and his actual achievement level;
2. Most definitions state that other handicapping conditions must be ruled out (such as mental retardation, emotional disturbance, and sensory impairments);
3. Most definitions exclude the culturally disadvantaged; and

4. Some, but not all, definitions assume brain damage, or a central nervous system dysfunction (e.g., Cruickshank, 1972).

The characteristics of children labeled "learning disabled" vary so broadly that it is impossible to list common characteristics. Identification procedures are not common from state to state, or even between school districts within a given state. In many school districts, children with reading problems are most apt to be labeled LD, although local priorities will change from time to time.

Visual Impairments

There are two bases for defining visual problems, legal and educational. From a legal point of view, blindness is defined as a visual acuity of 20/200* or worse in the better eye after correction. For educational purposes, blind children are defined as children for whom the printed word is not a usable medium of reading, and who thus need to read using means other than print. Partially sighted children are defined as those who can read print under special conditions such as enlargement or magnification. The distinction between legal and educational definitions of visual impairment is important for several reasons, and is discussed more completely in chapter 10. The important point to be made at this time is that educational definitions of visual impairment stress the *educational effects* of the condition, and attend to the level of vision loss only as it results in educational dysfunction.

Hearing Impairment

Hearing impairment, like visual impairment, is defined in terms of both degree of hearing loss and educational significance of the loss. Degree of hearing loss is measured in decibels (dB's), which refer to the level of intensity of sounds. The higher the dB level, the greater intensity of the sound, and hearing loss is measured in terms of dB levels at which sound can be heard by an individual at different frequency levels. In general, a hearing loss of 25 dB or more is thought to define a potentially significant situation. Smith and Neisworth (1975) present the following classification of hearing loss:

Slight: 27 to 40 dB
Mild: 41 to 55 dB
Marked or moderate: 56 to 70 dB
Severe: 71 to 90 dB
Extreme: 91 dB or more.

*The term 20/200 means that the person can distinguish at 20 feet what a person with normal vision distinguishes at 200 feet.

It must be noted that factors other than hearing loss, such as age at onset, cause, and physical origin are taken into account in classifying hearing losses (Myklebust, 1964).

From an educational point of view, a person is considered deaf if the hearing loss occurs at birth or any early age and is severe enough to prevent normal language development, while a hard-of-hearing person has either a less extreme loss or a later age of onset, and develops at least some level of spoken language. As with visual impairment, the educational definition of hearing impairment stresses the *effects* of the hearing loss rather than the medical definition of the loss itself.

Courtesy of The Ford Foundation (Robin Forbes).

Speech Impairment

Van Riper (1972) has defined defective speech as speech which interferes with communication, brings negative attention to the speaker, and causes social/emotional problems for the speaker. The primary types of speech impairment which are dealt with in special education are:

1. Articulation problems, such as omission, substitution, or distortion of sounds;
2. Stuttering, in which fixations, repetitions, or elongations of sounds disrupt the normal flow of speech;
3. Voice disorders, such as hypernasality, high or low speech, speech which is too loud or too soft, or monotone speech;
4. Impaired speech associated with conditions such as cleft-palate, mental retardation, cerebral palsy, or hearing impairment.

Speech therapy is the largest single area of special education in terms of the number of students served. The majority of speech therapists' time in the public schools is spent working with the most common types of problems, disorders of articulation. In addition, an area which has received increasing attention in the past ten years is language disorders, such as delayed language acquisition or selective dysfunctions in the use of oral language.

Crippling Conditions

Crippling conditions, or orthopedic handicaps, are neuromotor and other physical disabilities which limit a child's ability to function within his environment and result in special educational needs. The causes of orthopedic handicaps are too numerous to list here, but the most common and well-known condition resulting in orthopedic handicaps is cerebral palsy. Generally, crippling conditions may be due to brain damage, physical malformations in the muscular system, or direct damage to various parts of the body. Orthopedic impairments may be present from birth or may result from accident or illness at any point in life. Unlike hearing and visual impairments, the tendency has been to define crippling conditions from a medical rather than educational point of view, and this has often led us to overgeneralize concerning the educational implications of orthopedic conditions.

Giftedness

The area of giftedness, like learning disabilities, has seen a continuing controversy concerning definition. Some professionals in the field hold that outstanding intelligence, as measured by standardized intelligence tests, is necessary to be called gifted. Others stress notable achievement in academic areas as the most important criterion. Still others say that creativity or capacity for divergent thinking is necessary to be called gifted. A U.S. Office of Education report on the gifted (Marland, 1972) defines gifted persons as capable of outstanding performance in *one or more* of six areas: (1) general intellectual ability (IQ); (2) academic aptitude, (3) creative or productive thinking, (4) leadership, (5) ability in visual or performing arts, and (6) psychomotor ability.

By and large, giftedness has been defined and gifted children identified according to the characteristics of particular school programs being offered. For example, a special summer music school would define giftedness in terms of musical talent, while a special civics program would stress leadership skills. Where general programs for the gifted have been developed, the two most commonly used criteria for selection of students are general intelligence and creative/productive thinking. As with other traditional areas of exceptionality cited earlier, criteria for determining that a child is gifted vary so widely between school districts and states that no generalizable statements concerning identification criteria can be made.

Conclusion

The foregoing descriptions of traditional categories of exceptionality have been summarized as a basis for the discussion of categorical labels and service delivery systems in the next chapter. There the major movements of the 1970s are reported, and will serve as a rationale for the remainder of the book.

R E F E R E N C E S

Blatt, B. Some persistently recurring assumptions concerning the mentally subnormal. *Training School Bulletin*, 1960, *57*, 48–59.

Burke, P. J. Personnel preparation: historical perspectives. *Exceptional Children*, 1976, *43*, 144–147.

Cruickshank, W. M. Some issues facing the field of learning disability. *Journal of Learning Disabilities*, 1972, *5*, 380–388.

Deno, E. Special education as developmental capital. *Exceptional Children*, 1970, *37*, 229–237.

Dunn, L. M. Special education for the mildly retarded—is much of it justifiable? *Exceptional Children*, 1968, *35*, 5–22.

———. Children with mild general learning disabilities. In L. M. Dunn (ed.), *Exceptional Children in the Schools*. New York: Holt, Rinehart and Winston, 1973.

Franks, D. J. Ethnic and social status characteristics of children in EMR and LD classes. *Exceptional Children*, 1971, *37*, 537–538.

Gearhart, B. R. *Learning Disabilities: Educational Strategies*. St. Louis: The C. V. Mosby Company, 1973.

Goldberg, I. I., and Cruickshank, W. M. The trainable but noneducable: whose responsibility? *National Education Association Journal*, 1958, *47*, 622–623.

Graubard, P. S. Children with behavioral disabilities. In L. M. Dunn (ed.), *Exceptional Children in the Schools*. New York: Holt, Rinehart and Winston, 1973.

Grossman, H. (ed.) *Manual on Terminology and Classification in Mental Retardation, 1973 revision*. Washington, DC: American Association on Mental Deficiency,1973.

Hewett, F. M., and Forness, S. *Education of Exceptional Learners*. Boston: Allyn and Bacon, Inc., 1977.

Johnson, J. L. Special education for the inner city: a challenge for the future or another means for cooling the mark out? *Journal of Special Education*, 1969, *3*, 241–251.

Karier, C. J. Testing for order and control in the corporate liberal state. In C. J. Karier, P. Violas, and J. Spring (ed.), *Roots of Crisis: American Education in the Twentieth Century*. Skokie, IL: Rand McNally & Company, 1973.

Kirk, S. A. Research in education. In H. A. Stevens, and R. Heber (ed.), *Mental Retardation.* Chicago: University of Chicago Press, 1964.

———. Educating Exceptional Children. Boston: Houghton Mifflin Company, 1972.

Long, N. J., Morse, W. C., and Newman, R. G. *Conflict in the Classroom: The Education of Emotionally Disturbed Children.* Belmont, CA: Wadsworth Publishing Company, Inc., 1976.

Marland, S. P. (Submitter) *Education of the Gifted and Talented.* Washington, DC: U. S. Office of Education, 1972.

Martin, E. W. A national commitment to the rights of the individual—1776 to 1976. *Exceptional Children,* 1976, *43*, 132–135.

Myklebust, H. R. *The Psychology of Deafness.* New York: Grune & Stratton, Inc., 1964.

Quay, H. C., Morse, W. C., and Cutler, R. L. Personality patterns of pupils in special classes for the emotionally disturbed. *Exceptional Children,* 1966, *32*, 297–301.

Reger, R., Schroeder, W., and Uschold, K. *Special Education: Children with Learning Problems.* New York: Oxford University Press, 1968.

Rubin, E. Z., Simson, C. B., and Betwee, M. C. *Emotionally Handicapped Children and the Elementary School.* Detroit: Wayne State University Press, 1966.

Smith, R. M., and Neisworth, J. T. *The Exceptional Child: A Functional Approach.* New York: McGraw-Hill, Inc., 1975.

Special Education for Handicapped Children: First Annual Report of the National Advisory Committee on Handicapped Children. Washington, DC: U.S. Office of Education, 1968.

Van Riper, C. *Speech Corrections: Principles and Methods.* Englewood Cliffs, NJ: Prentice-Hall, Inc., 1972.

Vaughan, R. W., and Hodges, L. A statistical survey into a definition of learning disabilities: a search for acceptance. *Journal of Learning Disabilities,* 1973, *6*, 658–664.

Weintraub, F. J., Abeson, A. R., and Braddock, D. L. *State Law and Education of Handicapped Children: Issues and Recommendations.* Reston, VA: Council for Exceptional Children, 1975.

Wolfensberger, W. The origin and nature of our institutional models. In R. B. Kugel and W. Wolfensberger (ed.), *Changing Patterns in Residential Services for the Mentally Retarded.* Washington, DC: President's Committee on Mental Retardation, 1969.

Wright, J. S. The Washington, D.C. school case. In M. Weinberg (ed.), *Integrated Education: A Reader.* Beverly Hills, CA: Glencoe Press, 1968.

CHAPTER 2

SPECIAL EDUCATION
Emerging issues

M. STEPHEN LILLY

This chapter analyzes the major current issues in special education, and assesses the impact of emerging trends on its organization in general. Seven issues of major importance during the past decade serve as the basis for development of special education in the 1980s and beyond. Each of these issues will be discussed in detail: (1) Litigation in special education, (2) Free appropriate public education for all, (3) Positive and negative aspects of the use of traditional categorical labels in special education, (4) Appropriate education placement, (5) Role of the federal government in special education, (6) Role of parents in special education, and (7) Cooperation between special and regular education.

LITIGATION IN SPECIAL EDUCATION

The 1960s brought the first systematic use of the state and federal court system by parents of and advocates for handicapped children, as a means of assuring that children's rights are protected in the special education process. In the 1970s, this area of activity expanded significantly and the courts became a major force for change in special education. This section describes the principles of law which have been established through litigation, and summarizes the major court cases which have led to the affirmation of these principles. The cases presented here relate to provision of special education services. It must be recognized that this represents only a small portion of court cases regarding the handicapped, since areas of litigation have included not only education, but also such topics as architectural barriers, commitment, custody, employment, guardianship, sterilization, and voting.

With specific reference to education, the major areas of litigation have been (1) right to education, (2) right to protection in the classification (labeling) process, and (3) right to protection in the process of placement for special education.

Right to Education

Even with the expansion of special education in the 1960s, there remained a significant number of children of school age who were denied public education. This lack of service became a legal issue in the 1970s, through a series of court suits which established the right of *all* school-age children, regardless of type or severity of handicap, to a free, appropriate public education. The first landmark case in this area was Pennsylvania Association for Retarded Children (PARC) v. the Commonwealth of Pennsylvania, commonly referred to as the PARC case (1971). The PARC suit was filed on behalf of thirteen retarded children in the state of Pennsylvania who had been denied access to free public day school education, even though state law and constitution included a commitment to education of all children. In 1971, a preliminary order was issued in the case stating that once the Commonwealth of Pennsylvania undertook to educate all of its citizens, it could not deny access to free public education to any child, including children who are mentally retarded. It was ordered by the Court that *all retarded children in the state* be provided a free, appropriate public education by September 1972.

The PARC case was decided on the basis of constitutional and statutory principles; the consent order essentially affirmed that certain parts of the state law (which allowed exclusion of children who were "uneducable" or who had not reached the mental age of five) were in conflict with the state statutory commitment to education of all children. This was a very important decision, since it was the first court ruling dealing exclusively with exceptional children. The national significance of the decision was somewhat limited, however, due to the fact that it was settled by mutual consent of the parties involved.

While the PARC case was in its final stages, another suit was in the process of being heard in Washington, D. C., which would expand the PARC decision on three important dimensions. This class action suit, Mills v. Board of Education of the District of Columbia (1972), was filed on behalf of seven school-age children who were excluded from the District of Columbia schools because they had been labeled mentally retarded, hyperactive, emotionally disturbed, and behavior problems. The case focused both on children who were excluded and on children who were suspended or expelled. School officials in the District of Columbia argued that it was financially impossible to provide education for all children in the District. Presiding Judge J. Waddy rejected this argument, however, claiming that problems of finance can bear no more heavily on exceptional than on normal children. Judge Waddy ordered that every school-age child in the District of Columbia be provided a free, suitable public education within thirty days of the decision, and that no child be excluded from a regular public school assignment without provision of appropriate alternate educational services.

The Mills case is significant in three respects. First, it expanded the PARC decision to all areas of exceptionality, not just mental retardation. Second, it was decided by a judgment against the defendants, as opposed to the PARC consent decree. And finally, Judge Waddy based his decision in large part on the equal protection and due process clauses of the U. S. Constitution (Fifth and Fourteenth Amendments), citing the landmark 1954 Brown v. Board of Education school integration case as establishing that once a state undertakes to provide education to some of its citizens, it becomes a right available to all on equal terms.

The constitutional principles of equal protection under the law and due process for exceptional children served as the basis for a minor flood of right to education suits in the ensuing years. By the middle 1970s, these cases were so routinely being decided in favor of the plaintiffs that most were settled out of court with an agreement to provide services. At the present time, the right to education for all exceptional children is firmly established in federal and most state legislation, due primarily to the litigation of the early 1970s.

A final point to be made with respect to "right to education" litigation is that, while it set the stage for assuring education for all school-age children, it did not guarantee such education would take place. In 1975, three years after the Mills decision was handed down, a court master was appointed to help assure that the order was being carried out. In the PARC case, chaos ensued following the court order and for a substantial period of time it was impossible to tell how well the state was carrying out the mandates of the court. Judge Waddy, in issuing the Mills decree, expressed reluctance to accept on the part of the Court the administration of the schools of the District of Columbia. In fact, courts cannot administer schools. The movement from issuance of court decrees to full implementation of those decrees has been difficult and complicated. Litigation can be credited with setting the tone and *creating the expectation* of free, appropriate public education for all children, a principle which is now well established and widely pursued in the field of special education.

Protection in Classification

The majority of court suits having to do with protection of children's rights in the classification process have centered on use of discriminatory testing procedures in identification of children, particularly minority children, for special education services. The issue of misuse of tests for classification had been initially raised in the Hobson v. Hansen case on tracking* (Wright, 1968) in Washington, D. C., and became the first exclusively "special education" issue to be tested in the courts. The landmark case in this area is Diana v. State Board of Education (1972), a suit filed in Monterey County, California, on behalf of nine Mexican-American children whose primary language was Spanish, but who were placed in EMR classes after being given intelligence tests in English. Upon being retested in their native language, seven of the nine children scored above the cutoff point for EMR services. The court ordered the school district to reevaluate all Mexican-American and Chinese-American children in their native languages, and to rectify any misplacements which resulted from inappropriate testing.

A second case of significance in this area is Larry P. v. Riles (1972), in which the plaintiffs sought to have the San Francisco school district enjoined from use of IQ tests for the purpose of placing black students in EMR special classes. This suit was strengthened by the fact that 66 percent of EMR students in the city were black, as compared to 28 percent of students in the San Francisco school district as a whole. While the court refused to offer relief to students already in EMR classes, the school district was prohibited from using IQ test scores as the primary criterion for EMR placement of black children, if such procedures resulted in racial imbalance in EMR services.

As a result of these and other court suits, as well as mounting professional opinion, intelligence tests have become increasingly suspect as a determiner of mental retardation, an issue presented in greater detail in chapter 3. Litigation beginning with Diana and continuing through the present has been a significant pressure in drawing professional attention to the issues of nondiscriminatory testing and use of multiple measures in evaluation and placement of children.

Protection in the Placement Process

The third major area of concern in special education has been protection of children's rights in planning and delivery of special education services. To a certain extent, this overlaps with the testing issues presented above, since improper testing results in improper placement. The relief ordered in cases concerning inappropriate use of intelligence tests has nearly always involved changes in educational placement of children from special to regular classes.

In a broader sense, however, protection of children's rights in the placement process has been delineated by the courts in terms of due

---

*"Tracking" is a system in which all children in a school or school district are tested and placed in educational "tracks" of varying levels of difficulty. Since lower tracks teach less advanced skills, it is very difficult for students to work their way "up" a tracking system.

process procedures which must be followed in planning special education services. Specification of such due process requirements by the courts has been exhaustive, resulting in major changes in school district placement procedures. The requirements specified in Mills v. Board of Education of the District of Columbia (1972) are illustrative.

Whenever defendants [the school districts] take action regarding a child's placement, denial of placement, or transfer [for special education], the following procedures shall be followed:

1. Notice required hereinbefore shall be given in writing by registered mail to the parent or guardian of the child.
2. Such notice shall:
   (a) describe the proposed action in detail;
   (b) clearly state the specific and complete reasons for the proposed action, including the specification of any tests or reports upon which such action is proposed;
   (c) describe any alternative educational opportunities available on a permanent or temporary basis;
   (d) inform the parent or guardian of the right to object to the proposed action at a hearing before the Hearing Officer;
   (e) inform the parent or guardian that the child is eligible to receive, at no charge, the services of a federally or locally funded diagnostic center for an independent medical, psychological and educational evaluation and shall specify the name, address and telephone number of an appropriate local diagnostic center;
   (f) inform the parent or guardian of the right to be represented at the hearing by legal counsel; to examine the child's school records before the hearing, including any tests or reports upon which the proposed action may be based, to present evidence, including expert medical, psychological and educational testimony; and, to confront and cross-examine any school official, employee, or agent of the school district or public department who may have evidence upon which the proposed action was based.
3. The hearing shall be at a time and place reasonably convenient to such parent or guardian.
4. The hearing shall be scheduled not sooner than twenty (20) days waivable by parent or child, nor later than forty-five (45) days after receipt of a request from the parent or guardian.
5. The hearing shall be a closed hearing unless the parent or guardian requests an open hearing.
6. The child shall have the right to a representative of his own choosing, including legal counsel. If a child is unable, through financial inability, to retain counsel, defendants shall advise child's parents or guardians of available voluntary legal assistance including the Neighborhood Legal Services Organization, the Legal Aid Society, the Young Lawyers Section of the D. C. Bar Association, or from some other organization.
7. The decision of the Hearing Officer shall be based solely upon the evidence presented at the hearing.
8. Defendants shall bear the burden of proof as to all facts and as to the appropriateness of any placement, denial of placement or transfer.

9. A tape recording or other record of the hearing shall be made and transcribed and, upon request, made available to the parent or guardian or his representative.
10. At a reasonable time prior to the hearing, the parent or guardian, or his counsel, shall be given access to all public school system and other public office records pertaining to the child, including any tests or reports upon which the proposed action may be based.
11. The independent Hearing Officer shall be an employee of the District of Columbia, but shall not be an officer, employee or agent of the Public School System.
12. The parent or guardian, or his representative, shall have the right to have the attendance of any official, employee or agent of the public school system or any public employee who may have evidence upon which the proposed action may be based and to confront, and to cross-examine any witness testifying for the public school system.
13. The parent or guardian, or his representative, shall have the right to present evidence and testimony, including expert medical, psychological or educational testimony.
14. Within thirty (30) days after the hearing, the Hearing Officer shall render a decision in writing. Such decision shall include findings of fact and conclusions of law and shall be filed with the Board of Education and the Department of Human Resources and sent by registered mail to the parent or guardian and his counsel.
15. Pending a determination by the Hearing Officer, defendants shall take no action described, if the child's parent or guardian objects to such action. Such objection must be in writing and postmarked within five (5) days of the date of receipt of notification hereinabove described (pp. 880–882).

Faced with the imposition of "due process" procedures such as those outlined above in nearly all "right to education" cases that have been heard, the individual states began to incorporate such procedures into special education laws and regulations, and some state procedures are even more stringent than those imposed by the courts. For example, the Illinois Rules and Regulations Governing Special Education (1976) specify that impartial due process hearings may be requested by "parents, other persons having primary care and custody of the child, the child or the district" (p. 14), and thirteen potential reasons for requesting a hearing are listed, ranging from inadequate services to recommendation for graduation of an exceptional child. In addition, the Illinois Rules and Regulations specify procedures for requests for local and state hearings to resolve disputes between parents and school districts, and prescribe stringent timelines within which specific actions must be taken as a part of the appeal process.

Without doubt, the introduction of due process hearings into special education has tended to formalize many interactions between schools and parents, and at times the specter of a formal hearing can be intimidating to parents who are not satisfied with services being provided their child. Some states have published guides to the hearing process geared specifically for parents, and in most areas the stress is placed on solving disagreements before they reach the stage of a due process hearing. One undeniable outcome of the growth of hearing procedures is the establishment of an unequivocal mechanism for active involvement of parents in the planning of public school special education services, a goal long stated but seldom actualized until the courts established it as a necessity. This issue is discussed more fully later in this chapter in the section on parental involvement.

Summary

The 1970s saw an astounding increase in court cases related to special education, and during this decade, litigation emerged as a major force for change in the field. Subsequent chapters make reference to the role of litigation in specific areas of special education. The following sections of this chapter describe more fully some of the issues which were brought to the forefront in special education by the courts, and which are current issues of considerable professional interest and attention.

FREE, APPROPRIATE PUBLIC EDUCATION FOR ALL

Of the array of issues which exploded onto the special education scene in the 1970s, perhaps the most widely accepted and well-articulated new concept is "right to education" for all children. It might be argued that this is not a new concept at all, that it has been a hallmark of American education since the 1800s. However, as has been pointed out earlier, the right to education has in fact been restricted in the past. But the restrictions concerning education have been narrowing over time. While in the 1950s the schools did not serve children labeled "trainable mentally retarded," the 1960s saw an increase in public school services for this population. Development and expansion of special classes for children called "emotionally disturbed" from the 1930s through the 1960s resulted in fewer expulsions of children from schools and a broader concept of public school education. As pointed out in the previous section, however, while the focus of the schools has progressively expanded in terms of numbers and types of children served, there remained in the early 1970s provisions in most state laws which permitted certain children to be determined "ineducable" and thus to be removed from the realm of public school responsibility.

In the 1970s, court cases such as PARC (1971) and Mills (1972) helped to bring about a total commitment to public school responsibility for education of all school-age children. In fact, the "right to education" movement has resulted in a redefinition of education itself. The essential principle which has been established in "right to education" litigation and legislation is commonly called the "principle of zero exclusion," (Crowner, 1975) which holds that *every* child of school age, regardless of present level of functioning, is due a free, appropriate public education. Further, education has been functionally defined as moving a child from a present skill level to the next appropriate skill level, which means in practical terms that *no* child is ineducable. The principle of zero exclusion has been predicated on the following educational and legal tenets:

1. All children can learn, at some level of skill development;
2. If a state establishes a statutory requirement that all exceptional children are to be educated, this requirement cannot be waived because of the nature of the educational needs of individual children; and
3. Even if a state has not mandated special education for all exceptional children, it is still required to provide it, since the Fourteenth Amendment to the U. S. Constitution ("equal protection under the law") requires that once a state endeavors to provide a service to one citizen, that service must be available to all citizens of the state on an equal basis. Thus, if a state mandates free public education for normal children (which all states do), it must provide free public education for all children.

The implementation of the "principle of zero exclusion" in the public schools has resulted in tremendous growth in an area of special education that has received scant attention over the years: education of severely, profoundly, and multiply handicapped children. The two groups of children most apt to be excluded from public education in the late 1960s and early 1970s were children suspended or expelled for reasons of social behavior, and children with severe and/or multiple handicapping conditions. For the first group of children, treatment models existed but were not being implemented in many cases. For the second group, treatment models often did not exist since most prior service was largely custodial in nature.

In the early 1970s a very few special educators were focusing their efforts on severely and profoundly handicapped individuals. By the late 1970s, the number of professionals thus engaged had expanded substantially. School districts were increasingly accepting responsibility not only for financing private agency services for these children, but in many cases for providing services in the public schools. Education of the severely and profoundly handicapped rapidly became established as an important new area of emphasis in special education. In 1975, a new professional organization was begun, the American Association for Education of Severely and Profoundly Handicapped (AAESPH).

The increased emphasis on special education for the severely and profoundly handicapped is described in chapters 5 and 6, which deal exclusively with children who have been called moderately, severely, and profoundly mentally retarded and/or emotionally disturbed. These two categorical emphases are presented together because of the substantial overlap of functional problems and educational needs among children who are so labeled. The emphasis on severe and profound handicaps is also evident elsewhere, particularly in the chapter on crippling conditions, in which the limiting effects of such conditions which often accompany severe and profound mental impairment are discussed.

In summary, "education for all" is an idea whose time has come. Due to advances in special education litigation and both state and federal legislation, all states have now accepted the goal of zero exclusion. Acceptance of this *goal* has not always meant immediate implementation of the *practice* of zero exclusion, and development of systems for education of children traditionally excluded from the public schools, in particular children who are severely and profoundly handicapped, represents one of the major challenges currently facing the field of special education.

POSITIVE AND NEGATIVE ASPECTS OF CATEGORICAL LABELS*

The third current issue is the use of traditional categorical labels in special education. The subject of labeling in special education has been under intense discussion since the 1960s, and much of the discussion has been critical of present labeling practices, particularly in the areas of educable mental retardation, behavior disorders, and learning disabilities. Simches (1970) has stated: "We must develop identification systems which provide an understanding of the child so that programs can be built around the child's skills. We cannot continue to use taxonomy of labels that have a tendency to homogenize children into meaningless diagnostic label categories based primarily on psychometrics, medical findings, or psychiatric examinations" (p. 10). Weintraub, Abeson, and Braddock (1975) have recommended that "each state carefully reexamine its present system of defining and classifying children to ascertain if the system stigmatizes children beyond that which is necessary and whether the system is related to the educational needs of the child" (pp. 25–26).

To better understand the traditional categorization system, it is necessary to recall why it developed, as well as positive and negative factors in its use. As recounted in chapter 1, traditional categories of exceptionality developed one by one over time, with the early emphasis on obvious cases of severe mental retardation, incapacitating emotional disturbance, and sensory impairments. With the advent of compulsory schooling and increased complexity in society, milder conditions or situations were considered handicapping, and the spectrum expanded through acceptance of the category of learning disabilities in the mid-1960s. A part of this progression also included development of the notion of educable (mild) mental retardation in the 1920s, as well as the broadening of the concept of emotional disturbance to include behavior or conduct disorders encountered in the schools. Throughout this expansion of special education, a child-centered "disease" model was used in defining children to be served. It is this disease orientation, implying that the root of all learning

*A substantial portion of the information presented in this section is adapted from a paper prepared by this author as a part of the Vanderbilt Project on Classification of Exceptional Children, and published in chapter 16, "Schools," in Hobbs, N. (ed.), *Issues in the Classification of Children.* (2 vols.) San Francisco: Jossey-Bass, 1975a.

problems can be traced to a condition in the child, which has received increasing scrutiny of many special educators.

Data on behavioral effects of labeling are surprisingly sparse and, where available, not totally trustworthy. Jones (1972) has pointed out that "there is a stigma as perceived by teachers, pupils, school administrators, citizens and parents...No empirical study has been reported in the literature dealing with labels and stigma in the public school populations of exceptional children" (p. 554). Since there are limited empirical data to serve as a basis for discussion, any discussion of the effects of labeling must be based in large part on a logical analysis of the phenomenon. There has been considerable attention to such analysis by special educators over the past ten years, as is evident in the ensuing discussion.

In coming to a position regarding categorization of children, one must consider both the positive and the negative aspects of the traditional system of categories (keeping in mind that not all statements made about these aspects are applicable to all existing labels). Various special educators have claimed the following positive effects for traditional categories of exceptionality.

1. *Because some categories specify clear inclusion and exclusion limits, they reduce ambiguities and provide clear communication devices for professional exchanges of information.*

Although confusing ambiguities and varying standards do exist in the traditional classification system (for example, a child may be labeled brain-damaged in one school district, educable mentally retarded in another, emotionally disturbed or learning disabled in another, and not labeled at all in another), no one argues that doing away with the present system will reduce such ambiguities. They will, in fact, be increased, since reliance will then be placed on specific student behaviors rather than on broad deficit categories.

Under the present system, a given school district has a finite set of alternatives from which to choose when describing a child for administrative purposes. If, for example, the primary criterion for labeling a child as educable mentally retarded in a given school district is an individual intelligence test score between 55 and 75, this criterion defines clearly both the measurement conditions and the outcomes necessary to label a child EMR. Many professionals prefer this procedure to less clearly defined, more individually based measurement systems which rely on direct observation of classroom academic and social behavior (Clausen, 1972). These professionals believe that the traditional categories of exceptionality reduce subjectivity and ambiguity, and promote clarity of communication.

2. *In some cases traditional categories provide a description of a physical condition which has important educational implications.*

Categories of exceptionality were not developed in a vacuum; they nearly always relate in some degree to a child's ability to function adequately in school settings. In some cases educational implications of labels are direct and forthright. For example, it is self-evident that a visually impaired child or a child with a hearing problem will not be able to function well in a regular classroom without special assistance and attention to the problem.

In addition to providing short-cut descriptions of children, labels also sometimes open up opportunities for them which would not exist were they not so labeled. Students identified as visually impaired, for example, are eligible for braille materials and talking books as a result of their having been so identified. Likewise, orthopedically handicapped students receive a variety of physical therapy services. Various community agencies are mobilized to provide special recreational and other programs to handicapped individuals. In short, a label can open some doors at the same time that it closes others.

3. *Traditional categories of exceptionality provide a basis for determining the number of students needing special education services.*

Every category of exceptionality has one or more prevalence figure associated with it; these figures can be used as a basis for planning and securing funds for special education services. An argument for continued use of traditional special education categories is that if they are taken away, and if an adequate substitute system is not provided, funds will be cut off and children who need special education services will not receive them. If alternate categorization systems are to provide precise estimates of numbers of children for planning purposes, they must be precise in differentiating groups of children. To meet this criterion, they most likely would suffer from the same inflexibility for which the present categories have been criticized. The present system provides prevalence figures for planning and funding purposes as well as or better than any alternative system which has been proposed.

4. *Traditional categories provide a method for accounting for children being served through special education services.*

The increased emphasis on state and federal support for special education has resulted in a multitude of reporting procedures to be used in accounting for children served. At the federal level, for instance, reports are required from states summarizing services provided through various federal support programs. At the state level, detailed reports of various types are required from school districts to justify state reimbursement for special education services. Nearly all forms in use at both the federal and state levels require that numbers of children be listed by category of exceptionality. This provides a straightforward accounting method for services rendered and minimizes problems of data management and interpretation.

5. *Use of traditional categories at the local level enables a school district to collect reimbursement from the state for special education services.*

Nearly all states presently operate under a legislative or regulatory system whereby school districts are reimbursed for children identified and served through special education. Thus, in states using the traditional categories for reimbursement purposes (presently all but a few states), it is of direct advantage to school districts to account for children in this manner, since they receive up to 100 percent reimbursement of excess costs from the state for labeling children and providing services based on those labels. In addition to state reimbursement, some special incentives for labeling are present at the federal level with regard to certain types of handicapping conditions. For example, a school attended by a child certified as legally blind by an ophthalmologist and reported as such by the school district, may purchase approximately one hundred dollars' worth of educational materials annually through the American Printing House for the Blind for use in its school program. In a like manner, numerous educational materials and audiovisual aids are available through federal programs to teachers of children certified as hearing impaired.

6. *Traditional categories of exceptionality have provided a rallying point for securing both legislative and general public support for special education programs.*

As Gallagher (1972) has pointed out, much of the present support for special education has come about because of the "fine mixture of compassion, guilt, and social conscience...established over these many years as a conditioned response" to such labels as mentally retarded, learning disabled, and emotionally disturbed. "If we changed that now, if we unlabeled these programs, these financial resources, and much of the brains and talent they represent, would dissipate and much of the hard-won foundation that has been built will have been for naught" (p. 531). Many special educators are convinced that "deemphasis of children's disabling characteristics will diminish the wellsprings of sympathy which feed financial support into services for children having special need" (Deno, 1970, p. 229).

In short, the categories have served special education very well in securing funds for services to children—so well, in fact, that it is probably the major positive argument for continued use of the traditional categories of exceptionality. It would indeed have been very difficult to develop the present support base for special education without a relatively simple child-based system of problem identification.

While traditional categories of exceptionality have been defended on the basis of the arguments just reviewed, a number of difficult questions have been raised concerning the categories, particularly from an instructional point of view. Following are some of the negative aspects of traditional categories:

1. *These categories invite overgeneralizations concerning individual children.*

Even though, as pointed out earlier, traditional categories of exceptionality can identify certain child-based variables of importance in the educational process, there is a constant danger of overgeneralization. It is in this direction that the majority of errors in labeling have been made in school systems. Some school systems have assumed, for example, that children labeled educable mentally retarded are alike and should therefore be given the same curriculum. As Moss (1973) has noted, a label is useful only insofar

Courtesy of Telesensory Systems, Inc.

as the generalizations made with regard to that label apply to the specific child thus categorized. Unfortunately, it is much easier to go from the specific to the general than to move in the other direction. Iano (1972) points out that children in the various categories of exceptionality are not homogeneous. Regarding mental retardation, Leland (1972) states flatly, "There are no generalized behaviors specific to mental retardation" (p. 76). The effects of inviting such overgeneralizations are expressed in educational terms by Deno (1970): "Many workers are now pointing out that the introduction of categorical constructs based on presumed child defects merely adds a cluttering, unessential administrative and conceptual layer which interferes more than it aids in realizing the goal of individual instruction for all children, handicapped and nonhandicapped" (p. 232).

Recent studies indicate that labels can have a detrimental effect on teachers' approaches to children. For example, in a study by Gillung and Rucker (1977), teachers were given behavioral descriptions of children, some descriptions accompanied by labels of mentally retarded, emotionally disturbed or learning disabled, and other descriptions without such labels. In each case, teachers were asked to indicate an appropriate educational placement for the child described, choosing from a continuum of seven possible placements ranging from the regular classroom to a private school. Despite the fact that the behavioral descriptions were identical, teachers indicated that children who were labeled needed more intensive, and more separated, educational programs than those not labeled. The investigators conclude that "labels carry a negative connotation that results in lower teacher expectations for both regular and special education teachers" (Gillung & Rucker, 1977, p. 465). In another study similar in aim but different in design, Foster and Salvia (1977) asked teachers to rate the adequacy of academic performance and frequency of undesirable social behavior of a fourth-grade student, after viewing a videotape of the boy's classroom work. The behavior shown on the tapes was age and grade appropriate in all cases, but some teachers were told the boy was learning disabled while other teachers were told he was normal. The findings indicated that viewing the same videotape, teachers watching a "learning disabled" child rated him as less able academically and more socially inept than did teachers watching a "normal" child. Warning the teachers to be "objective" in their judgments tended to reduce the impact of the label on teacher ratings, but not remove it completely. Foster and Salvia conclude: "It seems that when teachers are asked to rate a labeled child, they are willing to rate in the absence of observable behaviors" (p. 53).

Label overgeneralization is not confined to categories based on psychological constructs, since orthopedically handicapped, visually impaired, and hearing impaired children also are grouped for educational purposes on the basis of the primary handicapping condition. An example of negative effects of such labeling can be seen in the area of the visually handicapped, where an explicit assumption was made for many years that legally blind children (children with vision of 20/200 or less in the better eye after correction) should read braille, since they "cannot see." Thus, in many classrooms and schools for the blind, legally blind children were taught braille to the exclusion of other reading methods. In the early 1950s, however, Jones (1961) found that over 80 percent of children with reported visual acuity of 20/200 were using print as their primary mode of reading. As a result of his findings, "the diminishing practice of requiring all legally blind children to read braille regardless of their functional vision was dealt a hopefully fatal blow" (Tisdall, 1968, p. 118).

If overgeneralization from labels is, as implied before, a major problem, what can be done about it? Specifically, educators can use "criteria based on how the children function in school rather than how they perform and are measured on clinical tests" (Ashcroft, 1963, p. 419). Behavioral assessments of children can be made in learning settings: "When diagnosis and treatment are based on direct observations and not on the supposition that one deviant behavior presupposes the presence of a syndrome of related events, time is spent in treatment of explicit behaviors rather than in what is frequently a fruitless search for correlate but often unrevealed behaviors" (Lovitt, 1967, p. 234). We cannot assume that any generalization associated with a categorical label applies to a specific child until we conduct a behavioral assessment of the child in an instructional setting. Further, once this is done, the label is no longer necessary or useful for instructional purposes, since it has been replaced with far more specific information.

2. *Traditional categories are self-sustaining in that they contribute to "reification" of the child labels used.*

The reification process with regard to labeling refers to the logical fallacy of applying a label to describe a behavior pattern, and then positing the label as the "cause" of the behaviors observed. The present author has explained the situation as follows: "Exceptionality is a psychological construct, created to make order out of chaotic classroom situations.... Eventually, as is often the case with psychological constructs, we cease to regard exceptionality as an explanatory concept and it becomes as real as the mumps in children" (Lilly, 1970, p. 48).

Whelan (1972) has described the problem of reification of the label "autistic":

> The most frequent misuse of labels is caused by reification. Simply stated, reification is a process which individuals use to label a behavior pattern, or individual, and then use the label to explain the origin of the behavior pattern that is labeled. For example, there are classical behaviors associated with the label autistic (Kanner, 1943; Rimland, 1964). The label functions as a brief communication device to describe behavior. It circumvents the necessity for listing all of the observed behaviors. There should be agreement among those who use the label as to what behaviors are being described, since accurate communication is necessary in concerted planning of a program to assist a child labeled autistic to acquire more organized behavior patterns.
>
> At this juncture in the reification process, a label has been used correctly as a general description of behavior. However, autistic is a label recognized by special educators as meaning that prognosis is guarded and that intervention programs have not been successful in changing total behavior patterns associated with the label. These are realistic meanings as long as they are not extended to mean that a child so labeled is worthless and, therefore, not worthy of concern or realistic assistance. The question of why a child labeled autistic exhibits certain behaviors must arise in the planning of behavior-change programs. If that question leads to formulation of procedures to change environmental conditions, rather than just change the child, then appropriate behavior-change procedures can be instituted. All too often, though, the question is usually answered by saying "The child behaves that way because he is autistic." The label that was initially used to describe behavior has now been used to explain the origin of behavior. A label is merely a brief description, organizational device and should not be used as an explanation. If it is, the explanation is myth, fiction, and usually functions to the detriment of the labeled individual (p. 43).

3. *Traditional categories ignore the interactive nature of instruction and assume that the root of instructional problems is in the child.*

Closely related to the difficulty of reification is a problem that results when only child-based labels are used for describing instructional problems. In nearly all cases of labeling (particularly if the label happens to be educable mental retardation, emotional disturbance, or learning disability), the first step in the labeling process is the teacher referral. The one certain aspect of such a situation is that a problem exists in the classroom. We do not know at this point the nature of the problem—specifically, whether or not it is due to a condition of the child. Adelman (1971) has pointed out that "learning problems result not only from the character- istics of the youngster but also from the characteristics of the classroom situation to which he is assigned." (p. 529)

Perhaps, then, instead of defining exceptional children, we should be- gin defining *exceptional situations within the school,* an idea suggested by the present author as follows: "An exceptional school situation is one in which interaction between a student and his teacher has been limited to such an extent that external intervention is deemed necessary by the teacher to cope with the problem.... [Such a definition] does not specify the basic nature of the problem, nor does it specify the child (or the teacher) as the causative agent in any given situation. In essence, it de- mands a complete analysis of the classroom situation before statements are made concerning the nature of the problem and steps necessary to bring about a solution" (Lilly, 1970, p. 48).

4. *Traditional categories remove the "burden of proof" for children's learn- ing from school personnel, by providing unalterable conditions of chil- dren as reasons for repeated failure.*

When confronted with a child who is either not learning or not behav- ing, many school personnel immediately initiate a search for the "cause" of that failure within the child. In the words of Lovitt (1967):

> A teacher, for example, might seek diagnostic solace as a means of rationalizing her own programming inadequacies. Such a teacher, when finding a child who does not adapt to her program or choice of curricular materials, could have her programming decisions greatly reinforced by a diagnostician who solves her dilemma with a report that the child is dyslexic or aphasic. As a result, when the child does not adequately perform, the teacher need only draw out her file and read the diagnosis to reassure herself that the student's poor performance is unalterably determined by some medical or psychological malady. Then no teaching obligation follows for altering the stimulus or consequence conditions of the program, nor is there any necessity for an assessment of possible errors within the teacher's management techniques (p. 234).

Not all educators, of course, use categorical labels as excuses for not teaching children. The vast majority of educators (both special and regular) are sincerely interested in bringing about the greatest possible growth in children, regardless of real or supposed child-based deficits. Even in per- sons of good faith, however, the tendency exists to look for the cause of failure in the student, as opposed to the program, a tendency both rein- forced and facilitated by use of child-based categorization systems.

5. *Traditional categories provide information to the teacher which is in large part irrelevant for instruction.*

If labels are to be applied to children for the purpose of improving their learning, such labels should have rather direct implications for instruction.

Many special education labels, however, are aimed at diagnosing, as opposed to treating the problem. Most often, the translation of these diagnostic labels into treatment alternatives is difficult if not impossible. Reger, Schroeder, and Uschold (1968) provide insight into this problem:

> What could the schools do with a diagnosis? Sometimes a child would be referred because he was unable to read, even though he was in the fourth grade. To be told that the child had a diagnosis of "primary reading disability" or "dyslexia" perhaps sounded impressive and informative, but in fact the schools knew whatever this meant in the first place.
>
> Referral, then, became notorious for being nothing more than having a label, a fancy medical term, applied to an already known problem. Further, the result often was increased confusion rather than clarification. "I knew the child couldn't read, but what is this business about 'dyslexia'—what does it mean?" The helping agency apparently suffered under the impression that labeling was explaining, but the child was the loser because the school could do nothing with the label; it had no bases for action. If anything, the school now felt completely helpless because the problem had been defined in terms not relevant educationally (p. 9).

6. *Placement of children in special education programs on the basis of traditional categories of exceptionality is often a one-way street, with little or no opportunity to escape the label or the treatment.*

Once a child is labeled as exceptional, what are his chances for escaping his label and returning to mainstream education? The answer, of course, depends on the policies of the school district in question and the steadfastness with which those policies are carried out. As a general answer to the question, however, Gallagher (1972) offers the following estimate: "In a number of large city school systems far less than 10 percent of the children placed in special education classes are ever returned to regular education. When one considers that the referral error could well be that high, it is easy to conclude that the bridge that should exist between special and regular education is, in fact, not really there. The traffic all goes in one direction" (p. 529).

This type of situation is, of course, consistent with the notion of child-based disability categories, which prescribe relatively permanent conditions of children as the basic causes of school problems. It is not, however, consistent with the notion of behavioral assessment of problem situations, and educational planning based on direct behavioral observation of classroom situations, as suggested earlier. To solve this problem of long-term special education placement based on a single labeling act, Gallagher (1972) has proposed that special education services for the "mildly handicapped" be offered on a contract basis, with a maximum contract length of two years. Such a contract "would be nonrenewable, or renewable only with a quasi-judicial type of hearing, with parents represented by legal or child advocate counsel" and also "would commit the special educational personnel to measurable objectives that would be upgraded on a six-month interval" (p. 532). This approach to special education services is designed to assure that relevant educational planning is done for children, and to eliminate the "school-lifetime" effect of the present categorization system.

7. *Traditional categories discriminate against minority groups and the poor through the use of culturally biased tests and subsequent "tracking" of children based on these test results.*

The single aspect of child categorization systems which has come under greatest fire in the last decade is the use of intelligence tests (both group and individual) for the purpose of classifying children. Specifically, critics charge that intelligence tests measure a very narrow range of behaviors—behaviors neither stressed nor valued in minority cultures—and consequently are used to classify blacks and other minorities as mentally retarded. The issue of discrimination in testing and placement has been discussed already and constitutes a strong argument against use of certain categorical labels, particularly educable mental retardation.

8. *Traditional categories tend to set special education apart from regular education, and to define instructional problems in terms that are formidable and threatening to regular educators.*

If a classroom teacher encounters problems teaching a child to read, the problem is not apt to be overwhelming or threatening to the teacher, who has probably dealt with similar problems before. If, however, it is reported to the teacher that the reading problem is due to "dyslexia" in the child, this report by itself can make the problem appear more formidable than it is. Likewise, explaining excessive out-of-seat behavior in terms of "hyperkinesis," "neurological impairment," or "emotional disturbance" introduces a level of unneeded complexity to the situation which tends to say to a classroom teacher: "It's too complicated for you to deal with. Let the experts handle it." The effect of such use of categorical labels has been to build a "mystique" around special education which makes rebuilding the bridge between regular and special education a more difficult task than it should be.

9. *Traditional categories create stereotyped public images of various types of exceptionality.*

In the late 1960s, in a series of television "spots," the general public was told that "one child in thirty is born mentally retarded." No mention was made of the relationship between poverty and mental retardation, or of the fact that black children are more likely than white children to be labeled retarded. In fact, the general public was led to believe that the established incidence of mental retardation is 3 percent, distributed randomly across the population. Moreover, no mention was made of degrees of severity, and the viewing public was not told that of this 3 percent, approximately 2.7 percent were not noticeably different outside of school from their neighborhood friends and playmates (President's Committee on Mental Retardation, 1970).

The effects of this simplified approach to informing the public about the handicapped have not been documented. It seems highly probable, however, that the public has a stereotyped and erroneous notion of "mental retardation"—a notion fostered by special educators trying to communicate with the general public. Similarly, although very little information is available regarding the response of children to labels, what is available indicates that these labels are not perceived in positive terms. In one study, for example, twenty-three high school boys enrolled in an EMR special class were questioned about their attitudes toward the class. Seventeen of the boys said that they lied whenever they were asked about their schoolwork (saying that they were enrolled in regular courses); and "not one of the twenty-three respondents indicated the special class as his preferred educational placement" (Jones, 1972, p. 561). The effects of stereotyping are certainly not confined to the area of mental retardation; all exceptionality has some degree of negative social implication and a number of labels used to describe problems of children and adults have undeniable stereotyping effects.

The foregoing presentation is indicative of discussion which has been occurring during the last decade concerning use of traditional categorical labels in the field of special education. In reviewing the pro and con arguments just presented, it is important to note that positive aspects of the traditional categories tend to relate to program administration (obtaining funds, planning for services, and accounting for services offered), while the negative aspects relate to instructional and civil rights concerns. This state of affairs has prompted many special educators to try to offer special education programs which use traditional categories in dealing with state and federal agencies, but ignore the labels in actual planning and implementation of the services at the local level (Blatt, 1972).

Another important point to note is that most of the debate concerning special education categories has been centered around the areas of educable mental retardation, behavior disorders, and learning disabilities. While many of the points made above apply to all categories of exceptionality, the abuses in the system have been primarily in the three areas just listed, and it is in these areas that the cries for reform have been most insistent.

In 1972, Nicholas Hobbs of Vanderbilt University was awarded a grant by the U. S. Department of Health, Education, and Welfare to study problems of classification and make a set of definitive recommendations on the topic. He approached the task by soliciting papers from respected professionals in all facets of work with exceptional individuals, and the products of the study include a publication of all solicited papers (Hobbs, 1975a) and a book presenting a summary and a set of specific recommendations (Hobbs, 1975b). Professionals involved in the *Project on Classification of Exceptional Children* cited numerous problems associated with the use of categorical labels, and recommendations were made that an increased emphasis be placed on funding of needed services, without inflexible reference to categorical grouping of clients. Coupled with issuance of numerous warnings concerning possible and documented misuses of categorical labels, however, Hobbs concluded that use of categorization systems is so embedded in our ways of thinking and approaches to problem solving that complete discarding of categories is impossible.

This author is not in disagreement with Hobbs on the latter point, and the organization of this book reflects not a total abandonment of categories of exceptionality, but rather an approach to categorization which is (a) potentially less threatening to those being labeled, and (b) potentially more conducive to development of better-quality treatment systems. Within the framework of this book, some traditional categories of exceptionality are maintained as separate entities, notably vision, hearing, and speech impairments, as well as exceptional gifts and talents. Other traditional categories of exceptionality, such as trainable mental retardation and orthopedic handicaps, are presented in rather nontraditional ways, with TMR being part of chapters 5 and 6, and orthopedic handicaps being presented not as an educational label which in and of itself defines a category of service, but rather as a set of impairments that affect learning in various regular and special education settings. And finally, in line with direct service and teacher-preparation trends in many states, the traditional categories of educable mental retardation, behavior disorders, and learning disabilities are combined in two chapters on mild learning and behavior problems. Thus, the aim of the present author, as represented in the organization of this text, is not to "throw away categories" but to move from the traditional categorical system in special education to one in which children are sorted and grouped on educationally relevant dimensions. *Exceptional children are defined in this book as children who require special services of a substantive nature and degree in order to assure optimum learning and educational development.* A focus on definition and classification *for the purpose of providing appropriate special education services* is a continuing theme.

APPROPRIATE SPECIAL EDUCATION PLACEMENT

Closely related to the debate concerning use of categorical labels in special education has been the discussion of regular versus special class placement for children labeled educable mentally retarded, learning disabled, and behavior disordered. The beginnings of this debate were described in chapter 1, and its escalation produced a movement termed "mainstreaming" which has had a profound effect on both special and regular education. Since the early 1960s, an increasing number of special educators had been calling for increased regular class experiences for students in special education, and three primary modes developed for achieving this goal:

1. Partially self-contained special classes, in which students spend the

majority of their day in the special class but attend selected regular classes with other children (often nonacademic classes, such as physical education, art, and shop);

2. Resource rooms, in which children receive short-term special help, usually on a tutorial basis, while spending the major part of the day in the regular classroom; and

3. Consulting teacher programs, in which children spend all or nearly all of the school day in the regular classroom, and the classroom teacher receives help from a special education "consulting teacher" in planning and implementing programs in the classroom to help the child.

Courtesy of The Ford Foundation (Tommy Wadeton).

Variations on these programs have abounded, and studies have been done to determine the relative efficacy of various administrative arrangements for serving students with learning and behavior problems. These studies are presented in some detail in chapter 3, but it will suffice here to say that no administrative arrangement for service to this group of students has been shown to be consistently and unequivocally better than another. The emphasis on increased regular class placement has been based on philosophical, not empirical arguments. The major beliefs which underlie placement of students with learning and behavior problems in regular education are listed below.

1. Students differ on a continuum of functional ability levels, and students in EMR, BD, and LD classes are more *like* than *different from* their peers in regular classes. Contrary to the popular notion that exceptional children are consistently and qualitatively different from children not labeled exceptional, the mainstreaming movement assumes that the overlap among students' abilities and interests outweigh the differences, and that it is possible to program across a wider range of variance in skill levels than is presently considered tolerable in many classrooms.

2. Traditional special classes, with curricula separate from regular education, tend to exacerbate rather than narrow the differences in functional skill levels between students in regular and special education. For example, an EMR curriculum which places proportionately less

emphasis on academic skills than the regular curriculum actually moves the child *away from*, not toward reintegration in regular education, since the more prolonged is the removal from a standard curriculum, the less able the student is to function in that curriculum. In short, special class placement can result in atrophy of skills critical for regular class functioning.

3. Closely related to the point just made, special class placement introduces the student into an "artificial" atmosphere in which the class size is smaller and the expectations are often reduced. Once the student is adjusted to this potentially more "protective" atmosphere, movement back into the larger group is often difficult.

4. Special classes isolate students from their peers, often requiring attendance in other than neighborhood schools. Even if the special class is in a student's home school, it is clearly recognizable as a separate unit from the rest of the school, and both the room and the students are often given derogatory names by other students in the school. While it can be argued that students recognize and sometimes make fun of their less able peers with or without special education, it is apparent in any school that special classes for students labeled EMR, BD, or LD can contribute to this derogation.

5. Related to the point just made, it is argued by many special educators that isolation of children with learning and behavior problems has negative implications not only for the students so placed, but for their "normal" peers as well. The point is made that we must all learn to live in a culture of diverse individuals, and to seek homogeneity of school groupings is to deny children the opportunity to learn to interact with less able peers on a personal and social basis. In short, it is posited that prejudice against those from whom one is different can be addressed and reduced only if opportunities for contact and interaction are available on an ongoing basis.

6. The final argument to be cited here in support of regular class placement of students with learning and behavior problems relates to point (1) above, and in particular, the classroom teacher's tolerance for diversity of skill levels in the classroom. It is argued that by focusing on solution of learning and behavior problems in the regular classroom to the maximum extent possible, the classroom teacher is learning techniques and approaches which will be used with other children in the room and reduce the necessity of future referrals to special education for similar problems. It is hoped that special education services provided in the regular classroom will enhance teacher skills and narrow the gap between regular and special education.

As mentioned earlier, approaches to "mainstreaming" have varied widely. In some cases, mainstreaming has been used as a professional excuse for cutting special education costs by reassigning children to regular classrooms without special help or supportive services, action which is clearly not consistent with the principles underlying the movement. Positive examples of mainstreaming range from establishing consulting teacher services on a statewide basis in Vermont (Egner & Lates, 1975) to a plan adopted in a school building in Urbana, Illinois, in which all teachers, including special educators, teach in a heterogeneous classroom and average class size has been reduced to fifteen, with highly individualized instructional programs in each classroom. Models for mainstreaming are further discussed in chapters 3 and 4.

Since its inception, the concept of mainstreaming has been expanded into a broader principle which applies not only to provision of regular class experiences for students with mild problems of learning and social behavior, but to placement of *all* exceptional children for the purpose of providing special education. This principle, known as "least restrictive placement" (LRP), holds that (1) students should be placed in special education services based on their unique educational needs, (2) a broad array of possible special education services should be available to any given student, and (3) placement of students in a special education arrangement should assure that the children are removed from the educational mainstream *only as necessary to meet their specific education needs.* Thus, the principle of least restrictive placement holds that placement in the regular curriculum is preferable to placement in a special class, special class is preferable to a segregated special school, special day school is preferable to a residential center, and so on. The LRP philosophy holds that any movement to a "more restrictive," i.e., more isolated setting must be justified on the basis of the individual child's educational needs. More restrictive placements cannot be justified on the basis of either convenience to a teacher and other students, or availability in a given locale of a limited range of service options. In determining least restrictive placement, the educational needs of the individual child are paramount.

Obviously the doctrine of least restrictive placement is inclusive of the mainstreaming movement described earlier. Mainstreaming, however, is only a subset of LRP: the doctrine of least restrictive placement applies to all of special education. For example, if a school district places children labeled trainable mentally retarded in a special school setting in which they have no opportunity for interaction with nonretarded peers, this placement must be justified on the grounds that the children's educational needs can be met in the special school, but not in a special class in a regular school. Likewise, if children are sent to a residential center for purposes of education, it must be demonstrated that their educational needs cannot be met in a program within the local community.

Inherent in the concept of least restrictive placement is the assumption that an array of special education service delivery alternatives is available to any given child. The desirable array of services is generally described in the framework of a "continuum of services," first described by Reynolds (1962) and later expanded upon by Deno (1970), Dunn (1973), and others. Deno describes a "cascade system...designed to make available whatever different-from-the-mainstream kind of setting is required

to control the learning variables deemed critical for the individual case"
(p. 235), and presents the cascade as follows in Figure 2-1:

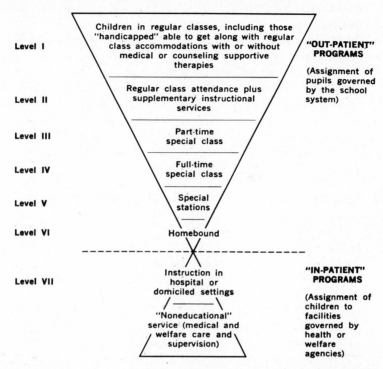

FIG. 2-1. The cascade system of special education service. The tapered design indicates the considerable difference in the numbers involved at the different levels and calls attention to the fact that the system serves as a diagnostic filter. The most specialized facilities are likely to be needed by the fewest children on a long term basis. This organizational model can be applied to development of special education services for all types of disability. Copyright 1970, The Council for Exceptional Children. Reproduced by permission.

As seen in the figure, it is assumed that each more restrictive level of service in the cascade will be needed by fewer children than the level which immediately precedes it, and that the cascade applies to all areas of exceptionality, no matter how mild or severe. Various forms of the cascade or continuum of services currently appear in most state legislation or regulations, and while implementation of the continuum of services concept is extremely difficult in many sparsely populated areas due to small numbers of children served, it is the single most widely used organizer for planning and development of special education services at the present time. An important point regarding the cascade of services is that it must be viewed *actively* rather than *passively*. Schools must generate programs at the "less restrictive" end of the cascade, and the educational goal for children in special education should always be to prepare each student to move into a less restrictive educational setting. The cascade of services should represent not a static collection of educational alternatives, but a continual challenge in the education of individuals with exceptional needs.

In summary, this section has described three principles which have had a significant impact on placement options that are available and preferred in special education: mainstreaming, least restrictive placement, and the cascade or continuum of services. These principles have evolved from statements of professional opinion, litigation, and legislation, and are principles upon which growing numbers of school systems are operating special education programs. The principles serve as the basis for much of the discussion presented in chapters 3–11.

ROLE OF THE FEDERAL GOVERNMENT IN SPECIAL EDUCATION

The fifth major issue of the 1970s is the dramatic expansion of the federal role in special education. The federal government's involvement in special education grew from practically nothing in 1960 to significant levels in 1970. For the most part, growth in the federal role during the 1960s was measured in dollars appropriated and spent. In the 1970s, however, while the financial investment of the federal government in special education continued to grow impressively, the major story is the increased federal influence in regulation of special education services.

The first federal legislation to introduce requirements for stringent safeguards concerning the rights of children in special education was Public Law 93-380, the Education Amendments of 1974. This legislation mandated assurance of due process procedures at the state and local level, assurance of education in the least restrictive environment, and establishment of a "goal of providing full educational opportunities for all handicapped children within each state, along with a comprehensive blueprint and detailed timetable toward the achievement of that objective" (LaVor, 1976, p. 101).

In 1975, the U. S. Congress passed and former President Ford signed into law P.L. 94-142, legislation which many consider to be the most important in the history of special education. Public Law 94-142 authorized, for the first time, federal money to be provided directly to local school districts for provision of special education services; the law stipulated that after 1979, 75 percent of all funds appropriated under the act flow through State Education Agencies (SEA's) directly to Local Education Agencies (LEA's) for support of services to children. In a regulatory vein, P.L. 94-142 requires the following assurances from SEA's:

1. A free appropriate public education is available to all handicapped children in the State between the ages of 3 and 18 in states with preschool special education mandates, and 5 and 18 in states without such a mandate;

2. By September 1, 1980, the mandate is extended to age 21 in all states except those in which such an age extension is "inconsistent with State law or practice, or the order of any court";
3. Each child receiving special education must have a written individualized education program (IEP) containing statements concerning present levels of educational performance, annual goals, short-term objectives, educational services to be provided, participation of the child in regular educational programs, date for initiation and anticipated length of services, and procedures for evaluating progress toward instructional objectives;
4. Each child must receive special education in the least restrictive environment, with removal from the regular educational environment only when the nature or severity of handicap demands such removal;
5. Due process procedures must be established in each State to assure that "handicapped children and their parents or guardians are guaranteed procedural safeguards" in provision of special education services; and
6. Diagnostic and assessment procedures must be established by each State to assure that racial or cultural bias is not present in special education identification systems.

P.L. 94-142 is significant legislation for several reasons. First, it expanded the educational rights which had been included in P.L. 93-380, and increased the federal regulatory control of special education. Second, it promised substantial federal investment in special education. Third, it established right-to-education and other issues presented in this chapter as national priorities in special education. And finally, it is permanent legislation, without an expiration date, a rarity in federal legislation that is indicative of the seriousness with which Congress approached this commitment.

ROLE OF PARENTS IN SPECIAL EDUCATION

Parents have been a major force throughout this century in development of special education services, especially for the more severely handicapped. Parents of moderately retarded children operated their own schools in the 1950s and 1960s, when public school education was not available. The same situation existed throughout most of the 1970s with regard to services for severely and profoundly handicapped children.

Parents' groups in special education include the National Association for Retarded Citizens (previously National Association for Retarded Children), the Association for Children with Learning Disabilities (ACLD), and the National Society for Autistic Children (NSAC). These organizations and their associated state and local groups have been very active in lobbying for state and federal legislation, and in serving as advocates for individual children at the local level.

The most significant factor in increasing parental involvement in special education in the 1970s was development of due process and impartial hearing procedures. Whereas the activities outlined above involved parents on a voluntary and therefore limited basis, the aim of the due process requirements is to have all parents involved in the planning of special education services for their children. This is, of course, a goal which can only be approximated in practice. While all due process procedures require that active involvement of parents be solicited by school officials, it is recognized that all parents will not want to become involved. In such cases it is required only that school districts maintain records of their efforts to solicit parent involvement.

In most state and federal legislation and regulations, parent involvement is expected at four points in the planning and provision of special education services. First, parental notification is usually required at the time of referral of the child for special education, and parental consent is customary before diagnostic assessment can be done. Second, parental involvement in planning conferences is expected and consent for actual provision of services is required. If parents do not believe the planning to be adequate or the proposed services to be appropriate, an impartial due process hearing may be requested. Third, parents must approve any significant changes in the student's educational program or the type of special education services being offered. And finally, parental involvement and consent is required to discontinue special education service for a child.

If at any point identified above, the parent is dissatisfied with the school district's plans or the actual services being provided, an impartial due process hearing may be requested. Generally, there are two levels of such hearings, local and state. At such a hearing, the parents and the school officials are assumed to be adversaries, and each may be represented by legal or other counsel. When a request for a due process hearing is made, an impartial hearing officer is appointed by the State Education Agency, and a formal hearing is held at which both sides present evidence and a verbatim transcript of the proceedings is kept. The impartial hearing officer, who may not be an employee of the school district in question, weighs the evidence, requests additional information if necessary, and issues a ruling. If either side (the parents or the school) do not wish to abide by the ruling, a state-level hearing may be requested. In this case, procedures similar to those described above are followed for the state hearing, and generally the impartial hearing officer in state proceedings makes a recommendation to the Chief State School Officer (for example, State Superintendent of Education) who issues a ruling that is binding on all parties involved. The only recourse available to a parent or a school district beyond the state-level hearing is to take the matter to court.

The process described above is accurate with minor variations for nearly all of the fifty states. Due process procedures were established with two goals in mind, to assure that parents have an opportunity to be heard and to cut down on the number of court cases in special education. Since it is a requirement of the courts that all administrative remedies must be exhausted before a suit will be accepted, the due process procedures serve as a means of solving many disputes without legal action.

An important point to note with regard to due process procedures is that no presumption of correctness is made for either side in a conflict. The role of the impartial hearing officer is to hear both sides and render a just decision. Neither side of a dispute, however, bears any greater burden of proof than the other. Due process hearings should not be likened to court suits, in which the parent is the plaintiff and the school official is the defendant, but rather to a dispute in which a referee is empowered to decide the outcome and solve the problem.

While the aim of due process procedures is to guarantee that the rights of children and their parents are protected, it must be pointed out that such is not always the case. Impartial due process hearings are an imperfect mechanism for assuring positive parental involvement for four reasons. First, the process itself is complex and it generally takes a parent (or professional) who is relatively sophisticated and experienced in special education matters to understand the complexities of the process. Second, the entire system depends on parents being aware of its existence, a problem which is complicated in rural areas or areas where contact between homes and schools is infrequent and largely negative. Third, many parents who understand the due process procedures are hesitant to request a hearing because of the potentially enormous amount of time and energy required to prepare for a hearing. And fourth, many parents who request a hearing and receive a favorable ruling report that they have "won the battle but lost the war," due to the ill feelings created in the school district by the process, and the aftermath of these feelings.

The impartial due process procedures which are existent in most school districts are not the final answer for involvement of parents in the special education process. They are, however, a significant first step, and the present challenge is to find ways to make these procedures more accessible to and usable by parents in general. In short, these procedures have created parental involvement, but not enough.

COOPERATION BETWEEN REGULAR AND SPECIAL EDUCATION

Until the advent of the movement toward mainstreaming, or least restrictive placement, special and regular education were two separate systems that coexisted within the educational enterprise, but which often did not overlap to any significant degree. In effect, special educators encouraged this separation through what Deno (1972) has called the Statue of Liberty philosophy: "Give me your defective, defeated and unwanted and I will love and shelter them" (p. 231). Also, the very labels used in special education have served as barriers which warn that these problems are too difficult to be solved by anyone without specialized training.

The mainstreaming movement has brought a significant shift in the extent to which regular and special education teachers and administrators interact, and the most successful of the resource/consulting teacher mod-

els for special education bring special educators into the regular classroom to work with students and teachers. The time of near-total
separation between special and regular education is past, and the special
education of the present involves classroom teachers and special educators working closely to meet the educational needs of students.

One of the major issues in special education during the 1970s centered
on preparation of regular educators to assume the new responsibilities
involved in mainstreaming. If mainstreaming is to succeed, classroom
teachers must be prepared to deal with learning and behavior problems in
the classroom, and inclusion of coursework in special education as a part
of regular education preparation programs has been the exception rather
than the rule. At the present time, only a few states require any background in special education for elementary and secondary teacher certifi-

Courtesy of The Muscular Dystrophy Association.

cation, and a common teacher objection to integrated special education is, "I'm not prepared to do it."

During the last half of the 1970s, substantial attention has been given to identification of skills of classroom teachers that will increase the probability that students with learning and behavior problems make appropriate progress in the regular classroom. Also, preservice and inservice training models have been developed and implemented for increasing these skills in classroom teachers. The Bureau of Education for the Handicapped, which awards grants to colleges, universities, and State Education Agencies for preparation of personnel for special education, has targeted an increasing amount of money each year for training of regular educators, both administrators and classroom teachers. One such initiative has involved awarding of grants to encourage colleges and universities to incorporate special education training into regular teacher preparation programs.

In summary, education of children with special needs is no longer the sole responsibility of special educators, and the 1970s has seen the beginning of removal of barriers between regular and special education, barriers that should have never been built in the first place. The special education literature has begun to reflect these efforts, which will be of paramount importance in the 1980s.

Special education is a field of continual development and refinement of knowledge. The issues delineated here will play a major role in shaping the future of special education, and to some extent, all education. The principles presented in this chapter will be evident throughout the discussion of specific areas of special education in the remainder of the book. Now that the general issues have been identified, we will move to a treatment of the various areas of special education service.

REFERENCES

Adelman, H. S. The not-so-specific learning disability population. *Exceptional Children*, 1971, *37*, 528–533.

Ashcroft, S. C. Blind and partially seeing children. In L. M. Dunn (ed.), *Exceptional Children in the Schools.* New York: Holt, Rinehart and Winston, 1963.

Blatt, B. Public policy and the education of children with special needs. *Exceptional Children*, 1972, *38*, 537–545.

Brown v. Board of Education, 347 U. S. 483 (1954).

Clausen, I. Quo vadis, AAMD? *Journal of Special Education*, 1972, *6*, 51–60.

Crowner, T. T. A public school program for severely and profoundly handicapped students: Zero exclusion. In L. Brown, T. Crowner, W. Williams, and R. York (ed.), *Madison's Alternative for Zero Exclusion: A Book of Readings.* Madison, WI: Madison Public Schools, 1975.

Deno, E. Special education as developmental capital. *Exceptional Chil-*

dren, 1970, *37,* 229–237.

Diana v. State Board of Education. Civil No. C-70, 37 RFP (N. D. CA, Jan. 7, 1970 and June 18, 1973).

Egner, A., and Lates, B. J. The Vermont consulting teacher program: case presentation. In C. A. Parker (ed.), *Psychological Consultation: Helping Teachers Meet Special Needs.* Reston, VA: Council for Exceptional Children, 1975.

Foster, G. G., and Salvia, J. Teacher response to label of learning disabled as a function of demand characteristics. *Exceptional Children,* 1977, *43,* 533–534.

Gallagher, J. J. The special education contract for mildly handicapped children. *Exceptional Children,* 1972, *38,* 527–535.

Gillung, T. G., and Rucker, C. M. Labels and teacher expectations. *Exceptional Children,* 1977, *43,* 464–465.

Hobbs, N. (ed.) *Issues in the Classification of Children (2 vols.).* San Francisco: Jossey-Bass, 1975(a).

——*The futures of children.* San Francisco: Jossey-Bass, 1975(b).

Iano, R. P. Shall we disband special classes? *Journal of Special Education,* 1972, *6,* 167–177.

Jones, R. L. Labels and stigma in special education. *Exceptional Children,* 1972, *38,* 553–564.

Jones, J. W. *Blind Children: Degree of Vision, Mode of Reading.* OE-35026. Washington, DC: U. S. Government Printing Office, 1961.

Larry P. v. Riles, Civil No. C-71-2270, 343 F. Supp. 1306 (N. D. CA, 1972).

LaVor, M. S. Federal legislation for exceptional persons: a history. In F. J. Weintraub, A. Abeson, J. Ballard, and M. L. LaVor, (ed.), *Public Policy and the Education of Exceptional Children.* Reston, VA: Council for Exceptional Children, 1976.

Leland, H. Mental retardation and adaptive behavior. *Journal of Special Education,* 1972, *6,* 71–80.

Lilly, M. S. Special education: a teapot in a tempest. *Exceptional Children,* 1970, *37,* 43–49.

Lovitt, T. C. Assessment of children with learning disabilities. *Exceptional Children,* 1967, *34,* 233–239.

Mills v. Board of Education of the District of Columbia, 348 F. Supp. 866 (D. D. C., 1972).

Moss, J. W. Disabled or disadvantaged: what's the difference?—A response. *Journal of Special Education,* 1973, *7,* 387–391.

Pennsylvania Association for Retarded Children v. Commonwealth of Pennsylvania, 334 F. Supp. 1257 (E. D. PA, 1971).

President's Committee on Mental Retardation. *The Six-hour Retarded Child.* Washington, DC: U. S. Government Printing Office, 1970.

Reger, R., Schroeder, W., and Uschold, K. *Special Education: Children with Learning Problems.* New York: Oxford University Press, 1968.

Reynolds, M. C. A framework for considering some issues in special education. *Exceptional Children,* 1962, *28,* 367–370.

Rules and Regulations to Govern the Administration and Operation of Special Education. Springfield, IL: Illinois Office of Education, 1976.

Simches, R. F. The inside-outsiders. *Exceptional Children,* 1970, *37,* 5–15.

Tisdall, W. J. The visually impaired. In G. O. Johnson and H. D. Blank (ed.), *Exceptional Children Research Review.* Washington, DC: Council for Exceptional Children, 1968.

Weintraub, F. J., Abeson, A. R., and Braddock, D. L. *State Law and Education of Handicapped Children: Issues and Recommendations.* Reston, VA: Council for Exceptional Children, 1975.

Whelan, R. J. What's in a label? A hell of a lot! In *The Legal and Educational Consequences of the Intelligence Testing Movement: Handicapped and Minority Group Children.* Columbia: University of Missouri Press, 1972.

Wright, J. S. The Washington, D. C. school case. In M. Weinberg (ed.), *Integrated Education: A Reader.* Beverly Hills, CA: Glencoe Press, 1968.

CHAPTER 3

LEARNING AND BEHAVIOR PROBLEMS
A traditional categorical overview

M. STEPHEN LILLY

It will be recalled from chapter 1 that special education for children with "mild" handicapping conditions (school learning and behavior problems) is a relatively recent phenomenon. While special education for individuals with severe sensory, intellectual, and emotional problems can be traced back many centuries, attention to milder problems of academic learning and social behavior was initiated during the last seventy-five years, in response to such developments as compulsory schooling and ability testing.

While special education for children with mild problems came late on the scene, it has experienced a rapid and impressive growth. Starting with services for the "educable mentally retarded (EMR)" in the early 1900s, and progressing through services for the "behaviorally disordered (BD)" and finally the "learning disabled (LD)," the mildly handicapped have become the largest group of children receiving special education. Prevalence figures presented by Hewett (1977) indicate that more than 50 percent of school-age children labeled "exceptional learners" would be included in the categories of educable mental retardation, behavior disorders, and learning disabilities.

The majority of introductory textbooks in special education contain separate chapters on the three categories of EMR, BD, and LD, treating each as a separate and distinct entity. In fact, each of the three areas has its own body of literature and an identity of its own. There is, however, growing professional evidence to indicate that continuation of rigid distinctions between categories of EMR, BD, and LD is neither educationally sound nor professionally justifiable.

The present chapter will provide an overview of the traditional categories of educable mental retardation, behavior disorders, and learning disabilities, as a precursor to description of a noncategorical system of providing special education services to children with mild learning and behavior problems. Following the categorical overview, a noncategorical model for definition, identification, and instruction of children with mild learning and behavior problems will be presented in chapter 4.

TRADITIONAL CATEGORICAL DESCRIPTIONS

Educable Mental Retardation

Definition
The most widely quoted and accepted definition of mental retardation is that offered by the American Association on Mental Deficiency (Grossman, 1973):

> Mental retardation refers to significantly subaverage general intellectual functioning existing concurrently with deficits in adaptive behavior, and manifested during the developmental period.

Within the field of mental retardation, the subclassification of educable mental retardation has generally been defined in two ways, level of measured intelligence and level of expected achievement or performance. The range of IQ* scores associated with educable mental retardation has varied according to the author(s) involved. Some definitions of EMR based on intelligence test scores are:

> 50-80 (Smith and Neisworth, 1975)
> 50/55-75/79 (Kirk, 1972)
> 50-75/80 (Chinn, Drew, and Logan, 1975)
> 50-70 (Hewett, 1977; Telford and Sawrey, 1977)

With reference to level of expected achievement or performance, Chinn, Drew, and Logan (1975) summarize the "educational expectations" of educable mentally retarded students as follows:

1. Second- to fifth-grade achievement in school academic areas.
2. Social adjustment that will permit some degree of independence in the community.

*The intelligence quotient, or "IQ" is a standard score designed to indicate where one stands in relation to one's peers in terms of performance on a test of intellectual functioning. Tests are designed such that the average IQ score in the population is 100, with approximately 68 percent of the scores falling between 85 and 115.

3. Occupational sufficiency that will permit partial or total support when an adult.

Obviously, the danger with definitions of exceptional conditions based on expected educational outcomes is that such definitions can become "self-fulfilling prophecies." If students are assigned to an EMR classroom in which the curriculum is set based on the expectations cited above, they will most likely not have ample opportunity to surpass these expectations, due at least partially to lack of instruction.

Prevalence

The most common method of determining the number of educable mentally retarded persons of school age is based on scores on intelligence tests. This is a seeming paradox, since level of measured intelligence is but one necessary criterion for establishing mental retardation according to the AAMD definition. Nonetheless, most estimates of the number of EMR students have been generated statistically, by taking a range of IQ scores (for example, 50–75), assuming that intelligence is "normally distributed" in the population, and determining the percentage of the population which would be expected to score within the specified range on a test of intelligence. An example of this approach is seen in Figure 3-1, presented by Telford and Sawrey (1977), which indicates that "about 2.5 percent" of the population is mentally retarded by purely psychometric criteria. This same approach is reflected in the report of the President's Panel on Mental Retardation (1962), in which it is estimated that of the 3 percent of the population called mentally retarded, 2.6 percent are in the mild range.

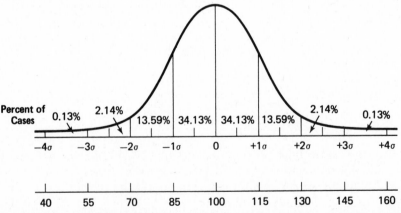

FIG. 3-1. Borderline intellect in the general population (Telford & Sawrey, 1977, p. 279).

Based upon more comprehensive definitions of mental retardation, which take into account more than scores on intelligence tests, generally reduced estimates of the number of mentally retarded individuals are generated. Hewett (1977) points out that "if a strict definition of mental retardation that employed precise measures of adaptive behavior and eventual social competence were used, the exact incidence of mild retardation would undoubtedly be closer to one percent overall" (p. 137).

In examining the incidence of children being labeled educable mentally retarded, there are still other factors which must be taken into account. First, educable mental retardation is primarily a school-related phenomenon, and the prevalence is very low in preschool and postschool years, but increases between the ages of five and twenty-one. Even students labeled EMR during their school years tend to "disappear" and are no longer identified as retarded after leaving school (Chinn, Drew, and Logan, 1975). Thus, the estimate of 2.5 percent to 3 percent of the population being mentally retarded must be made most cautiously, with due attention to the fact that this figure reflects only the school-age population.

A second factor that must be considered in interpreting EMR prevalence figures is that children are most often labeled in order to provide special education services. Often, labels are used in relation to services available in a given state or local school district. With the advent of services for learning disabilities in many locales, the number of students being served in special classes for the educable mentally retarded has steadily declined. Thus, the number of children labeled EMR has gone down as well. The response of many school districts to the controversy surrounding labeling has been to increase the use of the relatively nebulous and nonstigmatizing label "learning disability," and to decrease use of the more troublesome label "EMR." In many places, this has led to a decrease in the number of "EMR children," which is actually a decrease in the number of children receiving special education services under that label.

A third factor that must be recognized in any discussion of the prevalence of educable mental retardation is that it is not a phenomenon equally spread across all segments of the population. At least three identification biases can be pinpointed within the population of children labeled EMR:

1. More boys than girls are labeled EMR (Robinson & Robinson, 1976), a finding which is consistent across the areas of EMR, behavior disorders, and learning disabilities. This phenomenon is undoubtedly related to the fact that in-school and out-of-school social expectations tend to be more divergent for boys than for girls; that is, boys are apt to be "more trouble" and therefore more likely candidates for referral by classroom teachers.
2. As pointed out in earlier chapters, a highly disproportionate number of children labeled EMR are from lower socioeconomic status (SES) homes, a phenomenon which is *not* observed at more severe levels of retardation. This situation has been attributed to two factors:
   (a) the significant disparity between the values/aims of many low socioeconomic status homes and the schools' goals; and
   (b) the middle-class bias of all commonly used tests of intelligence, resulting in more low SES children scoring in the IQ range generally associated with educable mental retardation.

3. Minority students are consistently overrepresented in EMR school populations (Franks, 1971; Prillaman, 1975). This is clearly related to #2 above; the same factors operating in producing a high number of low SES students labeled EMR also work to the disadvantage of minority populations in the special education placement and labeling process.

Perhaps the most important thing to be said with regard to the number of individuals labeled educable mentally retarded is that caution is paramount. Determining the number of "EMR" individuals is not equivalent to establishing the number of persons with one arm. Educable mental retardation is not a unitary concept, and its definition and social usage change from community to community. Statistical approaches to determining prevalence are bound to yield oversimplifications which are not to be trusted. For a number of reasons, some pointed out above and others to be discussed later in this chapter, we choose not to join those who put forth "new and more reasonable" figures on the number of educable mentally retarded individuals.

Identification Techniques
The first step in identification of virtually all children labeled EMR is the teacher referral, which is usually the result of either inadequate academic performance, inappropriate social behavior, or both. After the referral, diagnostic data are collected using various standardized instruments, and a "diagnosis" of educable mental retardation is made. Traditionally, the single most influential factor in making such a determination has been the student's score ("IQ") on a standardized individual test of intelligence, most often the Stanford-Binet Intelligence Scale or the Wechsler Intelligence Scale for Children (WISC). If a classroom problem existed, as is evident by the fact of the teacher referral, and the IQ score fell within the prescribed range, the child was labeled EMR and provided the accompanying special education services.

Such heavy reliance on IQ scores in determination of educable mental retardation became the subject of substantial professional concern in the late 1960s and 1970s, due primarily to the emergence of the American Association on Mental Deficiency's definition of mental retardation, with its stress on deficits in adaptive behavior as essential to identification of an individual as mentally retarded. There has evolved, in the words of Chinn, Drew, and Logan (1975), "considerable professional concensus that important factors are involved in mental retardation beyond measured intelligence" (p. 7). In identification of educable mental retardation, it has been advocated that such factors as academic achievement and social adjustment in the home and neighborhood should be taken into account before a child is labeled EMR. Despite this professional concern, however, Prillaman (1975) found, in a study of EMR placement priorities in Virginia, that IQ was still regularly used as the single standard for labeling children educable mentally retarded. Chinn, Drew, and Logan (1975) point out that "many services are still operationally functioning with the single criterion of intelligence" (p. 8).

Characteristics

Perhaps the most common characteristic of children labeled EMR is that they have exhibited problems of academic learning and/or social behavior significant enough that they were referred for special help by a classroom teacher. Beyond this single unifying act of a teacher referral, generalizations concerning behavior of individuals labeled EMR are tenuous at best. In the words of Robinson and Robinson (1976), "retarded children constitute a very heterogeneous group" (p. 33).

Having delivered this warning concerning the futility of attempting to determine characteristics of *groups of individuals,* we will now share with the reader what has been put forward in the special education literature as "characteristics of the educable mentally retarded." At the end of this discussion, the reader will be reminded that such group characteristics are most often not based on empirical data, and are not particularly helpful in planning for individual children.

Kirk (1972) presents a list of seventeen "characteristics of educable mentally retarded children," broken down into physical, intellectual, academic, personal/social, and occupational characteristics. Smith and Neisworth (1975) summarize these characteristics as follows.

1. The EMR child does poorly on verbal and nonverbal intelligence tests, scoring most often between IQ 50 and IQ 80. This indicates a rate of development around one half to three fourths that of the average child. More specifically, the child may be slower in conceptual and perceptual abilities.
2. The EMR child is generally not ready for the usual school subjects (reading, writing, and arithmetic) at the age of six, but, rather, several years later. Progressing at a slower rate than most children, he will probably reach between second- and sixth-grade level.
3. While there are no personal or social traits common to all EMR children, the EMR child's interests correspond more closely to those of children of equal mental ages than to those of chronological peers.
4. The EMR person can do unskilled or semiskilled work at the adult level—approximately 80 percent eventually do (p. 307).

In a famous report of the President's Committee on Mental Retardation (1970), entitled *The Six-Hour Retarded Child,* the point was forcefully made that educable mental retardation is a school phenomenon, and that after school, at home and in the neighborhood, children labeled EMR tend to be very much like their family members and playmates. Furthermore, when they leave school, they adjust in much the same manner as others who live in the same neighborhoods and attend the same schools. In short, we must focus not only on characteristics of "EMR" children, but also on the characteristics of schools and classrooms which produce the *"Six-Hour Retarded Child."*

It must be pointed out that not all children labeled educable mentally retarded are poor, and not all fit the description of the *"Six-Hour Retarded Child."* A small percentage of children receiving EMR services have identifiable causes for what is undoubtedly an internal condition, such as brain damage due to encephalitis or febrile seizures. While this group of EMR children constitute a very small percentage of those children carrying the label of EMR in the public schools, they serve to emphasize once more the dangers involved in overgeneralizing from lists of general characteristics applied to groups of children.

Instructional Strategies

With a limited number of notable exceptions, the area of educable mental retardation has *not* developed a unique set of instructional methodologies. The vast majority of EMR curricula have borne striking resemblance to standard curricula *for younger children,* and the recommended instructional techniques have not been specially designed based on learning characteristics of the "mentally retarded." One notable exception to this general statement is the Social Learning Curriculum, developed by Herbert Goldstein and his associates at Yeshiva University, a curriculum covering a broad array of basic life skills and designed largely for the "EMR" population.

One reason for the lack of unique and nonoverlapping instructional approaches for children labeled EMR is the lack of agreement on generalized learning characteristics of this group of students. The EMR population is not, in fact, a homogeneous group of students, and this observation makes development of an "EMR instructional technology" a logical impossibility. It can be argued, for example, that the Social Learning Curriculum is appropriate not only for students labeled educable mentally retarded, but for a substantial subset of the total school population.

If anything, recent movements toward greater integration of students who have been called mildly retarded with students in the standard curriculum have discouraged the development of separate sets of instructional methodologies for special populations of students. If we accept as our goal the eventual integration of "EMR" students into the standard curriculum, we must teach them to deal with the content of that standard curriculum. Separate curricula can in fact lead students away from the mainstream of education by not presenting more complex skills necessary for success in the regular classroom. In effect, education of children labeled EMR must move from the "watering down" of the standard curriculum to an intensive analysis of the standard curriculum, intended to make it accessible to students who are having difficulty learning.

Service Delivery Models

Without question, the single most common method of delivering service to children labeled EMR has been the self-contained special class. As pointed out earlier, it was assumed for many years that special classes were the most effective means of educating children who were failing in the regular grades. EMR special classes generally stress academic skills, social competence, personal adequacy, and occupational skills (Robinson and Robinson, 1976). Primary classes generally stress "preacademic" readiness skills, oral language, and self-help, while intermediate programs move into direct academic instruction and development of "prevocational" skills such as on-time task performance and attention to directions for task completion. Secondary EMR programs are often work-study in nature, with students obtaining on-the-job work experience while continuing to learn functional academics.

Special classes for the educable mentally retarded were originally conceived and developed based on several assumptions.

1. Smaller class size makes possible more individualized attention for each student;
2. Grouping of children at similar skill levels makes possible more efficient instruction;
3. Homogeneous grouping improves the self-concept of low achieving students by avoiding comparisons with more able peers;
4. Special classes allow introduction of specialized curricula more suited to the needs of exceptional learners; and
5. Special classes require specially trained teachers whose qualifications for dealing with learning problems are greater than those of the classroom teacher.

Many of the assumptions underlying development of special classes for children labeled EMR have been called into question over the last ten to fifteen years, due primarily to mounting research data and changes in philosophical approach to special education. Evidence has accumulated that specialized curricula are the exception rather than the rule in EMR programs, and that very often the EMR program has consisted of little more than a "watering down" of the standard curriculum, a simplified presentation of some of the skills taught in the regular classroom. Also, in a series of efficacy studies ranging from poorly done to reasonably well conceived and executed, investigators were unable to demonstrate the superiority of special classes over regular classes in improving the academic and social performance of children labeled EMR (Dunn, 1968).

The past ten years have seen the emergence of new models for EMR services, involving increased contact with children and teachers in regular classrooms. Guerin and Szatlocky (1974) studied school programs for the "mildly retarded" in eight California school districts, and identified four models for programs aimed at increasing integration of students from EMR settings into regular education.

1. Programmed partial integration, in which students are housed in special classes and selectively placed in some regular classes during the school day;
2. Combination classes, in which 3–6 "EMR" children are placed in each regular class, and the money ordinarily used for special education is utilized to re-

duce regular class size;

3. Learning resource centers, in which all children are in the regular classroom and some leave the classroom for brief periods of time during the day for special help; and

4. Learning disability groups, in which all children are placed in the regular classroom and some receive individual tutoring by a special education teacher outside the classroom.

In summarizing the results of their research, Guerin and Szatlocky point out that:

1. Programmed partial integration was used most often, but led to the least integration of children and enjoyed the least amount of teacher support of the four options listed;

2. Combination classes and learning resource centers achieved the most integration and had the highest levels of teacher support;

3. There were essentially no differences between the behavior of children who had been labeled EMR and that of other children in the regular classrooms; and

4. More integration led to more self-directed behavior among children who had been labeled mildly retarded.

Walker (1974), in summarizing a research study on resource room services for children who had been labeled EMR, states that "the academic and social-emotional needs of the mentally retarded child can be met as well, if not better, in the resource room programs as in the special class" (p. 289).

Hewett (1977) has pointed out that "perhaps no other exceptional learner is experiencing such rapid changes in both special and regular education as the mildly retarded" (p. 142), and these changes are coming most quickly in the administrative arrangements governing provision of special services.

Behavior Disorders

Definition

Definition has been a source of some difficulty in the area of behavior disorders. Generally, any discussion of this area of special education includes a distinction between the term behavior disorders, which refers to behavior both frequent and disturbing enough that it is considered socially unacceptable, and social maladjustment, which is associated with juvenile delinquency. Also, as a rule, behavior disorders (or emotional disturbance) has been considered a unitary concept, with limited distinction between mild problems of social behavior as often encountered in the public schools, and more severe forms of behavioral deviations which render individuals incapable of carrying on normal day-to-day relationships. In this book, these two topics are separated, and mild problems of social behavior are discussed in this and the following chapter, while more severe problems are included in chapters 5 and 6.

The primary problem with regard to definition of the term "behavior disorders" is that the condition itself tends to be highly situational, and must be defined in terms of the actual behavior, the setting in which it occurs, and the reaction of others in the environment to the behavior. What might be "disturbed" or "disordered" behavior in one third-grade classroom can be well within the normal behavioral limitations of another third-grade classroom in the same school. What is acceptable behavior in one family or community might be cause for great alarm and concern in another setting. In short, behavior disorders are defined according to the reaction of others to the behavior of an individual.

Kirk (1972) defines a behavior disorder as "deviation from age-appropriate behavior which significantly interferes with (1) the child's own growth and development and/or (2) the lives of others" (p. 389). The role of the observer in determining behavior disorders is even more apparent in Graubard's (1973) definition:

> Behavioral disabilities are defined as a variety of excessive, chronic, deviant behaviors ranging from impulsive and aggressive to depressive and withdrawal acts (1) which violate the perceivers expectations of appropriateness, and (2) which the perceiver wishes to see stopped (p. 246).

Obviously, with the definitions cited above, precise measurement is impossible in determining the presence or absence of behavioral disorders in individuals. While it can be said that everyone exhibits behavioral excesses or lack of appropriate behavior at various times, behavior disorders are such deviations which are *frequent, consistent, intense,* and *public.*

There is often a tendency to assume that all behavior disorders consist of behavioral *excesses,* such as acting out, aggressive behavior. However, research by Quay, Morse, and Cutler (1966), using a checklist of problem behavior originally developed by Peterson (1961), identified three separate types of behavioral inadequacies: "conduct problems," "personality problems," and "inadequacy-immaturity." These dimensions of behavior problems are described as follows:

> The first dimension is composed of aggressive, hostile, and contentious behavior which has been labeled, at various times, conduct disorder, unsocialized aggression, or psychopathy. The second dimension represents anxious, withdrawn, introvertive behavior and has been labeled personality problem or neuroticism. The third dimension involves preoccupation, lack of interest, sluggishness, laziness, daydreaming, and passivity. (Quay, Morse, and Cutler 1966, pp. 297–298).

Prevalence

Given the definitions of behavior disorders presented above, it is clear that estimates of the number of school children with behavior disorders will vary widely. Schultz, Hirshoren, Manton, and Henderson (1971), in a survey of state education agencies, found that estimates of prevalence of "emotional disturbance" ranged from 0.5 percent to 15 percent. Smith and Neisworth (1975) report that estimates of the prevalence of behavior disorders "vary from 1 to 12 percent of the child population" (p. 325). Kelly, Bullock, and Dykes (1977), in a study of teachers' perceptions of behavioral disorders in their students, found that regular classroom teachers nominated 20.4 percent of their students as exhibiting behavioral disorders. Of this number, 12.6 percent were said to have mild problems, 5.6 percent were in the moderate category, and 2.2 percent were seen as having severe behavioral disorders. The number of children actually receiving behavior disorders services in the schools has never approached the higher figures mentioned above, and the U. S. Office of Education estimates that 2 percent of the school population is in need of special education designed for children with behavior disorders.

As with the discussion of prevalence of educable mental retardation, there are special factors which must be considered with regard to behavior disorders. By and large, these special factors are the same in the two areas. The following points must be made with reference to the prevalence of behavior disorders in children.

1. In every study of prevalence, substantially more boys than girls are found to be labeled as behavior disordered or emotionally disturbed. Kelly, Bullock, and Dykes (1977) found that boys outnumbered girls by two to one in the teacher nominations of behaviorally disordered children. In a study of actual service provision, Morse, Cutler, and Fink (1964) found that 83.2 percent of children labeled "behavior disordered" were boys.

2. Socioeconomic status and race are apparently interacting factors in labeling a child as behavior disordered. Graubard (1973) has stated that "casual inspection of institutions and special classes reveal that they are filled with low-achieving male minority-group members, far out of proportion to their number in the general population" (p. 255). Mackler (1967) found that special classes for the maladjusted in New York City consisted primarily of poor and minority students. Kelly, Bullock, and Dykes (1977) report that from kindergarten through grade seven, the teachers in their study reported twice as many black children as white children as having behavior disorders. Thus, the race and socioeconomic factors which enter into identification of children as EMR exist with reference to behavior disorders as well, even without the biasing effects of intelligence tests.

Identification Techniques

As with educable mental retardation, the initial step in the process leading to labeling a child as behavior disordered is nearly always a referral by a classroom teacher. Usually, the diagnostic process is followed as described previously with EMR, and a staffing team makes a decision that a child should receive "behavior disorders" services. It is clear from what has been presented thus far that absolute criteria do not exist for such identification decisions.

Perhaps the most important factor in identifying a child as BD is teacher judgment, supported by direct observation of the behavior of concern. In addition, however, some more formal measures are used.

Checklists have been developed to assist teachers in assessing the behavior of their pupils, such as the Walker Problem Behavior Identification Checklist (WPBIC, Walker, 1970). In addition, tests of personality such as the Rorschach Inkblot Test and the California Test of Personality are occasionally used. By and large, however, decisions concerning the labeling of a child as behavior disordered are made on the basis of teacher observation and teacher report data, in combination with information on school performance, most notably academic achievement.

Characteristics

It is apparent from the classification scheme presented above that children labeled BD display a wide variety of characteristics, ranging from behavioral excesses to lack of a sufficient behavioral repertoire. Thus, it is not possible to characterize the atypical behavior which leads one to be labeled BD. In this section, areas of performance which tend to correlate with behavior disorders in children will be described, keeping in mind that one should not generalize from such lists of characteristics to performance of an individual child.

As pointed out above, children who are labeled as BD tend to be more often male, poor, and minority. In addition, they are most often not achieving adequately in one or more academic areas. Rubin, Simson, and Betwee (1966) and Graubard (1971), among others, have conducted research which confirms that children labeled BD, on the average, score lower than their chronological-age peers in terms of academic achievement. Thus, it appears that a combination of academic and social behavior problems most often underlies referral of children by classroom teachers for special services.

As with educable mental retardation, perhaps the most important point to be made with regard to behavior disorders is that it is not a unitary concept, but rather a term which describes a variety of multifaceted children. In the words of Graubard (1973):

> Teachers are likely to find that many behaviorally disordered children have short attention spans, oppose authority, fight more frequently than the average child, have substantial fears and phobias, and avoid structured learning situations. Some behaviorally disordered children, however, may display exactly the opposite characteristics. The specific characteristics and problem areas of the individual child must be discovered and noted—not to medically diagnose or characterize the child but to gain information necessary for planning educational activities (p. 264).

Instructional Strategies

Unlike the area of educable mental retardation, in which development of separate curricula has largely overshadowed generation of separate instructional technologies, the area of behavior disorders is characterized by a number of unique and often mutually exclusive instructional approaches. Various authors have categorized instructional approaches in the area of behavior disorders as follows:

Kirk (1972)	Graubard (1973)	Morse, Cutler, and Fink (1964)
1. Psychodynamic	1. Psychodynamic	1. Psychiatric-Dynamic
2. Behavior Modification	2. Behavioral-Deficit	2. Psychological-Behavioral
3. Developmental	3. Behavior-Modification	3. Educational
4. Learning Disability	4. Ecological	4. Naturalistic
5. Psychoeducational		5. Psychoeducational
6. Ecological		6. Primitive
		7. Chaotic

Morse, Cutler, and Fink (1964) found, in a survey of special education teachers in the area of behavior disorders, that most teachers spent most of their time teaching academics, and viewed most of their students' problems as behavioral and educational in nature. The remainder of this section will provide "thumbnail" descriptions of the major types of instructional interventions listed above, focusing on those listed by Kirk (1972).

The psychodynamic approach to dealing with behavior disorders in children is largely Freudian in orientation, and focuses on intrapsychic conflicts and psychoanalytic intervention techniques. The overriding concern is for identification of not only behavioral symptoms, but inner causes underlying those symptoms. The most common intervention in the psychodynamic approach is individual psychotherapy, and it is seldom used as an *educational* intervention. Many hospitals, residential centers, and private clinics use the psychodynamic approach, but it is generally not used in schools due to the expense involved and questions concerning effectiveness of psychotherapy.

What Kirk terms the "behavior modification strategy" will be discussed here as a behavioral model for education, and will be presented in detail in chapter 4. Essentially, a behavioral approach to teaching demands that instructional problems be defined in specific terms which lead directly to instructional objectives and classroom interventions. Observable behavior is the purview of education, and the teacher's role is to bring about documented, positive changes in pupil performance. Continuous data collection on relevant student behavior is stressed, and instructional interventions are judged on the basis of student progress toward stated objectives. Behavioral approaches to education are becoming more widespread in special education, and will be explained in detail in the discussion of "data-based instruction" presented in chapter 4. Behavioral approaches to education are the antithesis of psychodynamic approaches.

Given the description of behavioral intervention strategies presented above, Kirk's (1972) "developmental strategy" becomes a subset of the behavioral approach. In discussing the developmental approach, Kirk refers primarily to the Madison School Plan, developed in Santa Monica, California (Hewett, 1977). The Madison School Plan is called developmental because it focuses on sequential progress through seven levels of educational goals, including attention, response, order, exploratory, social, mastery, and achievement. These developmental levels have been related directly to readiness for regular classroom performance, and have been labeled Pre-Academic I, Pre-Academic II, Academic I, and Academic II (regular classroom). Table 3-1 (Hewett, 1977) presents a description of curriculum emphases, teaching conditions, and consequences used across the four developmental levels of the Madison School Plan:

TABLE 3-1 Summary of Curriculum, Conditions, and Consequences on Four Levels of the Madison School Plan

	PRE-ACADEMIC I	PRE-ACADEMIC II	ACADEMIC I	ACADEMIC II (THE REGULAR CLASSROOM)
Curriculum	Emphasis on pre-academic skills of paying attention, actively participating, following directions, and exploring. De-emphasis on social and academic levels.	Emphasis on pre-academic skills of verbal participation and sociality. Emphasis on academic level with intensive remedial work.	Emphasis on academic skills. Regular-class curriculum content with remedial work as necessary.	Emphasis on grade-level curriculum and academic work.
Conditions	Primary use of teacher-child instructional setting with de-emphasis on group instruction. Interest and activity centers utilized.	Primary instructional setting is teacher-small group with provision of one-to-one instruction as needed.	Simulated regular classroom teacher-large group setting. Small group and individual instruction available as needed.	Teacher-large group setting with alternative settings as indicated or as possible.
Consequences	Check-mark system administered every 20 minutes, backed up by tangible and free-choice time exchange. Task-completion and activity rewards appropriate.	Check-mark system administered every 20 minutes and backed up by free-choice time exchange only. Social praise also emphasized as appropriate.	Numerical grading system for work accomplishment and behavior administered hourly. Social praise, grades, acquisition of knowledge and skill emphasized.	Regular school grading system with acquisition of knowledge and skill, social praise, and activity as available rewards.

(Hewett, 1977, p. 614)

The "learning disability strategy" to education of children identified as having behavior disorders posits that learning problems underlie many behavioral difficulties in the schools. Thus, the emphasis in this approach is on direct and intensive acceleration of academic performance. Proponents of such an approach argue that problems of academic learning and social behavior tend to occur in combination. Therefore, children identified as BD are most often deficient in one or more areas of academic performance. The "learning disability strategy" attaches greater importance, and therefore higher priority for intervention strategies, to acceleration of academic progress.

The psychoeducational strategy is, in Kirk's (1972) words, an "approach...concerned with *what* the child does.. .and *why* he does it" (pp. 408–409). Learning and behavioral difficulties are seen to be the result of a "vicious cycle" in which poor performance leads to lowered self-concept, which in turn leads to poorer performance, and so on. The psychoeducational approach deals with both the academic and behavior problems, and "proponents of the psychoeducational approach view acceptance of the child and positive interpersonal adult-child relationships as essential for effective treatment" (Kirk, 1972, p. 410). This author sees little more than semantic differences between the psychoeducational model presented by Kirk and other intervention strategies described above (with the exception of the psychodynamic approach, which is fundamentally different from all the other alternatives). Behavioral intervention programs have been observed which contained all of the positive attributes of the psychoeducational strategy described by Kirk, and which also had direct measures of student performance as evidence of program effectiveness. In this author's opinion, the "psychoeducational strategy" is not a unique instructional approach, but a set of instructional principles which are present in a variety of teaching strategies.

The ecological approach to instruction of children with behavior disorders was popularized in Project Re-Ed, a short-term residential treatment program begun in Tennessee in the mid-1960s. Proponents of the ecological strategy stress that behavior disorders are not conditions of children, but rather conditions of *children in interaction with their environment*. Thus, ecological strategies of education stress change in both the children *and* their environment. Project Re-Ed (Hobbs, 1969) has been designed on an ecological model, and consists of a four- to six-month residential program for students with behavior disorders, during which time the child receives academic and behavioral instruction while a "liaison teacher" works with the family, school, and community to produce a situation in which appropriate behavior is encouraged and maintained. Elements of the ecological model are seen in teacher consultation approaches to special education, in which the stress is on both modification of student behavior *and* modification of behavior of others in the student's environment (for example, teachers, parents, peers), so as to produce and maintain student progress.

Courtesy of The Ford Foundation (Eileen Arenholz).

In closing, one additional approach to modifying "disordered behavior" must be mentioned, because of its prevalence and the controversy that it is generating. A growing number of students are being given drug therapy for "hyperactivity," with medications being prescribed by family physicians. Drug therapy is particularly prevalent in residential schools, but in some communities one can expect a majority of students in special classes to be on one form of medication or another. Research on the use of psychotropic drugs to control hyperactivity in children indicates that drugs can bring about decreases in inappropriate behavior for some children, although some studies indicate that behavioral intervention strategies can control the troublesome behavior more quickly and more permanently. It has been contended that drug therapy produces rapid improvement in a very small percentage of cases (Omenn, 1973). Drug therapy has a number of detractors who cite inconsistent results, possible side effects, and possible habituation to the drugs used. Walker (1975) has warned against the "expedient" prescription of drugs for hyperactivity by general practitioners, pediatricians, neurologists, and psychiatrists, and has expressed "worry and dismay about the wholesale drugging of children whom adults find difficult to manage" (p. 358). Adelman and Compas (1977), in a review of research on stimulant drugs and learning problems, conclude that "it remains unproven that children taking stimulant drugs manifest important positive changes over the long term (and for many not even over the short term) in their learning and behavior at school and at home" (p. 409). Perhaps the most helpful development is the proposal that drug therapy be viewed as an *educational intervention*, and that its behavioral effects be assessed in every individual case (Strong, Sulzbacher, and Kirkpatrick, 1974). Obviously, if drug therapy is considered an educational intervention, it must be an *intervention of last resort*, used only after all other educational approaches have been exhausted. If this approach were to be adopted, the use of drug therapy would decrease dramatically.

Service Delivery Models

Perhaps more than any other area of special education, service delivery models for children with behavior disorders have spanned the entire continuum of services. By far the most popular approach to provision of special education services in the area of behavior disorders has been the self-contained special class. In addition, however, more restrictive educational settings have been used extensively, particularly at the secondary level with youngsters thought to be socially maladjusted.

In addition to segregated special services mentioned above, several models for BD services have been developed based on the assumption of regular class placement for students with behavior problems. Some of these models focus on direct work with students during part of the school day. Most notable among these are resource room models (for example, Glavin, Quay, Annesley, and Werry, 1971) and the crisis teacher model (Morse, 1962). In the resource room model, students spend most of the day in the regular classroom and go to the resource room for short, specified periods of time during the day. Instruction in the resource room is focused on intensive academic remediation and control of problem behaviors. The crisis teaching model differs from the resource room model in that children may be in the special classroom either at scheduled times or, often, on an episodic basis when the classroom situation "reaches the boiling point." Crisis teacher services are seen to be helpful to the classroom teacher, in making it possible to continue positive teaching in the classroom, and to the children, in helping them to deal with immediate problems at hand. Morse (1962) postulates that crisis teachers must be highly skilled in techniques of academic remediation and life-space interviewing, and must be a resource to the entire school.

Still other special education models aimed at keeping children with behavior problems in the regular classroom focus primarily on work with classroom teachers, as opposed to direct work with students. Tharp and Wetzel (1969) have described such a "consulting teacher" approach in which persons skilled in behavior analysis techniques help teachers and parents to solve specific academic and social behavior problems of children, in the setting in which those problems originally occur. A similar model has been in operation in Vermont for a number of years (Fox, Egner, Paolucci, Perelman, McKenzie, and Garvin, 1973), and will be discussed more fully in chapter 4.

One additional model for delivery of service to children with behavior problems deserves mention at this time. Some programs have used self-contained special classes as a model for services, but only as a stepping stone to more integrated services for the children enrolled. For example, in a program developed by Hill Walker and his associates at the University of Oregon (Mattson, Walker, and Buckley, 1970), children with behavior disorders were placed in highly structured special classes. In these classes, principles of behavior analysis and behavior modification were systematically implemented for a limited period of time, and as the children made academic and behavioral gains, they were reintegrated into the regular classroom. Contact with and support for the classroom teacher was initiated to aid the reintegration process. Another example of planned integration, mentioned in the previous section, is the Madison School Plan (Hewett, 1977), in which four levels of "readiness for regular classroom functioning" are established and children are systematically moved through the levels toward regular class placement, with specified criteria for moving from one level to another. At each level, curriculum, teaching conditions, and consequences are controlled and designed to successfully approximate regular classroom conditions. In the Madison School Plan, originated in the Santa Monica School District primarily through the efforts of Frank Hewett and Frank Taylor, the elements of several levels of the continuum of services are combined to produce an instructional system designed to move students ever closer to the mainstream.

While a good deal of research has been done on all of the service delivery models presented here, it can safely be said that no single model has proven most effective for all children labeled behavior disordered. The special class and special school models have the potential advantage of providing more systematic learning experiences, but they have the disadvantage of segregating children from their "normal" peers and thus depriving them of appropriate role models. The residential school provides even greater control over the child's environment, since it makes possible twenty-four-hour consistency in treatment of problem behaviors, but this is often more a dream than reality. A major problem which all self-contained models face, as well as resource room and crisis teacher models which remove children from regular classrooms, is that even if successful, they have solved children's problems in settings in which the problems did not originally occur. This leads to inevitable difficulties in returning the child to the original setting, since the patterns of reinforcement and instruction will most likely be the same as those which helped to exacerbate the problem in the first place. It is not at all unusual to find that a resource teacher has a set of problem behaviors under perfect control in the resource room, but upon returning to the regular classroom, the student exhibits the problem behaviors at the same rate and intensity as prior to the intervention. Glavin, Quay, Annesley, and Werry (1971) have concluded that "generalization (from the resource room to the regular classroom) does not occur fortuitously; it has to be engineered" (p. 137).

Yet another example of problems associated with generalization of learned behaviors across settings can be seen in residential programs. The Minnesota Learning Center in Brainerd, Minnesota, is a residential setting for students with marked behavioral difficulties, who have proven "too much" for their local school and/or community. As a part of the intake procedures, staff at the Minnesota Learning Center establish a contract with the referring agency, which outlines what levels of behavior would be acceptable for the youngster being referred. Upon reaching these desired levels of performance in the residential setting, the students are then returned to the community and the school whence they came. However, the fact that the child reached desired levels of performance at Minnesota Learning Center is by no means a guarantee that those levels of performance will carry over upon return to the original school and community. Intensive carryover services are provided by Minnesota Learning Center staff, and even this is often not adequate to ensure successful reintegration. In short, there seems to be ample evidence that behavioral difficulties are produced as a result of interaction between children and their environment, and changing the child without changing the environment is a short-sighted and ineffective approach to enabling children with behav-

Courtesy of The Ford Foundation (Tommy Wadelton).

ioral difficulties to function effectively with teachers and peers.

Because behavior problems tend to be disruptive and to have a significant effect on teachers and other students, there will always be pressures to remove children with behavioral excesses from regular classroom settings. Morse (1962), in building a rationale for crisis teacher programs, has stated that "if the regular school is to function, it is mandatory that we keep the classroom as free from teacher-exhausting, group-disrupting pupils as is possible" (p. 101). The Kelly, Bullock, and Dykes study (1977) cited earlier, in which teachers nominated 20.4 percent of their children as having behavior disorders, indicates that teachers are relatively intolerant of disruptive behavior in the classroom. In nearly all conversations with classroom teachers concerning "mainstreaming," the number one concern expressed is how to deal with problems of social behavior in the classroom.

In spite of these pressures toward segregation of children with behavioral difficulties, there has been a marked trend in the last ten years toward more integrated special services. Schultz, Hirshoren, Manton, and Henderson (1971), in their survey of state education agencies, found that forty-seven states listed special classes as the primary service option for "emotionally disturbed" children. Hewett (1977) has stated that "were the study to be replicated in the late 1970's, the resource room might well replace the special class, due to the trend of mainstreaming exceptional learners and providing regular classroom teachers with assistance through consultation" (p. 99).

Learning Disabilities

Definition*

Since the mid-1960s, the field of learning disabilities has been the fastest growing area of special education, and a large body of literature has developed around LD services. By and large, however, this growth has occurred in spite of, rather than because of, a general consensus among professionals as to what constitutes a "learning disability." The past decade has seen a proliferation of terms, and resulting definitions, to describe children with learning problems. McDonald (1968) has described a study by the Southern Regional Education Board, in which thirty-five professionals in the field of special education responded to a request to define the term "children with learning disorders." A total of twenty-two separate terms were used by one or more of the respondents as an exact synonym for learning disorders. In a similar vein, Cruickshank (1972) has identified more than forty terms used to identify essentially the same group of children.

The situation with respect to definitions is barely better than that re-

*This section is adapted from an article by the author, published in *Journal of Learning Disabilities* in February 1977 (Lilly, 1977).

garding terminology. Vaughan and Hodges (1973), in designing a study on practitioners' views of definitions, were able to assemble thirty-eight separate definitions of the term "learning disability." These definitions are available from a number of sources (McDonald, 1968; Kass & Myklebust, 1969; Kirk, 1972; Gearhart, 1973; Vaughan & Hodges, 1973), and will not be repeated here.

Perhaps the most widely accepted definition of learning disabilities is that proposed by the National Advisory Committee on Handicapped Children (1968):

> Children with special learning disabilities exhibit a disorder in one or more of the basic psychological processes involved in understanding or in using spoken or written language. These may be manifested in disorders of listening, thinking, talking, reading, writing, spelling, or arithmetic. They include conditions which have been referred to as perceptual handicaps, brain injury, minimal brain dysfunction, dyslexia, developmental aphasia, etc. They do not include learning problems which are due primarily to visual, hearing, or motor handicaps, to mental retardation, emotional disturbance, or to environmental disadvantage (p. 34).

Vaughan and Hodges (1973) report that the definition included in the 1970 federal legislation on LD, which is essentially the same as the one stated above, is currently used in forty-nine states as well as by the Association for Children with Learning Disabilities. They also report, however, that while this definition is most widely used, it is not the most popular among special education practitioners in the state of Colorado. In a study of acceptability of ten different definitions, eighty-seven respondents representing teachers, speech therapists, directors of special education, school nurses, social workers, and school psychologists rank the following definition by Baer (McDonald, 1968) as most preferred.

> A child with a learning disability is any child who demonstrates a significant discrepancy in acquiring the academic and social skills in accordance with his assessed capacity to obtain these skills. In general, these discrepancies are associated with special disabilities such as: gross motor, visual memory, visual discrimination, and other language related disabilities (p. 375).

Gearhart (1973) cites four generalizations which tend to link various definitions of LD.

1. Most definitions refer to both the child's capacity to learn and his/her present level of functioning, and posit a discrepancy between the two;
2. Most definitions exclude other special education categories, such as sensory handicaps, emotional disturbance, and mental retardation;
3. Most definitions exclude the culturally disadvantaged; and
4. Some definitions assume a central nervous system dysfunction (for example, Cruickshank, 1972).

These generalizations reinforce the notion of learning disabilities as a category designed to include children *not* includable under other, already existing special education categories. They do not, however, provide us with a sound operational definition of the term that will provide positive identification procedures and clear differential diagnosis.

It is this author's contention that a clear, operational definition of the term "learning disabilities" is not forthcoming, and that "rather than seek the consummate definition of learning disabilities, it would be better to examine the reasons why the term eludes precise definition" (Lilly, 1977, p. 115). Gearhart (1973) has stated that "of all the sub-areas of special education, learning disabilities is perhaps the most difficult to define" (p. 7). Wiederholt (1974) hypothesizes that this difficulty in definition is a result of the heterogeneity of children currently classified as learning disabled. This point of view is supported by Bryan (1974), who maintains that children labeled LD have not been demonstrated to differ consistently from "normal" children on such factors as auditory perception, auditory discrimination, visual perception, distractibility, hyperactivity, or presence of signs of neurological deficits. In short, "learning disability" must be defined *not as a condition of children*, but rather as a *rubric under which certain special education services are often offered.* Since these services are offered under other categorical designations as well, debate over definition of learning disabilities has offered added impetus to the movement toward noncategorical services for children with mild problems of academic learning and social behavior.

Prevalence

Given the situation described above concerning definition of learning disabilities, it is obvious that estimates of the number of LD children will vary widely. Estimates by state and local education agencies of the number of children with learning disabilities range from 1 percent to 30 percent of the school population (Bryan and Bryan, 1975), depending on both the definition being used and the purpose for which prevalence figures are being presented. Typically, states are providing learning disabilities services for 1 to 5 percent of the school-age population, although these figures are often confounded by inclusion of children receiving services under the auspices of either Title I programs (for economically disadvantaged children) or Title VII programs (for minority children).

Unlike the areas of educable mental retardation and behavior disorders, minority and poor children are not apt to be overidentified as learning disabled. In fact, learning disabilities has been described as a "middle-class phenomenon" (Weintraub, 1975), and if anything, the bias is toward provision of learning disability services in middle-class and upper-middle-class schools.

Identification Techniques

As with the areas of educable mental retardation and behavior disorders, the first step in designating a child as having a learning disability is nearly always a referral by a regular classroom teacher. Following the referral, it is recommended by many specialists in learning disabilities that a "multidisciplinary evaluation" of the child be completed, often including a medical evaluation, psychoeducational evaluation, and environmental evaluation (Hewett, 1977). Gearhart (1973) suggests the following steps in diagnosis of "learning disabilities."

1. Tests of visual and auditory acuity (vision and hearing loss)
2. Medical examination and medical history
3. Social history
4. Educational history
5. Administration of an individual intelligence test (most often Wechsler Intelligence Scale for Children or Stanford-Binet)
6. Administration of formal diagnostic instruments, such as the Illinois Test of Psycholinguistic Abilities, Bender Visual Motor Gestalt Test, Frostig Developmental Test of Visual Perception, Wepman Auditory Discrimination Test, Psychoeducational Inventory of Basic Learning Abilities, and formalized tests of academic achievement (the reader is referred to Gearhart (1973) for descriptions of these and other tests)

The complete list of diagnostic activities as compiled by Gearhart is seldom used in placing children for learning disabilities services, and is thought to be inappropriate by many special educators. Smith and Neisworth (1975) reject the interdisciplinary team approach for three reasons:

1. It is very costly.
2. Educational decisions are not made by educators.
3. The emphasis is on specifying the weaknesses or their causes which are hypothetical and unverified (p. 318).

One very important element of diagnosis not included in Gearhart's steps, but essential to the instructional planning process, is direct observation and recording of the child's performance in relevant areas of academic and social behavior. Lovitt (1967) stressed early in the history of learning disabilities the need for direct observational measurement of learning processes, as opposed to measurement of psychological processes which may or may not be related to a student's functional problem in the classroom. Haring and Bateman (1977) recommend functional analysis of behavior, a "method of evaluation based on thorough behavioral assessment of individual performance," (p. 106) as a viable approach to both identification and instructional planning. Functional analysis of behavior is summarized by Haring and Bateman as follows:

> The general strategy of evaluation is essentially a two-step procedure first of obtaining baseline data (a pretreatment measurement of the performance or behavior pattern) on the specific behavior to be changed and then assessing the conditions that maintain the behavior. These conditions include the stim-

ulus events, the responses, the contingency system, and the consequences within the learning environment in which the child is to perform. To illustrate briefly, if a child is referred for hyperactivity the first step in the evaluation procedure is to determine what behaviors are observable in his hyperactivity, e.g., foot tapping and ear pulling, and then to observe and count instances of those behaviors per minute (or other time unit) under a range of conditions. When the baseline data (rate of specific behaviors over several observations) are obtained, the second step is an assessment of the environmental conditions that cue and consequent foot tapping and ear pulling (p. 106).

Characteristics

Because children labeled LD comprise such a diverse population, lists of characteristics of "LD children" have always been perplexing and misleading. Telford and Sawrey (1977) have stated that "researchers and writers in the field have listed almost a hundred specific behaviors" associated with learning disabilities in children, and cite McCarthy and McCarthy's (1969) list of eight most frequently mentioned characteristics.

1. hyperactivity
2. perceptual-motor deficits
3. emotional lability
4. general orientation and laterality deficits
5. disorders of attention, such as distractibility and short attention span
6. impulsivity
7. disorders of memory and conceptual thinking
8. specific learning defects, particularly language deficits (p. 317).

Gearhart (1973) points out that there are actually only three universal characteristics of "learning disability children," (1) average intelligence or above, (2) adequate sensory acuity, and (3) underachievement in one or more academic areas. In addition, however, he also points out that "many of those children who fit the three mandatory characteristics also exhibit one or more of the following characteristics, *some of which are exact opposites* (italics mine):" (p. 10)

1. hyperactivity (restless, unable to sit still, etc.)
2. hypoactivity (not active enough)
3. lack of motivation
4. inattention
5. overattention (inordinate fixation on an object or activity)
6. perceptual disorders (visual, auditory, tactual, or kinesthetic perception)
7. lack of coordination
8. perseveration (persistent repetition of behavior)
9. memory disorders (auditory or visual memory)

From the above, it might be inferred that no one "learning disabled" child is like another, and this would not be an incorrect inference. What is not obvious from a discussion of characteristics of "LD" is that children labeled learning disabled are, on the whole, *very much like children who proceed through school labeled "normal."* It was pointed out earlier that LD is used more appropriately to designate a type of special education service than to describe a disability that can be found in children. Perhaps the most reasonable statement concerning characteristics of children called learning disabled was made by Jeanne McCarthy (1975) in her fifteen Ten Commandments of Learning Disabilities: "Thou shalt never again list a set of characteristics of children with learning disabilities. Thee are now acutely aware of the fact that each child with a severe learning disability is idiosyncratic unto himself" (p. 59). The same statement can most appropriately be applied to *all* children.

Instructional Strategies

As in the area of behavior disorders, instructional strategies associated with "learning disabilities" are well defined and clearly differentiated. This might seem incongruous, given the problems with definition of LD described earlier. In effect, however, various instructional approaches have stemmed from distinct, and often contradictory, definitions of the term "learning disabilities."

In this section, two major types of instructional strategies will be considered: (1) "basic ability" approaches in which major stress is placed on finding "underlying causes" of students' learning problems and instruction is targeted more toward these "causes" than toward the observable skill deficits; and (2) "direct skill" approaches in which the observable problems of academic and social behavior that led a teacher to refer the student for special help are the target of remedial instructional strategies. The "basic ability" approaches are further broken down into those which stress: (a) presumed neurological deficits in children labeled learning disabled; (b) perceptual disorders, most notably perceptual-motor problems and deficits in visual perception; (c) psycholinguistic abilities and disabilities, (or basic learning processes); and (d) combinations of the three areas just listed. "Direct skill" approaches are broken down according to (a) those which stress use of specified teaching methodologies, and (b) those which are methodologically eclectic and focus on careful specification and measurement of learning outcomes. In summary, instructional methodologies in LD are presented according to the following paradigm:

1. "Basic ability" approaches
   a. Neurological
   b. Perceptual-Motor
   c. Visual Perceptual
   d. Basic Learning Processes
   e. Integrated
2. "Direct skill" approaches
   a. Method-Oriented
   b. Outcome-Oriented

Basic Ability Approaches

If learning disabilities are viewed as deficits in children, rather than breakdowns in the teaching-learning process, then certain types of conceptual frameworks and instructional strategies ensue. Obviously, if the child is seen as the "carrier" of the problem, then the first step must be to identify the source of the problem "in the child." Thus, a heavy emphasis is placed on diagnosis, for the purpose of finding out what is behind the child's observable learning and/or behavior problems. This approach to diagnosis and remediation has sometimes been referred to as the "medical model," due to the emphasis on treatment, or at least recognition of underlying causes as opposed to remediation of "symptoms." As pointed out earlier, at least five "basic ability" approaches to understanding and remediation of learning disabilities can be identified.

1. *Neurological approaches*—Those who adopt a neurological approach to the study and treatment of learning disabilities assume that problems exhibited by children labeled learning disabled are caused by, or at least associated with, inadequacies in the brain structure or central nervous system. Indicative of this school of thought are Johnson and Myklebust (1967), who advocate use of the term "psychoneurological learning disabilities" to underscore their assumption that LD is neurological in origin.

The focus on neurological bases for learning problems was very strong in the early developmental stages of LD, and in the 1960s, many school districts established classes for children with "brain damage," "neurological handicap," or "minimal brain dysfunction." Such diagnoses are generally derived from clinical observations of "soft neurological signs"* by neurologists or pediatricians, and this diagnosis often represents the most substantive contribution of the medical profession to the special education planning process.

Several distinct teaching strategies have been developed based on the assumption of neurological defects in children. Strauss and Lehtinen (1947), in a book entitled *Psychopathology and Education of the Brain-Injured Child,* proposed detailed educational strategies based on specified theories of cortical functioning. Strauss and Lehtinen posited inattentiveness as a central problem of "brain-injured" children, and since they did not feel that brain damage itself could be treated, they recommended use of rather sterile learning environments which minimized the occurrence of "distracting" outside stimuli. Rooms for brain-injured children were to be located in nondistracting areas, teachers were to wear plain, unadorned clothing, and if necessary, children were to be put in cubicles for academic work, to protect them from extraneous visual stimuli. Strauss and Lehtinen saw this restrictive learning environment as temporary, with the children gradually learning to control their own behavior.

Cruickshank (1967), in *The Brain-Injured Child in Home, School, and*

---

*"Soft neurological signs" are behavioral characteristics, such as lack of balance or clumsiness, which are used to infer brain damage in the absence of known or actual brain trauma.

Community, described an extension of Strauss and Lehtinen's suggestions, proposing a classroom devoid of possible distractions, excluding
even a teacher's desk. Cruickshank recommended a learning cubicle for
each student, with blank walls and space enough only for a desk. In addition to the highly structured learning environment, Cruickshank suggested use of perceptual motor training.

Another leading proponent of neurological approaches to learning disabilities was Samuel Orton (1937), who proposed that poor language performance (particularly reading) can be a function of a lack of established
dominance in either hemisphere of the brain, resulting in "strephosym-
bolia," or twisting of visual symbols. Thus, according to Orton, a "brain-
injured" child might transpose letters in words (pat for tap) or write in
mirror images. Some of Orton's associates, most notably Gillingham and
Stillman (1965) have developed a highly structured phonic reading approach based on his theoretical constructs, and this approach will be discussed later as a method-oriented direct skill approach.

2. *Perceptual-motor approach*—A second major approach to building
instructional programs in the area of LD has been the perceptual-motor
approach, in which it is posited that adequate motor behavior is prerequisite to successful academic learning. The most comprehensive perceptual-
motor system, developed by Newell Kephart (1971), postulates that children develop cognitive structure after generalized motor behavior is established, and that "all behavior is basically motor,...the prerequisites of
any kind of behavior are muscular and motor responses." (Kephart, 1971,
p. 79) Kephart's theory is highly developmental, proposing that later cognitive structure cannot develop without an adequate perceptual system,
which in turn can develop only on the basis of generalized motor patterns.
In Kephart's (1971) own words, "efficiency of the higher thought processes can be no better than the basic motor abilities on which they are
based" (p. 81). In order to measure perceptual-motor abilities, the Purdue
Perceptual Motor Survey (Roach and Kephart, 1966) was developed,
which provides for observation in five areas: (1) balance and posture, (2)
body image and differentiation, (3) perceptual-motor match, (4) ocular
(eye) control, and (5) form perception. From the results of the survey, a
training program is developed which might include use of walking boards
("balance beams"), trampolines, movement and rhythm games, ocular
motor training, and form perception activities (for example, pegboards
and puzzles). The continual emphasis is on development of perceptual-
motor skills as a precursor to academic learning.

Another major perceptual-motor theorist is Bryant Cratty (1971), who
believes that adequate motor development is important to academic performance in the classroom, but is not convinced that perceptual motor
training will enhance the central nervous system or necessarily lead to improved academic performance in the classroom. Cratty sees motor activities as a helpful learning modality, which can lead to optimum arousal

levels, concept acquisition, increased self-control, longer attention span, and success experiences for children (Cratty, 1969). In short, Cratty argues for a wider variety of instructional activities, to include motor activities and games, without suggesting that such activities will have generalized effects on such peripheral areas as academic performance.

3. *Visual-perception approaches*—The visual perception approach to remediation of learning problems has been developed and popularized by Marianne Frostig, in her work at the Frostig Center of Educational Therapy in Los Angeles. Frostig has worked on the assumption that problems of visual perception can cause learning difficulties in students, and hypothesizes that improvement of visual perception skills in children will lead to increased academic achievement. Frostig has developed the Developmental Test of Visual Perception (1964), which tests eye-hand coordination, figure-ground discrimination, constancy of shape, position in space (for example, recognizing the same figure when it is rotated), and spatial relations. Remediation activities have been developed for each subtest of the Developmental Test of Visual Perception, consisting of worksheets and other activities. In working with children at the Frostig Center of Educational Therapy, visual perception activities comprise only a part of a more comprehensive remedial program.

4. *"Basic learning process" approaches*—A fourth major approach to remediation of learning problems has focused on what Kirk (1972) has called "the concept of intraindividual differences, the relationship of abilities and disabilities in the same child" (p. 55). The primary focus of such an approach is on identifying learning strengths and weaknesses of individual children, and programming either to capitalize on the strengths or to improve areas of weakness.

An example of "programming to learning strengths" is the work that has been done on matching children's "learning characteristics" with response requirements of materials with which they are taught. This matching of learner aptitude with characteristics of teaching materials, often called aptitude-treatment interaction (ATI), has been attempted most often in learner modality research. The aim of such research has been to match "visual learners" with materials that are primarily visual in nature and "auditory learners" with "auditory materials," thus maximizing student learning. Tests have been developed such as the Mills Learning Methods Test (1964), designed to assess auditory and visual learning characteristics of children.

A more comprehensive approach to assessing basic learning abilities and disabilities in school children is embodied in the Illinois Test of Psycholinguistic Abilities (ITPA), developed by Samuel Kirk (1968). The ITPA is based on a communication model developed by Osgood (1969), and is intended to separate and measure unique components of cognitive ability. The test is composed of twelve subtests which, according to Kirk (1972), measure the following five abilities:

   a. the ability to receive and understand what is seen and heard;

   b. the ability to make associations and understand interrelations of what is seen and heard;

   c. the ability to express oneself by verbal and motor responses;

   d. the ability to grasp automatically the whole of a visual pattern or verbal expression when only part of it is presented; and

   e. the ability to remember and repeat visual and auditory sequences of material (p. 55).

Administration of the entire ITPA yields a "learner profile" which displays areas of strength and weakness, according to subtest scores. This profile is then translated into a remedial program in which, in contrast to the modality approach summarized above, Kirk recommends direct work on remediation in areas of weakness. Remedial materials have been published which are directly keyed to ITPA subtests (Bush and Giles, 1969; Kirk and Kirk, 1971).

   5. *Integrated approaches*—Developers of various instructional programs for children with learning problems seldom recommend use of their programs to the exclusion of others, since they most often tap only a limited range of possible abilities and disabilities of children. Some systems, however, have been designed to be more comprehensive in the diagnosis and remediation of learning problems.

   Most often, such comprehensive systems borrow from and attempt to integrate the work of many of the individuals mentioned thus far in this section. One such integrative approach is seen in the work of Robert Valett, who has published a Psychoeducational Profile of Basic Learning Abilities (1966), a Developmental Survey of Basic Learning Abilities (1966), a Psychoeducational Inventory of Basic Learning Abilities (1968), and a handbook of suggested remediation procedures (1967). Valett defines six major areas of "psychoeducational growth and development," and lists learning abilities in each of these six areas as follows:

GROSS MOTOR DEVELOPMENT

1. Rolling	8. Skipping
2. Sitting	9. Dancing
3. Crawling	10. Self-identification
4. Walking	11. Body localization
5. Running	12. Body abstraction
6. Throwing	13. Muscular strength
7. Jumping	14. General physical health

SENSORY-MOTOR INTEGRATION

1. Balance and rhythm	5. Directionality
2. Body-spatial organization	6. Laterality
3. Reaction/speed dexterity	7. Time orientation
4. Tactile discrimination	

LANGUAGE DEVELOPMENT

1. Vocabulary
2. Fluency and encoding
3. Articulation
4. Word attack skills
5. Reading comprehension
6. Writing
7. Spelling

CONCEPTUAL SKILLS

1. Number concepts
2. Arithmetic processes
3. Arithmetic reasoning
4. General information
5. Classification
6. Comprehension

PERCEPTUAL-MOTOR SKILLS

1. Auditory acuity
2. Auditory decoding
3. Auditory-vocal association
4. Auditory memory
5. Auditory sequencing
6. Visual acuity
7. Visual coordination & pursuit
8. Visual-form discrimination
9. Visual figure-ground differentiation
10. Visual memory
11. Visual-motor memory
12. Visual-motor fine muscle coordination
13. Visual-motor spatial-form manipulation
14. Visual-motor speed of learning
15. Visual-motor integration

SOCIAL SKILLS

1. Social acceptance
2. Anticipatory response
3. Value judgments
4. Social maturity

Given this framework of basic learning abilities, Valett's assessment instruments provide an analysis of an individual student's areas of strength and weakness, and in turn, remediation suggestions are provided, keyed to the outcomes derived from use of the assessment instruments. As pointed out above, Valett's system represents an analysis of existing approaches, and actually overlaps the "basic ability" and "direct skill" paradigms. It is included here as an example of such integrative approaches.

SUMMARY OF "BASIC ABILITY" APPROACHES   This section has provided an overview of instructional strategies associated with learning disabilities based on an assumption that observable difficulties in learning are the result of more basic "causes" which must be identified and either (a) dealt with directly, or (b) taken into account in determining instructional interventions. The approaches outlined above are *not* an exhaustive list, nor should this presentation be assumed to be anything more than a brief summary of basic concepts and practices. For more detailed descriptions of these and other theories and programs, the reader is referred to the original sources listed herein, and to Haring and Bateman (1977) or Gearhart (1973).

The "basic abilities" approach to instructional programming for children labeled learning disabled has been under increasing attack during the past decade. Research on "basic ability" approaches has tended to yield either negative or equivocal results. For example, Cruickshank (1967) conducted research on nonstimulating, sterile classroom environments for "brain-injured" children, and found that such an environment did not lead to greater academic achievement than a "normal" learning environment. A good deal of research has been done on perceptual-motor approaches and visual perception models, testing the assumption that increasing skills in these "basic ability" areas will have resulting effects on academic performance. Reviews of these studies (Mann, 1970; Hammill, 1972; Goodman and Hammill, 1973; Larsen and Hammill, 1975) indicate that while intervention procedures can improve performance on perceptual-motor and visual perception measures, it is not at all clear that such improvement results in better academic performance. Likewise, reviews of research on aptitude-treatment interaction (Bracht, 1970; Arter and Jenkins, 1977) and on the ITPA (Hammill and Larsen, 1974) indicate that the promise of such "basic ability" approaches has not been fulfilled in current practice. For this reason, many special educators are placing primary emphasis on development of instructional interventions designed to directly remediate the academic and/or behavioral problems of concern, rather than searching for underlying causes of those problems and initiating instruction a "step removed" from the performance of primary importance. These "direct skill" approaches are the subject of the following section.

Direct Skill Approaches

Advocates of direct skill approaches to remediation of learning problems come from various theoretical frameworks, and are no more unified in their approaches than the "basic ability" advocates just reviewed. In fact, some direct skill teaching models claim support and even inspiration for their instructional systems from those who posit deficits in neurological processes as the underlying cause of learning disabilities. As described in this section, instructional strategies which focus on direct skills have a single common thread: a focus on teaching academic and social skills *without* direct instruction for "prerequisite" abilities such as visual perception or psycholinguistic functioning. Obviously, some approaches described in the previous section stress direct skill instruction, but in combination with attention to basic ability deficits.

Discussion of "direct skill" approaches will be focused on two types of instructional systems, those which are method-oriented and those which are outcome-oriented. For the purpose of this section, approaches which place a heavy emphasis on *telling teachers how to teach* are classified as methods-oriented, while outcome-oriented approaches stress direct and continuous measurement of student performance, regardless of the teaching procedure used.

1. *Methods-oriented approaches*—Instructional systems for children with learning problems which are methodologically based are too numerous to

be reviewed in any single chapter, not to mention a single section within a chapter. The special and regular education literature is replete with descriptions of instructional approaches, sometimes based on a given set of theoretical constructs, sometimes accompanied by research data related to effectiveness, and sometimes merely presenting a reasoned opinion on what might work. In this section, three exemplary instructional systems will be presented. These systems were chosen because: (1) they are (with the exception of the Fernald approach) *systems* for instruction, not isolated instructional procedures; (2) they have a basis in theory *or* research data, and (3) they are relatively well-known and widely recognized.

The first methods-oriented instructional system to be described was developed by Grace Fernald (1943) and is characterized as a multisensory approach to teaching word recognition. Fernald suggests a teaching procedure in which students choose the word to be learned, it is written (not printed) for them using large characters, and they trace the word repeatedly (saying it as it is traced) until they can write the word without looking. After several words are taught in this way, the children begin to write stories using the words and to read typed copies of their own stories. In addition, a file of learned words is kept by each student. Fernald's methods are precisely specified, and she recommends that they be followed without fail. In her book, Fernald presents impressive case studies to attest to the success of her teaching model. While the Fernald method is in use in many school districts and reading clinics, either in its original form or incorporated into other instructional programs, its efficacy has not been established through carefully controlled research studies. Multisensory instruction remains a "reasonable theory" rather than a demonstrated principle of teaching and learning.

A second major approach to remediation of academic problems, and specifically deficits in reading performance, was developed by Anna Gillingham and her associates (Gillingham and Stillman, 1965) based on the neurological theories advanced by Orton (summarized in the previous section). Based on Orton's conceptualization of language learning, Gillingham developed a highly phonetic approach to reading instruction in which students are taught vowel and consonant sounds which are then combined into single-syllable, phonetically regular words. Once words are learned, they are used in stories much like in the Fernald approach. Syllabication is used in teaching longer words, and "simultaneous oral spelling" is a continuous part of the instructional program. Gillingham's methods are spelled out in meticulous detail and are to be followed precisely by the teacher; neither the order of teaching nor the teaching methods are to vary. The Gillingham approach (sometimes called Orton-Gillingham) has a group of very zealous advocates within the learning disabilities community of parents and professionals and in some places, it is the sole method of instruction in reading programs for children called learning disabled. As with the Fernald approach, its efficacy has been argued on the basis of individual case studies rather than controlled experimental studies.

The final "methods-oriented" instructional system to be discussed is more comprehensive than the first two, in that instructional programs have been developed in the areas of reading, language, and arithmetic. This system, developed by Siegfried Engelmann and associates at the University of Illinois and later University of Oregon, is based on the following set of beliefs.

> Perhaps 90 percent or more of the children who are labeled "learning disabled" exhibit a disability not because of anything wrong with their perception, synapses, or memory but because they have been seriously mistaught. Learning disabilities are made, not born.
>
> The solution to the problem involves adequate instruction. The teacher must do what is required to teach, correct, and reinforce. The teacher frequently must avoid doing what comes naturally. The program that is used to teach the child must be designed so that it buttresses against all possible "misrules" or misunderstandings. Finally, the program must also provide for adequate practice of the skills taught and sufficient "applications" of what is taught (Engelmann, 1977, pp. 46–47).

Engelmann stresses that in instructional programming we must start with the task, not with the child, and posits that the only reason for a child to fail a complex academic task is "because he hasn't been taught certain skills required by that task" (Engelmann, 1969, p. 38). According to Engelmann, matching of children's learning characteristics to varying instructional approaches is absurd, because in all cases, the task to be taught is the same and therefore a detailed analysis of the task to be taught will yield but one teaching sequence and approach.

Engelmann and associates have adopted a behavioral approach to teaching, which can be defined as "getting a response to occur reliably in the presence of the appropriate stimuli" (Haring and Bateman, 1977, p. 176). The teaching act involves getting the student's attention, presenting a stimulus, and correctly reacting to the student's response. Great care has been taken in specifying means of clear-cut stimulus presentation, as well as proper teacher reactions to students' correct and incorrect responses. As the result of many years of research and systematic inquiry, instructional programs have been published under the name of DISTAR(*D*irect *I*nstructional *S*ystem for *T*eaching *A*rithmetic and *R*eading) in the curriculum areas of reading (1972, 1974), language (1971, 1972, 1976) and arithmetic (1972, 1975, 1976).

The DISTAR instructional programs have a strong theoretical base underlying the instructional procedures, and a central procedure within the system is called "concept analysis," in which three sets of characteristics are identified: "(1) the set of characteristics that define the concept, (2) the set that excludes nonexamples of the concept, and (3) the set that is irrelevant." (Haring and Bateman, 1977, p. 183) DISTAR applies the rules of concept analysis to learning reading, language, and arithmetic *operations*, and provides the teacher with absolute detail concerning both initial presentation and correction procedures. In DISTAR, children are taught in small groups, although the programs call for individual responding during instruction, as well as frequent tests and progress checks to provide the teacher with consistent feedback on specific areas of acceptable and unacceptable student performance. If a test item indicates that a student has not learned a concept or operation, the teacher is cued to the exact lesson to be repeated. DISTAR leaves no part of the teaching act to chance. In the words of Haring and Bateman (1977), "the programs specify what to say, where to point, how to signal the children to respond, when to praise, how to handle incorrect answers, and so on" (p. 188). Lest this seem to be "mechanical teaching," however, it must be pointed out that skilled DISTAR teachers learn to initiate and respond to student performance very "naturally" and enthusiastically, and DISTAR lessons are indeed enjoyable events for both teachers and children.

Unlike other direct skill approaches presented in this section, the developers of DISTAR have been continually involved in collection of research data on the efficacy of their instructional programs, and the outcomes are generally very impressive. Becker and Engelmann (1973) found that economically disadvantaged children taught with DISTAR from kindergarten through third grade performed above or near national norms in reading, arithmetic, and spelling, with the most impressive gains being in decoding skills. These outcomes were confirmed in an independent study by Abt Associates (1976) as a part of a federal government evaluation of national "Follow Through" programs for young school children. Given the rigorous methodology of the DISTAR programs, it is interesting to note that Abt Associates (1976) found that in nearly all sites studied, children receiving DISTAR instruction had significantly higher self-esteem than children being taught by other methods.

2. *Outcome-oriented approaches*—In the prior section, three instructional systems for children with learning problems were presented, each with its own unique set of instructional methods and procedures. All three focused on direct teaching of academic skills. In this section, another approach to remediation of learning and behavior problems will be introduced. This approach focuses less on direct methods to be used in teaching children, and more on procedures for monitoring, on a continuous basis, student performance in relation to stated instructional objectives. This system, which it will be recognized is not at all incompatible with the DISTAR approach (only less reliant on specific instructional methodologies), has been called "responsive teaching" (Hall, 1972), "direct and daily measurement" (Lovitt, 1977), and "data-based instruction" (Deno and Mirkin, 1977). For the purpose of this chapter, the most descriptive and generic of these terms, data-based instruction (DBI) will be adopted.

Data-based instruction will be presented in detail in chapter 4, and is presented here as a contrast to methods-oriented approaches to direct skill instruction. In data-based instruction, good teaching is defined as good outcomes, and instructional methodology is important only insofar as it relates to bringing about observable changes in student behavior. Instruction begins with the setting of specific instructional objectives, and teaching methods are changed if progress toward instructional objectives is not apparent. In chapter 4, data-based instruction will be presented as the preferred instructional strategy for children with problems of academic learning and/or social behavior.

Service Delivery Models

As with the other two areas of special education reviewed in this chapter, services for children labeled learning disabled cover the full gamut of available service delivery options. Very few "LD children" are educated in residential schools, but a substantial number receive their education in special day schools, which are most often private rather than public schools. A large number of children are also placed in self-contained special classes for learning disabilities.

By far the most popular approach to providing LD services in the school is the resource room, in which students receive instruction for limited periods of time (generally thirty minutes to two hours a day) while spending the major part of the day in a regular classroom. Resource room teachers often function as individual and small group tutors, and generally focus on intensive academic instruction. Reading is the most common area of instruction in resource rooms.

In addition to resource room services, teacher consultation approaches which stress cooperative work with classroom teachers and spe-

"Talking Typewriter." Courtesy of Responsive Environments Corporation.

cial instructional intervention in the regular classroom are often used in the area of learning disabilities (Lilly, 1971; Fox et al. 1973; Newcomer, 1977). The teacher consultation approach, with its focus on teacher change as well as pupil change, is a very attractive service model and is widely used in combination with a resource room program. Many would argue that it is impossible to operate a successful resource room without on-going consultation with classroom teachers.

At the present time, empirical data are not available to indicate reliably that one service delivery model is most appropriate for children labeled learning disabled. In comparison with the categories of educable mental retardation and behavior disorders, special educators involved in providing LD services have been most cognizant of the notion of least restrictive placement, and have endeavored to maintain regular class placements for students while providing special services on a resource or consulting basis. In a very real sense, the LD area has served as a catalyst for all of special education in development of resource and consulting service delivery models.

SUMMARY

We have presented the area of LD as the newest and perhaps the least unified category of special education. The term "learning disabilities" has been difficult, if not impossible, to define, and the variety of children labeled learning disabled defies precise description. Instructional strategies developed for children with learning problems have had widely variant theoretical or conceptual bases, and have rarely been validated through carefully designed research programs.

Perhaps the most important contribution of the LD area to the broader fields of special and regular education is the controversy which has accompanied the emergence of the LD category. When the field of LD came into existence in the 1960s, many special educators predicted that because it was such a broad, overarching concept, it would lead to less categorical approaches to special education service delivery. As has been reviewed elsewhere, and evidenced by the next chapter, these predictions were most certainly accurate.

Another major development in special education associated with the emergence of the category of LD has been movement toward special education services for children with mild learning and behavior problems in less restrictive settings. LD services marked the first major push in special education toward maintaining children in regular classrooms with resource and supportive services. This emphasis on closer relationships between regular and special education has now spread into other areas of special education.

The future of learning disabilities as a separate category of special education is unclear. Many parents of children labeled LD argue strongly that the category should be maintained and solidified, as assurance that their children will be neither labeled mentally retarded nor confused with children who are labeled mentally retarded. Many professional special educators argue for a tightening of the definition of LD, to define a distinct population of children, but there is little agreement on which parameters should serve as the basis for such tightening. The growing trend is to de-emphasize specific categories of exceptionality, particularly educable mental retardation, behavior disorders, and learning disabilities, and to provide special education services based on functional problems of children and teachers, with a minimum of child-based labels. A noncategorical approach to special education for children with mild learning and behavior problems, with an emphasis on functional analysis of problems and data-based, direct-skill approaches to instruction, is the subject of the following chapter. It is my strong opinion that the next ten years will see a marked increase in the provision of noncategorical special education services by states and local school districts, and a framework for such development is offered in chapter 4.

REFERENCES

Adelman, H. S., and Compas, B. E. Stimulant drugs and learning problems. *Journal of Special Education,* 1977, *11,* 377–416.

Arter, J. A., and Jenkins, J. R. Examining the benefits and prevalence of modality considerations in special education. *Journal of Special Education,* 1977, *11,* 281–298.

Becker, W. C., and Engelmann, S. E. *Technical Report 73–2.* Eugene, OR: University of Oregon, 1973.

Bracht, G. H. Experimental factors related to aptitude-treatment interactions. *Review of Educational Research,* 1970, *40,* 627–645.

Bryan, T. H. Learning disabilities: a new stereotype. *Journal of Learning Disabilities,* 1974, *7,* 304–309.

—— and Bryan, J. H. *Understanding Learning Disabilities.* New York: Alfred Publishing Company, Inc., 1975.

Bush, W., and Giles, M. *Aids to Psycholinguistic Teaching.* Columbus, OH: Charles E. Merrill Publishing Co., 1969.

Chinn, P. C., Drew, C. J., and Logan, D. R. *Mental Retardation: A Life Cycle Approach.* St. Louis: The C. V. Mosby Company, 1975.

Cratty, B. *Active Learning: Games to Enhance Academic Abilities.* Englewood Cliffs, NJ: Prentice-Hall, Inc., 1971.

—— *Perceptual-Motor Behavior and Educational Processes.* Springfield, IL: Charles C Thomas Publisher, 1969.

Cruickshank, W. M. *The Brain-Injured Child in Home, School, and Community.* Syracuse: Syracuse University Press, 1967.

—— Some issues facing the field of learning disabilities. *Journal of Learning Disabilities,* 1972, *5,* 380–388.

Deno, S. L., and Mirkin, P. K. *Data-based Program Modification: A Manual.* Reston, VA: Council for Exceptional Children, 1977.

Dunn, L. M. Special education for the mildly retarded: is much of it justifiable? *Exceptional Children*, 1968, *35*, 5–22.

Education as Experimentation: A Planned Variation Model. Boston: Abt Associates, 1976.

Engelmann, S. E. *Preventing Failure in the Primary Grades*. Chicago: Science Research Associates, 1969.

—— Sequencing cognitive and academic tasks. In R. D. Kneedler and S. G. Tarver (ed.), *Changing Perspectives in Special Education*. Columbus, OH: Charles E. Merrill Publishing Co., 1977, pp. 46–61.

—— and Bruner, E. *Distar Reading Level I*. Chicago: Science Research Associates, 1974.

—— and Carnine, D. *Distar Arithmetic Level III*. Chicago: Science Research Associates, 1972.

——, —— *Distar Arithmetic I*. Chicago: Science Research Associates, 1975.

——, —— *Distar Arithmetic Level II*. Chicago: Science Research Associates, 1976.

——, ——, and Becker, W. C. *Continuous Test for Distar Arithmetic I*. Chicago: Science Research Associates, in press.

——, and Osborn, J. *Distar Language Level II*. Chicago: Science Research Associates, 1971.

——, —— *Distar Language Level III*. Chicago: Science Research Associates, 1972.

——, —— *Distar Language Level I*. Chicago: Science Research Associates, 1976.

——, and Stearns, S. *Distar Reading Level III*. Chicago: Science Research Associates, 1972.

Fernald, G. *Remedial Techniques in Basic School Subjects*. New York: McGraw-Hill, Inc., 1943.

Fox, W. L., Egner, A. N., Paolucci, P. E., Perelman, P. F., McKenzie, H. S., and Garvin, J. An introduction to a regular classroom approach to special education. In E. N. Deno (ed.), *Instructional Alternatives for Exceptional Children*. Reston, VA: Council for Exceptional Children, 1973, pp. 22–46.

Franks, D. J. Ethnic and social status characteristics of children in EMR and LD classes. *Exceptional Children*, 1971, *37*, 537–538.

Frostig, M., Lefener, D., and Whattlsey, J. *The Marianne Frostig Developmental Test of Visual Perception*. Palo Alto: Consulting Psychologists Press, 1964.

Gearhart, B. R. *Learning Disabilities: Educational Strategies*. St. Louis: The C. V. Mosby Company, 1973.

Gillingham, A., and Stillman, B. *Remedial Training for Children with Specific Disability in Reading, Spelling and Penmanship*. Cambridge, MA: Educators Publishing Service, Inc., 1965.

Glavin, J. P., Quay, H. C., Annesley, F. R., and Werry, J. S. An experimental resource room for behavior problem children. *Exceptional Children*,

1971, *38*, 131–137.

Goodman, L., and Hammill, D. The effectiveness of the Kephart-Getman activities in developing perceptual-motor and cognitive skills. *Focus on Exceptional Children*, 1973, *4*, 1–9.

Graubard, P. S. Children with behavior disabilities. In L. M. Dunn (ed.), *Exceptional Children in the Schools*. New York: Holt, Rinehart and Winston, 1973, pp. 245–295.

—— The relationship between academic achievement and behavior dimensions. *Exceptional Children*, 1971, *37*, 755–757.

Grossman, H. J. (ed.) *Manual on Terminology and Classification in Mental Retardation*. Washington, DC: American Association on Mental Deficiency, 1973.

Guerin, G. R. and Szatlocky, K. Integration programs for the mildly retarded. *Exceptional Children*, 1974, *41*, 173–179.

Hall, R. V. Responsive teaching: focus on measurement and research in the classroom and the home. In E. L. Meyen, G. A. Vergason, and R. J. Whelan (ed.), *Strategies for Teaching Exceptional Children*. Denver: Love Publishing Co., 1972, pp. 403–414.

Hammill, D. D. Training visual perceptual processes. *Journal of Learning Disabilities*, 1972, *5*, 552–559.

——, and Larsen, S. C. The effectiveness of psycholinguistic training. *Exceptional Children*, 1974, *41*, 5–14.

Haring, N. G. and Bateman, B. *Teaching the Learning Disabled Child*. Englewood Cliffs, NJ: Prentice-Hall, Inc., 1977.

Hewett, F. M. *Education of Exceptional Learners*. Boston: Allyn and Bacon, Inc., 1977.

Hobbs, N. Helping disturbed children: psychological and ecological strategies. In H. Dupont (ed.), *Educating Emotionally Disturbed Children*. New York: Holt, Rinehart and Winston, 1969.

Johnson, D., and Myklebust, H. *Learning Disabilities: Educational Principles and Practices*. New York: Grune and Stratton, Inc., 1967.

Kass, C. E., and Myklebust, H. R. Learning disability: an educational definition. *Journal of Learning Disabilities*, 1969, *2*, 377–379.

Kelly, T. J., Bullock, L. M., and Dykes, M. K. Behavioral disorders: teachers' perceptions. *Exceptional Children*, 1977, *43*, 316–318.

Kephart, N. *The Slow Learner in the Classroom*. Columbus, OH: Charles E. Merrill Publishing Co., 1971.

Kirk, S. A., McCarthy, J. J., and Kirk, W. *Illinois Test of Psycholinguistic Abilities*. Urbana, IL: University of Illinois Press, 1968.

—— *Educating Exceptional Children*. Boston: Houghton Mifflin Company, 1972.

——, and Kirk, W. *Psycholinguistic Learning Disabilities: Diagnosis and Remediation*. Urbana, IL: University of Illinois Press, 1971.

Larsen, S. C., and Hammill, D. D. The relationship of selected visual-perceptual abilities to school learning. *The Journal of Special Education*, 1975, *9*, 281–291.

Lilly, M. S. A merger of categories: are we finally ready? *Journal of Learning Disabilities*, 1977, *10*, 115–121.

——— A training-based model for special education. *Exceptional Children*, 1971, *37*, 745–749.

Lovitt, T. C. Assessment of children with learning disabilities. *Exceptional Children*, 1967, *34*, 233–242.

——— *In Spite of My Resistance... I've Learned from Children.* Columbus, OH: Charles E. Merrill Publishing Co., 1977.

Mackler, B. *A Report on the "600" Schools: Dilemmas, Problems, and Solutions.* In R. A. Dentler, B. Mackler, and M. E. Warshauer (ed.), *The Urban R's: Race Relations as the Problem in Urban Education.* New York: Frederick A. Praeger Publishers, 1967, pp. 288–302.

Mann, L. Perceptual training: misdirections and redirections. *American Journal of Orthopsychiatry*, 1970, *40*, 30–38.

Mattson, R. H., Walker, H. M., and Buckley, N. K. *Assessment and Treatment of Deviant Behavior in Children: Final Report, U. S. O. E. Contract OEG 4–6–0613080571.* Washington, DC: Bureau of Education for the Handicapped, U. S. Office of Education, 1970.

McCarthy, J. M. Toward dispelling the mystique of learning disabilities. In S. A. Kirk and J. M. McCarthy (ed.), *Learning Disabilities: Selected ACLD Papers.* Boston: Houghton Mifflin Company, 1975.

McCarthy, J. J. and McCarthy, J. F. *Learning Disabilities.* Boston: Allyn and Bacon, Inc., 1969.

McDonald, C. W. Problems concerning the classification and education of children with learning disabilities. In J. Hellmuth (ed.), *Learning Disorders: vol. 3.* Seattle: Special Child Publications, 1968.

Mills, R. E. *The Teaching of Word Recognition.* Fort Lauderdale, FL: The Mills Center, 1964.

Morse, W. C. The "crisis teacher" public school provision for the disturbed pupil. *University of Michigan, School of Education Bulletin*, 1962, 101–104.

———, Cutler, R. L., and Fink, A. H. *Public School Classes for the Emotionally Handicapped: A Research Analysis.* Washington, DC: Council for Exceptional Children, 1964.

National Advisory Committee on Handicapped Children: First Annual Report. Washington, DC: U. S. Office of Education, 1968.

Newcomer, P. L. Special education services for the "mildly handicapped": beyond a diagnostic and remedial approach. *Journal of Special Education*, 1977, *11*, 153–165.

Omenn, G. S. Genetic issues in the syndrome of minimal brain dysfunction. *Seminars in Psychology*, 1973, *5*, 5–17.

Orton, S. *Reading, Writing, and Speech Problems in Children.* New York: W. W. Norton and Company, Inc., 1937.

Osgood, C. A behavioristic analysis. In: *Contemporary Approaches to Cognition.* Boston: Allyn and Bacon, Inc., 1969.

Peterson, D. R. Behavior problems of middle childhood. *Journal of Consulting Psychology,* 1961, *25,* 205–209.

President's Committee on Mental Retardation. *The Six-Hour Retarded Child.* Washington, DC: U. S. Government Printing Office, 1970.

President's Panel on Mental Retardation. *A Proposed Program for National Action to Combat Mental Retardation.* Washington, DC: U. S. Government Printing Office, 1962.

Prillaman, D. An analysis of placement factors in classes for the educable mentally retarded. *Exceptional Children,* 1975, *42,* 107–108.

Quay, H. C., Morse, W. C., and Cutler, R. L. Personality patterns of pupils in special classes for the emotionally disturbed. *Exceptional Children,* 1966, *32,* 297–301.

Roach, E., and Kephart, N. *The Purdue Perceptual Motor Survey.* Columbus, OH: Charles E. Merrill Publishing Co., 1966.

Robinson, N. M., and Robinson, H. B. *The Mentally Retarded Child.* New York: McGraw-Hill, Inc., 1976.

Rubin, E. Z., Simson, C. B., and Betwee, M. C. *Emotionally Handicapped Children and the Elementary School.* Detroit: Wayne State University Press, 1966.

Schultz, E. W., Hirshoren, A., Manton, A., and Henderson, R. Special education for the emotionally disturbed. *Exceptional Children,* 1971, *38,* 313–320.

Smith, R. M., and Neisworth, J. T. *The Exceptional Child: A Functional Approach.* New York: McGraw-Hill, Inc., 1975.

Strauss, A., and Lehtinen, L. *Psychopathology and the Education of the Brain-Injured Child.* New York: Grune and Stratton, Inc., 1947.

Strong, C., Sulzbacher, S. I., and Kirkpatrick, M. Use of medication versus reinforcement to modify a classroom behavior disorder. *Journal of Learning Disabilities,* 1974, *7,* 214–218.

Telford, C. W., and Sawrey, J. M. *The Exceptional Individual.* Englewood Cliffs, NJ: Prentice-Hall, Inc., 1977.

Tharp, R. G., and Wetzel, R. J. *Behavior Modification in the Natural Environment.* New York: Academic Press, 1969.

Valett, R. *A Psychoeducational Inventory of Basic Learning Abilities.* Palo Alto: Fearon Publishers, 1968.

—— *A Psychoeducational Profile of Basic Learning Abilities.* Palo Alto: Consulting Psychologists Press, 1966.

—— *The Remediation of Learning Disabilities.* Palo Alto: Fearon Publishers, 1967.

—— *The Valett Developmental Survey of Basic Learning Abilities.* Palo Alto: Consulting Psychologists Press, 1966.

Vaughan, R. W., and Hodges, L. A statistical survey into a definition of learning disabilities. *Journal of Learning Disabilities,* 1973, *6,* 658–664.

Walker, H. M. *Walker Problem Behavior Identification Checklist Manual.* Los Angeles: Western Psychological Services, 1970.

Walker, S. Drugging the American child: we're too cavalier about hyperactivity. *Journal of Learning Disabilities,* 1975, *8,* 354–358.

Walker, V. S. The efficacy of the resource room for educating retarded children. *Exceptional Children,* 1974, *40,* 288–289.

Weintraub, F. J. Legislation—initiation and implementation (part III). In S. A. Kirk and J. M. McCarthy (ed.), *Learning Disabilities: Selected ACLD Papers.* Boston: Houghton Mifflin Company, 1975.

Wiederholt, J. L. Historical perspectives on the education of the learning disabled. In L. Mann and D. Sabatino (ed.), *The Second Review of Special Education.* Philadelphia: Journal of Special Education Press, 1974.

CHAPTER 4

LEARNING AND BEHAVIOR PROBLEMS
Current trends

M. STEPHEN LILLY

The primary focus of this chapter is on a *noncategorical system* for identifying and serving children with learning and behavior problems in the schools. In addition, two major movements in special education for "mildly handicapped" children will be described: early (preschool) education and secondary/vocational education. No discussion of the education of students with learning and behavior problems is complete without at least a brief explication of these two areas, which will represent major thrusts in the 1980s. So the topics in this chapter include:

1. A noncategorical approach to learning and behavior problems.
2. Early education of children with learning and behavior problems.
3. Secondary/vocational education of students with learning and behavior problems.

A NONCATEGORICAL APPROACH TO LEARNING AND BEHAVIOR PROBLEMS

Based on the analysis of the traditional categories of educable mental retardation, behavior disorders, and learning disabilities presented in chapter 3, as well as the information presented in chapter 2, it is clear that a categorical orientation to providing special education for children with learning and behavior problems is less than desirable. The categories of EMR, BD, and LD are not clearly defined, nor do they adequately differentiate children for purposes of description and instructional planning. In fact, labels have been shown to have little practical value in actual delivery of special education services to children experiencing problems in regular classrooms.

The information presented thus far has supported the growing contention of many special and regular educators that future models of special education for the "mildly handicapped" must be based on something other than the traditional categories of educable mental retardation, behavior disorders, and learning disabilities, and that even the term "handicapped" should not be used. In some states, this less categorical system of providing special education services is not the future, but the present. For example, California has for many years combined the categories of behavior disorders and learning disabilities in offering services for "educationally handicapped" (EH) children, and recent legislation added educable mental retardation to this category of service. Massachusetts has enacted legislation which completely deemphasizes traditional categories of exceptionality and provides state funds for special education services based on the type of services required to meet individual needs. Nearly all states provide mechanisms by which local school districts can offer noncategorical special education services, even if the predominant funding system in the state is categorical in nature.

In this section, a non-categorical system for provision of special education services to children with "learning and behavior problems" will be outlined, with information presented under the subheadings used in the previous sections (definition, prevalence, identification techniques, characteristics, service delivery models, and instructional strategies). It must be pointed out that among persons who espouse noncategorical or less categorical special education, there is a broad array of points of view concerning appropriate instructional strategies and service delivery models. What is presented herein is one such point of view, based on two assumptions: (1) most children experiencing learning and behavior problems can be served in regular classrooms, *with special education supportive and consultative services for the classroom teacher;* and (2) a behavioral model of instruction is most effective and least prone to use of inappropriate labels, and therefore most beneficial for children with school learning and behavior problems. Thus, a behaviorally-based, teacher consultation approach to special services will be described. While readers are urged to attend very closely to the details of such a model, they must not leave this section with the mistaken impression that all who call for decategorization of special education services espouse a behaviorally-based, teacher consultation approach.

Definition

The purpose of most definitions of educable mental retardation, behavior disorders, and learning disabilities has been to be as clear and precise as possible, and to maximize the extent to which identification of such children is reliably done. Such quests for precision have generally been unsuccessful, and in defining "learning and behavior problems" no such attempt at precision will be made. Rather, a definition follows that is intended to reflect the reality of the school situation, in which the children most in need of special education services display a wide variety of behavioral characteristics, and where the need for special services is highly situational and often teacher- or classroom-specific.

> A child with learning and behavior problems is a child (1) whose regular classroom performance, in terms of academic and/or social behavior, is perceived to be inadequate, by a teacher, parent, or the child himself, and (2) for whom a team consisting of professional educators and the child's parents determine that special education services are necessary to provide the child with appropriate educational opportunities.

This definition stresses that the child's performance must be inadequate *from someone's point of view*, and that this inadequacy will result in a referral for special services. It does allow for someone other than the teacher to refer a student, most notably the parents or the students themselves. In addition, final declaration of eligibility is placed in the hands of a team consisting of professional educators and parents, a practice consistent with the due process procedures discussed in chapter 2. The definition is, by design, neither precise nor operational, since it is defining children so heterogeneous as to make precise definition impossible. It is intended to be a *reality based* definition, no more specific than the present state of knowledge will reasonably allow. Some operational guidelines surrounding the definition are presented in subsequent discussions of prevalence and identification techniques.

Prevalence

Obviously, a precise prevalence figure does not flow from the definition of learning and behavior problems presented above. Depending on local interpretation of the definition, a school district could reasonably choose to serve anywhere from 0.5 percent to 50 percent of the school population as "learning and behavior problems." It is doubtful, however, that the general public or those charged with providing money for special education (school board members, legislators, and so on) would accept a definition which would allow one half of the school population to receive special education services. Therefore it is proposed that a ceiling be placed on the number of children who can be identified at any given time as having learning and behavior problems severe enough to require special services. It has been suggested (Lilly, 1977a) that school districts be allowed to identify up to 8 percent of schoolchildren as having "learning and behavior problems" sufficient to require special education. The children who comprise this 8 percent would not be the same over time, since many problems tend to be situational and of short duration. The 8 percent figure sets an upper limit on the number of children to be served at a given time, without assuming that the "learning and behavior problem" population will be the same from month to month or year to year.

One might ask why the figure of 8 percent should be chosen as the upper limit of the number of children to be served at a given time. The figure is chosen as an aggregate of traditional prevalence estimates for the categories of EMR, BD, and LD. This is certainly not a scientific approach to establishment of the prevalence of a condition among the general public, but it represents a reasonable estimate that can be used for planning and monitoring purposes by local, state, and federal agencies. What is needed is general concensus on the approximate number of children with mild learning and behavior problems to be served in special education, rather than a continued futile search for the consummate set of categorical definitions that will yield unambiguous prevalence figures. Such definitions are not on the horizon, nor are they even conceptually possible at the present time. Thus, the task is to build a service delivery system in which we can function without such precise definitions. In building such a system, determination of a prevalence figure to be used for planning and monitoring is necessarily based on commonly shared values rather than clearly defined conditions.

Identification Techniques

In establishing identification procedures one has the option of merely combining techniques previously used for EMH, BD, and LD. This is, in fact, often the approach adopted. Such an approach usually involves administration of a complex battery of tests, including tests of intelligence, academic achievement, vision, hearing, social adaptability, and so on. The purpose of such testing is to determine the *cause* of the problem which has led to referral of the student for special education services. Most of the tests given are *norm-referenced* (meaning that norms exist which allow for comparison of the child's performance to that of other children of the same age or grade) and are standardized in terms of test items and administration procedures. Using these results, a multifaceted *diagnosis* is arrived at, which serves as the basis for program planning and instructional services.

A more functional approach to identification focuses on "a functional analysis of the process by which school learning problems are identified, the starting point of which is a teacher referral of a problem" (Lilly, 1977a, p. 119). As pointed out earlier, teacher referrals nearly always stem from problems of (1) academic learning and/or (2) social behavior. If we are to abandon the search for traditional categorical labels, then we can also abandon required use of the standardized tests which served as the basis for labeling a child EMR, BD, or LD. In place of such data collection "once removed" from the actual problem, we can instead focus on assessment of the functional classroom problem(s) which is (are) the basis for referral. Thus the data collected differ for each referral, since two children will seldom exhibit the same range and variety of learning and behavior problems. In addition, teachers (both classroom teachers and special educators) are more integrally involved in collection of assessment data, since the primary focus of concern is the student's performance in the classroom. Assessment procedures aimed at describing classroom problems and prioritizing them for solution necessarily reduce the role of school psychologists and others involved in formalized testing in the schools.

Once assessment data are collected and problems are more precisely identified and defined, the next step in a functional assessment and identification model is to convene a "staffing team" to determine whether the student in question is eligible for "learning and behavior problems" services. The essential members of such a staffing team are the principal, classroom teacher(s), special educator, and parents, with other professionals involved if they have *functional assessment data* that bear directly on the problem(s) leading to referral. The function of the staffing team has been defined as follows:

> The primary focus of the staffing team would be to determine if the pupil represents one of the *most severe functional problems* in the school, thus making him/her eligible for [special education] services. This is, in fact, a judgment for which no exact decision model exists. What constitutes a "severe functional problem" is highly situational, and thus the decision is best made at the school level. School districts could use test data for decision making at their discretion, but no specific test scores would be required (or even encouraged) for student selection. The focus would be on identifying functional school problems, and the upper limit of 8% would force schools to make priority decisions concerning which of those problems are most severe (Lilly, 1977a, p. 120).

Once a student is identified as eligible for special services, instructional planning can begin, and since all assessment data that have been collected relate to the student's functional problems of academic learning and social behavior, there is a direct connection between identification procedures and planning of instructional programs.

Functional identification systems such as presented above are not in widespread use at the present time, since most states still require use of standardized intelligence and achievement tests before children can be certified eligible for special education services. Such systems are in widespread use, however, for the purpose of instructional planning for children, and in states which have lessened requirements for formalized testing for placement, functional assessment systems have been used for identification purposes in many school districts.

It should be pointed out that an "imprecise" identification system such as the one presented here could be subject to abuse, resulting in special education being used as a "dumping ground" for poor and minority children. As pointed out in chapter 3, this is true to some extent in "categorical" special education, particularly with the categories of educable mental retardation and behavior disorders. Due process procedures currently in existence in all states offer protection against such abuse of the system, and it is critical that parents be fully informed of their rights in the placement process. With full and informed parental involvement, a noncategorical system offers the hope of *relevant* assessment leading to *nonstigmatizing* identification procedures.

Characteristics

Characteristics of children with "learning and behavior problems" will *not* be discussed in detail. As pointed out in previous remarks on characteristics associated with EMR, BD, and LD, global statements concerning characteristics of groups of children tend to be inaccurate in individual cases and divert our attention from careful assessment of individual strengths and needs. In general, children with learning and behavior problems can be assumed to have only the following in common:

1. They are referred for special education services, usually by a regular classroom teacher, because of problems of academic learning and/or social behavior;
2. They are judged eligible for such services by a staffing team; and
3. Their educational needs can be met while maintaining contact with regular class peers.

It is reasonable to assume that as with categorical services, disproportionate numbers of boys, as well as children from low socioeconomic status homes, receive "learning and behavior problems" services. It is probable, however, that such services can be offered closer to the "mainstream," with less stigma than categorical services, which could lead to better sex and socioeconomic balance as well as decreased concern over the issue of labeling.

Instructional Strategies

As is evident in the reviews of instructional strategies associated with educable mental retardation, behavior disorders, and learning disabilities, the special education practitioner has a wide choice of theoretical models of instruction from which to choose. One special educator might be committed to remediation of basic perceptual or perceptual-motor deficits, while another might subscribe to a certain method of instructon, such as "Orton-Gillingham" or "life-space interviewing." Some special educators maintain that they are "eclectic," which could mean either that they deftly pick and choose from a variety of instructional models, or that they have not mastered a single model of instruction. Most often, the instructional

Courtesy of The Ford Foundation (Eileen Arenholz).

biases of special educators will correspond rather closely to the major instructional models advocated in the university in which they were trained and/or the school district in which they work.

In this section, a specific model of instruction will be described in some detail, a model that is behavioral in orientation and focuses on direct and continuous measurement of pupil progress toward stated instructional objectives. This model, hereafter called data-based instruction (DBI), will be presented as the preferred model of instruction for the following reasons:

1. DBI focuses on the specific behavior of concern, and essentially ignores the underlying (internal) causes of the behavior. This focus on observable behavior makes coordination between special and regular education an easier task, since both sides are "talking the same language."
2. DBI avoids categorical labels, since the focus is on definition of academic and social problems in behavioral terms, thus leading to direct measurement and instructional intervention without necessity of further labeling.
3. DBI emphasizes functional assessment within the instructional setting, as described in a previous section and as contrasted with norm-referenced measurement which only incidentally relates to the problems being encountered by an individual child and his or her teacher.
4. DBI emphasizes the use of specific instructional objectives as the basis for teaching, which means that instruction is well focused and expected outcomes can be agreed upon by parents, teachers, and other school officials.
5. DBI does not rely on a specific teaching methodology, but rather provides for

evaluation of instructional effectiveness in each individual case. A teaching approach is not "good" or "bad" in a general sense, but might work with one child and not with another. These decisions are made not on the basis of subjective teacher judgment, but rather from data on student progress. Arguments over which teaching technique is "best" are rendered obsolete.

6. DBI is an individualized instruction model which operates on the basis of individualized instructional objectives and progress monitoring, but not necessarily one-on-one teaching. Instruction can be in groups, if it is effective in moving children toward stated instructional objectives.

7. DBI stresses collection of continuous data on student progress, so that teachers need not wait six weeks, two months, or an academic year to determine whether an instructional intervention is a success or failure.

8. If a student does not achieve an instructional objective, DBI focuses the teacher's attention on inadequacies in the instructional program, not inadequacies in the child.

9. DBI fits perfectly with the individualized education program (IEP) requirements of P.L. 94-142 as specified in chapter 2, in that any teacher who has implemented DBI will have readily available all required instructional elements of the IEP.

A data-based instructional model has eight essential steps. These are listed below and then discussed individually:

1. Statement of problem in behavioral terms.
2. Collection of baseline data.
3. Statement of instructional objectives.
4. Analysis of instructional objectives into teachable components (if necessary due to complexity of objective).
5. Determination of teaching-learning procedure and initiation of instruction.
6. Continuous measurement of student progress toward objective.
7. Charting of student progress data.
8. Instructional decision-making concerning adequacy of intervention.

STATEMENT OF PROBLEM IN BEHAVIORAL TERMS The first step in a data-based instructional model, as for that matter in any adequate instructional model, is to define the instructional problem in precise, behavioral terms. The need for precise behavioral descriptions of instructional problems has been discussed as follows (Lilly, 1977b):

No performance can be measured unless it can be reliably observed, and reliable observation depends on behavioral descriptions of problems. If a teacher's objective is to decrease a child's hyperactivity, for example, it is impossible to present unambiguous data in support of progress toward this objective, since hyperactivity in the classroom would not lend itself to direct and unambiguous measurement. However, if the objective is to decrease the frequency of inappropriate talk outs or leaving the seat without permission, then direct, reliable assessment is possible. Likewise, improvement of a child's performance in reading is too general to measure, while decreasing the error rate in oral reading or increasing the percentage of comprehension questions answered correctly represent objectives amenable to reliable measurement (p. 28).

Behavioral descriptions of problems prevent educators from implicitly "blaming" children for inadequate performance by using terms such as obstinate, aggressive, or dyslexic. Rather, problems must be described in *solvable* terms. Also behavioral problem descriptions help to narrow the focus of instruction: while it is impossible to solve a problem of "hyperactivity," leaving one's seat without permission is much more amenable to intervention. The key to knowing whether a problem is defined in behavioral terms is whether two people observing the behavior as described would agree on what they saw. For example, two observers would tend to disagree on when a child is "aggressive," but would be much more consistent in recording when the same child hit a classmate on the playground. Definition of problems in behavioral terms is the first, and most important, step in any feasible model of instruction.

COLLECTION OF BASELINE DATA   After problems have been defined behaviorally, the next step in DBI is to assess the present level of the problem. For example, if some students are constantly talking out, how many times do they talk out in a thirty-minute period? If the problem is not completing worksheets independently, what percent of the worksheet problems are done correctly in the allotted time? If the problem is not knowing how to borrow in subtraction, what percentage of subtraction problems involving borrowing does a student get correct?

Baseline data must establish with some consistency the students' preintervention performance in areas of concern, and this usually involves collection of one to five instances of baseline data for each behavior. One instance of baseline data is sufficient if the students obviously do not know the operation (for example, none correct on a page of two-digit multiplication problems). Three instances of baseline data are sufficient if the performance is relatively stable (for example, out of seat ten times in twenty minutes one day, twelve times the next day, nine times the third day). One need go beyond three instances of baseline data only when the data are inconsistent (for example, 20 percent correct the first day, 80 percent the second day, 40 percent the third day). Again, the purpose of collecting baseline data is to provide a picture of the students' performances prior to intervention, to serve as a basis for later determination of their progress.

Measurement of individual student performance in the classroom is both essential and demanding. Hall (1972) has described the progression from research studies employing outside observers in the classroom to development of observation procedures designed to be used by teachers, parents, and the children themselves. Hall defines the four major approaches to classroom observation of student behavior as follows.

One procedure which can easily be adapted to the new research approach is the *direct measurement of permanent products*. Teachers have long been used to recording spelling scores, the number of problems worked correctly on math tests, and whether or not assignments have been completed and handed in. In these cases, the behavior of a pupil results in a permanent product which can be observed and counted and lends itself very well to repeated measures of behavior over time.

Event recording is also a useful tool for observing behavior. It has been found that there are many behaviors which teachers and parents can reliably count and record as they occur. In many instances, to do so does not interfere with ongoing teaching or parental tasks. Thus, a teacher can count the number of times a given event (such as a talk out, an argument, a fight, the number of pupils who come in late) occurs by tallying with a pencil on paper or by using a small hand or wrist counter.

Time sampling is another tool for observing behavior. It has been shown that teachers and parents can use a time sampling procedure (McKenzie, Clark, Wolf, Kothera and Benson, 1968) to obtain an accurate estimate of the percentage of time children engage in ongoing behaviors such as wearing an orthodontic device. In time sampling, the pupil is observed at given invervals to determine whether the behavior of concern is occurring. By dividing the number of times the behavior occurs by the number of observations, the level of the behavior can be determined.

Duration, another measure which can be used in applied research, is recorded when time spent engaged in a behavior is an important dimension of the behavior—as it is in thumbsucking or in practice on a musical instrument. Wall clocks and stop watches can be used to measure the duration of certain behaviors (pp. 405–406).

Teachers must be careful in selecting procedures for collecting baseline data, since the same procedures must be used to gather progress data after instruction has been initiated. Thus, measurement systems must be chosen, taking into account both the nature of the behavior to be observed and the feasibility of continued use of the system in the classroom.

STATEMENT OF INSTRUCTIONAL OBJECTIVE   Based on the behavioral problem description and baseline data, the next step in DBI is to specify one or more instructional objectives which serve as a statement of intended outcomes. Several well-known texts are available on writing instructional objectives (for example, Mager, 1962; Wheeler & Fox, 1972) and the information will not be repeated here in detail. Suffice it to say that an objective must contain (1) the expected behavior, (2) the criterion for successful performance, and (3) the conditions in which the student is expected to perform. For example, an instructional objective in reading might be: "Given a list of 20 two or three syllable, phonetically regular words, the student will pronounce the words correctly with 90 percent accuracy, taking no more than five seconds per word." Obviously, this objective is amenable to measurement, and the specification of terms is clear and unambiguous.

ANALYSIS OF INSTRUCTIONAL OBJECTIVE INTO TEACHABLE COMPONENTS   Some instructional objectives are simple, and can be achieved in a single teaching step (for example, the student will not talk out more than two times during the independent work period, for three consecutive days). Other objectives, however, are more complex and require a number of instructional steps. For example, if a student cannot count to sixty by five's and cannot tell time to the nearest hour, then an objective calling for the child to tell time to the nearest five minutes is a complex multistep objective. In this case, an objective to tell time to the nearest five minutes is a *long range instructional objective* which must be broken down into smaller, individually teachable components. This process is called task analysis and yields a sequence of *enabling objectives* which, when successfully completed, will culminate in the student performing the *terminal objective* successfully. Task analysis is a relatively imprecise art at the present time, and teachers are encouraged to use task analysis without undue concern for finding the "correct," invariant sequence for teaching a given skill.

DETERMINATION OF TEACHING-LEARNING PROCEDURES   The search for instructional strategies has occupied a great deal of teacher time over the course of history, and educational researchers have invested considerable effort in searching for the "best teaching methods." Data-based instruction, however, minimizes attention to teaching methodology by accepting as valid any teaching procedure that produces progress toward the stated instructional objectives. In DBI, good teaching is good outcomes, and as long as teaching procedures are humane and not derogatory or damaging to children, they are judged only in relation to student progress data. This is especially important in bridging the gap between special and regular education, since it means that teachers need not necessarily learn a complete new set of instructional strategies previously associated only with special education, but rather can use their "favorite" procedures and see if they work.

One note of caution must be sounded with regard to teaching-learning procedures. In education, there is a tendency to set instructional objectives based on the materials being used (for example, reading objectives might be taken from the basal reading series chosen for use with the entire class). In DBI, however, the order of events is reversed. First, instructional objectives are determined, and then instructional techniques (including materials) are chosen in relation to those objectives. While this might seem to be a minor point, it is essential to the very concepts of special education and individualized educational programming.

CONTINUOUS MEASUREMENT OF STUDENT PROGRESS   Once instruction has been initiated, progress data must be collected on a continuous basis to determine whether the instructional intervention is successful. Some advocates of DBI suggest daily measurement of student progress (Lovitt, 1977), while others call for measurement at least twice a week (Lilly, 1977b).

In general, measurement of progress must be consistent and continuous, and the more often such data can be collected, the better. Progress data must be of the same nature as baseline data if any conclusions concerning student learning are to be made. This means that the teacher must take care in choosing baseline data collection techniques that can be maintained through the intervention period.

CHARTING OF STUDENT PROGRESS DATA*   If a teacher has data on the instructional objectives, the data must be maintained in such a way that they can be used both for instructional decision making and as evidence that an objective has or has not been reached. Perhaps the most efficient and effective means of keeping student performance data is through charting procedures that provide a visual display of data over time. While various charting protocols are available, the most important aim is to choose a procedure that will allow quick and easily readable data displays that can be readily understood by other teachers and parents.

Figure 4–1 is a sample chart showing data on percent correct for long-division problems. The chart clearly displays data for three days of baseline and six days of instruction. The vertical line designates baseline data collection and the beginning of instruction; the horizontal dotted line represents the criterion level for successful performance as stated in the instructional objective.

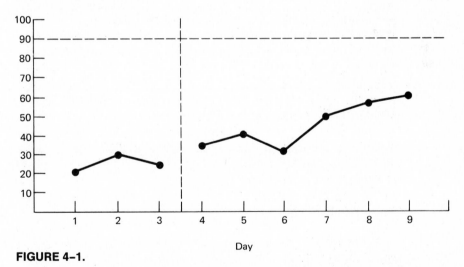

Day

FIGURE 4–1.

This is by far the simplest of a number of charting protocols which are available, and the most straightforward for teacher use. Other, more complex charting procedures might be more satisfactory to individual teach-

---

*This section is adapted from the following work by the author: Lilly, M. S. Evaluating Individualized Education Programs. In S. Torres, (ed.) *A Primer on Individualized Education Programs for Handicapped Children.* Reston, VA: Council for Exceptional Children, 1977, pp. 26–30.

ers. Any charting procedure can be used, as long as it serves its major purpose: to provide a visual display of student progress over time.

INSTRUCTIONAL DECISION MAKING   The only reason for collecting data on student performance in relation to specific objectives is to enable the teacher to make decisions concerning the adequacy of instructional interventions. While no infallible models exist for making these instructional decisions, the following guidelines apply:

1. Allow enough time for an instructional procedure to have an effect (at least one week).
2. Do not allow a student to continue more than two to three weeks without making progress.
3. When progress does not occur, blame the instructional program, not the child.
4. When progress does occur, celebrate with everyone involved.
5. Use progress charts in discussing school programs with parents.

The following questions must be asked in making instructional decisions (Lilly, 1977b):

1. Is progress sufficient to justify continuation of the present instructional procedures?
2. Do progress data indicate that the instructional objective and/or methodology is appropriate or inappropriate for the student?
3. Is the criterion level appropriate for the instructional objective?
4. If the objective is reached, what is the appropriate next step?

In summary, a data-based instructional model as just described provides a system for instruction that is noncategorical in nature, geared toward problems of concern for the regular classroom teacher, and sensitive to continuous measures of student progress. Only a brief overview of a data-based instructional system has been presented here. The reader wishing more detailed information is encouraged to read more extended works by Lovitt (1977) and Deno and Mirkin (1977).

Service Delivery Models

Children with learning and behavior problems are served in settings along the complete continuum of services as presented earlier, with a clear preference among most special educators for maximum contact with regular class peers. When resource programs began to develop rapidly in the late 1960s, the primary emphasis was on programs which removed the child from the regular classroom for brief periods of the day for either individual tutoring or small group work. Drawbacks of such a resource model, particularly in terms of generalization of learned skills or improved behavior back into the regular classroom, have been discussed earlier in this chapter.

The most normalized special education service delivery model is the "teacher consultation" model, which stresses not only direct work with children, but also supportive work with the classroom teacher so that whenever possible, problems can be solved directly in the regular classroom.

The author (Lilly, 1971) has described a "training-based model for special education" as an alternative to special class and resource room services. The training-based model was designed to meet three criteria.

1. It was to be a zero-reject model, in which "once a child is enrolled in a regular education program within a school, it must be impossible to administratively separate him from that program for any reason" (p. 745).
2. Responsibility for solving problems of academic learning and social behavior must rest with the regular educator, with special educators providing support and training for classroom teachers.
3. The goal of special education must be to create self-sufficient classroom teachers who can solve children's problems with a minimum of help from outside specialists, making teachers "able to handle problems rather than refer them" (p. 746).

The "training-based" model, as proposed in 1971, would make use of instructional specialists whose task would be to "work with the teacher in such areas as diagnosis of problems in academic skill areas, specifications of both individual and small group study programs, behavior management procedures, and group and individual reinforcement patterns" (p. 746).

An example of a "teacher consultation" model in practice is the consulting teacher approach, initiated in Vermont in the late 1960s through a cooperative arrangement involving the Vermont Department of Education, the University of Vermont, and local school districts. In Vermont, experienced teachers are trained at the university, in a two-year master's program, to be consulting teachers. The second year of the training program is a full-time internship in a school district, in which the trainee is expected to accept a consulting teacher position after graduation. A ten-step consultation model has been developed, as follows (Egner and Lates, 1975).

Step 1: Teacher makes written referral.
Step 2: Teacher and consulting teacher meet to determine baseline diagnosis procedures.
Step 3: Teacher and consulting teacher meet to determine student eligibility for services.
Step 4: Teacher and consulting teacher meet with parent to obtain permission to develop a learning program for the student.
Step 5: Consulting teacher directly observes the child in the classroom.
Step 6: Teacher and consulting teacher agree on instructional objectives and intervention procedures.
Step 7: Parents approve the proposed intervention procedures.

Step 8: Teacher implements intervention plan and takes daily progress measures.

Step 9: Intervention procedures are evaluated using student progress data collected by the teacher.

Step 10: Teacher and consulting teacher plan a follow-through program designed to assure that the student continues to make adequate progress.

Eligibility for consulting teacher services in Vermont is often defined in terms of the rate at which a particular student is achieving minimum instructional objectives expected for all students. These minimum objectives are established at a school or school district level, and are sequenced according to when children should be expected to master each given set of objectives during their school career. According to Egner and Lates (1975), "when entry level measures indicate that the child's performance is below the minimum skills the teacher may receive consulting teacher services" (p. 34).

Courtesy of The Ford Foundation (Tommy Wadelton).

Another early attempt to develop a teacher consultation model for special education was the Seward-University Project in Minneapolis, initiated in the early 1970s (Deno and Gross, 1972). This was a joint university-school district project in which Special Education Resource Teachers (SERT's) were trained and placed in individual schools to serve as "teacher/consultants" to whom regular classroom teachers could turn for help. While SERT's do some work with individual children, "the pressure is, and always should be, on turning over direct instruction and management of an effective program to the child, the regular classroom teacher, a peer, or a paraprofessional" (Deno and Mirkin, 1977, p. 16).

As mentioned above, the teacher consultation approach has "caught on" since 1970, and has been implemented in a number of school districts either as a separate program, or as an additional component of resource room programs. Recognition of the need for consultation with classroom teachers in cases in which students either never leave or are scheduled for return to the regular classroom is now widespread. Furthermore, with the current emphasis on provision of special education services in the least restrictive environment, no children with learning and behavior problems should be totally and permanently removed from the regular classroom setting. Therefore, it is necessary to assure that all special educators prepared to work with children with learning and behavior problems are trained to engage in effective teacher consultation. Such training is still not widespread, as is evident in Brown's (1977) observation that of approximately two hundred candidates interviewed for public school BD and LD teaching positions, none had specific training in the consultation process. Consultation training procedures are being developed, however, in a number of universities and school districts, and there is increasing pressure from practicing special educators for such training.

In summary, the teacher consultation approach to special education is the newest and most innovative model of service delivery. In fact, development of consulting teacher programs is so recent that in most instances they are still in the experimental stages. Few established, working models are available for close inspection, and of those which have been implemented, the Vermont program is by all accounts the most successful and most thoroughly documented. Consulting teacher models for special education will spread as more special educators are trained in the consultation process, and as least restrictive placement moves from promise to reality. While not all children with learning and behavior problems can be served through consulting teacher approaches, this author is confident that gradually, as is indicated in all models of the special education service continuum (see chapter 2), teacher consultation services will be the dominant service model for special education.

Summary

While the noncategorical approach does not solve all the questions raised in the prior discussion of EMR, BD, and LD categorical systems (some of which are unanswerable), it is this author's opinion that the weight of logic and available evidence support decategorization of services for children with mild problems. What is presented herein is an amalgam of theory and good practice, and the alert reader will observe elements of the proposed system at work in many school districts. It is predicted that special education in the future will continue to become less categorical and more focused on functional problems of children in regular classrooms.

It is tempting at this point to ask, "How will it all turn out?" The question itself is inappropriate, however, since the dynamic nature of special education means that it will always be a field in flux. What has been presented here is a description of the past, and a scenario for the not-too-distant future based on the trend-setting activities of the present. With the renewed interest in rebuilding the bridge between regular and special education, the current concern over categorization of children, and the emerging emphasis on functional approaches to solution of classroom problems, the future looks exciting for children and their teachers.

EARLY EDUCATION OF CHILDREN WITH LEARNING AND BEHAVIOR PROBLEMS

Early education of the handicapped has been described as "the most rapidly growing area in special education" (Haring, 1978, p. 27). Basically, this refers to formal educational programs for children who are below the normal age for public school programs; early education can begin at birth and generally includes programs for children up to age five.

Education of very young children with special needs has been a concern of a small, dedicated group of educators in the United States since the early part of the twentieth century (Hayden, 1978). Since the mid-1960s, however, this interest has blossomed into a substantial investment of public funds for programs for preschool children.

The first major investment of public funds in preschool education came in regular, not special education. In 1965, Project Head Start was begun as a federal preschool program for "disadvantaged" children. The purpose of the Head Start program was to provide systematic educational experiences that would help children overcome the effects of their "deprived" environment, thus enabling them to succeed in school. Head Start was clearly seen as a "compensatory" education, and spectacular results were predicted.

The rationale for Head Start and other preschool programs of the 1960s was derived primarily from the works of respected psychologists which indicated that intelligence and other human traits are more malleable at early ages than had generally been assumed (Hunt, 1961; Bloom, 1964). The decade of the sixties saw a strong movement away from the view that human potential is determined primarily through heredity, and the rise of the "environmentalist" point of view naturally led to concern for improving children's intellectual potential. Safford (1978) has summarized the effects of works such as those by Hunt and Bloom as follows:

The suggestion that *external* factors could substantively influence the rate and the course of children's intellectual development, already implied by sociological data, received empirical and theoretical support. This generated renewed interest in the role of *experience* in influencing children. . . . A new respect was accorded early education, in keeping with its potential to shape lifelong patterns of behavior (p. 5).

The early years of Head Start saw a focus on economically disadvantaged children, in the 3- to 5-year age range. Undoubtedly, many children were served in early Head Start programs who would eventually be identified as educable mentally retarded, behavior disordered, or learning disabled during their school careers. However, the focus in Head Start was on serving *disadvantaged*, not *handicapped* children.

In 1973, a new requirement was introduced in Head Start programs, a stipulation that at least 10 percent of all children served in Head Start be identified as "handicapped." Since it is necessary to demonstrate that the 10 percent mandate is being met in order to receive Head Start funds, this has resulted in substantial integration of handicapped and nonhandicapped children in Head Start programs nationwide. At the same time, the requirement that children must be labeled in order to meet the mandate has led to some questionable practices in identification and labeling of preschool children suspected of being mildly handicapped.

In addition to being included under Head Start since 1973, early education of the handicapped has come into its own in the last decade. In 1968, the Handicapped Children's Early Education Assistance Act was passed by Congress and signed into law by then-President Johnson. As a result of this legislation, demonstration preschool programs for the handicapped have been established throughout the country, programs covering the full gamut of the preschool-age range, and varying in both administrative and instructional focus. Preschool programs have been funded under the auspices of the Handicapped Children's Early Education Program (HCEEP), and have dealt with all levels of severity of handicap. In addition, P.L. 94–142 provides an incentive grant for each three-to five-year-old child receiving special education in a state.

In addition to federal assistance for early education programs, some states have also made commitments to preschool programs for the handicapped. Several states include the three- to five-year-old handicapped population as a part of their basic special education mandate, so that it is expected that *all* preschool children with handicaps who are over three years of age must be served. Several other states have legislation *permitting* school districts to receive state reimbursement for preschool special education programs for three- to five-year-olds. At the present time, it is very unusual for states to provide funds for special education for children under three years of age.

Thus far, the discussion has centered on preschool education for the handicapped, including all types and degrees of handicapping conditions. The remainder of the discussion of preschool education in this chapter will focus on a particular population: children with mild learning and behavior problems. While programs for this population have comprised the majority of special education preschool programs, they also present particularly vexing problems in relation to identification of children and evaluation of program effectiveness. The ensuing discussion will touch briefly on these topics: (1) Identification of mildly handicapped children at the preschool level; (2) Models for preschool programs; (3) Outcomes of preschool education for the mildly handicapped; and (4) Conclusions.

Courtesy of Responsive Environments Corporation.

Identification of Mildly Handicapped Preschool Children

Children are generally identified as being eligible for preschool programs for the mildly handicapped based on a two-stage process. First, a screening procedure is used in which all children of a given age (for example, three-year-olds) are given a "screening" test. Based on the outcomes of this testing, children who score below a certain level are given more complete batteries of psychological and educational tests to determine whether they are eligible for special education services. As with the assessment of school-age children with learning and behavior problems discussed in chapter 3, the aim is often to place children in a given category of exceptionality for the purposes of (a) providing an educational program, and (b) collecting state or federal funds related to provision of such services.

The identification and subsequent labeling of school-age children with learning and behavior problems for the purpose of providing special education services has been questioned in this chapter as well as chapter 3. However, the problem of labeling is even more complex at the preschool level. Whereas all children who are labeled as exceptional during their school years have presumably exhibited some academic or social behavior problems in the school setting, most preschool children are labeled not on the basis of performance in school, but rather on the basis of *predicted* school failure. Keogh and Becker (1973) have described the situation as follows.

> When early identification efforts are applied to exceptionalities of more educational or psychological definition, however, some subtle differences from the physical disability model must be considered. Basic to the question is this: When we seek to identify preschool or kindergarten children whom we fear may become learning failures, we are, in fact, hypothesizing rather than confirming. That is, the conditions which we view as atypical, namely, learning disability and failure in school, have not yet developed. Our concerns are that these conditions will develop. Yet, children who have not been exposed to a reading program cannot really be said to have reading problems; children who have not participated in a first grade program cannot be classified as first grade failures (pp. 5–6).

Keogh and Becker (1973) have described three major problems in early identification of learning problems.

1. While many tests have been developed for early identification of learning problems, it is not clear that the tests are valid predictors of school performance. While intelligence tests are widely used in assessment of preschool children, Keogh and Becker point out that except for children with extremely low IQ scores, "prediction of school failure on the basis of intelligence test score alone appears tenuous" (p. 6). Numerous other tests have also been used, with varying levels of predictive success. School performance in academic areas is a complicated phenomenon, and it would be very difficult to construct a test or battery of tests to predict school success in a reasonably accurate manner. With regard to predictive validity of preschool tests, Keogh and Becker state that "on the basis of present evidence, it seems reasonable to conclude that relationships between single, specific preschool test findings and later school achievement are too low to allow definitive prediction about individual children" (p. 7).

2. Unlike medical diagnoses, techniques for early identification of learning problems do not lead directly to specification of strategies for remediation. Early identification does not allow school personnel to make good matches between preschool children in need of services and specific educational programs.

3. The very fact that learning problems are predicted for preschool children can, in some cases, serve as a "self-fulfilling prophecy." Expectations are set, and a number of persons in a child's environment can be predisposed to respond to the child in a less than desirable manner. As Keogh and Becker point out, "effects may be particularly insidious in that preschool or kindergarten children have not yet developed the deficit con-

ditions for which they were identified" (p. 8).

The problems with early identification of mild handicapping conditions, as just presented, are not reason enough to forgo educational programming for preschool children. However, concerns for identification have led to a hesitance on the part of most special educators to label preschool children as EMR, BD, or LD. Generally, children with mild problems who are included in preschool special education programs are referred to as "high risk," rather than handicapped. In all special education, the concern for labeling is felt most acutely at the preschool level.

This section has not provided specific information on diagnostic techniques for preschool children but has attempted to highlight the major issues in identification. The reader interested in further information on diagnostic techniques is referred to Safford's (1978) book entitled, *Teaching Young Children with Special Needs*.

Programs for Preschool, "High Risk" Children

This section will describe both administrative arrangements and instructional programs for young children identified as having mild learning and behavior problems. Because there have been a large number of preschool demonstration programs, space does not permit a full explication of the variations of curriculum that have been demonstrated at the preschool level. More complete information on the material presented here is available in Karnes and Teska (1975) and Safford (1978).

In terms of administrative arrangements for preschool programs, the two most basic delivery systems are center-based programs, in which children attend school (usually on a half-day basis), and home-based programs, which stress delivery of instruction in the home either by the parents or by a teacher who comes into the home (Karnes and Teska, 1975). Center-based programs can either be segregated, comprised only of children identified as handicapped, or integrated, consisting of a mix of children with and without developmental delays. As mentioned earlier, because of the mandate that Head Start programs must enroll "handicapped" children, these preschool programs tend to be the most integrated. Because public schools are generally not empowered to serve normal children of preschool age, it has been particularly difficult to develop integrated preschool programs in the public schools. Most public school early education programs have only children who have been identified as "handicapped" or "high risk" enrolled.

With regard to educational programs, or curriculum, for young children with learning and behavior problems, very few generalizations can be made. Early education curricula have ranged from highly structured to open classrooms, and variation has been encouraged in the HCEEP programs funded by the Bureau of Education for the Handicapped. Starting with programs for the disadvantaged in the 1960s, there have been a large number of experimental, research-based preschool curricula which have yielded a great deal of data concerning program effectiveness. These data will be summarized in a subsequent section.

Karnes and Teska (1975) point out that nearly all preschool programs have placed a major stress on language development, with some programs based on specified models of language acquisition. While preschool curricula vary widely, an emphasis on language development is probably the common denominator that links nearly all preschool programs.

The aim of many early preschool programs was to improve the intellectual functioning (that is, the intelligence test scores) of the children enrolled, and this aim was reflected in many preschool curricula. In effect, many programs placed a major emphasis on the types of skills and knowledge necessary to perform well in a testing situation. This is not entirely inappropriate, since these same skills are often closely related to successful school performance.

Smith (1971) has outlined six broad areas of development which serve as the basis for preschool programs in mental retardation. While the list was developed in a specific area of exceptionality, it adequately describes major curriculum areas for preschool programs for "high risk" children. The six areas of curricular emphasis are:

1. Perceptual-motor development or physical fitness;
2. Verbal communication;
3. Cognitive skills;
4. Self-care and emotional development;
5. Social skills; and
6. Aesthetic and creative development.

It can safely be said that these areas encompass preschool curricula, with varying emphasis among the areas depending on the professional biases of program developers and school personnel who implement the curricula.

Outcomes of Early Education for "High Risk" Children

As mentioned earlier, there have been a large number of experimental preschool programs for disadvantaged and handicapped children. As a result of federal funding for these experimental programs, there is a rather large body of literature on the effects of preschool programs, literature which points to mixed results. This section will provide only a brief overview of the major findings of this research; for a more complete discussion, as well as a listing of original program references, the reader is referred to Karnes and Teska (1975).

Because the major purpose of most preschool programs of the 1960s was to improve the intellectual functioning of children, performance on intelligence tests was a major criterion variable in many early studies. The initial results of these studies were very encouraging; in general, experimental programs tended to raise IQ scores of children who were enrolled. It was not unusual to see average gains of 10–15 IQ points for students enrolled in experimental programs. However, these encouraging findings did not last; as they entered school, the differences in IQ scores between children who had been enrolled in experimental programs and those who had not attended preschool tended to disappear (Karnes and Teska, 1975). These findings, along with a major study designed to assess the outcomes of Head Start programs which produced essentially negative findings (Westinghouse Learning Corporation, 1969), led many to question the effectiveness of preschool programs for handicapped and disadvantaged children.

A major problem of early studies, however, is that they focused on the wrong outcome measures. Rather than examining preschool curricula to see how well they accomplished what they set out to accomplish, global measures of intelligence were used to assess program quality. In effect, the intelligence tests which were under serious scrutiny in other areas of education were made the primary indicators of success in preschool programs. The outcomes were not encouraging, but few people had confidence in the measures themselves.

Another shortcoming in early studies of the effects of preschool programming was that one could never be sure exactly how the stated curriculum was actually implemented in the classroom. In many cases, curricula were described in very sketchy detail, and rarely were any classroom observation data presented to indicate how curricula were actually implemented in the classroom or home instruction program (Karnes and Teska, 1975).

In spite of the disappointment of early evaluation studies, support for preschool education continued to grow. As outcome data provided a perspective for the field, different evaluation strategies were developed. In more recent studies, data have been gathered on more relevant variables such as school achievement, retention in later school years, and later referrals for special education services. Outcomes of these evaluations tend to favor children who have been enrolled in special preschool programs (Karnes and Teska, 1975; Hayden, 1978).

Conclusion

Early education of the handicapped is in a period of very rapid growth. Leading that growth is early education for "high risk" children. This area of special education has survived a period in which it was called into question based on evaluation outcomes that stressed the wrong measures of success. Early education of the handicapped has become a bona fide subspecialty in special education.

As early education becomes more widely accepted and implemented in the public schools of this country, some major issues need to be faced. Issues related directly to preschool programming for "high risk" children include:

1. How can children be identified as in need of special education at the pre-school level, with a minimum of risk regarding effects of labeling;
2. What areas of preschool curriculum are most important in terms of later school functioning;
3. How can children in preschool special education programs be assured of continuing contact with normal peers;
4. What types of follow-up are necessary to ensure carryover of learned skills when students move into regular school programs; and
5. What types of evaluation measures are most appropriate for immediate and long-term assessment of the outcomes of preschool programs?

The rationale for preschool programs for "high risk" children is impressive, and is accepted by the vast majority of special educators. This is not to say, however, that such programs will be accepted without question and flourish in the public schools. In most states, early education of the handicapped represents a substantial investment of new money in special education, an investment which will not be made without careful and on-going assessment. The development of early education programs for "high risk" children will be a most fascinating scenario to watch unfold in special education in the 1980s.

SECONDARY/VOCATIONAL EDUCATION OF STUDENTS WITH LEARNING AND BEHAVIOR PROBLEMS

Among the skills necessary for survival in an adult world, getting and holding a job must rank at or near the top. Consistent and steady employment is essential if one is to enjoy any level of independent life style as an adult.

In spite of the obvious importance of occupational skills to eventual independence, systematic vocational training has been the exception rather than the rule in many special education programs, particularly for the mildly handicapped. While vocational programs have been relatively prevalent for students labeled educable mentally retarded, and have been the most successful of all EMR programs (Brolin, 1976), they have not generally been available in numbers sufficient to serve the high school "EMR" population. In the areas of behavior disorders and learning disabilities, vocational programs at the secondary level have been virtually nonexistent.

While special education vocational programs have been generally limited in their scope and frequency, general vocational education programs in secondary schools have been well developed. The majority of high schools offer both general vocational coursework and specific vocational programs in areas such as carpentry, auto mechanics, and home economics. Further, the community college system has been growing at an impressive rate in most parts of the country, offering opportunities for advanced vocational training.

The current trend in vocational training for the handicapped, in particular for students with mild learning and behavior problems, is to attempt to open the general vocational education curriculum to a broader range of students rather than build "special" vocational programs for the handicapped. Typically, vocational programs in the high schools have very demanding and somewhat rigid entrance standards which have prevented many students with learning and behavior problems from enrolling. These standards were created to ensure that students who entered vocational programs would be able, motivated individuals who made the most of their training. The functional outcome of the entrance requirements, however, has been to exclude mildly handicapped individuals from vocational education programs, even though the factors which led them to be labeled handicapped might have little or no bearing on successful performance in the vocational program.

Albright and Phelps (1977) cite three factors, all external to the schools and related to federal legislation, which are helping to bring about a reanalysis of vocational opportunities for handicapped individuals. First, the Vocational Education Amendments of 1976 (P.L. 94–482) strengthened the federal government's commitment to vocational education for handicapped and disadvantaged ("special needs") populations. Since 1968, the Vocational Education Act has required that 10 percent of federal vocational education funds be spent on vocational programs for the handicapped (Brolin, 1976). In 1976, P.L. 94–482 expanded this provision with a requirement that these funds, along with a 20 percent setaside for programs for the disadvantaged, must be matched by state and local funds (Carlson, 1977). In other words, each state is eligible for vocational education funds, 30 percent of which must be spent on students with special needs, but in order to be received, the funds must be doubled at the state level.

A second factor cited by Albright and Phelps (1977) as bringing about increased attention to the role of vocational education for handicapped students is P.L. 94–142, discussed in chapter 2. P.L. 94–142 requires that an appropriate education be provided *all* handicapped students to age twenty-one, and since a major weakness of many public school special education programs has been the lack of secondary/vocational opportunities, the impact of P.L. 94–142 will be great in this area. In all of special education, we are furthest from meeting the full service requirements of P.L. 94–142 in the secondary schools, where the primary emphasis must be on vocational preparation.

The third factor that has sharpened our focus on vocational needs of special populations is Section 504 of the Vocational Rehabilitation Act of 1973, which "is designed to eliminate discrimination on the basis of handicap in any program or activity receiving federal financial assistance" (Albright and Phelps, 1977, p. 28). Section 504 will undoubtedly lead to a reexamination of entrance requirements for vocational training programs in high schools and community colleges, and will result in more handicapped individuals being served in these programs.

Carlson (1977) has accurately summarized the current situation:

> Generally, the handicapped and other special populations have not shared in the successful delivery system of vocational education across this country. There has been extensive dialogue over the years as to the need and the importance of assuring handicapped individuals training opportunities to become self-sufficient. However, this dialogue has not been translated into realistic vocational education programs and supportive services for the handicapped. In fact, the breadth of vocational offerings available to the "regular student" are generally not part of the curriculum provided for the special student.

The amount of attention being given this problem is significant at the present time, and its solution will be one of the major goals of special and regular education in the next decade.

Definition of the Population To Be Served

Because the vocational education community has used a different method of defining special populations to be served, it is necessary to describe briefly the terminology and definitions that have been used. The 1968 Vocational Education Amendments introduced the term "special needs students," which has become a common part of the language of vocational educators and secondary special educators. "Special needs students" are students who need vocational education programs and who are identified as handicapped or disadvantaged. Albright and Phelps (1977) cite the following definitions of handicapped and disadvantaged from the 1976 Vocational Education Amendments.

> The term handicapped...means persons who are mentally retarded, hard of hearing, deaf, speech impaired, visually handicapped, seriously emotionally disturbed, orthopedically impaired, health impaired, or persons with specific learning disabilities who by reason thereof require special education and related services, and who because of their handicapping condition, cannot succeed in the regular vocational education program without special education assistance or who require a modified vocational education program (Section 197.7) (p. 27).
>
> Disadvantaged is defined in the 1976 Vocational Education Amendments as: Persons (other than handicapped persons) who have academic or economic disadvantages; and who require special services, assistance or programs in order to enable them to succeed in vocational education programs (Section 197.16) (p. 27).

Albright and Phelps point out that both definitions stipulate that special services are necessary for the individual to succeed in the vocational education setting. Furthermore, the term "special needs student" is seen as positive in that it offers the opportunity to avoid the stigma associated with categorical labels used in special education. "The individual with special needs is defined by what she or he requires from us within the educational setting and not by medical or psychological labels" (Albright and Phelps, 1977, p. 27).

Factors in Integration of Special Needs Students in Vocational Programs

From what has been said thus far, it might be assumed that vocational and special educators are rushing toward a series of joint endeavors which will inevitably result in exciting new vocational programs for special needs students. While there is movement in this direction, there are also forces which must be overcome if these movements are to succeed. Maynard Reynolds, in describing lack of communication between vocational and special educators, says:

> The main problem is that we haven't done much together. We've been like a couple of neighboring kids looking at each other through knotholes in the backyard fence, each kid thinking that the other leads a strange, mysterious life; but as soon as the fence is torn down the mystery disappears and the kids discover how much they have in common (Wentling and Phelps, 1977, p. 13).

Meers and Conaway (1977), in describing reasons for past exclusion of handicapped individuals from vocational education programs, cite the following factors:

1. Many vocational educators have preconceived attitudes about the handicapped, mostly negative and not based on personal experience. This attitude is sometimes accompanied by a lack of skill (a direct result of lack of instruction) in meeting the individual needs of special students in the vocational setting.
2. Very few vocational educators have had any formal training to prepare them to work with special needs students. Inclusion of special education training in vocational teacher preparation programs is the exception rather than the rule.
3. Educational planning teams have not been used systematically to provide supportive help for vocational educators working with handicapped individuals. In many cases, vocational educators have been expected to "go it alone."
4. Special educators are not always familiar with the details of programs aimed at vocational placement of handicapped individuals. "In many cases, the non-vocational teacher involved in programs for the handicapped may not be familiar with teaching methods to accomplish this (vocational placement) goal" (Meers and Conaway, 1977, p. 31).

Perhaps the biggest overall problem facing vocational and special educators alike is the lack of adequate preparation for the roles they are expected to perform. With regard to preparation of vocational educators, Phelps and Clark (1977) point out that "a recent General Accounting Office (1976) report reveals that in 78% of the school districts sampled nationally, vocational educators were insufficiently trained in special education skills" (p. 40). In a like manner, Gillet (1978) surveyed ninety-five special education teacher preparation programs, and found that only twenty offered so much as a single course on career education for exceptional children. Only two special education teacher preparation programs required career education coursework for students concentrating in areas other than mental retardation. Clark (1977) has summarized the current situation with regard to teacher education as follows:

> The net result of the efforts of the primary teacher education disciplines involved has been the creation of a situation which essentially communicates the position, "We will attempt to be responsible for the needs of the field in our own way, within our own disciplines." Unfortunately, special needs students have not been receiving the "appropriate education" they needed as a consequence of this approach (p. 29).

While teacher education has been perceived by some as a negative factor in the move toward more cooperative efforts between vocational and special educators, there are encouraging signs of increased cooperation. Three national conferences have been held, two at the University of Illinois in 1976 and one at the University of Kentucky in 1977, designed to bring "vocational and special educators together to stimulate communication, cooperation, and, most importantly, action between and among the two fields" (Clark, 1977, p. 29).

School Vocational Programs for Special Needs Students

In spite of the problems just enumerated, progress is being made in developing vocational training opportunities for special needs students. These efforts will be *briefly* described in this section; the reader wanting further information on these programs is referred to Lake (1974), Brolin (1976), and Albright (1977).

As mentioned earlier, special education efforts at vocational training have come primarily in the form of work/study programs. "In this approach, students spend part of the day or week acquiring work experience and job skills in school and community work stations, while special education and vocational rehabilitation personnel jointly attempt to provide for needs of the adolescent while he is still in school" (Brolin, 1976, p. 42). Work/study programs have been primarily aimed at students labeled EMR, and have been among the more successful special education programs (Bitter and Bolanovich, 1966; Karnes, 1966; Halpern, 1972). However, as the need for vocational training for large numbers of mildly handicapped students in the secondary schools becomes apparent, it is unlikely that the work/study model is feasible or appropriate. Community job placements are limited in number, and supervision of job placement activities is very time consuming. Furthermore, involvement of vocational rehabilitation personnel in secondary programs for large numbers of mildly handicapped students is not likely to happen.

The factors just cited must also be taken in conjunction with two further considerations: (a) concern for placement of students in the least restrictive environment and (b) a general respect for the substantial capabilities of the general vocational education program. These factors in combination are leading many special educators to seek opportunities for students with learning and behavior problems in the secondary vocational education curriculum. Albright (1977) lists several sources of program descriptions which describe vocational education programs for the handicapped and disadvantaged. These program descriptions differ from those presented in the previous section on early education for the handicapped, in that most have been implemented in a nonexperimental mode and research data on program outcomes are limited. Nonetheless, the National Association of Vocational Education Special Needs Personnel has published a description of "100 Successful Vocational Special Needs Programs," with brief descriptions of program content and operation (Albright, 1977).

With the exception of work/study programs for EMR populations, vocational education for children with learning and behavior problems is in its infancy. Many programs have been developed, with varying levels of success, but very little of the school-based work which has been done has been translated into either full-scale school programs or initiatives in teacher education for vocational or special educators. In effect, the field has a number of limited pilot efforts which must be translated into widespread practice.

Conclusion

As with early education of the handicapped, vocational education for students with special needs will be one of the major growth areas in special education in the 1980s. The coming decade will see continued development of a limited number of vocationally-oriented special education programs established and run as separate self-contained operations. However, the major focus will be on development of programs in cooperation with vocational educators, so that students with learning and behavior problems can take full advantage of the considerable resources of secondary vocational education programs. Vocational education for the mildly handicapped is truly an area in which we must pool our resources and our talents for the maximum benefit of the students we serve.

SUMMARY

This chapter has described three major movements in education of students with learning and behavior problems: (1) noncategorical special education services, (2) preschool programming, and (3) secondary/vocational education. These three areas of concern will form the nucleus of much of the development work to be done in the field during the next decade and, as such, will serve to shape the special education of the future. As we continue to develop in these three areas, it is critical that we maintain an experimental focus and operate as much as possible on a research base. There are many unanswered questions in the three movements described in this chapter, and we can only answer those questions by being experimental in all of our new endeavors. The section on early education of the handicapped is a case in point; it is a more mature field today because of early research efforts that pointed out both positive and negative aspects of early developmental work. If we approach our tasks with an open mind and a commitment to learn from all our efforts, the next decade will see major, exciting efforts in each of these areas.

REFERENCES

Albright, L. Resources for special needs personnel development. *Journal of Industrial Teacher Education,* 1977, *14,* 46–55.

———. and Phelps, L. A. A new challenge. *Industrial Education,* 1977, *66,* 27–31.

Bitter, J., and Bolanovich, D. Development of vocational competence in the moderately retarded. *Mental Retardation,* 1966, *4,* 9–12.

Bloom, B. S. *Stability and change in human characteristics.* New York: John Wiley & Sons, Inc., 1964.

Brolin, D. E. *Vocational Preparation of Retarded Citizens.* Columbus, OH: Charles E. Merrill Publishing Co., 1976.

Brown, V. L. "Yes, but..." A reply to Phyllis Newcomer. *Journal of Special Education,* 1977, *11,* 171–177.

Carlson, R. E. Legislation and special needs teacher education: The Vocational Education Amendments of 1976 (P.L. 94-482). *Journal of Industrial Teacher Education,* 1977, *14,* 19–22.

Clark, G. M. Guidelines and strategies for coordination of special needs teacher education. *Journal of Industrial Teacher Education,* 1977, *14,* 28–35.

Deno, S., and Gross, J. The Seward-University Project: a cooperative effort to improve school services and university training. In E. N. Deno (ed.), *Instructional Alternatives for Exceptional Children.* Reston, VA: Council for Exceptional Children, 1972.

Deno, S. L., and Mirkin, P. K. *Data-Based Program Modification: A Manual.* Reston, VA: Council for Exceptional Children, 1977.

Egner, A., and Lates, B. J. The Vermont Consulting Teacher Program: case presentation. In C. A. Parker (ed.), *Psychological Consultation: Helping Teachers Meet Special Needs.* Reston, VA: Council for Exceptional Children, 1975, pp. 31–62.

General Accounting Office. *Training Educators for the Handicapped: A Need to Redirect Federal Programs.* Washington, DC: U. S. General Accounting Office, 1976.

Gillet, P. Career education: a survey of teacher preparation institutions. *Exceptional Children,* 1978, *44,* 516–518.

Hall, R. V. Responsive teaching: focus on measurement and research in the classroom and the home. In E. L. Meyen, G. A. Vergason, and R. J. Whelan (ed.), *Strategies for Teaching Exceptional Children.* Denver: Love Publishing Co., 1972, pp. 403–414.

Halpern, A. *Longitudinal Evaluation of Work/Study Programs for the Educable Mentally Retarded in Oregon.* Working paper #62. Rehabilitation Research and Training Center in Mental Retardation, University of Oregon, 1972.

Haring, N. G. (ed.) *Behavior of Exceptional Children.* Columbus, OH: Charles E. Merrill Publishing Co., 1978.

Hayden, A. H. Special education for young children. In N. G. Haring (ed.), *Behavior of Exceptional Children.* Columbus, OH: Charles E. Merrill Publishing Co., 1978.

Hunt, J. M. *Intelligence and Experience.* New York: The Ronald Press Company, 1961.

Karnes, M. M. Work study programs. In S. G. Di Michael (ed.), *New Vocational Pathways for the Mentally Retarded.* Washington, DC: American Personnel and Guidance Association, 1966.

Karnes, M. B., and Teska, J. A. *Children's Response to Intervention Programs.* In J. J. Gallagher (ed.), *The Application of Child Development Research to Exceptional Children.* Reston, VA: Council for Exceptional Children, 1975.

Keogh, B. K., and Becker, L. D. Early detection of learning problems: questions, cautions, and guidelines. *Exceptional Children,* 1973, *40,* 5–11.

Lake, T. (ed.) *Career Education: Exemplary Programs for the Handicapped.* Reston, VA: Council for Exceptional Children, 1974.

Lilly, M. S. A training-based model for special education. *Exceptional Children,* 1971, *37,* 745–749.

———— A merger of categories: are we finally ready? *Journal of Learning Disabilities,* 1977a, *10,* 115–121.

———— Evaluating individualized education programs. In S. Torres (ed.), *A Primer on Individualized Education Programs for Handicapped Children.* Reston, VA: Council for Exceptional Children, 1977b, pp. 26–30.

Lovitt, T. C. *In Spite of my Resistance...I've Learned from Children.* Columbus, OH: Charles E. Merrill Publishing Co., 1977.

Mager, R. F. *Preparing Instructional Objectives.* Belmont, CA: Fearon Publishers, 1962.

McKenzie, H. S., Clark, M., Wolfe, M. M., Kothera, R., and Benson, C. Behavior modification of children with learning disabilities using grades as tokens and allowances as back up reinforcers. *Exceptional Children,* 1968, *34,* 745–752.

Meers, G. D., and Conaway, C. Vocational education's role in career education for handicapped students. *Journal of Career Education*, 1977, *3*, 19–34.

Phelps, L. A., and Clark, G. M. Personnel preparation for vocational programming of special needs students. *Journal of Career Education*, 1977, *3*, 35–51.

Safford, P. L. *Teaching Young Children with Special Needs*. St. Louis: The C. V. Mosby Co., 1978.

Smith, R. M. *An Introduction to Mental Retardation*. New York: McGraw-Hill, Inc., 1971.

Wentling, R. L., and Phelps, L. A. An interview with Rupert N. Evans and Maynard C. Reynolds. *Journal of Industrial Teacher Education*, 1977, *14*, 9–18.

Westinghouse Learning Corporation—Ohio University. *The Impact of Head Start: An Evaluation of the Effects of Head Start on Children's Cognitive and Affective Development*. June 1969.

Wheeler, A. H., and Fox, W. L. *Behavior Modification: A Teacher's Guide to Writing Instructional Objectives*. Lawrence, KA: H & H Enterprises, Inc., 1972.

CHAPTER **5**

SEVERE/PROFOUND HANDICAPPING CONDITIONS
Administrative considerations

BARBARA WILCOX*

Special education is in transition. Perhaps nowhere is the historical contrast in special education more striking, the implications for service delivery more wide ranging, and the task more complex and challenging than in the area of services to severely handicapped students.

The severely handicapped have borne numerous pejorative, socially stereotyped, and educationally irrelevant labels: they have been called idiots, imbeciles, mongoloids, and cretins; they have been described as trainable, subtrainable, multihandicapped, autistic, schizophrenic, semi-independent, and developmentally young. The expectations attached to these labels have hardly been flattering or functional. Consider for example, the general descriptions (see Table 5–1) of persons labeled "moderately, severely, or profoundly retarded," that are presented in a widely used introductory text (Dunn, 1973). Other authors set equally low expectations: "Most will remain dependent throughout their lifetimes" (Anderson, Greer, and Dietrich, 1976, p. 11); "in general, trainable students do not learn to read from even first grade books (Kirk 1972, p. 231)."

Similar statements supporting the stereotype assumption that severely handicapped are incompetent and can, therefore, be denied social, educational and vocational opportunities are unfortunately common. The

*The author thanks Nancy Dodd and Joseph Jenkins for their help with this and the following chapter.

TABLE 5-1 Typical Adaptive Behavior Expectancies for Persons with General Learning Disabilities by Four Levels of Intellectual Functioning

INTELLECTUAL LEVELS (APPROXIMATE IQ SCORES FOR NATIONAL SAMPLE ON WHOM TEST WAS STANDARDIZED)	AGE LEVELS		
	PRESCHOOL (UNDER 6)	SCHOOL AGE (6–18)	ADULT (OVER 18)
Mildly retarded (60 ± 5 to 75 ± 5)	Slightly slow in walking, talking, and caring for self; but usually indistinguishable from average children and therefore unidentified before entering school	Capable of learning academic skills between the 3rd- and 6th-grade levels only; therefore literate	Capable of vocational, personal, and marital independence; thus most lose identification in adulthood. The more retarded may need some supervision and guidance
Moderately retarded (35 ± 5 to 60 ± 5)	Noticeably slow in learning self-help skills; but usually do learn to walk, feed self, and speak simply; toilet training will be minimal at this age	Capable of school learning between kindergarten through 3rd grade; therefore still typically illiterate	Capable of employment in supervised unskilled occupations, often only in sheltered workshops; very rarely attempt marriage or unsupervised independent living
Severely retarded (20 ± 5 to 35 ± 5)	By 6 may finally have learned to walk and feed self, but very little toileting, speaking, or other self-help skills at this age	Capable only of rudimentary learning of nonacademic skills in areas of self-care, and elementary speech	Some capable of performing chores and other simple tasks even in home or sheltered workshop; need permanent care from parents, relatives, or society
Profoundly retarded (below 20 ± 5)	Usually learn at best minimal ambulatory skills; rarely any feeding, speaking, toileting, or other self-help skills; many permanently bedbound	Some capable of some ambulation and feeding; many continue permanently bedbound and helpless; never learn to speak	Incapable of any self-maintenance or vocational usefulness; need permanent nursing care

SOURCE: Dunn (1973) adapted from Sloan and Birch, 1955, p. 262.

School Code in Illinois incorporates in its definition of "trainable mentally handicapped" the statement that such children are "incapable" of being educated through ordinary classroom training, but "may be expected to benefit from training...designed to further their economic usefulness in their homes or in a sheltered environment" (Section 14–1.05). Work activity centers, the sheltered vocational environment into which most severely handicapped students go (Greenleigh Associates, Inc., 1975), are licensed to serve only those who are "inconsequential producers" (Pomerantz and Marholin, 1977).

These low levels of public and professional expectation are compounded by the fact that severely handicapped students have routinely been denied public school services. This denial of service was often done as a matter of administrative convenience, because professionals lacked the skills to design and implement appropriate educational programs, or as a result of general social intolerance, fear, and ignorance. Prior to the consent agreement in *PARC v. Commonwealth of Pennsylvania* and the more encompassing decision in *Mills v. Washington, D. C. Board of Education*, severely handicapped, or, indeed, mildly handicapped students could be denied access to public schools for a number of reasons: (1) if there were "no room in the class" or "no class available;" (2) if they did not have a mental age of five years, or a chronological age of eight years; (3) if they were not toilet trained or ambulatory; (4) if they exhibited behavior problems or evidenced multiple handicaps; (5) if there were not sufficient funds for special education programs; or (6) if it were decided that the student could no longer "benefit" from the program. These exclusionary procedures were justified by the assumptions that severely handicapped students could not learn, and that, given limited resources, it was more cost-effective to invest in the educational futures of children who were more likely to benefit.

As a result of this social unresponsiveness and relative professional naivete, the educational opportunities available to severely handicapped students were generally restricted to placement in public or private institutions, or to private homebound instruction. Dissatisfaction with these limited options gave rise to parental efforts through the National Association for Retarded Children (now the National Association for Retarded Citizens) to organize and staff private educational services. It is only recently (late 1950s and early 1960s) that "trainable level" students have been accommodated by public school systems, and only with the signing of P.L. 94–142 (1975) have all children, regardless of the severity of their handicap, become the educational responsibility of the public schools. The passage of this legislation acknowledges that the severely handicapped do, indeed, benefit from systematic instructional procedures and that there are enormous social and financial costs incurred as a result of *not* educating these students to be more independent and productive.

While there has been a significant increase in federal involvement with special education in general, the financial and regulatory impact on services to the severely handicapped has been particularly dramatic. As described earlier (Lilly, this volume) the federal government's major attempt to oversee special education is in the Rules and Regulations for P.L. 94–142. While *all* handicapped students may expect to benefit from this legislation, the severely handicapped should profit the most since they have most frequently been excluded from public school programs, and since the priorities of the Act are directed to the unserved and the more severely handicapped special student. The law is procedurally important in that it applies basic constitutional rights of "equal protection" and "due process" to severely handicapped students, and is financially significant in that federal funds are to be provided directly for the provision of special education services.

Though federal involvement is typically regulatory in nature, there have also been significant attempts to influence by incentive, especially through the activities of the Bureau of Education for the Handicapped (BEH). The Bureau's commitment to the provision of quality educational services to the severely handicapped is reflected in its priority statements beginning in 1972. By priority funding of university training programs preparing teachers and other personnel to work with severely handicapped students, and through support of exemplary special projects and model demonstration centers for the severely handicapped, BEH has fostered the development of exemplary training programs and service delivery models. In addition to its very tangible contributions to services for the severely handicapped, BEH has provided an important model through the strong public commitment of its leadership (for example, Martin, 1975, 1976; Sontag, 1976; Burke, 1977; Thompson, 1977).

While the issue of "appropriate special education placement" typically focuses on the assignment of children with learning and behavior problems to regular or special classes ("mainstreaming"), the question assumes a somewhat different form when applied to the provision of educational services to severely handicapped students. The general guideline of "least restrictive placement" subsumes two controversies: (1) placement of severely handicapped students in a self-contained school, versus their placement in a self-contained class in a regular attendance center (Sontag, Burke, and York, 1973), and (2) direct provision of services by the local education agency (LEA) versus provision of services by a private agency through a contractual agreement with the public schools. In the latter case, the LEA is ultimately accountable for the quality of the program regardless of who provides the service. These placement controversies raise issues similar to those in racial segregation cases. While current practice is still characterized by segregated services (viz., self-contained school; Kenowitz, Zweibel, and Edgar, in press), professional opinion increasingly favors integration, i.e., dispersal approaches provided within the public school system (Brown, Nietupski, and Hamre-Nietupski, 1976; Sherr, 1976; Sontag, 1976; Bricker and Iacino, 1977). While P.L. 94–142 legislates services in the least restrictive educational environment, programs for severely handicapped are struggling to operationalize the parameters of restrictiveness. Because of the immediate and long-range implications, a more detailed consideration of the least restrictive placement issue is presented later, and the concept of "least restrictive" is applied not only to the question of the location of the educational program, but to other aspects of educational services as well.

The newly won right to a "free appropriate public education" has perhaps its greatest impact on severely handicapped students. Crowner (1975) has expanded the zero-reject model for general special education (Lilly, 1971), to a zero-exclusion model in which no student, regardless of the degree or condition of his handicap is denied access to the services of public school personnel. Crowner makes the distinction between public school services and programs. "Services," taken as the more general term, is used to connote the fact that public school resources are available not only in classrooms, but in all settings where they are required. For example, there may be instruction in the student's home to provide extended therapy, early intervention, or parent training activities, as well as in community and vocational environments for secondary-level severely handicapped students.

The *appropriate* in "free appropriate public education" assumes special importance as it is applied to services for severely handicapped children and young adults. The requirement of *appropriate* educational programs, rather than simply *educational* programs, forces a number of changes in the educational system. Service delivery models appropriate for students with mild learning and behavior problems are probably not sufficiently comprehensive for more severely handicapped students. Physical facilities and transportation systems must undergo modification to make them accessible and appropriate for students with physical handicaps and/or mobility problems. Additional personnel resources—physical and occupational therapists, physicians and/or nurses, mobility aids, and parent/family coordinators—are often required to design and implement appropriate instructional and therapeutic programs for students with unique and complex special education needs. The curriculum content offered by regular and special education must be radically reconceptualized if it is to prepare severely handicapped students to function adaptively in complex, integrated, community-based postschool environments (Brown et al., 1976). The delivery of an appropriate educational program is additionally dependent upon the application of a technology of direct instruction that includes precisely delineated and task analyzed instructional objectives, systematic behavior management procedures, and frequent formative evaluation and data-based program revision.

Federal and state legislation that has allowed parents access to the educational records of their child, mandated their participation in the design of his or her individualized educational program, and established due process and impartial hearing procedures have certainly affected parents of severely handicapped students as much as any other parent group. Arguments for increased parent involvement and parent training efforts, specifically for parents of children with severely handicapping conditions, can be advanced from both socioeconomic and instructional positions, and are discussed later.

The remainder of this chapter will identify the challenges that severely handicapped students present to the educational system, and chapter 6 will examine the state of the art of providing these students with quality educational services.

DEFINITION AND CHARACTERISTICS

Historically, problems of definition and labeling have characterized special education and have consumed enormous professional energy that might otherwise have been invested in direct service or in the development of improved instructional technology. Categorical labels for special students are justified only to the extent that they benefit directly or indirectly the students who are labeled. A variety of reasons are advanced for continuing or discontinuing the use of categorical labels in special education, and both positions are supported by recent events. On the one hand, there is significant professional and legislative pressure to minimize the use of labels on the grounds that they are educationally irrelevant and

Courtesy of the Easter Seal Program for Multiple Handicapped Children (Steve Neiman).

socially detrimental. For example, with the signing of P.L. 94–142, students can no longer be denied services because they belong to a particular disability group; all must be served. At the same time however, there are forces which serve to perpetuate categories because labels are politically and financially expedient. Teacher certification is usually based on student disability areas. P.L. 94–142 provides money to state education agencies and local school districts based on child counts by category, and BEH often requests and funds proposals on varied categorical bases.

While it is generally believed that the essential first step in developing services, programs, and curricula for a target population is to arrive at a "precise" written definition of that population, such an undertaking may be neither functional nor necessary in accomplishing the intent of education—to change student behavior. Currently, there is no universally accepted definition that permits reliable exchange of educationally relevant information pertaining to students who will here be imprecisely referred to as severely handicapped. A number of types of definitions have been proposed which vary in both their explicitness and their relationship to instruction.

Several definitions of the term "severely handicapped" describe a range of behavioral excesses or deficits that characterize the population. Sontag, Burke, and York (1973) provide an example of such a definition.

> [Severely handicapped students are those] who are not toilet trained; aggress toward others; do not attend to even the most pronounced social stimuli; self-mutilate; ruminate; self-stimulate; do not walk, speak, hear or see; manifest durable and intense temper tantrums; are not even under the most rudimentary forms of verbal control; do not imitate; manifest minimally controlled seizures; and/or have extremely brittle medical existences (p. 21).

Similarly, Abt Associates (1974), and Sailor and Horner (1976) use the term "severely handicapped" to refer to students exhibiting complex problems in sensory, motor, communication, self-care, or social behavior. Their approach of defining a population by behavioral descriptors creates the possibility of two types of classification errors. A child who is indeed severely handicapped may be rejected for services because of failure to display one or more of the behaviors described in the definition. Conversely, children who are not severely handicapped may be so classified if they display one or more of the behavior descriptors (Sontag, Smith, and Sailor, 1977).

The definition formulated by the Bureau of Education for the Handicapped as part of federal policy includes much of the Sontag, et al., (1973) definition and also includes as a defining characteristic the fact that the severely handicapped have not been served by public educational programs.

> Severely handicapped children are those who because of the intensity of their physical, mental or emotional problems or a combination of such problems need educational, social, psychological and medical services beyond those

which are traditionally offered by regular and special education programs, in order to maximize their full potential for useful and meaningful participation in society for self-fulfillment (*Federal Register*, 1975, p. 7412).

A definition based on historical exclusion from regular or special education does not seem particularly useful since appropriate programs are now mandated for all special students.

Another strategy has been to define severely handicapped by reference to an absolute level of functioning. The severely handicapped are variously defined as students who do not demonstrate the developmental competence displayed by the average two-year-old (York and Williams, 1977), three-year-old (Robinson, 1976), or six-year-old (Haring and Cohen, 1975). The implication of this type of definition is that once severely handicapped students demonstrate the skills of non-handicapped two-, three-, or six-year-olds, they will no longer be labeled "severely handicapped" or receive all their educational services from programs serving the severely handicapped. Definitions which reference absolute functioning levels, though admittedly arbitrary, do carry reasonable information regarding the probable content of instruction and do allow for the removal of the label "severely handicapped" based on demonstrated student progress: as students acquire more and more skills, they lose the label.

Most traditional approaches to the identification of severely handicapped students have referenced their rate of development to that of their nonhandicapped classmates. The American Association of Mental Deficiency (AAMD) classification scheme is the most salient example of this approach. The use of standardized measures of intellectual functioning may not be inappropriate if the purpose is simply to identify a portion of the population in need of services. However, it fails to provide educationally relevant information regarding student performance in specific curriculum domains, or to provide sensitive estimates of performance of students with sensorimotor or expressive language impairments. A strict peer-referenced definition has the additional disadvantage of not reflecting student progress if it occurs, and thereby, making the severely handicapped label quite permanent. Consider for example, a child of eight who performs only those skills characteristically displayed by nonhandicapped two-year-olds. For purposes of illustration, using the old formula of $IQ = MA/CA \times 100$, one can compute this child's IQ as $2/8 \times 100$, or 25. Suppose that as a result of an intensive and comprehensive educational program, this student begins to gain skills, and that after two years of intervention his repertoire includes those skills characteristic of nonhandicapped four-year-olds. Recomputing the IQ ($4/10 \times 100 = 40$), one sees some progress but not enough to move the student convincingly out of the severely handicapped range. However, if one considers the *rate* of learning during instruction, a rather different picture emerges. In two chronological years the student has acquired the equivalent of two "mental years" of skills, a rate of learning equal to that which typifies normal development (1 mental yr./1 chronological yr. $\times$ 100 = 100). Should a student whose skills are being developed at this rate continue to be defined as severely handicapped? One might make a strong case to the contrary.

Approaches which define the severely handicapped as those students manifesting multiple categorical disabilities (for example, retarded/emotionally disturbed, learning disabled/physically handicapped) might be rejected on the basis of the inadequacy that exists in the present system of disability categorization. Categorical descriptors have been nominally combined with no information about educational characteristics or service delivery needs. A more useful approach to definition makes reference to the number of curriculum domains in which student performance is impaired. Bricker and Iacino (1977), for example, include as part of their working definition the requirement that at least two independent observers agree that the child's current behavior repertoire is significantly deficient or impaired in two or more major curriculum areas (sensorimotor, language, motor, and social self-help skills).

In contrast to both norm-referenced and skill deficit definitions are a number of recent approaches which attempt to define students on the basis of intensity of the educational programs required to produce educational change (Hobbs, 1975; Gold, 1976; Lilly, 1977; Bricker and Iacino, 1977). This service-need formulation is based not so much on child problems as on the probable intensity and duration of support needed from the special education system. Within the framework of this approach, no student would be classified as severely handicapped until the educational system had demonstrated that less intense and less restrictive services were insufficient to effect functional and generalizable gains.

In spite of all of this attention to the question "who are the severely handicapped," it remains far less important *what* students are called than *whether* their skills can be effectively enhanced by educational intervention. While a definition may serve as a general organizer, it does not add a great deal of knowledge and it does not solve problems (Meyen, 1975). For present purposes, the term "severely handicapped" will be used to collectively refer to students who have traditionally been labeled moderately, severely, or profoundly retarded; autistic, autistic-like, or severely emotionally disturbed; and multihandicapped. Severely handicapped undoubtedly encompasses a more heterogeneous group than does any other special education category. Students labeled severely handicapped may manifest sensory impairments, physical abnormalities, crippling conditions, or bizarre behavioral repertoires. They share no common etiology. A severe handicapping condition may result from a variety of factors usually classified according to time of onset. *Prenatal* causes may include chromosomal aberrations (the most common of which is Down's syndrome), specific genetic disorders, various maternal conditions (Rh factor, alcoholism, infections such as rubella or syphilis), or uncontrolled patterns of central nervous system development (resulting in cerebral palsy, hydrocephalus, or spina bifida). *Perinatal* factors refer to complications of delivery or of the period immediately following birth and might include direct injury to the head or brain, infection, or placement in an atmosphere deficient or overly rich in oxygen. *Postnatal* factors contributing to severe handicapping conditions may include accidents, infection (meningitis, encephalitis), the advent of seizure activity, or general environment conditions such as poor nutrition. In spite of this heterogeneity in characteristics and etiology, severely handicapped students share the fact that each, in some way, exhibits significantly discrepant behavior and demands intensive and sustained intervention from the educational community. The problems of facilitating communication among practitioners and of grouping individuals for effective instruction will not be solved by building a better definition, but rather by the systematic use of behavioral descriptors and technology in the design and development of educational programs.

LEAST RESTRICTIVE ENVIRONMENT FOR SEVERELY HANDICAPPED STUDENTS

Traditionally, severely handicapped students have been the responsibility of either noneducational agencies (e.g., the mental health system) or agencies in the private sector (private schools, private residential facilities, etc.). There are those who contend that because of this experience, both the private sector and the mental health system are better equipped to deliver expanded educational services to severely handicapped students. However, a number of factors argue strongly for public school programs for severely handicapped students.

1. Public schools are the most widely available educational service delivery system; programs are already "in place" and can be expanded to include severely handicapped students (Sherr, 1976).
2. Public schools are the expected source of educational services in programming for all children, handicapped or nonhandicapped, and are thus most normal for severely handicapped learners.
3. The public school system has operational liaisons with community supportive agencies and therefore is readily able to access extensive supportive services (Sherr, 1976).
4. Since public schools already have responsibility for providing services to the majority of exceptional children, these services can be extended to include programs needed by severely handicapped, and to include younger and older age groups as well (Hobbs, 1975).
5. Since public schools are expected to provide a continuum of special services, they have readily available options for students whose development in one or more areas progresses beyond the severely handicapped range. Thus public school programs would facilitate appropriate transitions to less restrictive settings.
6. Public school services are cost-effective in that they do not require duplication of services/facilities. There is no need for parallel systems (Sherr, 1976; Hobbs, 1975)

7. Public schools have a state and local tax base making them less dependent upon private or federal funding to finance services.
8. Public law has mandated public school responsibility for the design and monitoring of educational programs to all special students. This new responsibility, coupled with factors identified above may effectively result in public schools directly providing all educational services.

Considering the practical, legal, and ideological arguments, one would expect to see significant increases in public-school-based programming for severely handicapped learners. The precise nature and character of those programs will be much influenced by the application and interpretation of the doctrine of least restrictive placement.

Least Restrictive Placement

Both P.L. 94–142 and Section 504 of the Rehabilitation Act require that state and local agencies follow a policy of providing services in the least restrictive educational environment. The concept of least restrictive placement for appropriate educational services seems to incorporate two notions: (1) education with children who are not handicapped, and (2) maintenance in a regular educational environment. Both of these aspects are to be operationalized "to the maximum extent possible." It is clear from the language of the law that least restrictive placement must be determined on the basis of child need rather than system convenience. Appropriate educational programs must be designed to meet student needs; students are not put into available programs or the least restrictive of existing alternatives. The law permits the removal of the child from the "regular educational environment" only if "the nature of severity of his handicap is such that education in regular classes, even with supplementary aid and services, cannot be achieved satisfactorily." Though this may seem to be a general statement condoning the removal of severely handicapped students from the regular educational environment, this is, in fact, not the case. The "mainstream" for a severely handicapped student is more a regular *school* placement (regular attendance center, neighborhood school, and so on) than placement in a regular *class per se.* Severely handicapped pupils clearly have the right to the least restrictive educational placement regardless of whether the school system can presently or conveniently absorb these students into the educational mainstream.

> In a few school districts, many severely handicapped children are today being integrated into the everyday activities of the public schools. How far can this concept be pushed? The answer lies in the field's acceptance of the rightness and necessity of the least restrictive educational environment. Once this is understood and accepted, it makes little sense to group the severely handicapped in homogeneous, unrealistic settings, which do not reflect a normal society. With careful planning and creative problem solving, all of our severely handicapped children can indeed be well served in self contained classes within the public schools (Sontag, 1976, p. 154).

Since the determination of least restrictive placement is an individual question (what is restrictive for one student may not be restrictive for another), and since the law is not specific regarding how to judge "the maximum extent possible," the following are offered as general guidelines against which a proposed placement can be evaluated to determine the extent to which it is restrictive or nonnormalizing.

1. *Presence of nonhandicapped students in the same educational facility.*

This criterion is both clearly stated in the law and easily evaluated. One needs to simply ask whether nonhandicapped and severely handicapped students attend the same school.

2. *Presence of nonhandicapped peers.*

This criterion, an extension of the first, examines the extent to which the nonhandicapped students in the educational setting are peers of the handicapped students. Peers are most often defined in terms of age equivalence. For example, the peers of a handicapped secondary-age student would be nonhandicapped secondary-age students. But the environment is restrictive if the secondary-age student's "peers" are elementary aged or preschoolers.

3. *Interaction with nonhandicapped students in school environments.*

While the mere presence of both nonhandicapped and handicapped students in a school building is clearly a step toward educational integration and the realization of least restrictive educational placements for severely handicapped students, such a placement remains restrictive to the extent that there fails to be planned and functional interaction between the two groups. Segregation of severely handicapped into wings, floors, or pods of regular school buildings, with separate access, lunchroom, and recreational facilities, does not represent the spirit of least restrictive placement. It would seem that, at a minimum, severely handicapped students could integrate with nonhandicapped peers in hallways, lunchroom, and playgrounds.

4. *Ratio of handicapped to nonhandicapped.*

As the ratio of handicapped to nonhandicapped students in an educational setting exceeds that of the population as a whole, placement becomes restrictive. Thus, a school should provide compelling justification for housing multiple classes of low prevalence students within the same building when the services required by these students are not so unusual as to be unavailable if classes are dispersed throughout the system. While the severely handicapped are a low incidence group, making it administratively effective to cluster students for services, one must bear in mind that the ability of the student, rather than administrative convenience, is the final criterion.

5. *Equality of access to educational facilities.*

The educational and nonacademic facilities available to severely handicapped students must be comparable to those available to their nonhandicapped peers. If nonhandicapped students normally have access to libraries, cafeterias, gymnasiums, and locker room facilities, then the same resources must be available to handicapped students. A placement in which severely handicapped students have lunch in their classroom, or do not have access to locker room facilities after physical educational activities, must be considered restrictive. Similarly, a program which provides vocational training and placement for nonhandicapped secondary-level students but does not do so for severely handicapped secondary-age students is discriminatory and restrictive.

6. *Quality of educational services.*

The educational placement of severely handicapped students is restrictive to the extent that educational and supportive services are not available from competent professional personnel. Programs for severely handicapped students designed and delivered by uncertified teachers or by professionals who are unfamiliar with severe handicapping conditions, are restrictive no matter how well intentioned.

7. *Normal organization of school day.*

The length and organization of the school day for severely handicapped students should approximate that of non- or less-handicapped age peers. If nonhandicapped students attend school from 8:30 A.M. to 3:00 P.M. five days a week, then so should severely handicapped students. An arrangement whereby handicapped students arrive at school late and depart early because it is convenient for social, financial, administrative, or logistical reasons is untenable. Similarly, the organization of the school day should be patterned after the system in effect for nonhandicapped

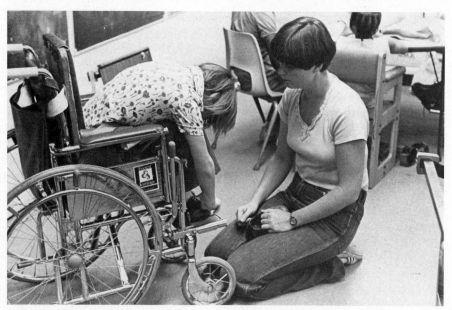

Courtesy of the Easter Seal Program for Multiple Handicapped Children (Steve Neiman).

students. If nonhandicapped elementary students attend class in rooms that are self-contained with one teacher providing instruction in all curriculum domains, then similar self-contained arrangements are justified for a class of severely handicapped students. However, if classrooms attended by nonhandicapped students include team teaching activities, and relevant support staff (art, music, and so on), then so should services to a classroom attended by severely handicapped students. Since nonhandicapped high school students typically travel through the school building taking classes in different settings, the educational environment for severely handicapped students might be considered restrictive unless they have similar opportunities to move through the school environment.

One must recognize that each student, regardless of functioning level, is in need of individualized attention and planning. The law certainly acknowledges the need for individualization when it requires that handicapped students be educationally integrated to "the maximum extent appropriate." However, any adjustment made in the educational plan or placement of a child because of a severe handicapping condition must be carefully scrutinized to minimize the possibility that such a placement might encourage rather than reduce developmental discrepancies between severely handicapped and nonhandicapped students.

MODELS FOR SERVICE DELIVERY TO SEVERELY HANDICAPPED STUDENTS

Sontag, Burke, and York (1973) delineated two basic approaches for the provision of services to severely handicapped students. A clustered approach to service delivery has as its extreme the grouping of severely handicapped students for both educational and residential services. A dispersal approach has as its extreme the integration of severely handicapped students into classrooms of less- or nonhandicapped peers. Intermediate models include self-contained schools or centers for severely handicapped, self-contained wings in regular educational facilities, and self-contained classrooms dispersed throughout school buildings or throughout school districts. Evaluation of service delivery systems is no longer restricted to the questions of cost-effectiveness and administrative feasibility, but must now also be referenced against an interpretation of least restrictive placement as it has been operationalized here.

There are those (for example, Sontag, 1976) who maintain that service delivery models such as the "continuum" and the "cascade" have not enhanced the options available to severely handicapped students, but have instead had the effect of legitimizing arrangements such as institutional placement and self-contained educational facilities for more severely handicapped students. It is clear that few current service delivery formats approach normalized, least restrictive educational environments. Traditional models for serving severely handicapped students (residential placement, self-contained schools or centers) are now inappropriate for the following reasons:

1. Exposure to nonhandicapped student models is absent or minimal;
2. Severely handicapped students tend to learn "handicapped" skills, attitudes, and values;
3. Teachers tend to strive for the resolution of handicapping problems at the expense of developing functional community referenced skills;
4. Most comparisons between students are made in relation to degrees of handicap rather than comparing skill levels of the students to the criteia of nonhandicapped skill performance;
5. Lack of exposure to severely handicapped students limits the probability that the skills, attitudes and values of *nonhandicapped* students will become more constructive, tolerant, and appropriate. (Brown, Wilcox, Sontag, Vincent, Dodd, and Greunewald, 1977).

It is difficult to justify maintenance or creation of facilities and models that obviously do not support the principle of least restrictive placement.

It is likely that somewhat different service delivery models will be required in different locations throughout the country. The problems of a major urban area confronting the return of a large population from institutions will certainly require different solutions than the problems of delivering least restrictive services in a sparsely populated area. While a tutorial arrangement in a regular classroom might be the least restrictive solution in a sparsely populated area, self-contained classrooms in regular attendance centers may be less restrictive in an urban surrounding. Similarly, a center-based parent program might be appropriate in an urban area while home-based programming would be less restrictive in a rural area (McKenzie, Hill, Sousie, York and Baker, 1977; Smith and Pasternack, 1977). Demographic, geographic, socioeconomic and ethnic characteristics of different areas can naturally be expected to affect the form of service to severely handicapped students. As a general guide, however, one should expect that the prevalent model of services would move from segregated and self-contained schools (Kenowitz, Zweibel, and Edgar, in press) to self-contained classes in regular educational centers. As such movement occurs it should be accompanied by descriptions of procedures employed to expand the integration of severely handicapped students with their nonhandicapped peers (see, for example, Russo and Koegel, 1977) and reports of the outcomes of that integration on the various attitudes and behaviors of nonhandicapped and handicapped students.

While discussions of "least restrictive" have usually focused on the question of the physical location of the student's educational placement, the application of the concept is by no means so limited. Criteria of restrictiveness could be generated and applied to domestic living arrangements, vocational and postschool employment options, and prosthetic devices and adaptive equipment, as well as to curriculum content and instructional delivery format. Consider for example, domestic living arrangements for secondary-age and adult severely handicapped. At least the following domestic living arrangements seem available as long-term options: (1) independent apartment living, (2) independent apartment living with follow-up, (3) staffed apartments or co-resident apartments, (4) clustered apartments, (5) group homes, (6) developmental homes, (7) intermediate care facilities, and (8) sheltered care facilities. Applying the criteria of least restrictive setting, the domestic living situations which satisfy the integration and normalization components of least restrictive placement include only (1) through (5) above. Professionals should strive to bring domestic living alternatives in line with the mandate for least restrictive environment. Similarly, vocational opportunities for adult severely handicapped should attempt to incorporate the concept of least restrictiveness by developing a continuum of vocational opportunities ranging from traditional sheltered employment, to competitive employment in enclave units in regular vocational settings, to community-based placements in which severely handicapped workers are integrated with the nonhandicapped work force.

Considering the concept of least restrictive as it might be applied to the design and selection of prosthetic devices, adaptive equipment, and/or functional alternatives, one would be guided to employ as few prostheses as possible. When prostheses are used, they should be selected to maximize the possibilities of independent functioning (for example, wheelchairs that can be self-propelled by students should be preferred over chairs that must be mobilized by an adult), to train for performance without the prostheses or adaptive equipment, and to train students to use prostheses which are most frequently and realistically available. *Dynamic* prostheses that require response from the individual and hence aid development of balance, head control, and so forth, are to be preferred over the more restrictive *static* prosthetic devices that simply provide necessary support, or position the body in place without requiring active participation and learning by the handicapped.

Prosthesizing a student's educational environment with computer-assisted instruction may actually be considered restrictive since it does not train responses to naturally occurring stimulus events, does not teach functional application of skills, and is not a system available in most educational environments. With such a prosthetic system, one might expand a repertoire while paradoxically limiting the handicapped student's ability to function in a normalized setting.

While the concept of "least restrictive" is beginning to be applied to areas other than educational placement (see, for example, Skarnulis, 1976; Pomerantz and Marholin, 1977; York and Williams, 1977), considerably more must be done if severely handicapped students are to have available opportunities which are least restrictive and most normalizing in all their aspects.

Administrative Accommodations

In order to effect a significant change in the quality and quantity of services delivered to severely handicapped individuals, public school administrators will be required to accommodate on a variety of levels in a number of different domains.

Transition, Planning, and Public Relations

The transition from no services or services in restrictive settings to integrated public school services for severely handicapped students will not, in all likelihood, be easy. The vested interest of those in residential or segregated educational settings, and the lack of past interaction among parents, administrators, special and regular class teachers, and nonhandicapped students must all be overcome by careful planning and education. Attitudes must be changed so that the public supports, both financially and ideologically, the education of all children in the least restrictive educational settings. There must be careful planning for transition to the public schools, including such tasks as the hiring of competent and qualified teachers for severely handicapped students, and inservice programs for administrators, as well as regular classroom teachers and students.

Physical Plant Modification

Since the construction and maintenance of special segregated facilities for severely handicapped learners is neither financially nor ideologically tenable, the public school administrator faces the task of redesigning and modifying existing facilities to accommodate severely handicapped pupils (Orelove and Hanley, 1977). Since most school buildings were constructed for ambulatory students who experience few sensory or motor impairments or for those students who possess some degree of physical disability but who are generally able to self-locomote, it is clear that existing educational facilities must be modified to varying degrees to accommodate severely handicapped students. Stairways, unmodified bathroom facilities, curbs, and conventional classroom furniture may all present major obstacles to physically impaired individuals, and thereby, may foster dependence on able-bodied adults or peers. On one hand, administrators will be required to modify existing physical facilities to accommodate the motoric and sensory disabilities of handicapped students. On the other hand, they must take care to avoid overreacting to special physical needs of severely handicapped students by creating a sterile, abuse-resistant school environment characterized by indestructible walls and floors, shatterproof glass, heavy-duty furniture and equipment, sheltered light fixtures, and so on. Such an environment may tend to perpetuate the image that students in that environment are deviant or non-normal. The appearance of the school building itself is variable, and can contribute to a placement being more or less restrictive (Wolfensberger, 1972).

Time and Locus of Instruction

If educational efforts for severely handicapped are going to be directed toward teaching students to function in society, there are obvious implications for instructional delivery and concomitant requirements for administrative support. If students are being prepared to function in heterogeneous adult environments, then a majority of their training experiences must be conducted in such natural settings. While simulation and/or repeated practice tasks may characterize early instruction, there must be eventual verification of academic, social, self-help, vocational, and domestic performances in the criterion environment. For example, if students are to be taught to use community mass transit, they must actually spend time outside of school waiting for buses and subways, and boarding and riding them to selected functional destinations in the community. Administrators must be tolerant of the logistical problems that will arise as a result of moving education into the real world. With community mobility training as an example, administrators must be willing to negotiate the insurance problems which will arise as a function of students spending time outside the school building, must initiate or support teacher-initiated public relations efforts with both parents and mass transit officials, and must support educational schedules that allow for necessary community-based training. With vocational training efforts in particular, school administrators will be required to tolerate departures from the form and location of education activities. The simulated workshops in a classroom or elsewhere in the school building must be replaced by student movement into a variety of community job placements. Administrators may no longer be able to define their services by the number of days or hours in the school building, but may instead have to rely on descriptions of program options (Vincent and Broome, 1977) and documented success in meeting academic, social, vocational, and community living goals delineated by individualized education programs.

Extensive Family Involvement

It seems clear that as a result of P.L. 94–142, parents will become increasingly involved in the educational programs that serve their handicapped children. In the past, the majority of attempts to involve parents have been directed toward "parent training" and reflected an attitude that parents of exceptional children were by definition targets of special training efforts themselves. Several recent trends (notably consumer education and educational accountability) have expanded the options available to parents of severely handicapped children. For example, Vincent and Broome (1977) describe a program serving young severely handicapped students in which parents have a variety of options for participation, beginning with participation in the IEP Conference and including classroom observation, classroom participation, frequent telephone or written contacts, home visitations, parent meetings, and involvement with curriculum task force groups. Still other roles for parents might include legislative lobbyist, builder of special equipment, trainer of other parents, student and/or program advocate, data collector, and general program volunteer. Just as school districts are responsible for having a range of educational service options, so should programs offer a range of parent participation opportunities. Certainly "training" activities where parents are taught to position, feed, carry, manage, and instruct their children should remain an important component of this continuum.

In addition to replacing the term "parent training," it might also be appropriate to replace "parental involvement" with *family* involvement, since a sibling, grandmother, or a concerned neighbor might assume responsibility for a number of roles in the educational system with respect to the severely handicapped student. To effect a range of family involvement options is not as easy as it sounds. Not only is it a novel approach for home-school interactions, but it may also require overcoming a number of existing counter productive parent-professional interaction patterns (see Roos, 1977). However, both economic and learning theory arguments make the parent-professional "partnership" imperative for those providing services to severely handicapped students.

Flexible Staffing

If students are to spend significant amounts of time learning or demonstrating skills in a natural environment, and if this is to occur in a normalized fashion (for example, one or two students ride the bus, shop and eat lunch out with one teacher, rather than a whole class riding, shopping, and eating together), administrators will need to support frequent teacher absence from the school building. Similarly, if adequate educational programming requires frequent home visits by the teacher, then provisions should be made in the daily schedule to acknowledge these activities as a legitimate part of the teaching role. Perhaps administrators will find it necessary to hire a different type of staff. In addition to teachers for self-contained classrooms, they will also hire specialists in job analysis and training, community mobility training, domestic living training, and so on. In all likelihood, special "parent advisor" or "family coordinator" positions will be required to establish and maintain family involvement in the school program and the necessary communication between home and school. Additionally, programs serving severely handicapped students may need to have mobility aides who are shared among a number of classrooms and whose job it is to assist nonambulatory students through the building, or to assist with feeding programs for physically involved students. The administrative comfort of traditional staffing patterns and schedules will be abandoned for severely handicapped students if they are to receive appropriate educational programs.

Cooperative Models for the Delivery of Services

It is obvious that no discipline will be equipped to design and deliver singlehandedly the complement of services required by severely handicapped students. Significant input may be needed from a variety of specialists—parents, physicians, biomedical engineers, audiologists, occupational therapists, physical therapists, nutritionists, social workers, and behavior management consultants—in addition to the traditional educational staff. Clearly, this creates the demand for a system which can both integrate information and coordinate services from a variety of disciplines, and which can do so in an integrated, least restrictive manner. A number of models have been proposed for the use of many disciplines and for the design and provision of services to severely handicapped students (Hart, 1977). A major problem with a multidisciplinary approach has been the absence of the requirement to integrate independent evaluations and recommendations from various disciplines to achieve a group consensus regarding priorities for a particular student. An interdisciplinary approach attempts to focus independent professional evaluations into a total program by requiring a group/team consensus concerning the program. While this certainly is a step toward more integrated services, there is still the problem that multiple discipline involvement is limited to making recommendations rather than actually implementing and reevaluating specific interventions. Responsibility for implementation is diffused among disciplines and the persons most obviously responsible for the student, namely the teachers, may find themselves without resources to effect qualitative change in the programs delivered.

The transdisciplinary model has evolved in an attempt to alleviate the compartmentalization and fragmentation of services that have characterized both multidisciplinary and interdisciplinary service approaches. While a transdisciplinary approach may include the same team members as other approaches, it is novel in that there is considerable role release among the professionals, and the ultimate decision-making power rests with the classroom teacher. Thus, rather than having the communication specialist deliver direct speech and language services to a student, the specialist would consult with the teacher to develop programs and train the teacher to actually integrate and deliver those programs. Similarly, a physical therapist on a transdisciplinary team would spend less time delivering isolated direct therapy to handicapped students, and more time training teachers in positioning and handling techniques which would facilitate both instructional and physical therapy goals throughout the day. A transdisciplinary approach requires that specialists take on more of a training role and that educators acquire specialized content and personnel-coordinating skills not traditionally expected of classroom teachers.

There are several arguments for an educational (rather than clinical) model for the delivery of multiple disciplinary services. The first, and very practical consideration, is that there are simply not enough specialists (physical therapists, occupational therapists, etc.) to provide sufficient direct services to severely handicapped students. Thus training teachers to implement certain aspects of specialists' roles increases the services available to children. Secondly, since teachers are the professionals responsible for students the greatest part of the day, they are in the best position to integrate and coordinate information from a number of sources into a coherent educational program (D. Bricker, 1976). Instead of a student receiving instruction on head control only in a scheduled physical therapy period, the teacher can program head control activities during feeding, play, and academic instruction. Finally, since the severely handicapped are frequently characterized by a failure to spontaneously generalize newly acquired skills to new situations or activities, training skills in the environment where they will actually be required (viz., the classroom rather than the therapy room) enhances the probability that the trained skills will actually be functional to the child.

It is clear that the realization of transdisciplinary services can be accomplished only with careful selection and training of individuals in various disciplines, and within the context of a data-based approach to services. All programs, regardless of the originating discipline, must be continuously monitored and revised, with decisions made on the basis of student performance data, not personal allegiance to particular techniques or systems. To advocate a service delivery approach in which a variety of disciplines cooperatively devise and implement the most appropriate comprehensive educational programs for severely handicapped students, is far easier than to realize such a system. If such cooperation is to occur, the following problems (at least!) must be avoided.

1. Misunderstanding or lack of respect for paradigms and techniques utilized by other disciplines;
2. Lack of common terminology;
3. Feelings of territorial rights;
4. Competition for time of students; and
5. The tendency for individuals to regard themselves primarily as diagnosticians or programmers rather than as contributors responsible for evaluation, programming, and follow-through (Crowner, 1975).

Despite these difficulties, effective transdisciplinary services to severely handicapped students are being realized in a number of locations (for example, Carter, Filler, Fundakowski, and Peterson, 1977; Sousie, Edelman, Fox, Fox, Williams, and York, 1977; and Sternat, Messina, Nietupski, Lyon, and Brown, 1977). With effective transdisciplinary models in place it should be possible to generate the necessary data to evaluate the model in terms of feasibility, cost, and educational effectiveness.

Ideal Services

While it is likely that the form of ideal services will vary somewhat across locations, certain components should be visible in any system that purports to provide comprehensive services to severely handicapped students:

1. Early Identification and Intervention

Local and state agencies and medical personnel should work to actualize a high risk infant registry and to follow up such children with appropriate enrichment and educational activities. Intervention should be continuous and coordinated to provide maximal gains to the infant, as well as maximum support and training to the family unit (Haring, 1976).

2. Integrated Services from Many Relevant Sources, Including Parents

Programs must have some articulated plans for bringing together and coordinating the resources necessary to solve the problems of severely handicapped students. Simply having the expertise available does not guarantee that it will actually be brought to bear, or that it will culminate in an educationally relevant plan (D. Bricker, 1976; Hart, 1977).

3. Curricula Organized Around Longitudinal Skill Sequences Designed to Facilitate Acquisition of Vital Independent Functioning Skills

The goals of programs serving severely handicapped students should not represent isolated or convenient educational objectives. Rather, the curriculum should represent part of a thoughtful, long-range, coordinated attempt to build the social, self-help, motor, communication and conceptual performances required for more independent functioning (Brown, Nietupski, and Hamre-Nietupski, 1976; York and Williams, 1977).

4. A Continuum of Educational, Vocational, and Home-Living Arrangements which Emphasizes and Facilitates Movement to Less Restrictive Environments

If students are to be involved with systematic educational programs from birth to twenty-one years, then one might reasonably expect skills to be developed over that period. As new skills emerge and increased competence is demonstrated, students must have available increasingly less restrictive and more normalized options in educational, vocational, and home-living areas.

5. Data-Based Approach to Evaluation of Instruction and Systems Efforts

All aspects of services, from personnel preparation activities and service delivery models to specific educational programs for communication and self-help objectives, should be subjected to evaluation of both cost and educational effectiveness. No aspect should be exempt from empirical verification or analysis, for it is only by maintaining an experimental perspective that the most appropriate and efficient problem solution will be realized.

CONTINUING CHALLENGES

Without doubt enormous progress has been made in the provision of services to severely handicapped individuals. Without doubt much remains to be done. Administrators, teachers, parents, university trainers—anyone concerned with the delivery of educational services to severely handicapped students—will continue to confront problems on a number of dimensions.

Community Education and Public Attitude

In addition to the myriad of problems related to educational technology, educators of severely handicapped students will be faced with larger societal issues as well, and will, in all likelihood, have to assume some responsibility for public education and attitude change. Presently, nonhandicapped citizens may be quite willing to make episodic and tax-deductible contributions to upgrade the services available to the severely handicapped, or to "dance for those who can't" as evidence of their commitment to handicapped minorities. However, special educators need to work from this level of involvement to shape a higher order commitment which is expressed not only by charity and volunteer work, but also by a willingness to hire and accept handicapped workers in community employment, to advocate accessible mass transit and barrier-free stores and services, to support group homes and community living facilities located in residential neighborhoods, and to bear the cost of quality educational services to these long-neglected citizens. Naturally, teachers of the severely handicapped must justify this social and financial support by documenting their effectiveness in producing personal, social, and academic gains in their students. It is imperative that programs for the severely handicapped be planned with care and staffed with competent professionals, for unless the emphasis on quality is maintained, severely handicapped students are unlikely to demonstrate sufficient behavior change to maintain active public support. The cost of special education for severely handicapped pupils far exceeds the per pupil expenses of regular education. Therefore, professionals must take care to educate the public as to the relative short-term and long-range social and financial benefits of public school services, as compared to institutional or other programs which restrict the ultimate functioning of severely handicapped individuals (see Crowner, 1975).

Personnel Preparation

Despite the number of people involved in the provision of services to severely handicapped students, the ultimate success of those services rests with the classroom teacher. Because the pressure to implement programs for severely handicapped is so intense and the shortage of trained personnel so acute, conditions exist which actually undermine the benefits that the severely handicapped have gained through legislative and judicial mandates. School districts may respond to current pressures by hiring staff who are not trained or qualified to work with severely handicapped students. Since in many states there is a surplus of elementary and secondary teachers and categorically-trained teachers of the mildly handicapped, school districts may transfer these surplus teachers into classrooms for severely handicapped. The probable outcome of such a practice would be failure on a massive scale, since most graduates of programs that prepare teachers of the mildly handicapped are not likely to possess the skills to toilet train, to eliminate self-destructive and self-stimulatory behavior, to train eye contact and imitative responding, to systematically teach community survival skills, and so on. The role of the teacher of severely handicapped students is exceedingly complex and extends far beyond the traditional teaching role. There is a direct relationship between the level of a student's disability and the level of instructional competence required of the teacher: the more pronounced the disability, the greater and more precise the skills required of the teacher (Sontag, Burke, and York, 1973).

It is obvious that school districts, state departments of education, and teacher-training programs must cooperate to plan quality inservice and preservice training programs, and to develop and implement certification standards that will ensure the delivery of the necessary range of services by high caliber personnel. Though there is currently a large demand for teachers of severely handicapped, it is hoped that the number of programs training teachers, especially at the preservice level, will be limited because the long-range need of this low-prevalence population will be for quality rather than quantity. Furthermore, the staff resources to support training programs (sufficient faculty expertise, well-articulated competency–based programs, available practicum sites, severely handicapped students, master teachers, interdisciplinary resources, and so on) are not widely available. If the demand for quality teacher-training efforts is to be met, coordination and quality control is required on a national level.

> [There is a] need to generate statements of standards for preservice training in terms of practicum sites, staff qualifications, student-staff ratios, competency statements, and evaluation procedures, and professional standards that are exclusionary in the sense of admitting only the most highly qualified people to the task of educating this low incidence population (Sontag, Smith, and Sailor, 1977, p. 10).

Debilitating Contingencies in Service Systems

Pomerantz and Marholin (1977) offer a systems analysis of the contingencies operating against the provision of effective, normalized vocational rehabilitation services to the severely handicapped. Their analysis applies to other domains of education and service-delivery systems as well. In general, there are inadequate standards for funding or certifying educational, vocational, or home-living programs for severely handicapped citizens. There is a lack of emphasis on student behavior change as a measure of program accountability, and student attendance or per pupil cost are examined more carefully than are behavioral gains effected by the programs. Further, it is rare that programs are differentially funded according to their effectiveness.

Across service systems in general, there is a lack of incentives for teachers, trainers, or programs to place individuals into less restrictive environments. For example, the placement of a client from a sheltered workshop into competitive community employment usually means the loss of a more able worker, which in turn decreases workshop income, and is therefore ultimately undesirable to the agency sponsoring the workshop. Furthermore, such a placement leaves a vacancy in a program that may receive funding based on the number of clients in attendance per day.

Planning for transition to less restrictive programs at the educational level may require that teachers spend significant time analyzing the criterion environment, adapting materials, providing inservice training to the receiving teacher, and so forth. If there is no system support for the necessary planning activities, and if teachers must plan transitions in addition to their ongoing classroom management and curriculum development activities, then one of two things will occur. The transition may fail altogether because neither the student nor the receiving program is adequately prepared for the change, or the quality and quantity of services to ongoing classroom activities will fail because teacher time and energy is invested in transition. A subtle, but equally devastating contingency is the tendency on the part of many disciplines to focus their energy and service on those students who are likely to "profit the most" rather than on those who need it the most. Such priorities serve to exaggerate and compound the problems of the more severely handicapped.

If parents, professionals, and others concerned with severely handicapped students are going to realize comprehensive, functional, and less restrictive services, they must work to eliminate such debilitating contingencies. Instead, systems and regulations must be developed which articulate and enforce standards, which focus on documented child behavior change as measures of program quality, which provide active support, resources and incentives for transition activities, and which reinforce student independence and competence.

Research Needs

Given the relative naivete of the field, it is unlikely that any one person, program, or system has the long range answers to many of the problems posed by severely handicapped students. New problems are constantly appearing and new techniques for their solution constantly offered. If the field is indeed going to meet the myriad needs of the severely handicapped, the long standing dichotomy between training and research, service and science, must be broken down. Efforts must be combined to generate effective and valid problem solutions (W. Bricker, 1976; Gaylord-Ross, 1977; and Williams, Stepner, Scheuerman, Broome, Conte, Crowner and Brown, 1974).

Historically, special education has been guided more by sociopolitical ideology than by an empirical data base, and researchers with exceptional populations may have generated a science of the artificial and trivial by concentrating on experimental laboratory tasks rather than on the performance of individuals in natural settings. Science for its own sake is no longer tenable, and researchers are under tremendous pressure to be relevant and to justify the potential utilization of basic research efforts. Though the revolution in mental retardation service delivery was effected independent of input from the research community (Gaylord-Ross, 1977), practitioners are now in need of assistance from researchers to validate their efforts, monitor and refine their techniques, develop maximally effective training procedures, and refine instructional technology. It is past the time when the general community should allow educators to be visionary and proclaim what could or should be done in designing services for the severely handicapped student. It is time to demand that programs be designed, services delivered, and effects documented. Clearly, it is the day for a marriage of service and research.

There is a critical need for longitudinal educational research relating to the problems of the severely handicapped. Topics of such investigation could include empirical evaluation of service models for the delivery of auxiliary or supportive services, validation of teacher competencies proposed by various training programs, documentation of the effects of institutionalization, data-based design of optimal community-living arrangements, and monitoring of attitudes toward severely handicapped students as a function of their presence in integrated educational settings. A major area in need of "the service of research" (W. Bricker, 1976), is curriculum development. With increased public attention to severely handicapped students has come a plethora of published programs and curriculum sequences for severely handicapped learners. Unfortunately, there has been very little empirical verification of the appropriateness of these sequences, and, with few exceptions, there seems to be no inclination to engage in systematic and empirical curriculum development activities. The relative merits of cognitive-developmental or logical task analytic approaches to curriculum design should be determined by data rather than theoretical chauvinism. A collaboration of research and program delivery at this point would be mutually beneficial and could be expected to increase the quality of the instruction to severely handicapped students.

At a more molecular level, there are literally thousands of questions

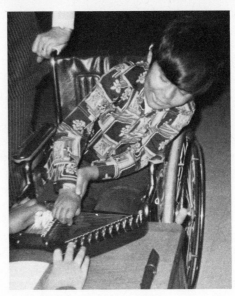

Courtesy of The Muscular Dystrophy Association.

which should be empirically investigated rather than answered with dogma or reference to history. For example, while there is now an emerging technology for programming generalization of newly acquired responses (Baer and Stokes, 1976), there is little information on which procedures are most effective. Is it more effective to bring a student to criterion on an objective and then introduce variation in training settings, task materials, teachers, and cues to respond, or is it more efficient to begin programming generalization across these dimensions with the very initiation of training? If rate is an important aspect of a complex performance being trained, is it "better" to build the entire behavior chain before focusing on rate of responding, or is it "better" to build rate before each new component is added to the chain? These are simple questions with tremendous implications.

A similar question in need of research relates to the setting of criterion levels for student performance. Most commercially available curricula prescribe specific criterion performance to be demonstrated before moving students on to a new phase of training tasks (for example, 90 percent correct on two consecutive days; three consecutive correct responses; and so on). A criterion, by definition, is an arbitrary point at which the teacher or trainer is willing to accept that learning has been demonstrated. Rather than continuing to set arbitrary performance levels, teachers and/or curriculum developers might look to research for information regarding optimum criterion levels for different types of outcomes or different types of tasks. As an illustration, research from the mastery learning literature (Block, 1972) reveals that learning to a criterion of 85 percent correct will result in optimum student enjoyment of the material presented, while learning to a criterion of 95 percent correct produces most efficient long-term retention. It seems likely that training to various criterion levels may differentially affect the ease of response or stimulus generalization, the acquisition of simple motor chains versus chains composed of multiple concepts and operations, and so on. Applied studies analogous to the laboratory studies of overlearning may yield important implications for severely handicapped students.

A related question concerns the extent of the data system and the form of the data decision rules needed to make appropriate changes in management or instructional interventions with severely handicapped students. With early programming efforts, trial by trial data was gathered daily; more recent authors (for example, Brown et al., 1976) have suggested moving away from such fine-grained data collection to intermittent or probe systems for monitoring student performance. Systematic study can provide information on how much data can be faded before adversely affecting program decisions for severely handicapped students. Indeed, this research could show whether the collection of data per se actually affects child progress.

As demonstrations of the effectiveness of instructional procedures with severely handicapped learners increase, a body of research on programmatic and instructional variables should be simultaneously generated. For example, it has been repeatedly demonstrated that severely handicapped students can acquire expressive object labels when training procedures utilize a program sequence in which students are brought to criterion on a match-to-sample task, which is followed by training on a receptive labeling/object identification task which, in turn, is followed by direct training on expressive labels. While it is generally valuable to know that this is sufficient for establishing object labels, there remains a question whether the entire sequence is necessary or if it actually facilitates acquisition of the type of response. Perhaps after match-to-sample training, students can be probed for mastery of the expressive task without training on object recognition.

In addition to the need to investigate instructional and programmatic variables per se, there is a tremendous need to develop and validate procedures which can be used for perhaps the most challenging subset of the severely handicapped population: the nonverbal, severely physically impaired student who, because of profound physical involvement, is unable to speak and lacks the prerequisite motor control for any voluntary movement beyond gross approximations to touching/pointing or eye contact. The student response mode in current instructional procedures is, in general, limited to one or more of the following: independent verbal production, imitations of verbal models, independent motor responding, or imitation of motor models. The teacher selects and presents content, and verifies student learning on the assumption that these response modes are available. For example, the teacher might train a student to touch, pick up, point to, give to another, play appropriately with, model the use of, and/or verbalize the label for an object, and then verify that the student could do these tasks to some criterion. Every instructional procedure the teacher employs for training the label "ball" explicitly relies on the student's motor and verbal response capabilities. Students who lack such response capabilities will not fit existing program models. While some exploratory work has been done, there is a clear need to further delineate and evaluate instructional procedures that may be applicable to students with severely limited response modes.

There are an unfortunate number of procedures both long standing and currently in vogue which are zealously defended or advocated without being subjected to careful empirical scrutiny. For example, certain programs or programmers advocate training the functional use of objects prior to or as the initial activity in language-training intervention. Another *Zeitgeist* in the language-training area is total communication (pairing manual signs with verbalizations) and the assumption that such pairing facilitates the development of verbal language skills in severely handicapped students. If one examines the literature available to support either functional object use as a prerequisite to other language acquisition (Bricker and Dennison, 1973; Vincent-Smith and Chatelanant, 1973; Williams, 1977) or total communication as a speech facilitator (Miller and Miller, 1977; Stremmel-Campbell, Cantrell and Hale, 1977) it appears that the research is inconclusive at best. While the notion of training functional object use has intuitive appeal and documentation in the developmental literature, experimental support for functional object use as a prerequisite to further language training has yet to be provided. The equally appealing total communication procedures have yet to be so adequately described that they can be replicated and their effects on acquisition, maintenance, and generalization of student communication documented. If future work were to show that total communication is indeed a language facilitator, additional questions would be raised; for example, how or when does one most effectively fade manual signs while maintaining verbal communication? Professions should not advocate procedures without simultaneously advocating their data-based evaluation.

The educational, medical, and social needs of severely handicapped students are both complex and extensive. The training needs of teachers of these students are similarly overwhelming. The research needs of the field as a whole, however, are perhaps most pressing of all. Unless direct service and teacher-training program efforts are carefully coordinated with ongoing formative evaluation and empirical documentation, professionals working with the severely handicapped run the risk of losing the rare opportunity to systematically develop a field of training and service that is both responsive and accountable.

REFERENCES

Abt Associates, Inc. *Assessment of Selected Resources for Severely Handicapped Children and Youth* (vol. 1). Cambridge, MA: Abt Associates, 1974.

Anderson, R. M., Greer, J. G., and Dietrich, W. L. Overview and perspectives. In J. M. Anderson and J. G. Greer (ed.), *Educating the Severely and Profoundly Retarded.* Baltimore: University Park Press, 1976.

Baer, D. M., and Stokes, T. F. *Discriminating a Generalization Technology: Recommendations for Research in Mental Retardation.* Paper presented at the Fourth International Congress of the International Association for the Scientific Study of Mental Deficiency, Washington, DC; August 1976.

Block, J. H. *Student Evaluation: Toward the Setting of Mastery Performance Standards.* Paper presented at the Annual Meeting of the Americal Educational Research Association, Chicago, 1972.

Bricker, D. Educational synthesizer. In M. A. Thomas (ed.), *Hey, Don't Forget about Me!* Reston, VA: The Council for Exceptional Children, 1976.

——, and Iacino, R. Early intervention with severely/profoundly handicapped children. In E. Sontag (ed.), *Educational Programming for the Severely and Profoundly Handicapped.* Reston, VA: The Council for Exceptional Children, 1977.

Bricker, W., Service of research. In M. A. Thomas (ed.) *Hey, Don't Forget about Me!* Reston, VA: Council for Exceptional Children, 1976.

——, and Dennison, L. Functional classification, imitation, comprehension, and production in preschool children. In D. Bricker and W. Bricker (ed.), *Infant, Toddler, and Preschool Research and Intervention Project—Year III,* IMRID Behavioral Science Monograph No. 23, George Peabody College, 1973.

Brown, L., Nietupski, J., and Hamre-Nietupski, S. The criterion of ultimate functioning. In M. A. Thomas (ed.), *Hey, Don't Forget about Me!* Reston, VA: The Council for Exceptional Children, 1976.

——, Wilcox, B., Sontag, E., Vincent, B., Dodd, N., and Gruenwald, L. Toward the realization of the least restrictive educational environments for severely handicapped students. *AAESPH Review,* 1977, *2,* 195–201.

Burke, P. J. The determination of adequacy—Our Gethsemane? *AAESPH Review,* 1977, *1* (8), 2–4.

Carter, R., Filler, J., Fundakowski, G., and Peterson, C. Utilizing a transdisciplinary approach to the education of the severely handicapped. AAESPH National Conference, San Francisco, October 1977.

Crowner, T. T. A public school program for severely and profoundly handicapped students: Zero exclusion. In L. Brown, T. Crowner, W. Williams, and R. York (ed.), *Madison's Alternative for Zero-Exclusion: A Book of Readings.* Madison, WI: Madison Public Schools, 1975.

Dunn, L. M. (ed.). *Exceptional Children in the Schools: Special Education in*

Transition (2nd ed.). New York: Holt, Rinehart and Winston, 1973.

Gaylord-Ross, R. J. *Mental Retardation Research, Ecological Validity, and the Delivery of Educational Programs.* Unpublished manuscript. New York: Yeshiva University, 1977.

Gold, M. W. Task analysis: A statement and an example using acquisition and production of a complex assembly task by the retarded child. *Exceptional Children*, 1976, *43*, 78–84.

Greenleigh Associates, Inc. *The Role of the Sheltered Workshop in the Rehabilitation of the Severely Handicapped.* Report to the Department of Health, Education, and Welfare. Rehabilitation Services Administration, New York, 1975.

Haring, N. G., and Cohen, M. Using the developmental approach as a basis for planning different kinds of curricula for severely/profoundly handicapped persons. In *Educating the 24-Hour Retarded Child.* Arlington, TX: National Association for Retarded Citizens, 1975.

——. Infant identification. In M. A. Thomas (ed.), *Hey, Don't Forget about Me!* Reston, VA: The Council for Exceptional Children, 1976.

Hart, V. The use of many disciplines with the severely and profoundly handicapped. In E. Sontag (ed.), *Educational Programming for the Severely and Profoundly Handicapped.* Reston, VA: The Council for Exceptional Children, 1977.

Hobbs, N. (ed.) *The Futures of Children.* San Francisco: Jossey-Bass, 1975.

Kenowitz, L., Zweibel, S., and Edgar, E. Determining the least restrictive educational opportunity for the severely and profoundly handicapped. In N. Haring and D. Bricker (ed.), *Teaching the Severely Handicapped* (vol. 3). New York: Grune and Stratton, Inc., in press.

Kirk, S. A. *Educating Exceptional Children* (2nd ed.). Boston: Houghton Mifflin Company, 1972.

Lilly, M. S. A training based model for special education. *Exceptional Children*, 1971, *37*, 745–751.

——. *Legislative Working Paper Prepared for the Task Force on Finance.* Springfield, IL: Illinois School Problems Commission, 1977.

McKenzie, H. S., Hill, M. G., Sousie, S. P., York, R., and Baker, K. Special education training to facilitate rural community-based programs for the severely handicapped. In E. Sontag (ed.), *Educational Programming for the Severely and Profoundly Handicapped.* Reston, VA: The Council for Exceptional Children, 1977.

Martin, E. Federal commitment to education of the severely and profoundly retarded. In *Educating the 24-hour Retarded Child.* Arlington, TX: National Association for Retarded Citizens, 1975.

——. On education for the severely and profoundly handicapped and Justice Douglas. *AAESPH Review*, 1976, *1*, 115–123.

Meyen, E. L. Preparing educational personnel for the severely and profoundly retarded. In *Educating the 24-hour Retarded Child.* Arlington, TX: National Association for Retarded Citizens, 1975.

Miller, A., and Miller, E. E. Cognitive-developmental training with elevated boards and sign language. *Journal of Autism and Childhood Schizophrenia*, 1973, *3*, 65–85.

Orelove, F. P., and Hanley, C. D. School accessibility survey. Unpublished manuscript, Urbana, IL: Department of Special Education, University of Illinois, 1977.

Pomerantz, D. J., and Marholin, D. Vocational habilitation: A time for change. In E. Sontag (ed.), *Educational Programming for the Severely and Profoundly Handicapped.* Reston, VA: The Council for Exceptional Children, 1977.

Robinson, C. C. Application of Piagetian sensorimotor concepts to assessment and curriculum for severely handicapped children. *AAESPH Review*, 1976, *1*, (8), 5–10.

Roos, P. A parent's view of what public education should accomplish. In E. Sontag (ed.), *Educational Programming for the Severely and Profoundly Handicapped.* Reston, VA: The Council for Exceptional Children, 1977.

Russo, D. C., and Koegel, R. L. A method for integrating an autistic child into a normal public-school classroom. *Journal of Applied Behavior Analysis*, 1977, *10*, 579–590.

Sailor, W., and Horner, R. D. Educational and assessment strategies for the severely handicapped. In N. G. Haring and L. J. Brown (ed.), *Teaching the Severely Handicapped*, (vol. 1). New York: Grune and Stratton, Inc., 1976.

Sherr, R. D. Public school programs. In M. A. Thomas (ed.), *Hey, Don't Forget about Me!* Reston, VA: The Council for Exceptional Children, 1976.

Skarnulis, E. Less restrictive alternatives in residential services. *AAESPH Review*, 1976, *1*, 40–84.

Smith, J., and Pasternack, R. Cooperative special education services in remote and sparsely populated areas. In E. Sontag (ed.), *Educational Programming for the Severely and Profoundly Handicapped.* Reston, VA: The Council for Exceptional Children, 1977.

Sontag, E. Federal leadership. In M. A. Thomas (ed.), *Hey, Don't Forget About Me!* Reston, VA: Council for Exceptional Children, 1976.

————, Burke, P. J., and York, R. Considerations for serving the severely handicapped in the public schools. *Education and Training of the Mentally Retarded*, 1973, *8*, 20–26.

————, Smith, J., and Sailor, W. The severely and profoundly handicapped: Who are they? Where are we? *Journal of Special Education*, 1977, *11*, 5–11.

Sousie, S., Edelman, S., Fox, T., Fox, W., Williams, W., and York, R. *An Interdisciplinary Approach to the Development and Implementation of Educational Programs for Learners in Need of Intensive Special Education.* Burlington, VT: Center for Special Education, University of Vermont, 1977.

Sternat, J., Messina, R., Nietupski, J., Lyon, S., and Brown, L. Occupational and physical therapy services for severely handicapped students: Toward a naturalized public school service delivery model. In E. Sontag (ed.), *Educational Programming for the Severely and Profoundly Handicapped.* Reston, VA: The Council for Exceptional Children, 1977.

Stremmel-Campbell, K., Cantrell, D., and Hale, J. Manual signing as a language system and as a speech initiation for the non-verbal severely handicapped student. In E. Sontag (ed.), *Educational Programming for the Severely and Profoundly Handicapped.* Reston, VA: The Council for Exceptional Children, 1977.

The School Code of Illinois. Springfield, IL: Illinois Office of Education.

Thompson, P. *The Severely Multiply Handicapped—What are the Issues?* Keynote address in proceedings for the Regional Topical Conference, Salt Lake City, University of Utah, 1977.

Vincent, L. J., and Broome, K. A public school service delivery model for handicapped children between birth and five years of age. In E. Sontag (ed.), *Educational Programming for the Severely and Profoundly Handicapped.* Reston, VA: The Council for Exceptional Children, 1977.

Vincent-Smith, L., and Chatelanant, G. An evaluation of a new assessment procedure: Functional use of objects, receptive vocabulary, and expressive vocabulary. In D. Bricker and W. Bricker (ed.), *Infant, Toddler, and Preschool Research and Intervention Project—Year III.* IMRID Behavioral Science Monograph No. 23, George Peabody College, 1973.

Williams, W. The relationship of object-function to concept learning in severely handicapped individuals. Burlington, VT: CENSE, University of Vermont, 1977.

———, Stepner, J., Scheuerman, N., Broome, R., Conte, S., Crowner, T., and Brown, L. A partial delineation of what the practitioner needs from the researcher in developing public school programs for selected low-functioning individuals. In L. Brown, W. Williams, and T. Crowner (ed.), *A Collection of Papers and Programs Related to Public School Services for Severely Handicapped Students.* Madison, WI: Madison Public Schools, 1974.

Wolfensberger, W. *Normalization: The Principle of Normalization in Human Services.* Toronto: National Institute on Mental Retardation, 1972.

York, R., and Williams, W. Curricula and ongoing assessment for individualized programming in the classroom. In R. York, P. Thorpe, and R. Minisi (ed.), *Education of the Severely and Profoundly Handicapped People.* Hightstown, NJ: Northeast Regional Resource Center, 1977.

CHAPTER **6**

SEVERE/PROFOUND
HANDICAPPING CONDITIONS
Instructional considerations

BARBARA WILCOX

While the primary focus of chapter 5 was on administrative considerations in providing special education and related services to severely
handicapped students, this chapter focuses on assessment and instructional programming. Severely handicapped students present a unique and
formidable challenge to the educational system, in terms of both content
of instruction and teaching methodology. The current chapter will examine the nature of this challenge.

ASSESSMENT

The present section will outline a system for the educationally relevant
assessment of severely handicapped students, specifying both *what*
should be assessed and *how* the assessment should be conducted. This
system will be compared to both historical and current practices in the
assessment of severely handicapped learners. A brief overview of measurement techniques will be presented along with special measurement or
assessment considerations for various performance domains.

What Should Be Assessed?

In the past, formal systematic assessment of the severely handicapped
has focused on two relatively undifferentiated factors: intelligence and

adaptive behavior. Furthermore, assessment has generally been conducted more to meet administrative requirements (for example, determining the prevalence of students with severe handicapping conditions)
than to generate appropriate educational programs. Typically, standardized measures have compared student performance on an artificial sample
of behavior in a contrived setting, to the average performance of a set of
chronological age mates. The outcome of the assessment is usually expressed as a single number (scaled score, age-equivalent, percentile, and
so on) and provides only information regarding relative standing: performance is average, above, or below. Because of the very nature of norm-
referenced instruments, little educationally relevant information is produced: there is no description of the content of the pupil's repertoire, indicating what skills should be developed next, or suggesting strategies likely
to be effective with individual children. Assessment is inferential, infrequent, and indirect.

Over the past decade there has been growing disillusionment with traditional norm-referenced procedures and increasing documentation of
their short-comings (see for example, Jenkins and Pany, 1978; Jones, 1970;
Filler, Robinson, Smith, Vincent-Smith, Bricker, and Bricker, 1975; Larsen, 1977). The problems of norm-referenced measurement are even more
acute when applied to severely handicapped students. In addition to the
pragmatic complaint that standard batteries generate no useful information, and the technical question of their appropriateness for the severely
handicapped since frequently this population was excluded from the
standardization sample, there is a problem that severely handicapped are
often untestable under standard conditions. These students may frequently present sensory impairments which restrict their ability to process events during assessment (for example, visual or auditory stimuli are
not functional in presenting items to a student who is blind or deaf). They
may have motor or language impairments which prevent them from providing a response in a standard manner (for example, the student may not
be able to vocalize an object label, manipulate puzzle pieces, or directly
point to objects in a display), or physical problems which prevent the delivery of the test in the standardized format (for example, the student cannot be physically manipulated into an upright sitting position). There are
several reviews of norm-referenced assessments used with severely handicapped (Sailor and Horner, 1976; Faris, Anderson, and Greer, 1976); however, these describe the content areas covered by the instruments and
summarize procedures for administration and scoring rather than review
the technical or programmatic adequacy of the measures.

A welcome and necessary complement to norm-referenced procedures is criterion-referenced measurement (Popham, 1971) or instructional-program-based tests (Becker and Engelmann, 1976). In this
approach there is an emphasis on basic skills and performance mastery.
The repertoire of the learner is compared with actual instructional content and objectives of the curriculum rather than with the performance of

other students. Specific information about performance competencies (objectives mastered) is retained rather than lost in the translation to standard scores. Brief comparisons of norm-referenced and criterion-referenced strategies are presented in Table 6-1.

The advent of criterion-referenced and instructional-program-based assessment has provided an important bridge between assessment and programming. What is to be evaluated is student performance on curriculum items. The curriculum items might be developed from either of two basic approaches: using normal developmental sequences as the basis of assessment and programming, or using an analysis of ultimate functioning to isolate important functional skills. Using either criterion-referenced approach, the strategy which serves as a basis for curriculum development also serves as the basis for assessment efforts.

Despite the fact that the criterion-referenced assessment techniques provide considerably more instructionally-relevant information than their norm-referenced predecessors, they do not in and of themselves constitute a sufficient or comprehensive approach to evaluating severely handicapped learners. Like traditional assessment, a criterion-referenced approach also limits its focus to the *behavior* of the target student(s). Though knowledge of an individual's current repertoire in communication, motor, social, cognitive/conceptual, and self-help domains is probably the most useful information for further instruction, other factors must be examined if assessment is to be truly functional. For some time now, proponents of behavioral approaches to education have maintained that assessment is appropriate for every aspect of training: antecedents and consequences as well as the response itself (for example, Bijou and Peterson, 1968; Bijou and Wilcox-Cole, 1975). While there is clearly a need to delineate responses in a student's repertoire, there is an equal need to identify antecedent and consequent events that will affect student performance.

In attempting to assess antecedent events, one asks under what *conditions* do students respond to an educational task: verbal instruction, modeling, or physical guidance? To what types of *materials* can they respond: real objects, three-dimensional object representations, simple line drawings, symbolic representations (printed words or symbol systems)? What are functional forms for teachers' input: is the student physically capable of responding to visual, auditory, gustatory, olfactory, and/or tactile stimuli? To which *people* in the environment is the student most responsive: mother, father, teacher, physical therapist? While answers to these questions have obvious instructional and programmatic importance, they are rarely systematically evaluated.

Other, and perhaps more subtle, antecedents that relate to successful instruction may include the identification of expectations that parents and others hold for student performance, the priorities of parents regarding skill acquisition in various curriculum domains, the physical characteristics of the environment, and the availability of opportunities to respond. It is important for programmers to know whether the environment

TABLE 6-1   Comparison of Norm-Referenced (NRM) and Criterion-Referenced (CRM) Measurement Strategies

DIMENSION	NRM	CRM
Definition/ Purpose	Intent is to identify individual differences; determine relative standing in group; select limited number from group; has "competitive" orientation.	Designed to assess individual's status with respect to a particular criterion or standard of performance regardless of the relation of his/her performance to the performance of others on task; document that certain skills are or are not in repertoire; has "competence" orientation.
Standard of Reference	Standard against which any individual is compared is relative and depends on performance or others taking the test; is determined after the test is taken.	Individual performance is compared to a predetermined standard; standard is absolute and usually determined by instructional objectives or mastery learning requirements.
Item selection	Items are those which discriminate among examinees; usually items with degree of difficulty of .50.	Items are basic concept items necessary for progress through the program; items taken from the students' curriculum, task analysis, or experts' opinions.
Relevance to Instruction	Measures are taken on tasks other than those which may be the focus of education or training; difficult to translate into instructional implications.	Assessment of specific skills in a curriculum or skill reference; supplies information to teacher so that program changes can be made.
Frequency of Measurement	1. Infrequently administered (once a year or every several years); 2. Emphasizes pre/post-testing; 3. Insensitive to instructional manipulations.	Emphasizes direct and daily measurement; sensitive to instructional interventions.
Testing Situation	Usually tested in artificial situation outside of classroom.	Assessed in learning environment or in environment where the target performance is expected to occur.
Reporting of Scores	Usually represented as a number (any one of a variety of derived scores: stanines, standard scores, rank, etc.).	Describes what student can/cannot do; reporting may be awkward but is more informative.
Teacher Role	Teacher has minimal responsibility; assessments usually selected and interpreted by psychologist.	Teacher more involved in measurement and decision-making.

presents physical barriers, as well as whether parents allow the student to respond and take risks. In order to adequately plan educational programs, social and physical characteristics of a student's environment must be carefully assessed.

An assessment of consequences in the environment would include specification of the typical consequences for any performance (what usually happens if a student does not comply with an instruction? How are toilet accidents handled?), as well as the identification of functionally reinforcing and punishing stimulus events. A number of strategies are available for determining functional reinforcers: asking parents, teachers, or the students themselves; observing high probability activities; conditioning reinforcing events; or sampling potential reinforcers. Confronted with students with few communication skills or students who lack motor prerequisites to interact with objects in the environment, it becomes more likely that some systematic reinforcer sampling will be required (see for example, Fredericks, Riggs, Furey, Grove, McDonnell, Jordan, Hanson, Baldwin, and Wadow, 1976; Wilcox and Orelove, 1976). If this is the case, it must be emphasized that the evaluation of consequences should take place in the context of instructional efforts, rather than prior to or separate from any attempts at intervention.

When assessing functional consequences, one may be confronted with a discrepancy between what is functional and what is natural or normal (Wolfensberger, 1972; Brown et al., 1976). While primary consequences, such as candies or bits of food, may be the most powerful for a student, they are clearly not normal in an educational setting and have small, if any, logical relation to performance on various instructional tasks. An excessive or continuing reliance on primary consequences may actually restrict student performance in response to naturally occurring environmental demands.

Because of the unique and complex problems presented by severely handicapped individuals, several additional areas must be examined before assessment can be considered complete. Assessment should attempt to identify: (1) significant interfering behaviors that will have to be eliminated prior to, or during, the course of skill building (for example, various self-injurious behaviors; repetitive or stereotyped nonfunctional movement; phobias); and (2) behaviors or physical characteristics which will need to be managed in the course of presenting instructional tasks (for example, certain reflexes, body position, seizures, muscle tone). Evaluation of interfering behaviors is achieved primarily through collection of direct observational data. Evaluation of physical characteristics that may influence instructional goals/activities requires the cooperation of trained medical and allied medical personnel (physicians, physical therapists, occupational therapists, ophthalmologists, and otologists). Students must be examined to determine (a) their general health condition, range of motion, and reflexes; (b) the structural and functional condition of appendages and eyes, ears, nose, and mouth; (c) any pattern of seizures; (d) special nutritional considerations; and (e) the effects of particular kinds/dosages of medication. This information is necessary to plan appropriate physical and medical management routines, as well as to design mobility prostheses and/or adaptive equipment.

Characteristics of the Ideal Assessment Procedure

It is apparent that the outcome of an assessment of severely handicapped students requires considerably more than a number representing a relative level of "general intellectual functioning," or "adaptive behavior." In addition to considerable expansion of what should be assessed, the *format* for conducting the assessment must also be significantly revised in order to provide the necessary information. In contrast to the usual indirect, infrequent, and inferential assessment, assessment of severely handicapped must be direct, frequent, and based on a model of "zero-inference" (Brown et al., 1976).

Direct Measurement

Assessment should not be focused on psychological constructs presumed to underlie performance, but rather should address the target performance itself. Direct measurement imposes two requirements: that items assessed be those which are components of the curriculum sequence, and that they be presented in the format of a behavioral objective (Mager, 1962) so that they are unambiguously defined and capable of being quantified. Direct measurement emphasizes a closer alignment between assessment procedures and instructional goals. To strengthen this interface, assessments may be keyed into curriculum materials, or curriculum sequences may provide their own assessment in the form of placement tests or comprehensive checklists. Direct assessment provides a sufficient sample of items in every behavioral domain to provide information useful in instructional planning.

Like a behavioral objective, a direct assessment item should contain a behavioral description of what the student will do, under what circumstances, and to what criterion level he or she will perform. A checklist entry that simply states "Lifts head while lying on abdomen" (Meyers, Sinco, and Stalma, 1973, p. 35) is not adequate since there is neither a statement of conditions under which behavior is to occur nor a statement of how well the pupil must perform in order to pass the item. Is the student to lift head in response to verbal cues, visual stimuli, physical prompting, or simply at any time? Does the child begin with chin on the mat or with the side of the face lying on the mat? How high must the head be lifted to qualify as "lifted up?" How long must it be held off the horizontal surface? How many times or with what latency must the head be raised?

Many times ambiguously written items are scored with an equally ambiguous code such as:

0 = No competence
1 = Moderate competence
2 = Competence

Such an approach does not begin to meet the requirements for direct measurement. Criterion-referencing is not an excuse for the lack of precision in defining assessment and training items; direct measurement requires explicitly stated assessment and curriculum objectives. The requirements of reliability of an assessment instrument are more easily met when there has been specification of directly observable behavior, as well as the conditions under which an individual is required to perform and the criterion level for successful performance.

Frequent Assessment

For severely handicapped students, learning tasks must be refined into very small units. It is essential for the educator to utilize frequent measurement to determine whether severely handicapped students are making progress, whether that progress is adequate, and whether they have mastered one learning task and are ready to advance to another. Common strategies for gathering frequent measures of student performance include trial-by-trial data collection, daily performance samples, or systematic data probes on a less than daily basis.

Repeated or frequent measurement is necessary to assure that results reflect the actual performance of the individual. A single assessment conducted on an unusually good or an unusually bad day can be both confusing and detrimental to instructional planning. Multiple measures can compensate for fluctuation and provide a more representative picture of student functioning. Frequent measurement also permits the teacher to closely monitor the effects of instruction and make program/instructional/curricular changes if sufficient change is not evidenced. Traditional pre-tests and post-tests at the beginning and conclusion of the school year provide no time to implement program changes if the student has not shown progress. Valuable instructional time has been lost. In addition, attempts to analyze student gains may still be misleading, as is evidenced in the following example by White and Liberty (1976:)

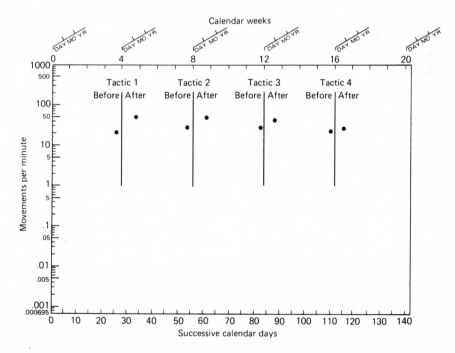

FIG. 6-1 In White and Liberty, 1976.
(Courtesy of J. T. Spaulding and M. Waechter).

Assume that the data in this first figure represent four different tactics for teaching a student math facts. The object of the analysis is to determine which tactic produces the largest change and, therefore, should be tried first with future students. Rank the tactics in order of effectiveness (one equals the most effective, four equals the least effective). Consider only the difference or gain between the "before test" and the "after test" for each tactic—do not consider just the final, or "after," rates.

Most people, including the authors in the absence of additional information, would rank the tactics in exactly the order they are presented. Tactic one appears to have produced the greatest change, and tactic four appears to have produced the least change.

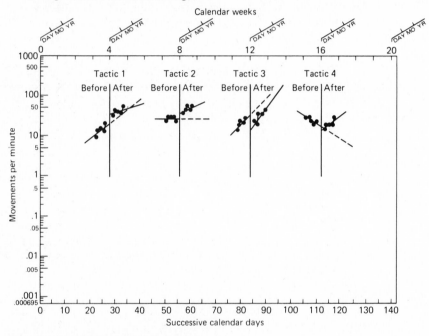

FIG. 6-2   In White and Liberty, 1976.
(Courtesy of J. T. Spaulding and M. Waechter).

Now look at Figure 6-2. The data are from exactly the same sources, but now we can see that an assessment was made for five days before the tactics were tried and for five days after each tactic was started. The last data point in each phase (i.e., the periods before and after the change) are the same data points that were shown in Figure 6-1. Note that changes are found not only between the last data points in each phase. Changes are occurring almost daily. In tactics one and three, the data indicate that the child was getting better even before the new tactics were introduced. In tactic two, apparently no progress was being made before introducing the change in programs; and in tactic four, the child apparently was getting worse before the teacher tried the new approach. The lines drawn through the data summarize the daily progress. The dotted lines in the "after" portion of the data indicate where we might have expected the child to go if we had simply left the program alone. Those lines allow us to examine where the child is in contrast to where he would have gone and how he is now changing in comparison to how he was changing.

The difference between the prediction (dotted line) and the child's actual performance (solid line) is greatest after the use of tactic four. Since the lines are moving apart in those data, we can assume that the benefits of the new program would increase even further if we were to leave it in effect. The next greatest difference was produced by tactic two—the change is from no progress to some progress. In tactics one and three, however, where the child was already making some progress before the change, the change did not seem to enhance performance as well. If we rank the results of the new program now, one would have to say that tactic four produced the most favorable change, then tactic two, then tactic three, and least of all, tactic one. What appeared to be the best approach, now appears to be the worst, and vice versa (White and Liberty, 1976, pp. 40–42).

The complaint that the time required for frequent assessment takes time away from teaching is more than counterbalanced by the fact that frequent measurement provides invaluable information with regard to the effectiveness of various instructional procedures and provides the most reliable basis for moving students through curriculum sequences.

Zero-Degree Inference

An assessment of severely handicapped students requires not only that assessment be direct and frequent but that it be based on a "zero-degree inference strategy:"

Most teachers assume varying degrees of instructional inference in relating to students, regardless of their functioning levels... [F]or example, teachers of nonhandicapped students often teach the rational counting of wooden pegs. After a student has performed to criterion on this task, it is usually inferred that the student can also rationally count eating utensils, money, and completed work units. This, of course, represents a relatively high degree of instructional inference. Implicit in relatively high degrees of instructional inference is the assumption that from specific training on circumscribed or core tasks students will abstract the critical factors, strategies, rules and concepts from this training environment, and apply them in new and varied environments...

To our knowledge it has not been empirically demonstrated that the teaching of a few critical skills has resulted in substantial increases in general developmental functioning levels of many severely handicapped students. Thus, teachers of severely handicapped students can rarely, if ever, infer that because a student performs a particular skill in an artificial setting, she can also perform that skill in other and more natural settings... No inferences are made that training to criterion on any task in one situation will result in criterion performance in similar but different situations requiring similar but slightly different actions. Stated another way, each time a situation changes, it will be necessary to empirically verify that severely handicapped students can perform the skills required by that new situation (Brown et al., 1976, pp. 5–6).

Applied to the design of assessments, this zero-degree inference strategy

Courtesy of the Easter Seal Program for Multiple Handicapped Children
(Steve Neiman).

requires that any particular skill be evaluated on a variety of materials, in a
variety of places, by a number of different adults, and using a number of
different cues to respond. While there is a need to be explicit regarding what
is being assessed (viz., to state it as a behavioral objective) there is a concomitant need to be "consistently inconsistent" and make multiple evaluations of student performance. A student might not be able to execute the
target skill (for example, pincer grasp with controlled release) when performance is probed by a strange adult in an unfamiliar setting on an artificial task (for example, "put cube in cup"). However, one should not
necessarily infer that the same student could not respond in the presence of
a known adult in a familiar situation on a functional task (for example,
grasping finger food in the family kitchen in the presence of mother). Students should be given a variety of opportunities to demonstrate competence. This point is highlighted by recent data showing that the results of a
Piagetian assessment of object permanence display significant variation as
a function of the objects used in testing (Hupp, 1978). An accurate description of student abilities clearly requires a comprehensive assessment.

Assessment procedures provide more useful information if they include
a graduated assessment and if they are designed to include functional,
naturally occurring tasks. A graduated assessment first probes for independent performance of the skills under consideration. If the student is unable
to perform, the task can then be re-presented with additional cues or
prompts to respond (for example, verbal instruction, demonstration, or
physical guidance). If the desired performance still is not evidenced the

student might be provided opportunities to execute each step of the task in question. By employing a graduated assessment of a target skill area, much more information is provided than the simple fact that the student could not perform the skill as defined by the assessment instrument.

The requirements set forth in P.L. 94–142 for the design and monitoring of an Individualized Education Program (IEP) for each student receiving special education services will do a great deal to promote the requirements of an assessment as delineated here. The IEP requires assessment of child performance on educational tasks in various curriculum domains, and incorporates an emphasis on direct assessment of the entering repertoire. Statement of annual goals and specification of short-range objectives further adhere to the requirements of direct assessment: training targets must be identified in such a way that their attainment can be measured. The requirement that "objective criterion and evaluation procedures" be identified as part of program planning decreases the distance between assessment and programming, and builds teacher accountability based on child-behavior-change data. The addition of time lines for the achievement of short-term goals increases the likelihood that child assessment and program evaluation will be conducted more frequently than has usually been the case.

Performance Measurement of Severely Handicapped Students

Frequent and ongoing measurement of student performance has been emphasized as a general requirement of behavior change technology (for example, White and Liberty, 1976; Bijou and Wilcox-Cole, 1975) and is particularly important to programs for severely handicapped where the concern is to document behavior change or progress through small steps in a task analysis or a skill sequence (Haring, 1976). Various types of data and recording strategies are presented in detail in a number of sources (see, for example, Axelrod, 1977; Gentry and Haring, 1976; Kazdin, 1973). What is unique to the severely handicapped population is the nature of the behaviors being measured. The concern is for head control more often than oral reading rate; for functional money skills more often than division facts; and so on. The behaviors are generally components of larger skill clusters or are management problems of the kind and degree not frequently encountered in regular classrooms (for example, seizuring, fluid intake, self-injurious behavior). The practitioner assessing severely handicapped students must adopt techniques to generate a level of description and degree of calibration useful for program decision-making for the particular presenting problems. The following should serve as general guidelines for the collection of student performance measures.

1. Recording procedures and the type of data collected must be compatible with the performance and criterion conditions established in behavioral objectives.

2. Measurement procedures should be minimally disruptive to the delivery of instruction.
3. Data should be collected on *all* important aspects of a student's program (including physical and medical intervention).
4. The type of data and the manner in which it is summarized and displayed should be understandable to all participating parties.
5. Performance data should be used to make changes in program or instructional delivery according to *predetermined* decision rules.
6. It is more appropriate to monitor limited aspects of many behaviors than to comprehensively describe performance on a limited number of skills.

Special Considerations

The characteristics of severely handicapped students present some special challenges to those responsible for their assessment and programming. Areas requiring further development or special consideration are briefly described below.

Functional Alternatives

If due to a sensory or motor impairment, an assessment/training objective is not appropriate for a student, it must be adapted to meet that student's needs. For example, if an objective states that pupils should verbally label objects, an alternative objective may have to be formulated for nonverbal pupils. If an objective states that pupils should perform a specific motor movement, an alternative objective may have to be formulated for motorically impaired students. Similarly, if objectives state that pupils should respond to verbal cues, alternatives must be designed for deaf pupils, while objectives requiring discriminations on the basis of visual cues must be reformulated for visually impaired students. In general, the reformulation of objectives may include modifying either the way of presenting a task, the way a student is to respond to the task or the actual task itself. When confronted with a need to adapt either the task or the way a student responds, one strategy is to translate the behaviors into their functions (York and Williams, 1977). For example, the function of walking is to move the body through space, the function of speaking is to communicate information, and the function of grasping is to manipulate objects in the performance of specified tasks. After translating behaviors into their functions, a teacher can then devise and/or select alternative ways for pupils with sensory and/or motor impairments to execute these same functions. Specific functions will remain as instructional priorities but the description of the skill will change. Often this will involve the use of adapted equipment or prosthetic devices, or having an adult perform some response for the student. Long-range programming should always involve a transfer of the performance of selected functions from reliance on caregivers or prosthetic devices to normalized independent performance. An assessment device must provide information to monitor this transfer from functional alternatives to more normalized student responding.

Sensory Assessment

There is a clear need to expand and refine existing audiometric and ophthalmological techniques so that severely handicapped students can be accurately evaluated for the presence of functional loss of hearing and/or vision, and subsequently fitted with proper hearing aids or lenses. While there has been some important progress in sensory evaluation of nonverbal multihandicapped children largely through the application of operant conditioning procedures (for example, Bricker and Bricker, 1969; Newsom and Simon, 1977), further development and dissemination is necessary before the severely handicapped can more routinely have access to a complete range of services.

Early Identification

While early screening and identification receives great attention in special education, it is simultaneously and paradoxically both more and less important for severely handicapped students. On the one hand, it is less important because the problems presented by these children are typically quite obvious and frequently apparent at birth. In fact, Haring, Hayden, and Beck (1976) suggest that as many as 50 percent of children who subsequently are recognized as severely handicapped can be identified by one month of age. On the other hand, screening is more important for these children if it leads to educational programming. Since it is of prime importance to have access to severely handicapped children at the earliest possible time (Haring, Hayden, and Beck, 1976; Vincent and Broome, 1976; Haring and Bricker, 1976), the existence of an early screening or infant identification network enhances the probability that children will receive necessary educational and related services as early as possible. The basic rationale for early assessment and intervention includes:

1. Dealing with development problems when they are least complex.
2. Building prerequisite responses to prevent cumulative deficiencies.
3. Reducing the likelihood of developing related disabilities (e.g., severe contractures in a child with cerebral palsy).
4. Reducing the likelihood that the child will develop undesirable or inappropriate behaviors.
5. Providing support to the family and/or primary care-giver.

Vocational Assessment

Traditional vocational assessment has been concerned with evaluating the "potential" of severely handicapped workers. Scores on intelligence tests, aptitude tests (examining dexterity, manipulation, and strength), simulated work samples, and behavior ratings are used to make judgments whether individuals can perform adequately on completely unrelated tasks in completely different situations. Individual performance on, for example, a manual dexterity test is used to predict the likelihood of success in a service occupation or assembly job. As Gold (1973) points out, such techniques may yield statistically significant information which is devoid of practical application. Traditional approaches to vocational assessment suffer from all the criticisms of norm-referenced assessment, and are discussed in detail elsewhere (Gold, 1973).

Combined with this kind of predictive correlational assessment has been a vocational training approach which emphasizes general job readiness skills (good work attitude, cooperation, promptness) to the exclusion of training on specific job-related skills. When an individual was deemed to be "ready" for job placement, then an effort was directed at finding an appropriate job. Needless to say, the success of such an indirect, inferential approach to the vocational training and placement of severely handicapped workers has not been impressive.

Belmore and Brown (1976) take a radically different approach to vocational assessment. Rather than wait to observe "vocational readiness" in their students, they proceed to identify vocational settings in the community and delineate the skills required in those settings. The resulting job inventory then serves as the basis for assessment and training efforts. It is the vocational environment itself which is most carefully scrutinized and the student is trained on the various behaviors demanded by that environment. The assumption underlying the job skills inventory is that transportation, social, emotional, and health variables are as important to job success as job skills per se. The job inventory strategy is impressive in its thoroughness. The demands of the social environment are delineated (for example, worker norms regarding dress, patterns of social interaction, frequency and manner of supervision, specific employer rules), and work skills specific to the job are identified (requisite physical, motor, interpersonal, academic, machine/tool, and hygiene skills are listed). Finally, the skills necessary to support performance on the job are identified. The latter category includes an inventory of transportation skills, clothing and money management skills, as well as time-telling and time-management skills. All this information complements a detailed task analysis of the job itself. The job skills inventory serves to assess trainee performance relative to the particular job in question and provides explicit information regarding the areas in which the student needs direct instruction. The job skills inventory is a *strategy* for vocational assessment rather than a static collection of information. An inventory must be completed for each job in which severely handicapped students are to be placed. Indirect and before-the-fact assessments are replaced by measurement and direct training in the relevant vocational setting.

Community Living Assessment

Like vocational assessment, the assessment of community living skills (and their subsequent training) has typically been unsystematic and inferential. If students could prepare a simple meal using the appliances and other facilities at school or a training center, it was assumed that they could prepare other meals using appliances and arrangements particular to the home or domestic living situation. Similarly, students trained to wash and dry clothing using powdered detergent, liquid bleach, and the equipment in a training center laundry room, were presumed to be able to adequately perform laundry tasks using liquid detergents, dry bleach, and a coin-operated machine in the local launderette. In short, trainers operated with strategies based on very high degrees of inference. In addition, there was an emphasis on self-help skills *per se* without any consideration of the numerical skills, sight vocabulary, communication, or mobility skills necessary for community living (Barrett, in press).

In order to adequately devise a community living curriculum, and to assess student performance on the various sub-skills, it will be necessary to adapt both curriculum and assessment procedures to the actual community environment of the students. It is irrelevant and inappropriate to assess and train students on bus-riding skills if the community in which they live has no mass transit system. The independent community mobility objectives for such students would more appropriately assess their ability to walk or ride a bike from selected points of origin to selected functional destinations, or their performance on cluster skills necessary to use taxi cabs as transportation. A functional community living assessment, like the job skill inventory, would require the teacher/trainer to survey the opportunities and demands particular to each student's community. A rudimentary outline of a community living assessment might be first broken down into home/domestic-based and community-based tasks. These two areas could then be further broken down into specific behavior routines required of the student (cleaning, cooking, communication, clothing management, simple repair, mobility, use of stores and services, leisure-time activities, and so on). The next step would be to inventory the student's actual community and domestic environments to determine what specific skills were required for adequate functioning. A general ecological inventory should identify: (1) the objects in the environment (What particular kitchen appliances are available to the student? What particular recreational activities are available in the community?); (2) the functional reading and math skills (time telling, calendar use, written instructions and so on) for functional use of those objects; (3) the physical demands of tasks as set up in the particular environment (Must laundry be carried up or downstairs? Must pans be lifted up for storage?); and (4) the judgment or problem-solving skills required. Finally, the community living assessment must delineate the parameters of normal performance of the task and the student's life space by asking questions such as the following:

1. On what occasion is the response performed? Is the task performed daily, weekly, or monthly? Is one time of day more suitable than another?
2. What is the response rate of a nonhandicapped performer? For example, how long a time does one reasonably spend shopping for groceries?

3. What is the appearance of an average person engaged in the same activity? For example, what is the relative level of dress of patrons of particular restaurants? What kind of attire is worn to church?

Such an ecological, community-referenced strategy for assessing community living skills is clearly a considerable undertaking. At the same time, because it is based on zero-inference strategy, it is probably the only approach that will yield instructionally relevant information regarding student performance.

The State of the Art

It has been the position here that assessment of severely handicapped students must be expanded from the traditional focus on the response repertoire of the learner with respect to the content area being evaluated. Both characteristics of the learner (functional reinforcers and antecedents, available response modes, physical/medical constraints for responding, etc.) and characteristics of the learning environment (availability of certain types of consequences, physical and social demands, etc.) must be carefully examined. In addition, the entire process of assessment must be executed in a significantly different fashion to yield educationally relevant information. Of the myriad of assessment instruments currently in use with or being developed for severely handicapped students, surprisingly few approach the complete assessment as it has been conceptualized here. In all likelihood the adequacy of any assessment would depend more on the skills of the evaluator (ability to build in missing components), than on the adequacy of the assessment package per se. Despite this disclaimer, there are materials available which provide a solid basis for an educationally relevant assessment of severely handicapped students. Perhaps the most refined of such instruments is the *Minimum Objective System for Pupils With Severe Handicaps* (Williams and Fox, 1977) which incorporates finely delineated developmentally sequenced objectives (skill sequences) in communication, motor, self-help, and social domains. Items are presented as functional behavioral statements and can be translated directly into educational programs. Administration includes provisions for functional alternatives as well as multiple measures, and provides fine grain information regarding student performance by scoring items as mastered, acquired, or performed with one of several levels of teacher assistance. The Behavior Characteristics Progression (Office of Santa Cruz County Superintendent of Schools, 1973) also provides a good initial framework for the design of a comprehensive assessment system.

CURRICULUM CONSIDERATIONS

Early work with the severely handicapped consisted of applications of behavior management techniques or simple demonstrations that the population could benefit from systematic instruction, especially in the area of self-help skills (Berkson and Landesman-Dwyer, 1977). Barrett (in press) characterizes the selection of instructional outcomes for severely handicapped students as falling into one of four categories: eliminative education, cosmetic behavior control, basic skills emphasis, and "special need savants." *Eliminative education*, which includes the bulk of the behavior management studies, focuses on the removal of excessive or inappropriate behaviors from students with already abnormally limited repertoires. The approach typically focuses on the deceleration of behaviors per se without attention to the building of a normal or socially appropriate behavioral repertoire. The result is to remove from students the only effective means they may have for interacting with their environment. Instruction guided by the philosophy of *cosmetic behavior control* emphasizes compliance, task-attending, and normal appearance (for example, being clean and properly dressed). The focus is on socially appropriate *appearance* rather than on *performance* of the social and academic skills required by the environment. The *basic skill approach* focuses on instruction on elemental skills such as object sorting, identity matching, cross-modal matching, and object and quality naming without intentional or sequential programming toward functional life competencies. While it is clearly within the capabilities of instructional technology to effect mastery of these basic skills by severely handicapped students, it is questionable whether such basic skills are, in fact, related to the cumulative skill development required for independent living. A contrast to the basic skills approach is one that emphasizes instruction in complex specialized skills, such as making change, telephoning, and reading price tags and restaurant menus. Severely handicapped students who have mastered these complex skills often have not been taught the mobility, social, or communication skills necessary to execute the behaviors in the flow of daily activity. While the teaching of such specialized skills (creating *"special need savants"* according to Barrett) serves as a poignant reminder that severely handicapped students are indeed capable of learning sophisticated tasks, it should also remind educators of the shortcomings of teaching any skill in isolation.

In the past, the almost inevitable placement of severely handicapped students in large residential facilities, and the lack of any effective instructional technology, helped justify teaching severely handicapped students isolated skills, such as color naming and shoe tying. However, recent socio-legal and technological advances have moved the field beyond the point where instruction on isolated skills is justifiable. The need is to develop effective functional curriculum sequences and instructional procedures which address the needs of the whole student, and which develop academic, social, motor/mobility, communication, community living, and vocational competence. If students are to be enrolled in public school programs for as long as twenty-one years, it is mandatory that instructional objectives be cumulative components of longitudinal skill sequences designed to lead students from current levels of performance to functioning in a least restrictive environment. Unfortunately, a major problem facing educators of severely handicapped students is the lack of such functional, integrated and longitudinal curricula.

> There are many incomplete and partial curricula available; however, most of them have rather serious deficits. Unfortunately, also, many curricula for more able children have been "adapted" to the severely handicapped and have in most instances caused more harm than benefit. It is indeed unfortunate that the area which most needs a well-developed, sequential, and carefully planned curriculum has, in fact, the most inadequate one (Sherr, 1976, p. 100).

Strategies for Curriculum Development

Assuming that it is both necessary and possible to develop functional longitudinal skill sequences, one might proceed according to one of two basic strategies. York and Williams (1977) have suggested that the curricular outcomes of these strategies be entitled, "skill sequences based upon normal development" and "skill sequences based upon the logical analysis of the living environment." Within the developmental approach there are two related, though distinct, strategies, one organized around normative developmental milestones and the other focusing on stages and structures of cognitive development as delineated by Piaget. A developmental milestones approach, perhaps best exemplified by the *Developmental Pinpoints* (Cohen, Gross, and Haring, 1976), assumes that the content for a curriculum for retarded children should be taken from the data available on development in normal children, and that the specific skills should be taught in the same sequence that they are acquired by the normal child. Curriculum sequences organized around a Piagetian cognitive-developmental approach (Stephens, 1977; Bricker and Bricker, 1970; Robinson, 1976) focus less on skill acquisition per se than on the development of cognitive structures presumed to be prerequisite to later functioning (for example, object permanence, conservation, means-ends relationships). The assumptions underlying a developmental approach to curriculum development are that handicapped children follow the same sequence as normal children but do so at a slower rate, and that development is not arbitrary, but proceeds from the simple to the complex in a fashion generally consistent across children.

Deriving a curriculum from a logical or task analysis of the living environment, one begins not with normal development but with the terminal behaviors that an individual must be able to perform in order to function in selected environments (such as group homes, vocational placements, and recreational settings). After identifying the basic skill requirements of these selected environments, the skills are broken down into components which are then logically ordered from simple to complex in an instructional sequence. The standard for generating the curriculum is not infant development but adult behavior. The latter is broken down until skills have been identified which are currently in the repertoire of the target student. This analytic approach to curriculum development is based on the cluster of procedures known as task analysis. Task analysis is not a single set of operations but rather includes several different strategies for generating what should be taught. The different approaches to task analysis work well with different types of instructional content. One approach which works particularly well with complex motor performances is described by Gold (1975). In this system the teacher/trainer decides how the task is to be performed, describes skilled task performance, and agrees upon a particular strategy or method that the learner will use to solve the problem. This method is then divided into discrete movements or teachable component skills. This approach to task analysis (division into discrete motor skills) is illustrated by various investigators who have taught severely handicapped students complex assembly and vocational tasks. Table 6–2 presents an illustration of a task analysis generated using this approach.

A second approach to task analysis, which is perhaps more appropriate for "cognitive" than for motor performances, is represented by Becker, Engelmann, and Thomas (1974), and Resnik, Wang, and Kaplan (1973). In this system the target skill is analyzed into its component concepts and operations, and those concepts and operations are taught or verified prior to asking the student to combine them in the terminal performance. Table 6–3 presents an illustration of a task analysis generated under this approach. An assumption underlying this approach to task analysis and curriculum is that the target performances can be broken down, the component skills taught, and then recombined into a final performance. An important distinction here is between component and prerequisite skills. Component skills are those steps that skilled performers actually execute as they perform the terminal task. The prerequisite behaviors, in contrast, are not actually performed in the course of terminal performance though they facilitate the learning of the higher-level skill (Resnik, Wang, and Kaplan, 1973). Thus, when reading a clock indicating 7:35, a component skill would be counting by fives to thirty-five, while a prerequisite skill for time telling in general might be counting by fives to fifty-five. Prerequisite skills are taught separately, while component skills are executed in a format approximating actual performance of the task.

Relative Advantages of Curriculum Strategies

Both developmental and logical task analytic approaches have particular advantages for generating curriculum sequences for severely handicapped students. One advantage of a developmental approach to skill sequences is that it is generally understood and easy to explain. Most people have some knowledge of normal child development and are familiar with the general sequence of skills. In addition, there are theoretical bases for the sequence. There is extensive literature on normal child de-

TABLE 6-2   Sample Task Analysis: (Brushing Teeth[1,2])

1. Remove toothbrush and toothpaste from cup
2. Unscrew toothpaste cap
3. Squeeze appropriate amount of toothpaste onto brush
4. Lay toothbrush down
5. Screw cap back on tube
6. Pick up brush in preferred hand
7. Lean over sink
8. Brush in down motion over top teeth from one side of mouth to the other
9. Spit out excess at least once
10. Brush in up motion over bottom teeth from one side of mouth to the other
11. Spit out excess at least once
12. Brush in down motion over back of top teeth from one side of mouth to the other
13. Spit out excess at least once
14. Brush in up motion over back of bottom teeth from one side of mouth to the other
15. Spit out excess at least once
16. Brush back and forth over crowns of top teeth from one side of mouth to the other
17. Spit out excess at least once
18. Brush back and forth over crowns of bottom teeth from one side of mouth to the other
19. Spit out excess at least once
20. Pick up cup
21. Turn on cold water faucet
22. Fill cup with water
23. Rinse mouth with water
24. Spit out excess at least once
25. Pour excess water out of cup into sink
26. Replace cup next to sink
27. Rinse toothbrush in water
28. Turn off cold water faucet
29. Replace brush and paste in cup

(Hamre, 1974, p. 392)

[1]The analysis represents an initial breakdown of the toothbrushing sequence. If performance data does not show student progress, the content of particular steps might be broken down into more specific fine motor movements (e.g., grasping, turning, releasing) or aspects of the method changed (e.g., using an electric rather than a traditional toothbrush).

[2]Statements of conditions and criteria for performance on each step or the task as a whole have been omitted.

velopment which has been broken down into sequences in language, motor, social, and cognitive domains. The curriculum developer need not sit down and logically derive all skill sequences. Another advantage to normal developmental sequences is that they begin at or near a zero skill level, so the mapping of development begins with the very basic skills of an infant and proceeds through adult functioning. A final advantage to a developmental approach is the frequency of its use: a developmental model is basic to most physical, speech, and occupational therapy approaches, so its use might be expected to facilitate interdisciplinary programming for severely handicapped students.

Skill sequences based upon an analysis of the living environment also

TABLE
6-3 Sample Task Analysis: Sums to 10 Using Objects[1,2,3]

1. *Counting and One-to-One Correspondence*
   A.   The child can recite the numerals in order.
   B.   Given a set of moveable objects, the child can count the objects, moving them out of the set as he counts.
   C.   Given a fixed ordered set of objects, the child can count the objects.
   D.   Given a fixed unordered set of objects, the child can count the objects.
   E.   Given a numeral stated and a set of objects, the child can count out a subset of stated size.
   F.   Given a numeral stated and several sets of fixed objects, the child can select a set of size indicated by numeral.
   G.   Given two sets of objects, the child can pair objects and state whether the sets are equivalent.
   H.   Given two unequal sets of objects, the child can pair objects and state which set has more.
   I.   Given two unequal sets of objects, the child can pair objects and state which set has less.

2. *Numerals*
   A.   Given two sets of numerals, the child can match the numerals.
   B.   Given a numeral stated and a set of printed numerals, the child can select the stated numeral.
   C.   Given a numeral (written), the child can read the numeral.
   D.   Given several sets of objects and several numerals, the child can match numerals with appropriate sets.
   E.   Given two numerals (written), the child can state which shows more/less.
   F.   Given a set of numerals, the child can place them in order.
   G.   Given numerals stated, the child can write the numeral.

3. *Comparison of Sets*
   A.   Given two sets of objects, the child can count sets and state which has more objects or that sets have same number.
   B.   Given two sets of objects, the child can count sets and state which has less objects.
   C.   Given a set of objects and a numeral, the child can state which shows more/less.
   D.   Given a numeral and several sets of objects, the child can select sets which are more/less than the numeral; given a set of objects and several numerals, the child can select numerals which show more/less than the set of objects.
   E.   Given two rows of objects (not paired), the child can state which row has more regardless of arrangement.
   F.   Given three sets of objects, the child can count sets and state which has most/least.

4. *Seriation and Ordinal Position*
   A.   Given three objects of different sizes, the child can select the largest/smallest.
   B.   Given objects of graduated sizes, the child can seriate according to size.
   C.   Given several sets of objects, the child can seriate the sets according to size.
   D.   Given ordered set of objects, the child can name the ordinal position of the objects.

---

[1]Adapted from Resnick et al., pp. 684–685.

[2]If use of this analysis as a training sequence did not produce student progress then individual prerequisite skills could be further broken down.

[3]Statements of criterion performance on each prerequisite skill have been omitted.

enjoy the advantage of being relatively easily understood. An analysis of the skills required for functioning in the least restrictive environment ensures that the sequences are based upon skills actually required for independent functioning, and thereby decreases the chance of teaching skills that are irrelevant or nonfunctional. Priorities are determined and assigned to those behaviors essential to survival in the environment. Employing this general approach, Mithaug and his colleagues (Mithaug and Haring, 1977; Mithaug, Hagmeier, and Haring, in press) conducted an extensive survey to determine the work expectations and skills required for entry into sheltered workshops in the Northwest. The results of the survey have direct implications for the design of a prevocational curriculum for students who might one day seek entry to those work settings.

> Clearly, training activities could be misdirected either by focusing upon areas not critical for entry into a workshop, or by not implementing activities considered essential. [. . . The survey] tells us that for entry into any of the . . . workshops, there are no limitations imposed as a function of the client's ability to read, write, compute, speak, stand, his nut-bolt assembly skills, matching or sorting rates, ability to use money, his verbalizations, learning capacity for complex tasks (requiring more than five responses), verbal reaction to corrections from supervisor, verbal reaction to corrections from peers or social initiative with fellow workers. [. . . It also] suggests that those skill areas considered critical by employers include: personal hygiene; promptness; responsiveness to instruction, mode of learning new tasks; on-task endurance; distractability when working alone, when working independently in a group, or when working on an assembly line; minor and major deviances from shop behavior standards; social contact patterns with supervisor; supervisor attention required when working independently; and the effects of supervisor corrections on the client's performance (Mithaug and Haring, 1977, p. 269).

Sequences based upon a task analysis make no assumption about student abilities or potential. The task of the teacher is to simply move students from their current skill level to the point where they can perform the tasks necessary for survival in target environments.

While both developmental and task analytic curriculum strategies have particular advantages, each has disadvantages and potential for being misused. For example, one might well question the application of sequences based on normal development to programming for students whose development is obviously not normal: for instance, those who have been out of their natural home for years, or those who manifest significant sensory and/or motor impairments. Since something has already gone wrong with normal development, it becomes less necessary to know how skills normally develop than to know a reasonable teaching sequence for producing those skills. The question to be asked is "How do you teach this skill?" not necessarily "How does it normally develop?". Adherents of a developmental approach frequently assume that *normal* development is synonymous with *necessary* development. This simply may not be the case.

Curricula and skill sequences based on normal development often fail to focus attention on the development of functional alternatives. Once one deviates from the normal sequence (for example, a student is physically unable to walk), a curriculum based on a normal developmental model is of little use in determining a training sequence for the functional alternative.

It may also be dangerous to assume, as Cohen et al. (1976), suggest, that if a child can perform the most advanced item in a developmental cluster, that child has indeed mastered all of the earlier skills. A related dilemma in the use of a normal developmental sequence is the question of when to begin "intervention" rather than to continue to "induce the progression through the normal developmental sequence." Another disadvantage of a curriculum based on a normal developmental sequence is that it may ignore functional application of skills that are delineated. There may be no consideration of the requirements placed upon an individual to function in a particular environment. For example, while "puts cube in cup" is an item from many developmental sequences (Cohen et al., 1976), it is hardly an appropriate *training* objective for older severely handicapped students, nor does it have any obvious survival value. Sequences should build toward the application of skills in the tasks of daily living and should not necessarily focus on skills whose only characteristic is that people can normally execute them.

A criticism of cognitive-developmental approaches might be the tendency of some to teach the particular tasks described by Piaget. For example, while children typically can track an object as it is moved behind several barriers prior to the onset of language, there is no empirical validation that students *must* be able to perform this task before they can effectively benefit from language instruction. Given this lack of a data base, it is difficult to justify object permanence training per se on either its functional or face validity.

A major disadvantage to using curricula and skill sequences based upon an analysis of functioning within a given environment is simply that such analyses are generally unavailable. As a result, teachers may be required to develop their own curricula from nothing. To be maximally effective such analyses will have to be individualized for each student and for each community or domestic living environment in which the student is expected to function. While this is clearly an advantage in ensuring the generalization of skills to the natural environment, it may, at the same time, limit student performance to those environments specifically analyzed. Another problem of sequences based on logical analyses is that such a strategy does not serve as the basis for other related disciplines and may, as a result, impede interdisciplinary endeavors.

A final danger of a strictly logical, task analyzed curriculum is that important developmental data will be ignored. The information that children typically are able to imitate actions involving objects before they imitate simple gross motor responses, and that they imitate visible before invisible responses, might be very useful to a teacher who is structuring an

Courtesy of the Easter Seal Program for Multiple Handicapped Children.

imitation-training program. Given the normal developmental data, it would certainly seem appropriate to begin training with responses involving object manipulations and with behaviors which the students themselves could actually observe.

A general misuse of both developmental and task-analytic sequences is instruction on isolated skills. Instructors may select objectives and then devise separate tasks for teaching each skill. One might, for example, have a gross motor objective of sitting unsupported, a fine motor objective of using thumb in opposition with finger grasp, a perceptual-motor objective of taking objects out of containers, and a language objective teaching the prepositions *in* and *out*. Five separate programs or tasks could be derived for teaching these skills. However, since skills are rarely performed in isolation and are generally used in relation to other skills, it might be more appropriate for the teacher to work all five objectives into a single task centering around, for example, a feeding or social skills program.

While they have been presented as relatively discrete, developmental and task-analytic approaches to curriculum design are not necessarily incompatible. They may acquire differential importance or usefulness as a function of the age of the student under consideration. For young severely handicapped students a developmental approach is clearly more normal, while for secondary-level students, the impending reality of the postschool environment makes curriculum sequences based on an analysis of ultimate functioning seem infinitely more useful.

Regardless of whether one proceeds from a developmental or task analytic approach, a curriculum based on longitudinal skill sequences is theoretically and methodologically justifiable. Such sequences which begin with near zero level functioning and proceed to skills associated with independent adult performance readily serve as the basis for educational assessment. Identification and description of students can be done on the basis of placement along a skill sequence rather than on the basis of general labels such as autistic, profoundly retarded, and so forth. This use of sequences facilitates coordination of assessment, individual programming, and evaluation. Skill sequences ensure that there will always be something to teach. Rather than wait until a student is "ready" to learn, the teacher teaches or verifies the presence of earlier skills in the sequence, and proceeds to training on the next objectives in the sequence. Skill sequences might be expected to provide considerable stability to programs for severely handicapped students. Rather than simply teaching skills which are easy to identify or convenient for teacher presentation, a skill sequence ensures that necessary, albeit sometimes obscure or difficult, skills will be developed. What distinguishes curricula for severely handicapped students from curricula designed for their less or nonhandicapped peers is not that the domains differ, but that within each curriculum domain, objectives are taken down to a level near zero functioning.

Establishing Student Priorities

Though the use of planned instructional sequences should facilitate the process of designing IEPs, there will undoubtedly be occasions that require decisions regarding priorities among instructional objectives (for example, in situations where there are limited resources, limited remaining years in the educational system, or lack of agreement among those participating in the IEP conference). The following are offered as general guidelines to aid in establishing priorities.

1. *Frequency of use.* In general, priority should be given to those skills which students are required to perform frequently over skills which, though valuable, are less frequently demanded by the physical or social environment. For example, while one needs to brush one's teeth at least once a day, one may need to wash one's hair only once a week. Because of the relative frequency of use, tooth brushing would assume priority over hairwashing for initial training.

2. *Parental preference.* Parents or primary caretakers play an important role in programming for the generalization of skills to home and community environments. Identifying as instructional priorities those behaviors which parents want their children to develop enhances the probability that generalization training will be effectively implemented. If future cooperation with parents is desired, this too should be facilitated by deference to parental priorities. For example, if parents indicate a preference for a language board over manual signing as a communication system for

their nonverbal child, it seems likely that they would use a language board in the home to make communication demands on the child. They might not be so inclined to carry through on a program requiring them to learn, teach, or use manual signs.

3. *Relationship to other independent performances.* Skills which will support independent student functioning in a variety of task situations should, in general, be given priority over objectives which are not integral components of other tasks. Since coin matching and sorting are prerequisites to more complex, functional behavior such as shopping, eating in restaurants, and using mass transit or pay telephones, these skills are training targets that should take priority over traditional and similar tasks of matching and sorting shapes. Similarly, telephone use is to be preferred over less pervasive skills such as naming days of the week, months, and seasons, since use of the telephone supports a variety of social, vocational, and personal safety objectives.

4. *Relative effect on the social environment.* Objectives which might be expected to have a positive, normalizing effect on the social environment may be preferred over objectives which may not affect the acceptance or tolerance of the severely handicapped student. Teaching a child to play a common and age-appropriate group table game might be a recreational/leisure-time objective to be preferred over training in an isolative game or a physical sport.

5. *Immediacy of effect.* In general, training objectives should reflect attempts to develop skills which will provide the students with some immediate control over their environment. In the area of language development, for example, the general objective of communication should be an earlier and higher priority goal than the development of verbal language per se. Once the student can control the environment through gestures, signs, or a communication booklet, then attempts should be made to make communication take the most normal, least restrictive form possible. Choosing an alternative that is temporarily more functional to the subject does not preclude later instruction on the "normal" skills.

6. *Functionality.* The term "functional skill" or "functional application" refers to behaviors which are actually and frequently demanded by daily activity and whose mastery significantly affect a student's performance in his or her environment. The term is not new to special education, though clearly it has taken on new meanings as services to severely handicapped students have evolved. Initially, functional activities referred almost exclusively to safety and hygiene skills. Functional reading, for example, meant mastering a sight vocabulary consisting of words such as poison, warning, danger, stop, keep out, women, men, and so on. More recently, however (Brown et al., 1976), the term "functional" refers to activities which support maximum independence and integration of severely handicapped people in normal community, vocational, and domestic situations. Functional reading, then, would consist of training on printed stimuli to which students must respond in their daily environment. No

skill is justifiable per se, but only so far as it can be shown to relate to the criterion of ultimate functioning (Brown et al., 1976). Skills that foster independent and integrated performance are to be preferred over objectives which do not provide central support for independent survival.

Conclusion

The signing of Public Law 94–142 and other recent landmark legislation appears to promise a better life for severely handicapped children and adults. Today, the gap between that promise and reality is enormous. Bridging the gap will require the continued efforts of many dedicated parents, competent teachers, committed public schools, empirical program developers, responsive administrators, quality university training programs, and a well-educated community. If the next decade is to reflect increasing integration of severely handicapped citizens, there must be both a focus on quality and a strong committment to the belief that all individuals can learn.

R E F E R E N C E S

Axelrod, S. *Behavior Modification for the Classroom Teacher.* New York: McGraw-Hill Inc., 1977.

Barrett, B. Communitization and the measured message of normal behavior. In R. York and E. Edgar (ed.), *Teaching the Severely Handicapped* (vol. 4). New York: Grune and Stratton Inc., in press.

Becker, W. C., and Engelmann, S. *Teaching 3: Evaluation of Instruction.* Chicago: Science Research Associates, 1976.

———, ———, and Thomas, D. *Teaching 2: Cognitive Learning and Instruction.* Chicago: Science Research Associates, 1975.

Belmore, K., and Brown, L. A job skill inventory strategy for use in a public school vocational training program for severely handicapped potential workers. In L. Brown, N. Certo, K. Belmore, and T. Crowner (ed.), *Madison's Alternative for Zero Exclusion: Papers and Programs Related to Public School Services for Secondary Age Severely Handicapped Students.* Madison, WI.: Madison Public Schools, 1976.

Berkson, G., and Landesman-Dwyer, S. Behavioral research on severe and profound mental retardation (1955–1974). *American Journal of Mental Deficiency*, 1977, *81*, 428–454.

Bijou, S. W., and Peterson, R. F. A psychological assessment of children: A functional approach. In P. McReynolds (ed.), *Advances in Psychological Measurement* (vol. 2). Palo Alto: Science and Behavior Books, 1971.

———, and Wilcox-Cole, B. The feasibility of providing effective educational programs for the severely and profoundly retarded. In *Educating the 24-Hour Retarded Child.* Arlington, TX: National Association for Retarded Citizens, 1975.

Bricker, D. D., and Bricker, W. A. A programmed approach to operant audiometry for low functioning children. *Journal of Speech and Hearing Disorders,* 1969, *34,* 312–320.

———— Toddler Research and Intervention Project Report: Year 1. Nashville, TN: George Peabody College, 1970.

Brown, L., Nietupski, J., and Hamre-Nietupski, S. The criterion of ultimate functioning. In M. A. Thomas (ed.), *Hey, don't Forget about Me!* Reston, VA: The Council for Exceptional Children, 1976.

Cohen, M., Gross, P., and Haring, N. G. Developmental pinpoints. In N. G. Haring and L. J. Brown (ed.), *Teaching the Severely Handicapped* (vol. 1). New York: Grune & Stratton Inc., 1976.

Faris, J. A., Anderson, R. M., and Greer, J. G. Psychological assessment of the severely and profoundly retarded. In R. M. Anderson and J. G. Greer (ed.), *Educating the Severely and Profoundly Retarded.* Baltimore: University Park Press, 1976.

Filler, J. W., Robinson, C. C., Smith, R. A., Vincent-Smith, L. J., Bricker, D. D., and Bricker, W. A. Mental retardation. In. N. Hobbs (ed.), *Issues in the Classification of Children* (vol. 1). San Francisco: Jossey-Bass, 1975.

Fredericks, H. D., Riggs, C., Furey, T., Grove, D., Moore, W., McDonnell, J., Jordan, E., Hanson, W., Baldwin, V., and Wadow, M. *The Teaching Research Curriculum for Moderately and Severely Impaired.* Springfield, IL: Charles C Thomas, Publisher, 1976.

Gentry, D., and Haring, N. G. Essentials of performance measurement. In N. G. Haring and L. J. Brown (ed.), *Teaching the Severely Handicapped* (vol. 1). New York: Grune & Stratton, Inc., 1976.

Gold, M. W. Research on the vocational habilitation of the retarded: The present, the future. In N. R. Ellis (ed.), *International Review of Research in Mental Retardation* (vol. 6). New York: Academic Press, 1973.

———— Vocational training. In J. Wortis (ed.), *Mental Retardation and Developmental Disabilities: An Annual Review* (vol. 7). New York: Brunner/Mazel, 1975.

Hamre, S. An approximation of an instructional model for developing home living skills in severely handicapped students. In L. Brown, W. Williams, and T. Crowner (ed.), *A Collection of Papers and Programs Related to Public School Services for Severely Handicapped Students.* Madison, WI: Madison Public Schools, 1974.

Haring, N. G. Infant identification. In M. A. Thomas (ed.), *Hey, Don't Forget about Me!* Reston, VA: The Council for Exceptional Children, 1976.

————, and Bricker, D. Overview of comprehensive services for the severely/profoundly handicapped. In N. G. Haring and L. J. Brown (eds.), *Teaching the Severely Handicapped* (vol. 1). New York: Grune & Stratton, Inc., 1976.

————, Hayden, A., and Beck, R. General principles and guidelines in programming for severely handicapped children and young adults. *Focus on Exceptional Children,* 1976, *8,* 1–14.

Hupp, S. Effects of Object Preference and Object Manipulation Training on Object Performance. Unpublished manuscript. University of Illinois, Department of Special Education, 1978.

Jenkins, J. R., and Pany, D. Standardized achievement tests: How useful for special education? *Exceptional Children*, 1978, *44*, 448–456.

Jones, R. L. Accountability in special education: Some problems. *Exceptional Children*, 1973, *39*, 631–642.

Kazdin, A. E. *Behavior Modification in Applied Settings*. Homewood, IL: The Dorsey Press, 1975.

Larsen, L. Community services necessary to program effectively for the severely/profoundly handicapped. In E. Sontag (ed.), *Educational Programming for the Severely and Profoundly Handicapped*. Reston, VA: The Council for Exceptional Children, 1977.

Mager, R. F. *Preparing Instructional Objectives*. Belmont, CA: Fearon Publishers, 1962.

Meyers, D. G., Sinco, M. E., and Stalma, E. S. *The Right to Education Child: A Curriculum for the Severely and Profoundly Mentally Retarded*. Springfield, IL: Charles C Thomas, Publisher, 1973.

Mithaug, D. E., and Haring, N. G. Community vocational and workshop placement. In N. G. Haring and L. J. Brown (ed.), *Teaching the severely handicapped*. (vol.2). New York: Grune & Stratton, Inc., 1977.

———, Hagmeier, L. D., and Haring, N. G. The relationship between training activities and job placement in vocational education of the severely and profoundly handicapped. *AAESPH Review*, in press.

Moreland, A. G. Effectiveness of four instructional procedures for teaching object identification to non-verbal severely physically impaired students. Unpublished manuscript, Urbana, IL: University of Illinois, Department of Special Education, 1977.

Newsom, C. D., and Simon, K. M. A simultaneous discrimination procedure for the measurement of vision in nonverbal children. *Journal of Applied Behavior Analysis*, 1977, *10*, 633–644.

Popham, W. J. (ed.), *Criterion-referenced Measurement: An Introduction*. Englewood Cliffs, NJ: Educational Technology Publications, 1971.

Resnick, L. B., Wang, M. C., and Kaplan, J. Task analysis in curriculum design: A hierarchically sequenced introductory mathematics curriculum. *Journal of Applied Behavior Analysis*, 1973, *6*, 679–710.

Robinson, C. C. Application of Piagetian sensorimotor concepts to assessment and curriculum for severely handicapped children. *AAESPH Review*, 1976, *1* (8), 5–10.

Sailor, W, and Horner, R. D. Educational and assessment strategies for the severely handicapped. In N. G. Haring and L. J. Brown (ed.), *Teaching the Severely Handicapped*. (vol. 1). New York: Grune & Stratton, Inc., 1976.

Sherr, R. D. Public school programs. In M. A. Thomas (ed.), *Hey, Don't Forget about Me!* Reston, VA: The Council for Exceptional Children, 1976.

Stephens, B. A Piagetian approach to curriculum development for the severely, profoundly and multiply handicapped. In E. Sontag (ed.), *Edu-*

cational Programming for the Severely and Profoundly Handicapped. Reston, VA: The Council for Exceptional Children, 1977.

The Office of Santa Cruz County Superintendent of Schools. *Behavior Characteristics Progression.* VORT Corporation, 1973.

Vincent, L. J., and Broome, K. A public school service delivery model for handicapped children between birth and five years of age. In E. Sontag (ed.), *Educational Programming for the Severely and Profoundly Handicapped.* Reston, VA: The Council for Exceptional Children, 1977.

White, O., and Liberty, K. Behavioral assessment and precise educational measurement. In N. G. Haring and R. L. Schiefelbusch (ed.), *Teaching Special Children.* New York: McGraw-Hill, Inc., 1976.

Wilcox, B., and Orelove, F. P. *Conventions for using Sensory Stimulation/ Reinforcer Sampling with Low Functioning/Profoundly Retarded Students.* Unpublished manuscript, Urbana, IL: University of Illinois, Department of Special Education, 1976.

Williams, W., and Fox, T. *Minimum Objective System for Pupils with Severe Handicaps.* Burlington, VT: Center for Special Education, University of Vermont, 1977.

Wolfensberger, W. *Normalization: The Principle of Normalization in Human Services.* Toronto: National Institute on Mental Retardation, 1972.

York, R., and Williams, W. Curricula and ongoing assessment for individualized programming in the classroom. In R. York, P. Thorpe, and R. Minisi (ed.), *Education of the Severely and Profoundly Handicapped People.* Hightstown, NJ: Northeast Regional Resource Center, 1977.

CHAPTER **7**

CRIPPLING CONDITIONS

VERNA HART

Traditionally, each of the types of handicapping conditions has had distinctive characteristics. Retardation was historically based on intelligence scores, blindness has been legally defined by the degree of visual acuity, and deafness has been determined by the amount of decibel loss. Characterizing crippling conditions in such a precise manner presents a much greater difficulty.

Even giving a title to this chapter is difficult. "Orthopedic conditions" would cover some of the children, but not all. "Health impaired" would cover others. However, the title "crippling" was chosen to be used in its broadest concept, covering various types of disabilities.

"Crippling" is very difficult to define and specify. At what point is a person said to be crippled or disabled enough to need special educational services? The difficulty with the lack of specific criteria can be illustrated by the problems encountered in determining prevalence of crippling conditions: one set of numbers is derived by special educators, and others that are decidedly larger come from health statistics.

Table 7–1 presents figures that are typical of the discrepancies found in such numbers. The total prevalence of crippling conditions as reported by educational agencies is 328,000 children. Numbers obtained from health statistics prevalence figures come to many times the "education" figure. Adding just two of the figures, those reflecting chronic activity limitations that make the child unable to engage in school activities, and the

TABLE 7-1   Prevalence of Crippling and Other Health Impairments for Children under 17 Years of Age

Total for education purposes	328,000[1]
Chronic circulatory conditions	683,000[2]
Under 6 years	218,000
School age	465,000
Active rheumatic fever and chronic rheumatic heart disease	68,000
Other specified heart disease	65,000
Unspecified disorders of heart rhythm	523,000
Congenital anomalies of circulatory system	388,000
Chronic activity limitations	2,305,000[3]
Unable to engage in regular school or preschool activities	135,000[4]
Diabetes	86,000[5]
Epilepsy	188,000[5]
Diseases of the urinary system	389,000[5]
Kidney trouble or disease	70,000[5]
Absence of major extremities	70,000[6]
Selected musculoskeletal impairments	66,554,000[7]
Paralysis, complete or partial	158,000
Back or spine	210,000
Upper extremities and shoulders	120,000
Lower extremities and hips	1,281,000
Disease of bone	86,000[2]

[1]Based on estimates obtained from national agencies—organizations, plus state and local directors of special education. *Statistical Abstract of the United States, 1976;* U. S. Department of Commerce, Bureau of the Census, Washington: U. S. Government Printing Office, 1976.

[2]Prevalence of Chronic Circulatory Conditions-United States, 1972, *Vital and Health Statistics,* Series 10, Number 94, September 1974.

[3]Health Characteristics of Persons with Chronic Activity Limitations-United States, 1974, *Vital and Health Statistics,* Series 10, Number 112, October 1976.

[4]Limitations of Activity Due to Chronic Conditions-United States 1972, *Vital and Health Statistics,* Series 10, Number 111, June 1977.

[5]Prevalence of Chronic Conditions of the Genitourinary, Nervous, Endocrinal, Metabolic and Blood and Blood-Forming Systems and of Other Selected Chronic Conditions, *Vital and Health Statistics,* Series 10, Number 109, March 1977.

[6]Prevalence of Selected Impairments-United States, 1971, *Vital and Health Statistics,* Series 10, Number 99, May 1975.

[7]Prevalence of Chronic Skin and Musculoskeletal Conditions-United States, 1969, *Vital and Health Statistics,* Series 10, Number 92, August 1974.

number of children having complete or partial paralysis, the total comes to 293,000 or close to the figure reported as the total number by the educational sources. Thus, the actual prevalence of crippling conditions is difficult to ascertain. As data gathering under P.L. 94–142 becomes more sophisticated, figures should become more accurate.

Another problem in discussing the topic is the wide variety of conditions that are covered under the broad term "crippling." While cerebral palsy is a crippling condition, those who possess cerebral palsy can differ among themselves as much as blind do from deaf or retarded from gifted. Therefore, the term crippling covers a broader area than does other handicapping conditions.

Multiple handicaps are also present to such a degree in some crippling conditions that they are the rule rather than the exception, while they are virtually absent in other conditions. Thus crippling can refer to a child who is minimally handicapped as well as one who is so incapacitated that independent movement is impossible. Yet they all come under the general term of crippling.

Also encountered in discussing crippling conditions are the great changes that have taken place and continue to evolve in the field. Parts of the country that have kept pace with the most recent medical and educational advances may have an entirely different population of crippled children than those who have not. Educational programs that have had a long history may serve a different type of child than those that have recently begun, because of a tradition of serving specific types of handicapping conditions.

All of these problems make it very difficult to make specific statements about crippling conditions that will apply to all such children in varying localities. Children who are deemed in need of specific educational facilities in one location may be viewed entirely differently in others. Thus, this chapter will be organized differently than the others, with changes that have occurred during past years discussed along with some of the more recent developments. Since so many of the crippling conditions reflect medical problems, changes in this area will continue to evolve much more rapidly than changes in the other areas of special education.

DEFINITION AND PREVALENCE

Who are the children with crippling and other health impairments? What type of children are found in classes for the orthopedically impaired? The answers to these questions would depend upon what point in history the question was asked, for the types of orthopedic conditions that have resulted in special education placement have varied considerably in the relatively recent period of time that children have been provided public school special education services.

Previous Population (1900–1970)

The role of special education for children with crippling conditions has experienced more change than any other program for exceptional children, because the types of children who are eligible for such services have changed during the years. The schools and classes that were originally established (from the early 1900s into the 1960s) for children with crippling or other health problems were constituted using a medical model: the children were deemed in need of educational placement because of a health problem or medical condition, not because of an educational need per se. Frequently these classes for crippled children were found in hospital settings. This allowed the children in need of frequent hospitalization to continue their education while they were convalescing from surgery, blood transfusions, or long-lasting medical problems. Very often the classes were assigned a secondary importance in the life of the child, with the medical problems assuming precedence over all others. Speech, physical and occupational therapy usually were considered more important than educational activities.

Separate schools were built in many communities so that children with ambulatory problems, whether from a lack of vitality or from orthopedic handicaps, could be placed there for education. This was necessary because many of the regular school buildings were multistoried and had elevators that were to be used for freight only—if there were any elevators at all. A single school was often set aside for crippled children but also was used for all children in the system who had ambulatory problems. A child who broke a leg while attending a regular classroom was transferred to the school for crippled children for the duration of the period that the leg was in a cast or that the child was using crutches. This was to prevent the child from being injured by normal peers crowding into school halls or stairways, and to prevent the necessity of climbing stairs to get to classrooms. This protective attitude was also apparent in the assumption that children who have orthopedic problems would be more comfortable away from the curious stares of more normal peers. Also, a child whose only "handicap" was a missing finger or an extra thumb could very well be assigned to a classroom for crippled children. Thus classrooms were frequently established to "protect" the children, both from their environment and from other people, by adapting their physical surroundings and isolating the setting. Educational needs of the children were a secondary factor in most special education placements for children with orthopedic handicaps.

Acquired or Adventitious Handicaps

The types of conditions presented by children placed in rooms for crippled and other health impaired just a few years ago would seem odd to us in this day of medically advanced technology. Most of the children were born normal and because of some type of infection or disease became handicapped later in life. This meant that the children had a period where they were able to go through the normal stages of development. For the most part, it meant that the children still had learning abilities that were unaffected by the illness but that they had some type of residual problems as a result of the disease. In the 1940s, 1950s, and even into the 1960s, classrooms were for the most part filled with children who had the residual effects of *poliomyelitis*. These residual crippling conditions were usually limited to some type of orthopedic problem involving the arms or legs, with the children remaining capable of learning in the manner of their normal peers.

Heart conditions also necessitated placement in a special school or class because the victims lacked the stamina and vitality to partake in a regular educational program. *Rheumatic fever* often left its victims with a rheumatic heart condition. This illness often reoccurred and the children were confined to bed for long periods of recuperation. The children were enrolled in hospital classes and were then taught at home during their long confinement. During periods between reoccurrences, the children were enrolled in special schools or classes.

Children with *Legg-Perthe's Disease* also found themselves enrolled in special classes. This painful condition results when changes take place in the head of the thigh bone and is most common in active elementary school-aged boys. Enforced rest is necessary for the affected leg to allow the involved hip joint to heal. Although there is usually little actual medical treatment except enforced rest of the involved joint, the children must use crutches; thus they were placed in a room of crippled children where they could be monitored to see that they were adhering to the immobilization rules necessary for the hip to heal itself. *Amputations* were also a reason to place a child in a special class for the physically handicapped. Even though the child might have been fitted with an artificial limb, the child was placed in the protective environment of the orthopedic classroom or school. This was for protection from the stares of the other students and to allow any physical or occupational therapy that might be necessary for mobility.

Asthma was another condition that often resulted in placement in a special class. The knowledge that stress could bring on an attack was the rationale for special class placement, for it was felt that the child could function better within this sheltered environment without any additional stress. *Childhood diabetes* was another condition which was listed as requiring special education. Although the condition required no educational adaptations, teachers were instructed to watch for the frequency of urination and the amount of water consumed, and to use first aid methods if the child went into a coma or shock.

Epilepsy also demanded placement in special education. Epilepsy is a condition where there is a disturbance in the electrical brain potentials, resulting in a seizure. Children who had their seizures reasonably well controlled were often placed in special classes so that the nurse assigned to the building could administer their medication. Children who had uncontrolled seizures were sometimes admitted to special education classes or to the school for physically handicapped, but were often admitted to special schools that were built in the more populated areas where only children with histories of epilepsy were enrolled. Even in these programs, however, uncontrolled seizures or the presence of an additional handicap could lead to exclusion and eventual confinement in a special residential institution that the various states built and staffed specifically for those with epilepsy.

Because the special schools were more academically oriented, this placement was felt preferable to that of the residential institution. Frequently only a select few received any educational training after placement within the institution, the major emphasis being on controlling the medical problems and protecting the child from the curious and critical public. Emphasis was also placed on protecting the public from the curse of epilepsy, so often described in negative terms throughout our historical literature.

Arthritis and *scoliosis,* a lateral curvature of the spine, were also conditions that led to placement either in special schools or special classes for the physically handicapped. As is true in most of the other cases mentioned, there was no difference in the learning style of the children but there were medical problems sufficient to recommend placement where there were medical resources available. In essence, the special classes and schools were for children with a wide range of medical conditions, but with little more than *physical adaptation of the environment* necessary for planning and delivering appropriate education.

Within the last twenty years, advances in medical practice and technology have all but eradicated most of the above conditions. Polio has, for the most part, been eliminated because of the development of an effective vaccine. It still occurs, unfortunately, and medical personnel persistently warn of a possible increase because of a laxity in vaccinating vulnerable children. However, there is currently available the means to totally eradicate the disease.

Techniques in open heart surgery have been perfected, as have medications promoting better cardiac functioning, so that children with heart conditions who formerly would have been doomed to an early death or an entire life of restricted activities are now able to enjoy a comparatively normal life. The discovery of penicillin has had its effect in controlling strep throat with its resulting rheumatic fever and rheumatic heart conditions. Preventive drugs are able to control the disease so that even if an individual has rheumatic fever, the recurrences of the past are no longer as prevalent.

The use of cortisone as well as antihistimines that have been developed for those suffering from allergies have been helpful in controlling asthma attacks. Children who were formerly completely segregated from their normal peers are now able to run and play with them because of the advances in medical technology regarding allergies and asthmatic conditions.

Diabetes is another condition for which medical breakthroughs have aided treatment. Before the discovery of insulin, children were doomed to an early death. With the advances made in treating this disease there is a chance for a more normal childhood, although greater success must be made before children affected with this disease will be able to live a normal life span. Even though diabetic children may eventually become blind or suffer heart or kidney conditions because of the damage caused by this disease, children who have it today are rarely confined to special class settings on the basis of the disease alone.

Epilepsy is another disease where great advances have been made. The discovery of new anticonvulsive medications, the development and use of tranquilizers in combination with other medications, and the education of the public to the actual cause and treatment of epilepsy have all aided in the decline of separate facilities for children and adults with epilepsy. The separate schools and institutions that were once used exclusively for those with epilepsy have all been turned to other uses.

New treatment for arthritis and new techniques for treating those with scoliosis allow the children to continue in regular classrooms and allow mobility during treatment, in contrast to the bed rest and casting that were so popular a few years ago. Surgical rehabilitation for limbs and replacements for joints require briefer periods of hospitalization and allow ambulation that would have been thought impossible just a few short years ago.

Congenital Conditions

Some conditions are present from birth and are diagnosed during the birth process or very shortly after because of their visibility or because of the medical complications their presence demands.

Hemophiliacs, those whose blood lack normal clotting abilities, previously also were enrolled in special classes and hospital settings. Because very insignificant bumps, bruises, or movements often started extensive internal bleeding with resulting joint problems and excruciating pain, these children spent considerable time in the hospital for blood transfusions, or in a protected environment where their activities could be monitored and restricted. Hemophiliacs are now able to live much more normal lives with the development during the late 1960s of new plasma concentrates, recent gains in knowledge of obtaining, storing, and administering blood to those in need, advances in medications, and home administration of treatment.

The children whose mothers took *thalidomide* during their pregnancies and who were born with limb deformities have been able to achieve remarkable gains through the use of artificial limbs developed to meet their needs. The large numbers of thalidomide children and their militant parents have marshalled medical and technological resources directed to their needs, .with the subsequent development of adaptive equipment which allows largely independent functioning.

A major cause of congenital handicapping conditions during recent years has been the *Rh blood incompatibility*. Within one generation, the specific cause of this problem has been determined and its treatment successfully developed so that within another generation, death and birth defects from Rh disease should be almost eliminated (Apgar and Beck, 1974).

The presence of an Rh factor in a person's blood makes no difference as far as that particular person's health is concerned. However, the pregnancy of an Rh negative mother by an Rh positive father can result in damage or death to the unborn baby. Although this condition does not usually happen in the first child, the mother with the Rh negative blood reacts to the baby's Rh positive blood as if it were an invading virus and her body begins to manufacture antibodies to destroy the foreign blood cells (Apgar, 1974). This happens during the first pregnancy only if some red blood cells of the Rh positive baby happen to spill into the circulation system of the Rh negative mother. During childbirth many more of the baby's cells from the placenta enter the mother's circulation and trigger her antibody production. These antibodies remain in the mother's system throughout her life, ready to attack an invading Rh positive organism. Such an attack can happen during subsequent pregnancies when the antibodies cross through the placenta connecting the child to the mother and proceed to destroy the red blood cells of the unborn Rh positive baby. The damage may be very mild or it may result in the baby's death.

Unless the mother has had a transfusion that contained Rh positive blood prior to the first pregnancy, the first infant will not be affected. However, subsequent pregnancies can result in the further manufacture of antibodies and can affect the developing Rh positive fetuses. These affected babies can be born with a wide range of problems, depending upon the severity of the attack by the mother's antibodies. Although the majority of babies born under such a condition are not severely involved, antibodies that are numerous or strong enough to harm the unborn child's red blood cells can result in jaundice, deafness, mental retardation, or cerebral palsy.

Although the Rh problem was identified in the 1940s, it was not until the late 1950s that physicians were able to determine whether the fetuses in subsequent pregnancies had Rh negative or Rh positive blood, or the degree of damage that the mother's antibodies may have done to the baby's red blood cells. At that time, a procedure called amniocentesis was perfected which allows a small amount of the amniotic fluid surrounding the infant to be withdrawn and studied for destroyed red blood cells. Such a study allows the doctors to monitor the developing fetus during the pregnancy and to induce labor or take by Caesarian section those in-

Courtesy of The Muscular Dystrophy Association.

fants that are in danger of dying (Center for Disease Control, 1975). The new technique allows the infant to remain in the uterus as long as possible, lessening the possible complications of a premature birth.

In the 1960s a means was developed to transfuse the infant while still in the uterus. This allows those infants too young to otherwise survive a premature birth an opportunity to remain longer in the uterus, reducing the dangers of premature delivery.

Amniocentesis and in-uterine transfusions are necessary only after the mother has started producing antibodies. A new means has been developed so that eventually these may no longer be necessary. A vaccine, if given to the Rh negative mother within seventy-two hours after the birth or abortion of an Rh positive baby, can prevent the mother from producing the damaging antibodies. If the mother becomes pregnant again, there will be no antibodies to attack the cells of an Rh positive baby. This procedure cannot help those mothers who have already developed antibodies and they must still depend upon amniocentesis and transfusion to protect their babies.

The Current Population

We can see therefore that several types of physical conditions that resulted in children needing special education are presently either nonexistent or limited in their effects. This is not to say that special educational facilities have become unnecessary to house children with orthopedic or other health impairments. On the contrary, conditions are such that there is currently a great demand for such facilities.

Where many of the conditions that were considered to demand such placement have been partially or totally eliminated by advances in medical science, that same medical progress has been responsible for an increase in other types of conditions in which the children need special education. Many children who would formerly not have survived their early years are now living life spans that require educational programs.

Congenital Conditions

It is interesting to note that the present population of children with crippling impairments have a much higher prevalence of congenital conditions. Medical advances have eliminated or decreased many of the acquired conditions that were formerly so prevalent. It has also kept alive many of those children who previously would not have survived either the birth process or the first few years of life. One such example of longer life spans is for children with *spina bifida.*

The cause of spina bifida is unknown although considerable study has been given to the condition. The incidence has been followed closely in this country as well as abroad (Congenital Malformations Surveillances, 1975). Both long-term as well as seasonal variations in its incidence have been reported, in this country as well as in England, Scotland, and Ireland, with unexplained cause. The incidence of spina bifida reflects rather substantial racial difference, with a much greater incidence among whites than among blacks.

Spina bifida develops during the early fetal period when the spinal column of the fetus is being formed. Normally, each segment of the spinal column forms a complete circle of bone, allowing complete protection for the spinal cord and the meninges, the covering of the cord, that lie within it. In spina bifida, the sides of the bone fail to come together and leave an opening. If there is no deformity or misplacement of the spinal cord, the condition is called *spina bifida occulta*. This condition usually causes no problems and requires no treatment. If part of the meninges containing the spinal nerve roots and spinal fluid protrudes through the bony protection to form a sac or cyst on the child's back, the sac, completely covered with skin, is called a *meningocele*. Spina bifida with a portion of the spinal cord itself and membranes protruding is called a *myelomeningocele*. The skin may not completely cover this type of protrusion.

Formerly considered inoperable, children with spina bifida were protected as much as possible so that the membrane would not leak or puncture and thus drain the cerebrospinal fluid within it. Normal life spans were impossible not only because the membrane might puncture, but also because the membrane that protected the spinal cord and fluids was vulnerable to leakage, as well as to viral and bacterial infections that could enter the central nervous system and result in death. Untreated infants usually expired during the first year of life. Prenatal detection of open spina bifida lesions now can be determined early in a pregnancy through the study of alpha feto-protein obtained during amniocentesis (Swingard, 1975).

Hydrocephalus often accompanies myelomeningocele. Hydrocephalus, which literally means "water brain," results when the cerebrospinal fluid which circulates through and around the brain and spinal cord is not absorbed into the bloodstream. New fluid is constantly being formed, and the pressure that is built up as this new fluid is added to that which already exists causes the bones of the head, which are fairly flexible at birth, to expand. The heads of children with untreated hydrocephalus continue to grow, with the fluid inside the head often pressing on the brain as well as on the optic and auditory nerves, causing brain damage as well as visual and auditory sensory losses. Hydrocephalic children who may have survived the initial birth experience were doomed to very limited lives until surgical techniques were developed to deal with these problems.

Currently most infants who are born with myelomeningocele are operated on within a few hours after birth. The neurosurgeon replaces the membrane and its contents back within the spinal column. If it is indicated, the surgeon also may perform an operation to prevent hydrocephalus by shunting the excess fluid that accumulates within the skull to another body cavity. Such shunts in the past had to be replaced frequently because of the growth of the child or because they became blocked and the pressure, unable to be relieved, built up in the skull. New developments now have produced different kinds of shunting procedures and materials so that the shunt expands its length within the child as the child grows, thus eliminating the need for such frequent surgical procedures.

Much of the successful outcome of surgery for myelomeningocele depends upon the skill of the surgeon performing the operations. Additional trauma to the spinal nerves can increase the lack of innervation to parts of the body. Spina bifida can occur at any point on the spinal column but occurs most often in the lower regions. The placement of the opening has much to do with the resulting handicap of the individual, because there is usually damage done to the nerves as they expand into the opening or as they are replaced into the spinal column. The parts of the body those particular nerves innervate thus retain a certain amount of damage. The more common spina bifida with lower openings usually affects the legs and the body organs that the lower nerves innervate. The children have accompanying difficulty in walking. Placement of the opening will also affect the urinary tract and cause particular problems in toileting for these children, because they are unable to feel sensations in the affected area and thus are unable to cooperate in moving their muscles in a voluntary manner. Until mandated special education occurred, many children with spina bifida were refused admission to schools, not because of an inability to partake in an educational program, but because they (1) presented problems in transportation and in traveling to the lunch room, and (2) lacked the ability to control their bowels and bladder. Various techniques have been addressed to the lack of toileting control, from credeing (applying external pressure to empty the bladder), to surgically creating a direct opening and then placing a bag on the outside of the body for a continual collection of urine. Conditioning the bowels to move at a particular time each day and catheterizing the children so that there can be extended periods of dryness have also been used. There are pros and cons to each of these methods and physicians and other professionals continually discuss the problems. No matter which technique is used, the children remain frequent targets of urinary tract infections and it is often these, not the spina bifida, that cause an early death.

Cerebral palsy is another handicapping condition that has been eased by medical advances. Cerebral palsy is a neuromuscular disability that results from injury to the brain before, during, or after birth. It results in varying types and degrees of disturbance of voluntary motor functioning. Such disorders of movement are usually observable in gross motor, fine motor, and postural functioning, but may vary from a mild involvement with little limitation of activities, to a moderate involvement where walking, self-help, and communication are all affected, to a severe involvement where there is almost total incapacity.

Conditions that have been identified as causing such a defect or lesion in the brain are (1) anoxia, or lack of oxygen during prenatal development or the birth process; (2) birth trauma; (3) heavy use of alcohol by the mother during pregnancy; (4) hyperbilirubinemia, in which there is excessive destruction of red blood cells or an interference with bile excretion causing jaundice; (5) abnormalities of the chromosomes; (6) Rh blood incompatibilities; (7) complications of twin pregnancy delivery; (8) prenatal conditions such as rubella (German or three-day measles); (9) complications of the placenta; (10) thyroid disease; and (11) kidney infection and diabetes in the mother. The largest group in risk of suffering cerebral palsy consists of children who are born prematurely.

The incidence of cerebral palsy is now one half of what it was in 1960. An estimated 10,000 cogenital cerebral palsied babies were born in 1976 (Sternfeld, 1977). Although the incidence of cerebral palsied children has decreased both in this country and abroad, the primary cause of cerebral palsy, *prematurity,* has not decreased. Prematurity is as prevalent as ever but the decreasing cerebral palsy figures reflect the progress that has been made in the care of the premature newborn child. The use of neonatal intensive care units not only has resulted in a higher survival rate for premature children, but has also helped to prevent central nervous system damage.

A specific portion of the premature population is still a problem in the prevention of cerebral palsy; those children who weigh less than 1,500 grams (3.3 pounds) at birth. If the children weigh between 1,000 grams (2.2 pounds) and 1,500 grams and do not have respiratory difficulty following birth, they do not present a problem. However, about 15 percent of those with respiratory difficulty have damaged nervous systems. If the child weighs less than 1,000 grams, the rate of damage goes up to one baby in three (Sternfeld, 1977). Generally, the more premature the child, the greater the risk of cerebral palsy (Apgar and Beck, 1974).

It is not the act of prematurity itself that creates cerebral palsy, but the fact that the child is probably much more susceptible to difficulties in the birth process and to the stresses of life during the first few days. The prematurity might also reflect the fact that the child has had an unfavorable environment within the uterus or generally poor development during pregnancy.

Congenital cerebral palsy comprises about 85 percent of the cases, with the cause of the cerebral palsy often creating additional handicapping conditions. Although the prevalence varies from study to study (Haynes, 1974), mental retardation is present in at least a third of cerebral palsied children, with ranges of intellectual ability from profound retardation to giftedness. A third of the children also have seizures, while another one third have abnormal electroencephalograms but no seizures. A third have eye problems, usually as a result of some type of eye muscle inadequacy. Problems in hearing, speech, kinesthetic perception, and learning are also frequent. The resulting combination in each child presents a multihandicapping condition to which can be added those social and emotional problems caused by the child and family adjusting to the effects of the multiplicity of problems within our society (Scherzer and Gullo, 1975). About 35 percent of severely involved cerebral palsied children die before their fifth birthday. Those who survive the first five years have a life expectancy of forty to forty-five years.

Cerebral palsy is primarily a motor disorder whose classification is based on the type of motor abnormality presented, with the motor abnormality related to the localization of the brain damage (Scherzer and Gullo, 1975). *Spasticity*, caused by damage to the motor cortex is responsible for 50 percent of the cases of cerebral palsy. The motor symptoms include hypertonicity (too much tone) in the muscle movements which creates *muscle tightness*, a Babinski sign (a backward extension of the great toe when the lateral part of the sole of the foot is stroked, indicating an upper motor neuron lesion), and spasmodic alternations between muscle contraction and relaxation. Up to 80 percent of cerebral palsied children with a history of prematurity exhibit spasticity (Scherzer and Gullo, 1975).

A different form of motor movement with *uncontrollable, involuntary rhythmic movement* is related to a lesion primarily in the basal ganglia area of the brain. This form of cerebral palsy, called *athetosis*, comprises about 25 percent of the cerebral palsied population. Because of the increasing use of blood transfusion for the affected babies and vaccination of Rh negative mothers, the incidence of athetosis is decreasing.

Ataxia, another form of cerebral palsy, results from a fixed cerebellar lesion with resulting *muscular incoordination*. Ataxic children lack a sense of balance and have abnormal depth perception. Ataxia represents about 10 percent of the cerebral palsied population. Although each of these three types may be observed singly, varying mixed combinations of athetosis, spasticity and/or ataxia may also be observed.

The presence of cerebral palsy may not be possible to observe at the time the lesion takes place. It is not until motor patterns emerge as a result of the maturation of an abnormal nervous system that the different types of cerebral palsy can be classified. The three major types of cerebral palsy emerge with the maturation of the brain from its functioning primarily on a brain stem level at birth to gradually higher levels. It is no longer acceptable practice to wait until the specific types of motor abnormalities appear to make a diagnosis, but delayed motor milestones, abnormal reflex patterns, and abnormal tone and posture are used as indicators long before the obvious motor patterns appear (Johnston and Harryman, 1975; Scherzer and Gullo, 1975).

Cerebral palsy is also classified as to involvement of the four limbs (Pearson and Williams, 1972). Paraplegics only have the legs involved. Hemiplegics have involvement of both the upper and lower limbs on the same side. When both arms and legs are involved, the legs to a greater extent than the arms, diplegia results. These usually reflect an upper motor neuron lesion and would therefore be spastic. Quadriplegics have all four limbs involved. Because of the amount of damage to the brain, the muscles of the face, trunk, mouth, and throat areas are affected as well. This type may be either spastic or athetoid in classification.

Cerebral palsy is also classified according to the severity of involvement (Pearson and Williams, 1972). Mild involvement usually needs no specific treatment. There are no speech problems, there is enough functioning for independent activities of daily living, and the students are able to work without assistance. Very often a mild involvement is of the hemiplegic type.

Moderate cerebral palsied involvement demands treatment. The students are inadequate in self-care, have problems in speech, and trouble with walking. The moderately involved student benefits from positioning, or being placed in particular positions that will aid motor functioning. Changes in muscle tone can be brought about through proper positioning.

Very severely involved spastic students cannot move independently at all. They become rigid and frightened of movement, creating additional problems to therapists and educators. Intervention demands a multidisciplinary approach with pediatrics or medicine, neurology, orthopedics, physical and occupational therapy, speech therapy, social work, and education all contributing to the total development of the students. Severely involved students have a poor prognosis for independent self-care, speech, and ambulation. Often bladder and bowel control is lacking. Because of their problems with positioning, handling, and education, these students present sometimes overwhelming challenges.

Muscular dystrophy is another condition that has been affected by increases in medical advances. There is no known etiology or cause for muscular dystrophy. The disease follows a dominant hereditary pattern, but usually affects only male members of a family. It has been found that about 20 percent of all females manifest subclinical evidence of the disease but it usually never fully develops. Women act as carriers for the disease. Since individuals with muscular dystrophy do not procreate, it is through the female carrier that the disease is transmitted. Female members of a family that have a muscular dystrophy member can be tested to ascertain whether they are capable of transmitting the disease.

The disease is characterized by a progressive muscle weakening over a long period of time. The chief symptoms of the disease are the increasing muscle weakness and crippling as the affected muscles supporting the skeleton contract and lose their ability to function.

Pseudohypertrophic (Duchenne), or childhood form, is the most common type of muscular dystrophy. The symptoms may begin during the first few years of life but may not become too noticeable until the child begins to stumble and fall. As the disability progresses, it involves more muscles and the child gradually loses his ability to walk. As the gradual degeneration and wasting of muscle tissue takes place, it is replaced with fat and fibrous tissue. Although there may be periods of remission, the disability progresses and the child is eventually confined to bed. The body becomes increasingly deformed and an attack of some type of acute infection usually causes death before or during the teen years.

There are other types of dystrophy, some of which affect females. Most have similar prognoses or outcomes; some may be disabling but not fatal. In spite of research that has been directed to the total dystrophy population, there has been little progress made in preventing death and disability. Postural drainage, treatment of contractures, and antibiotics have all aided children with the disease, but a cure still is not known.

Sickle cell anemia is another condition that has received additional emphasis during the past few years. Found almost exclusively among blacks, although there are some cases reported among whites found in small areas of some Mediterranean countries, it is estimated to occur in one in every four hundred black children. Sickle cell anemia seems to have originated among people living in a wide geographical area stretching across central Africa. Originally felt to be a protection against malaria, because the sickle cell carriers had a blood system that prevented malaria parasites from multiplying, the disorder has tremendous implications if found in the schoolchildren of today.

Carried as a recessive gene, about 10 percent of blacks in the United States possess the abnormal, recessive gene. When two people with recessive genes produce a child, the genetic pattern of sickle cell anemia appears. The chances are one in four that this child will have normal genes, two in four that the child will carry one normal and one abnormal gene, and one in four that sickle cell anemia will occur. Those who have one normal and one abnormal gene are said to have sickle cell trait and are carriers of the disorder, although they usually possess no outward symptoms (Apgar and Beck, 1974).

Sickle cell anemia is a very painful, serious disorder that can affect almost every part of the body, and which produces enormous amounts of suffering and illness. The condition occurs within a part of the body where there has been a decrease in the normal amount of oxygen. The abnormality takes place in the hemoglobin molecule, distorts its shape and causes it to clump together with other affected molecules. The distorted shape of the red blood cells make them look like tiny sickles, thus giving the disorder its name.

Once they are formed, the sickled cells tend to stick together even more and can cause a temporary obstruction in the small blood vessels. This in turn can cause a decrease in the supply of oxygen and cause even more sickled cells. The seriousness of the problem created by the sickled cells depends upon the place in the body where the blockage occurs and the length of time it endures. Although sickle cell anemia can begin at any age, the symptoms most frequently occur before the age of two. Those first symptoms usually are swelling of the fingers or toes. Preschool children can often have severe bouts of pain, *sickle cell crises*, that are mistaken for other types of problems. The pain during a crisis is so severe that it cannot be relieved even when the child is in the hospital under pain-relieving drugs. These crises, while occurring often in young children and teenagers, decrease in frequency in adulthood. Severe anemia can result in sudden death in the young affected children (Apgar and Beck, 1974).

Males seem to contract sickle cell anemia to a greater degree than females, except for pregnant women and those who have recently delivered babies. These women have a high mortality rate as well as a greater chance for miscarriage, premature deliveries, and stillborn babies. Because of this, women should be screened for sickle cell trait before pregnancies.

Sickle cell anemia and sickle cell trait can be identified by means of routine blood tests. Although it can be identified, there is at the current time no cure for the disease. The main treatment usually lies in prevention and relief of the symptoms. Avoiding fatigue, exposure to cold, and stress are preventive measures.

There is a great deal of work being carried on currently to discover more about sickle cell anemia and sickle cell trait. In the past, half of those with sickle cell anemia failed to reach their twentieth birthday, and few of those who survived lived past forty (Apgar and Beck, 1974). The picture has improved but there is much more to be done.

The educational implications are important when considering sickle cell anemia victims as crippled and health-impaired children. The children will usually be found in regular classrooms if the condition has not resulted in severe debilitation. Frequent and prolonged hospitalization and the necessity of daily blood transfusions in prevention and treatment may cause particular children to receive most of their schooling in that type of setting. Damage to the joints and heart, constant pain during a sickle cell crisis, or resulting neurological damage may necessitate special class placement, resource room, or itinerant help. Sickle cell anemia is a medical condition, however. Unless there has been extensive damage to the neurological system, most of its victims will remain within the confines of regular education.

Cystic fibrosis is another disease where the life span has been prolonged. A chronic, noncontagious disease that mostly affects whites, it is inherited through a recessive gene. Until two decades ago, infants with the disease died before they reached their second birthday. Infants now diagnosed early and given comprehensive care can survive to reach their twentieth year, with the severity of the involvement of the lungs usually determining the length of survival.

In cystic fibrosis, an inborn error in metabolism results in a lack of enzyme that is essential to normal functioning of the glands which control the production of saliva, sweat, and mucus. Consequently, the lungs produce a gluey, sticky mucus that clogs the air passages and makes it difficult to fight off infections, blocks the pancreas and intestines, and interferes with the digestion of food. Because the electrolyte level of the body is affected, a high degree of salt in the sweat is used for diagnostic purposes. Although it is not completely accurate, lesser amounts of salt can identify carriers of the recessive gene (Apgar and Beck, 1974).

Symptoms such as failure to grow in spite of an enormous appetite, continual fussiness, persistent runny nose, coughing and wheezing, and foul-smelling stools can signify presence of the disease. Vision and heart disease and clubbing of the fingers may also accompany the condition.

Another disease that is inherited, although through a single dominant gene, is *osteogenesis imperfecta*. This congenital condition causes fragile bones that fracture easily. Such fractures may affect the development of bone and may result in shortened height. The condition can be associated with deafness and with a blue discoloration of the whites of the eyes although only one or two of these major symptoms of the disease may be present.

Infections

Some of the conditions that are found in classes for crippled children result from different types of infectious diseases. The incidence of such diseases has decreased following the discovery of antibiotics. However, the success of antibiotics has contributed indirectly to the increase in certain types of exceptional children. Many conditions such as *spinal meningitis* and *encephalitis* were previously fatal to the affected children. The use of antibiotics has led to a decrease in the number of cases, but not all children are immediately diagnosed and given the proper dosage for controlling the diseases. Although late administration of drugs might save the child's life, it may not save a severely infected child from damage that the disease caused to the brain before being brought under antibiotic control (Kappelman, 1972). Of the 1,359 cases of encephalitis reported in 1976, 257 were characterized as presenting residual problems (Sternfeld, 1977).

Delay in diagnosing, controlling, and immunizing against other bacterial and viral infections can also result in an increase in the numbers of children with varying degrees of handicapping conditions. Sternfeld (1977) estimates that almost 1,000 cases of cerebral palsy can be prevented annually if children are immunized with the basic immunization agents that are now available against measles, rubella, whooping cough, mumps, diphtheria, and tetanus.

Traumatic Conditions

Many children are born normal and later become handicapped because of some type of trauma. There are increasing numbers of children enrolled in special education because of handicaps caused by traumatic conditions.

Although not a handicapping condition, *accidents* often lead to severe handicapping conditions and are mentioned as a causal factor that should be considered when discussing the current population of handicapped children found in educational settings for children with orthopedic impairments. Accidents are a result of our increasingly complex and industrial society. Although accidents have always been present, there are many more ways in which debilitating accidents can happen than ever before.

The major source of handicaps from accidents involves automobiles. Hundreds of thousands of injuries are suffered each year in car accidents. Although the figures have fallen recently, there have been close to 50,000 people killed each year in automobile accidents. It is not those who die that are of concern here but those who live, handicapped from the injuries that they suffered. Accidents are a leading cause of handicapping conditions, and the types of handicaps resulting from such accidents cover the broad gamut of special education: blindness, deafness, orthopedic handicaps, seizures, retardation, and emotional disturbance.

There is a big difference in teaching children who have an acquired handicap and those who are congenitally handicapped. Children who are adventitiously handicapped were usually normal at one time with normal abilities to learn. They usually are able to remember what they were like before the accident and can readily realize how different they are at the present time. This can lead to tremendous emotional implications in a classroom when the child faces problems in learning that were not there before injury. Former athletes and gifted learners sometimes become nonambulatory and retarded because of an accident. Such students may refuse to learn, may become extremely depressed, or may exhibit behaviors that are unacceptable to others.

It is important, however, for the teacher to remember that the child at one time had normal learning abilities and, hopefully, that the core of learning is still accessible and new learning can be imposed. Some recovery of former functions may be possible, some may not. The teacher must become an ally to help the student recover all that is possible while at the same time laying a firm foundation for new learning to take place by techniques that were not formerly necessary.

Some handicapped children have injuries that have been afflicted by abusive parents. *Child abuse* has become a national concern and is currently receiving attention from leaders in special education because of the large numbers of children in special education placement that have been abused.

In 1974 at their annual convention, the Council for Exceptional Children adopted a resolution recognizing abused and neglected children as exceptional children. Also in 1974 Congress passed the Child Abuse Prevention and Treatment Act (P.L. 93–247), which established a National Center on Child Abuse and Neglect and authorized grants to study the child-abuse problem.

In 1976, the Council for Exceptional Children was awarded a grant to demonstrate the effectiveness of a national training curriculum developed by the National Center on Child Abuse and Neglect to orient educators to the problems of child abuse. The curriculum is organized into two components, one which is highly specialized for educators, and the other for persons in many different disciplines. Modules of instruction include the physically abused child, the neglected child, the emotionally maltreated child, the sexually abused child, reporting child abuse and neglect, referring cases of child abuse and neglect, and the courts and child abuse and neglect. The educators' module includes procedures for identifying, reporting, and referring children who are known or are suspected of being abused and neglected and also provides training in the skills needed by teachers and administrators to effectively carry out these responsibilities (Insight, 1976). The curriculum was tested in local, metropolitan, regional/state, and national settings in an attempt to alert special educators to the needs of abused and neglected children.

When abuse and its effect in producing handicapped children is discussed, cause and effect become a part of the discussion. Kline and Hopper (Soeffing, 1975) have completed extensive reviews of the literature in the education, medical, psychological, social work, and law areas and found no study that established a definite cause-and-effect relationship between handicap and abuse. Some studies they reported do indicate a correlation between the two but it is difficult to determine whether the abuse led to the handicap or some type of deviancy in the child was responsible for the abuse. Studies that have been completed with abused children indicate that the portion of abused children with IQ's below 70 is ten times greater than at higher IQ levels, and children with a history of head trauma and/or neurological impairment score significantly lower than other children on tests of intelligence. One condition appears to result from abuse alone—physical injury, particularly brain damage—and a large percentage of the abused children who receive hospital care suffer permanent brain damage (Soeffing, 1975). Since damage to the brain often results in orthopedic problems, it is of significance to discuss it. Even casual, manual whiplash shaking of children can cause later mental retardation and brain damage. Since the shaking of infants and children leaves no sign of injuries, minimal damage may go unnoticed until the child's entrance to school.

It is anticipated that the figures of child abuse will go even higher in the years to come. With improved reporting techniques and mandatory reporting for suspected abuse, the figures will undoubtedly rise. In reporting the 1975 National Data on Child Neglect and Abuse, the Children's Division of the American Humane Association (1976) summarized figures from twenty-nine states and territories where the data were detailed and specific, as well as data received from additional sources.

The data reflect that about half of the cases reported as suspected abuse or neglect were validated as such. Neglect was more prevalent than abuse, with no difference noted in the sex of the child involved. Agency personnel and individuals were almost equal as sources of reporting, with medical and other sources far behind. Natural parents were found to be the most frequent child abusers. Step-parents, other relatives, adoptive parents, and baby-sitters followed in that order. The natural parents were responsible for 82.47 percent of the abuse with the mother responsible for 56.70 percent of that total.

The validated types of abuse reported included: (1) minor physical injuries such as contusions, abrasions, and unspecified, with no visible injuries: 31,142 children or 51.3 percent; (2) Sexual abuse: 6,696 or 10.7 percent; (3) major physical injuries with bone fractures: 1,516 children or 2.4 percent; (4) burns and scalding: 1,680 or 2.7 percent; (5) congenital and environmental drug addiction: 33 children or 0.1 percent; and (6) unspecified physical abuse: 20,557 children or 32.8 percent. Neglect was also reported with 100,544 verified cases of physical neglect, or 78.1 percent of the total. Medical neglect was found in 12,396 cases, or 9.6 percent; emotional neglect that included psychological impairment and failure to thrive in 10,045 cases, or 7.8 percent; and education neglect in 5,714 cases or 4.5 percent. Some of the children were reported in more than one category (American Humane Society, 1975).

It is difficult to fathom 139,267 cases of neglect and abuse in the United States in one year, and to estimate the damage inflicted on the victims. Undoubtedly, child neglect and abuse will be a contributing factor in referrals to special education services for some time. If only a portion of the 44,913 verified cases of abuse result in orthopedic conditions, abuse will be a leading cause of referrals to special education.

Burns and their incidence resulting in handicapping conditions have also increased with our technological advances. While one usually thinks in terms of burns resulting from fire, tissue injury can result from excessive exposure to not only thermal sources but chemical, electrical, friction, or radioactive agents. The effects of burns will vary according to the type, intensity, and duration of the agent as well as the part of the body involved. Any burn that involves an area of the body that is greater than that covered by the palm of the hand can produce shock and a poisoning to the system caused by the substances derived from the body's burned tissue.

The seriousness of a burn usually depends upon the degree and extent. A first-degree burn consists only of a reddening of the unbroken skin. If the skin is broken and blistered, it is considered a second-degree burn. Third-degree burns cause destruction of the skin and underlying structures. In spite of advances in care in this area, burns that cover more than one half of the body are usually fatal in children and, depending on the type and extent, burns covering little more than 10 percent of the body surface can be fatal to a small child. The pain, which is more severe than any other injury, the accompanying shock, as well as the infection that presents such a ready appearance in the open body areas, all present dangers.

Sterility, relief from pain, proper care of the wound, control or prevention of infection, prevention or relief of shock, maintenance of water and electrolyte balance within the body and proper nutrition are all part of the treatment. However, deep burns will not heal themselves and prolonged and painful skin grafts may be necessary. Chronic anemia and permanent deformity may accompany the burns. Also accompanying the burns may be extreme emotional problems that remain after the burns have healed. The presence of such emotional problems can present a study in and of itself.

Epilepsy has been mentioned as a condition that was often uncontrolled and resulted in special class placement or in institutionalization. Because seizures are such a common accompaniment to other types of handicapping conditions they will be discussed, although seizures themselves are not usually a legitimate reason for special educational placement. Controlled seizures in particular should make no difference in a person's activities, if that person is conscientious about taking the necessary medication and following the doctor's precautions.

The etiology of epilepsy is unknown, although electroencephalographic (EEG) studies of the brain would note a direct relationship between changes in electrical brain potentials and the occurence of seizures. The actual seizure itself can be described as similar to an overcharge of electricity with the fuse blowing. The seizures themselves may differ considerably and each individual may have characteristic patterns of behavior during a seizure.

The *petit mal*, or "little sickness" seizure, comes and goes within seconds. There is a momentary loss of consciousness but no falling. There may be an associated but meaningless jerk, or movement of some part of the body or head. Often these attacks are viewed as momentary lapses and are overlooked as seizures.

During a *psychomotor* seizure, there is a momentary loss of consciousness which is accompanied by some type of repetitive behavior that is completely out of context, such as picking lint off clothes when there is no lint present, or the clapping of hands. This type of behavior begins abruptly and may be contrary to the person's ordinary characteristic behavior. The actions appear purposeful but are irrelevant to the situation. This attack is usually followed by a brief period of amnesia, or loss of memory.

A *grand mal*, or "big sickness" seizure, is usually much more dramatic and frightening to those who observe it. The seizure itself is usually preceded by an aura, or warning. The aura differs among individuals but may consist of flashes of light, the appearance of black spots, distinctive odors, a sense of falling, or a meaningless muscle jerk that is visible to the observer. Following the aura, the epileptic may utter a cry or other sound as he falls to the floor. The person loses consciousness and the total body twitches and jerks. The person may salivate, urinate, and defecate during the seizure. The seizures vary in time although they are usually a few minutes in duration, and may take place during the person's waking or sleeping hours. Following the seizure, there is usually a period of stuporous bewilderment when the person is extremely drowsy and wishes to sleep. Amnesia follows the attack and the victim will have no recollection of it. Often the only evidence the epileptic will have that there has been an attack is the presence of sore muscles, bruises from the extremities hitting something, or blood from biting the tongue or cheek.

A *Jacksonian* seizure is a focal seizure that begins with a twitching or numbness in one part of the body and spreads to include the greater portion of the body. Consciousness may be lost in the later part of the attack.

There is little that the observer can do during a seizure, other than to make the area safe for the person. In the event of a grand mal, turning the head to the side allows the saliva to run out of the mouth and not choke the victim. Room needs to be provided so that the person thrashing about does not sustain physical injury during the seizure. It used to be recommended that a hard object be placed in the mouth to prevent the victim from biting or chewing the tongue, but this is no longer recommended because of the severe jaw lock that the victim may exhibit. Pieces of metal and wood bent and broken, and bitten fingers of well-meaning helpers often have been the result of such practice.

There are many effective drugs that have been developed for epilepsy. Each may be used alone or in conjunction with others. Dosages must be particularly tailored for each individual, so there may be a period of time between the diagnosis of epilepsy and its control. About 85 percent of the epileptic population is controlled by skilled use of drugs; thus, most epileptics are able to lead normal lives. The remaining 15 percent may have partial control with fairly infrequent seizures or may have frequent, uncontrolled seizures. It is often this latter group of children that appear in special education settings, because of the handicap that the seizure accompanies. Cerebral palsied children, because of the damage to the brain, often have accompanying seizures.

Heredity plays a role in epilepsy, but its exact role is not known. Thirty-five percent of those with seizures of an unknown cause have a positive family history. However, there is no history in the remaining 65 percent. Some seizures can be directly connected to the onset of a handicapping condition while other seizures begin in infancy and may be related to fevers.

Once a child has had a febrile (fever-induced) seizure, it is important to know whether or not additional seizures can be anticipated. Physicians also want to know if the seizures have a reoccurring pattern before a diagnosis of epilepsy is made. The interaction between the child's age, sex, and family history all relate to whether there will be a reoccurrence of the seizure. An additional indicator as to whether a febrile seizure will lead to epilepsy is the length of the seizure. Those lasting longer than twenty to thirty minutes have a much greater likelihood of future epilepsy. The indication of an abnormal EEG two weeks after the seizure increases the chances, as does frequency. Febrile seizures can be prevented by continuing a child on anticonvulsants for a prolonged period of time (Carter, 1975).

Both experimental and clinical studies indicate that recurring or prolonged seizures can cause irreversible damage to the brain (Carter, 1975). Children who already are severely brain damaged may suffer such seizures, further compounding their problems. However, convulsions alone do not appear to cause impairment or mental deterioration. (Epilepsy Foundation of America, 1971).

In an educational setting, there is little that a teacher can do to prevent seizures. The best way to deal with a seizure is to react calmly, not for the benefit of the person who is seizuring, but for the benefit of the other students and adults in the room who are observing the seizure. If a student indicates an aura, the teacher can often help the child to the floor, remove anything from the environment that may be harmful to the victim, turn the head to the side to prevent choking, and continue to teach. The other students who are observing will take their cues from the teacher that this is not a catastrophic happening and act accordingly. Their attitudes will aid the epileptic after the seizure to avoid the stigma that can result from a teacher's hysterical response to a seizure. If the child has difficulty breathing or if a seizure lasts longer than fifteen to twenty minutes, the teacher should seek medical aid. The teacher should also report any seizure to the student's parents as well as to the school nurse.

The teacher should also note that the period of time that the student was seizuring and sleeping after the seizure will be time not spent learning. If the child was in the middle of a lesson, it will be necessary for the teacher to go back over work covered as well as to continue the lesson so that the child will have a continuity of material.

It is important for a teacher to take note of the events that took place in the classroom just prior to the child's seizure. Particular events might be found that relate to the onset of the seizure. In observing the events, a teacher may become aware that some children can self-induce a seizure to avoid unpleasant tasks. It is important to have data to support this; thus, careful observation and the recording of all events just prior to a seizure should be made. Consultation with the child's physician can result in carefully developed plans to control this aspect of the child's behavior.

The teacher should also be aware of the school district's position regarding the dispensing of anticonvulsive medication. If the child is under frequent medication, the parents will often send the teacher the medication that must be taken during the school hours with instructions to administer a specified dosage at a particular time. The teacher should be aware of the school procedures to follow in this event. Some districts specify that a school nurse is the only one allowed to give the medication, others demand a note from the parents and/or doctor, and others will not allow the teacher to touch the medication but will allow the teacher to remind the child to take it. Because there are usually legal ramifications underlying specific procedures, the teacher should become knowledgeable about them.

Leukemia is a variety of cancer that affects the blood and blood-forming organs. It is characterized by an enormous increase in the number of white blood corpuscles, enlargement of the spleen, lymph glands, and liver. It can take several forms, depending upon the particular types of white blood cells predominating.

Leukemia is another of the conditions where medical advances have made tremendous impact. Formerly, no matter whether a child suffered an acute or chronic attack, death resulted in anywhere from a few weeks to a month in the former case to perhaps a few years in the latter. Current treatment now enables leukemia victims prolonged remissions free of the boils, anemia, pneumonia, flu, hemorrhages from the mucus membranes, digestive disturbances, and dimness of vision that can accompany the condition. Such treatment means that children no longer must be confined to medical settings while they suffer an increasingly debilitative disease, but are able to be educated in a much less restrictive environment while in their remissive and "symptom free" stages.

Summary

If the students in classes for crippling and other health-impaired children twenty years ago were compared with the students of today, one would find an almost completely different population. Although many of the seizure and cardiac conditions still exist, they are not currently the primary conditions that lead to placement in special education, but the accompanying handicaps in children who have many others.

The severity of handicapping conditions that are found in classes today would have been unthought of just a few years ago. In fact, most educators would have considered the children uneducable and would have resisted acceptance of them in their classes. Court cases, public laws, and medical science have all contributed to this different population.

One major difference in the special classroom for crippling conditions stands out from all the rest. Whereas children were previously placed in classrooms for the crippled because of a medical condition, they are now placed there because of particular learning problems. Formerly, children placed in such classes could be taught by the same techniques used with normal children if allowances were made for lowered vitality or lack of movement. Today, the children present severe learning problems caused by extensive brain damage, mobility problems that tax even experts in the field, and mental abilities that run the gamut from profoundly retarded to the gifted. Many children with relatively uncomplicated orthopedic problems are now routinely educated in regular classrooms.

Enlarging the concept of "education" to include much more than the ability to read and write or to learn traditional subject matter, children who previously would have been excluded are now allowed access to public education. In fact, passage of P.L. 94–142 caught many school systems out of compliance, and educational placements were developed for children that had been excluded from educational settings up to that time.

ASSESSING THE CHILDREN

Assessment of children with crippling and other health conditions is a most challenging task. The children represent a wide range of types of disabilities from those who are able to ambulate without help to those who are unable to make any independent movements. Their learning abilities run the broad range of intellectual development from those who are capable of learning in a normal manner if adaptive equipment is available to those who must be programmed for the simplest of self-help tasks. There will be those who have but a single handicapping condition and those who may have five or six handicaps, any one of which could make them eligible for special education services.

Problems in Assessment

A proper assessment for each child becomes very important to find the appropriate placement and to develop the best educational plan for that particular child. It may be that some of the children will be able to attend regular classes with their normal peers, others may be placed in special classrooms with those who have similar learning problems and handicapping conditions, and still others will receive their instruction at home because transportation would be too demanding for their fragile bodies.

The need for assessing the various aspects of the total child becomes particularly important, for many of the children are multihandicapped with each handicap not only adding to the major crippling handicap, but multiplying the problems associated with it. Obstacles encountered in assessing cerebral palsied children will be discussed here as typical of difficulties met in assessing children with crippling conditions.

There are no tests that have been standardized on a representative cerebral palsied population. A test, to be valid, should be used only on a population similar to those on whom it was standardized. This means that any formal standardized test given to handicapped children could penalize them if it were not standardized on children like them. Also, such tests often require behaviors that orthopedically handicapped children cannot perform. Any test item that asks for mobility penalizes the cerebral palsied student, as does any item that is timed, because of motor problems. Items that require visual responses can depress the test scores of children who have additional visual problems. Items that require auditory skills can be penalizing if the children have the type of hearing loss frequently found among cerebral palsied children. Verbal responses can also be discriminatory because of the frequent speech problems exhibited by cerebral palsied children, particularly if the examiner testing the children is not used to such speech and has difficulty understanding it. Even a need to point to a correct response can be unfair if the children have contractures and are unable to extend their arms because of cerebral palsy. Items that ask questions relating to activities engaged in by normal children can be nonmeaningful to children who have spent their entire lives inside their homes because their parents felt they were too difficult to move, or because they were embarrassed by the stares of others, or because they could not face the pity, revulsion, or questioning of the general public. Even for those children who have had the benefit of informed parents who have taken them out into the community, the experiences are not the same as for normal children, for children who observe activities from the sidelines do not derive the same benefits as those who engage in the activities. Catching a fast ball appears easy from the sidelines. It's another matter when it's tried.

Psychologists, educators, and child development experts have been advocating experience as a primary goal for children. Yet some handicapped children come to school without even having been in all the rooms of their own homes. To expect the children to bring the same experiences to the testing situation as normal children who have had the freedom to roam their neighborhoods, have been far beyond their neighborhood limits and have had full use of all their perceptual and intellectual skills while engaged in these activities, is unfair. However, the test scoring procedures that determine intellectual and academic functioning do not allow the children with more limited experiences any scoring adjustments. Because of this, the children will test less well than the children who have had more experience, even though the basic intellectual potential may be the same. This fact should be remembered when assessing children who are being considered for placement with their "normal" peers. If the children are assessed in all the various areas of development decreed by law, they will be penalized in each because of the presence of moderate or severe cerebral palsy. Cerebral palsy is such a debilitating disease that the resulting handicaps permeate every area of educational endeavor.

However, there are children whose cerebral palsy is mild and who will be able to take a traditional test and do comparatively well on it. They might not do as well as they would have without the problems of this handicapping condition, but the condition is of a degree that they have made compensations, will be able to learn as normal children learn, and should be placed in a regular school environment.

Many of the children who are referred for formal assessment cannot be adequately appraised by a standardized instrument. For those who are capable of performing on such an instrument, such tests can be given, but only with due attention to problems of standardization, how this child compares to the standardization group, and ways in which the test might be discriminatory with the particular child being tested.

Even children who are able to cooperate in a formal assessment should have that information supplemented. It is important to observe the children in a variety of settings and a number of different situations to note the behavior in each. The children should be assessed in the areas of gross and fine motor, perceptual and conceptual development, social/emotional development, communication skills, and in the ability of self-care. With multiply handicapped children, it is necessary to have a comprehensive team with members representing different disciplines to appraise the children and interpret their behavior in light of each particular team specialty. Assessment teams are composed of different types of personnel; the team that assesses each child should be as broadly representative as possible because of the multiplicity of problems that orthopedically handicapped children represent.

Teams, during their assessment, can use the multidisciplinary, the interdisciplinary, or the transdisciplinary model. The pros and cons of each of these approaches has been discussed (Hart, 1977) and it is hoped that a real effort is made when constructing the team to use a model that will be most useful in assessing the potential of the children and in planning a program where each of the team members has assessment input and is also accountable for implementation of at least part of the program.

During the assessment, there should be some type of medical input. For example, an excellent individualized education program can be devel-

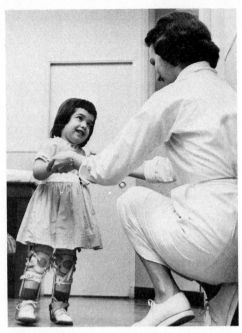

Courtesy of the United Cerebral Palsy Association, Inc.

oped for a child with muscular dystrophy that is totally impractical because of the child's prognosis for decreasing motor and performance skills. Thus, medical input into a total assessment can provide the prognosis for a particular handicapping condition. Any medical restrictions on physical participation in particular activities should be considered. Are there medical services that the children should be receiving? Are there behaviors that are of significance and for which the teacher should be watching? Are there medications that are being administered that may have educational implications for the children or teacher? An example of this is the child who lacks complete seizure control and is given heavy dosages of anticonvulsant medication. The dosage affects the child's alertness during school hours and the child may sleep most of the day. Communication between the doctor and teacher might result in some sort of compromise whereby the dosage is adjusted so that the child is less affected during school hours. If no compromise is possible, it is important for the physician to know that the child is sleeping most of the day and is unable to take an active part in the learning environment.

A variety of medical services is usually indicated by the mere presence of an orthopedic handicap, for such handicaps often entail a multitude of accompanying problems. These problems may indicate a need for the services of an ophthalmologist who can provide input as to the effect of the crippling condition on the eye, and whether there are visual acuity or muscle problems. An otologist can provide information as to the status of the ears. Has the crippling condition also affected the ears? Is there some type of physical anomaly that affects hearing? An orthopedic doctor should inspect the bone structure of the children and examine their limbs, joints, and spines in terms of restrictive conditions as well as situations that can be aided either medically, surgically, or by bracing. A physiatrist can be of assistance as a link between the orthopedic physician who is interested in the bone and the neurologist who is interested in the nerves and the damage that has been caused to them by the handicapping conditions. The physiatrist can work closely with the occupational and physical therapist in determining therapy for each child, as well as with the teacher in providing information as to the appropriate positioning to aid each child to achieve the greatest movement and interaction with the environment. All of these professionals can assist the teacher and parent by providing types of activities or exercises that will help the child to achieve maximum movement as well as to avoid contractures (muscle shortening) and stiffness that can restrict voluntary movement.

An audiologist should add any information regarding hearing loss. Is there a medical condition causing the loss that can be corrected surgically? Will medication help? Are there special diagnostic tests that can aid in a diagnosis of the child's problems? If there is a loss, of what type and what significance is it?

A psychologist should also be involved in the assessment of each child. A psychologist may be at a loss to assess severely involved children if experience with this particular population has been limited. Many of the children will be unable to respond to a formal instrument so the examiner must use other means to assess the functioning level and potential for learning. The psychologist may be comfortable in using some of Haessermann's adaptations (Haessermann, 1958; Jedrysek, 1972). Others have made their own adaptations. Of crucial importance is whether the psychologist can obtain an accurate assessment of the child's functioning level. It is necessary for the psychologist to know of some of the problems that result from specific disabilities so that any particular child is not presented with test materials that are inappropriate or in a manner that does not permit responses because of particular handicapping conditions. A psychologist who is knowledgeable about the handicapping conditions as well as able to assess the children and get an accurate idea of their functioning level can be of great help to the educator planning an educational program. Those who lack the skills can be of no help to the teacher and of great detriment to the child, because the assessment can be reported in such a negative way and project such poor prognosis that the child is believed incapable of learning. A psychologist with little expectation for gains can pass that attitude to others who will be working with the child. Others' expectations in turn are lowered and the lack of gains in a child may become a self-fulfilling prophecy rather than a reflection of true potential.

A speech clinician as a team member can evaluate the method and level of communication skills of the child. Because orthopedic disabilities are often accompanied by speech problems, a nonverbal means of communication may have to be developed for the child to communicate needs. A well-trained speech clinician can provide information as to the types of nonverbal communications that might be appropriate for each child, as well as whether the child might be able to use the many communication devices that are currently available.

An assessment should also include some indication of the family involvement and expectations for the child. A social worker on the team should be able to appraise the parents and siblings as part of the assessment process. Whether the family members are able to carry out suggestions that have been made by professionals is important. Family members can provide information as to the person who will be best able to provide the greatest amount of information about the child and the person with whom cooperative efforts can be set up between school and home. Previous experiences of the child and whether the child related positively or negatively to them can be supplied by family members if the child is unable to provide them. Since most children with orthopedic handicaps have spent a great deal of their lives in hospitals, under doctor's care, and in treatment that is often painful and grueling, it is important to know an individual child's reactions to those experiences. It is also important to know how the other members of the family regard such treatment and the efforts that must be extended to get the child to appointments, through surgery or hospitalizations, and the view taken toward the expenses involved. A few years ago, the author was involved in an infant education program. At that time, it cost about $12,000 a year for each of the first six years of a spina bifida child's life to provide adequate medical services. Today the figure would be even greater. Expenses included the neurosurgery for the initial placement of the spinal cord, membrane and fluid back within the spinal column; shunt operations and revision; urogenital surgery, treatment and care; braces; physical therapy; walkers; crutches; etc. The cost did not include transportation to and from the medical centers for care, baby-sitters for the child's siblings while the child was taken to medical centers or while the child was visited during hospitalization, or the time deducted from the parents' paychecks for lost work while they were with the child for medical treatment or during the frequent hospitalizations. This can cause a tremendous drain on a family's resources and the attitude of the other family members toward the child can be a reflection of this tremendous outlay and the sacrifices made by family members. It is important for the social worker to assess the family attitude and involvement with the idea of involving the total family in the educational program that will be developed for the child.

The membership of the assessment team will vary for each child, according to individual needs. Music therapists, adaptive physical educators, urologists, cardiologists, dental specialists, and others, when appropriate, should play an active part in assessing the child's needs, and in helping to design a program that will aid the child to develop to the greatest degree possible.

Of particular importance in designing an educational program is the information gained by the educator during the assessment period. The learning stages, process, and content demonstrated during the assessment process by the child should all be examined. Learner variables should be scrutinized to determine the type and amount of material received by the child and whether sensory or perceptual problems were exhibited. Special education placement procedures usually specify norm-referenced tests to determine eligibility for placement. This type of test was discussed previously as a test standardized on a normal population of children. Though any such test is not valid when used with exceptional children, such tests are usually required and/or attempted. Criterion-referenced tests are also used. By this means, each child is measured against his own growth to determine whether set instructional objectives have been attained.

While determining the achievement level of each child, additional observations are made. What are the basic skill levels in the various academic areas being tested? How does the child attack problems encountered during the testing? How does the child face frustration? What causes frustration? What seems to reward the child during the testing situation? Does the child complete tasks? How long does it take? Does the handicapping condition contribute to the length of time involved? How willing is the child to try new things? How much dependency is shown? What are the strengths and weaknesses shown in the perceptual and cognitive areas? Is adaptive equipment necessary for the child to respond? Does it help if such equipment is used? Does positioning the child aid responses? What social skills are revealed? How does the child relate to adults? How does the child relate to peers? If there has been no situation observed where the child has to interact in some ways with peers, such a situation should be created. Often orthopedically handicapped children are raised in an adult environment and have gained no skills in relating to their peer group. Some children reach the teen-age years with social skills restricted to interaction on a preschooler's parallel play level.

Placing the Child

After the child has been assessed and the staff has reached a decision as to the child's strengths and weaknesses and the type of environment where these strengths and weaknesses can be served, a decision must be made concerning the most appropriate, least restrictive environment for educating the child. The most desirable and least restrictive environment is in the regular classroom with normal peers, if the child has the potential for that placement. It has been mentioned previously that the range of abilities and handicaps in children with orthopedic problems runs to broad extremes. When deciding on the most appropriate placement, it will be necessary to keep this range in mind, for children will need placements along the same broad range.

SERVICE DELIVERY MODELS

There are probably more settings that serve the orthopedically handicapped than any other type of handicapping condition. Many are served in public schools in regular classrooms, in itinerant services, in resource settings, and in self-contained classrooms with other children with orthopedic problems or other types of handicapping conditions. Children will also be found in classes that have been set up in agencies such as the United Cerebral Palsy, Easter Seal, Association for Retarded Citizens, etc. Not too many years ago, most classes were found in those locations. With mandatory education, the numbers of such classes are decreasing and only very young children or adults above school age are still being served in large numbers by private agencies. Agency efforts are now expended on other aspects of handicapping conditions since public money is currently available for education.

Very young physically handicapped children are also being served in the home. Itinerant services, with or without some type of group meetings for the children and/or their parents, are also a means of serving the young child. Services for preschool children take many forms: some children are served in self-contained classes, others in special classes with a few normal children integrated into the setting, some attend regular preschool classes consisting predominantly of normal children, others are served in their homes with occasional group sessions held for socialization purposes. Still others are served in the home with the parents meeting regularly once a week to once a month for parent training. Because some of the physically handicapping conditions are identifiable at birth, those children are often enrolled in educational programs in infancy. The variety of services for very young children can accommodate the diversity of needs of the parents, infants, and handicapping conditions.

Some older children also are served in their homes where they are tutored individually. Other homebound children are connected by phone or radio to a teacher and other children. These children spend varying hours "in class." Switches or conference call telephones allow them to ask the teacher questions and allow them an opportunity to answer the teacher's questions. All can hear the questions of others and soon learn the voices of their various "classmates." Such students can thus participate in a more normal educational setting by becoming a part of a classroom, even though it is "at a distance." This service delivery model allows one teacher to serve a number of children and cuts the costs to the local school district. This allows widely separated children in rural areas to become members of a single class. Such phone lines have also been used so that physically handicapped students can enroll in college classes (Schemeller, 1975).

Hospitalized orthopedically handicapped children are also served by their school district itinerant teachers who are hired to serve all of the hospitalized and homebound students within the district. Some districts have a regulation that only children who will be out for a prolonged period of time will be served by this means. Children who will be out of school only a short time have assignments made by their regular teachers.

Some children are served by itinerant teachers who may teach children from one or more school districts, depending upon the numbers of children needing service, the numbers of teachers available, and the rules under which they operate. Usually, the itinerant teacher contacts the child's local district and coordinates the assignments the child's teacher will cover during the period of hospitalization. The itinerant teacher then tries to keep the child current with those assignments. The itinerant teacher may serve such children in hospital locations individually at their bedsides, or in a central hospital location where a class is held.

Teaching such a class is an interesting experience. There may be long-term children who will be enrolled throughout the school year because of some type of chronic orthopedic condition that requires prolonged hospital care. Others will be there only a short time but will need to keep current with their studies. Others will attend for varying periods of time, with the population changing constantly and the children often missing the class periods because of medical conditions.

Televised classrooms are also available, and in hospitals or home settings they represent a slight change from the radio and telephone classrooms. The children are able to see the classroom, and vice versa, as a part of some types of televised classrooms. Other television classes have packaged cassettes or video tapes of specific lessons that the children are able to view when they are played through the television sets in their homes or hospital rooms. The parent and/or the itinerant teacher are responsible for checking each child's individual assignments which accompany the tapes. Tapes have a weakness in that they do not provide the socialization needed by many of the isolated children and also do not allow for a great deal of individualization. It then becomes necessary for the teacher to individualize for each particular child. Because of the wide diversity of handicapping conditions and the multiple problems that may accompany them, such individualization is imperative.

Children with mild orthopedic handicaps can usually be placed with normal peers in regular classrooms. There may or may not be a need for some type of special education itinerant help. Any medical or therapeutic help can usually be obtained within the school on a regular basis from staff assigned to the building on either an itinerant or permanent basis. Such services may also be scheduled after school hours so that the children do not miss academic work while in therapy. Since any children who are scheduled for therapy during school hours will miss something of what goes on during the class period, it is important to schedule therapy after school hours or at periods during the day when the child will not miss an opportunity for academic or social interaction with peers.

It is important to remember that some children with moderate and severe degrees of orthopedic handicapping conditions will also be assessed as functioning on a level where placement within the regular classroom is most appropriate. This entails more problems than for the mildly handicapped, for the necessity of adaptive equipment for moderately and severely involved children is much greater than for those who are mildly involved. Children may be so physically involved there is little ability to move even one part of their bodies and yet their intellectual skills allow them to compete and learn with normal peers. The problem then becomes one of finding a means to transport them to school, a way to position them in the classrooms, and a way for them to indicate their needs and to ask and answer questions within their physical limitations.

Other students will be placed in resource classes where they can have assistance with their studies but will also spend at least part of the day with normal children. Services necessary for this least restrictive placement might consist of help from the special education teacher while attempting to learn to use a communication device, from the physical or occupational therapist for therapy, or from an adaptive physical education teacher.

Children who have severe orthopedic handicapping conditions are more often found in self-contained special classes. Reasons for forming and placing the children in such a setting include: (1) the amount of time that it takes the child to perform tasks when there is little movement; (2) the amount and types of intensive therapy necessary to maintain this movement, to keep contractures from forming; and (3) the amount of individual attention the child must have in assuming adequate performance (Sternat and Messina, 1977). Children should only be placed in a special class if that is the most appropriate for their educational needs. If the same type of intensive work can be carried on in a less segregated setting, it should be done there.

If a segregated setting is the least restrictive, it is important that physical and occupational therapists integrate their work with the child into the classroom rather than removing the children for therapy. This will allow the teacher and aides the opportunity to observe the therapy needed and the types of positioning necessary to prevent contractures. In this manner, communication between teacher and therapist is assured, and the small amount of time spent with the child by the therapist can be multiplied because the teacher, aides, and hopefully, the parents, will know the procedures and be able to carry them out throughout the day (Utley, Holvoet, & Barnes, 1977).

Patterns of service delivery systems for intervention vary with the different ancillary services delivered to the child. Children may be serviced in their homes, hospitals, or schools by some type of medical personnel. Various types of therapy may be offered: occupational, physical and speech. Thus children who are preschoolers and served in their homes, or who are older and physically unable to travel to a center, can partake of the same types of services provided to the school or hospitalized children. Sometimes the therapists serve the children by arriving in vans fully equipped for the children's needs. If it is possible the children are served inside the vans, using all of the equipment provided. Otherwise, the therapists bring in the equipment from the vans and serve the children who are unable to leave their rooms. Often such equipment is left for a period of time so that the parent or teacher can continue to use it between visits from the therapists.

The value of such educational and therapeutic intervention has proven to be most useful when applied early in a child's life. Children with orthopedic handicaps who are identified early and who have maximum intervention will have fewer of the accompanying handicaps such as blindness and deafness, because the cause of these accompanying handicaps can often be prevented or corrected. Early physical therapy services with instruction given to the parents on how to position and brace the child at home, should result in children being free of contractures and able to use their braces and crutches (or walkers) to the maximum. By the time they are of school age, the children should have learned how to climb steps and walk inclines. They should know how to fall so that there is no fear and so they will not hurt themselves when they do fall, which is inevitable. Parents should be instructed in the emotional climate necessary for their children's development so that they are not overprotected but rather allowed to get the normal amount of bumps and bruises that will allow them to learn from the world about them. The children should be aware of their environment and use their perceptual and conceptual skills to obtain information from it. If there is an accompanying sensory handicap, the children should know how to use their residual senses to obtain maximum input from them. They should have had experiences with actual objects so that they can begin to mentally process these objects in a more abstract symbolic form such as with pictures, figures, and words. They should have language experiences so that they can use language as a learning tool. Furthermore, work in each of these skill areas should begin as early as possible in the lives of crippled children.

Children with the skills listed above may be able to be placed with their normal peers. The school principal may need to be sold on the idea that they will not fall down the steps, injure themselves, and sue the school. Some crippled children may need surgery so that their toileting problems can be better accepted by teacher and peers. Sometimes transportation will have to be provided for them. But aside from such problems, it does mean that they will be able to attend the least restrictive setting and become a member of their peer group.

Children placed in such settings still need to be served by the special educator. Problems encountered by the children or the teachers need to be examined so that help can be supplied. Sometimes simple intervention can be given with very little effort. One child was able to go on a field trip when the special education teacher brought a wagon for his use. Another child was able to carry his books and materials to classes even though both hands were busy with his crutches, when a backpack was provided. Although neither of these illustrations directly deal with learning in the regular classroom, they are illustrative of the type of help that teachers request and that allow children to partake of their "mainstream" or least restrictive placement to the fullest.

ADAPTIVE EQUIPMENT

The types of aid which orthopedically handicapped children must have to be able to function within a regular classroom varies from child to child. Some adaptive equipment will be the type that can be found or made from things around the house. A seminar held at Indiana University resulted in a publication that shows how to use bleach bottles and other usually discarded items for splints, spoon holders, and other adaptive aids (Slominski, 1970). Corrugated cardboard can be used to make corner chairs, book holders, and stools. Items such as bolsters and rolls can be developed at home from coffee cans, towels, rolls of paper towels, etc., and used for positioning.

These items have been mentioned because it is often assumed that all equipment must be purchased and must be tailor made to each child's specifications. Although it is true that equipment should meet the specific body specifications and needs of the individual child, equipment can also be used by other children if it is adjustable. Such adjustability seems mandated to meet the needs of the growing child and the further use of equipment after one child has outgrown it.

Adaptive devices are of several types (Campbell, Green and Carlson, 1977; Lowman and Klinger, 1969; Robinault, 1973). Some are for positioning, some for locomotion, some for communication and education, others for life support and still others for personal grooming and hygiene or for household aids. Some can be used to position the child for the greatest comfort, mobility, or hand use, to prevent contractures, or to develop head support. Positioning equipment varies from such items as wheelchairs to corner chairs that can be used independently or used within a wheelchair. The muscle extension pattern often exhibited by spastic children is broken up by the corner chair because it keeps the children's shoulders forward and they remain in a flexed position that allows them better use of their hands. An extension pattern, once the children are in it, prohibits movement, and the children continue to further extend themselves, with shoulders and head pressing farther back, prohibiting movement. Many adaptive devices are used to break up the extension patterns children exhibit. The physical positioning of children thus becomes important, for proper positioning can aid in movement.

Children who are positioned properly while seated in regular classroom chairs or in their wheelchairs should have their hip joints, knees, and ankles bent at 90-degree angles. This helps to prohibit contractions and shortening of the muscles that result in the joints being pulled out of line and in their eventual lack of use. Adaptive equipment may consist of adjustable straps to secure children in chairs, to prevent falls, and to prevent the body from leaving the 90-degree sitting position to go into an extension pattern that can result in the child slipping from the chair.

Pillows, sandbags, rolled towels, and covered coffee cans of differing sizes can be used to help position individual children. Small juice cans, soup cans, and/or dowels are sometimes placed on chairs to position the children's legs to prevent scissoring or frogging of the legs. Prone boards can be purchased or made from patterns available from most Cerebral Palsy and Easter Seal Centers. Prone boards can be propped against a table or other surface to allow the children who can support their body weight to be placed on their stomachs in a flexed position to gain better head control, use of the hands, and standing tolerance. It also allows eye contact with peers and teachers and if used at home, allows the children opportunity to eat at the family table.

Wedges of wood or foam can be used by the children who are placed prone, face down, on the floor. Standing tables, which hold the orthopedically handicapped in an upright position, may also be used for some children.

More involved equipment may be indicated for profoundly involved children. Such children are unable to move themselves and must rely on others to care for all their needs. Adaptive equipment can allow the child to accomplish some of those movements independently as well as respond to the environment, even though the responses may be in different and alternative forms.

Communication and education equipment may consist of a head piece with points attached for children who have fairly good head control but are unable to move their hands or feet voluntarily. Such a head stick or stylus will allow the child to type out messages on a typewriter that has been adapted by a plastic or metal template lying over the keys of the typewriter so that only the surfaces of the keys are available to poke. The head stick is thus able to touch the individual keys without sticking between the keys or without touching two letters at one time. Such templates can be made or purchased. Other equipment uses a foot, hand, or head indicator connected to electronic equipment to record or type the messages received.

Slings may be constructed to help move arms. Slings can also be used to facilitate eating or shaving when there is little use of the arms or limited arm and wrist rotation needed for such self-care activities.

All types of projection instruments are available for those who cannot view their environment in the normal manner. Ceiling projectors are available for those who are on their backs. Automatic page turners can be used by those who are unable to turn pages of books. The variety of adaptive equipment is limited only by the ingenuity of the person trying to adapt equipment to the needs of the handicapped individual.

Crippled children who have difficulty in handling textbooks or in reading them are now eligible for talking-book services through the Library of Congress and its regional libraries. Records, tapes and cassettes, and the equipment to use them are available, without charge, to those who qualify.

A large amount of money has been spent by the federal government and by private sources to develop communication devices for children so severely involved that they cannot communicate independently but must rely on artificial means. A very simple communication device allows the child who has only the use of the eyes to look at a pictured object to communicate basic needs. Eye movements to look at a picture of a bed, glass of water, toilet, or food can communicate to others what is wanted. Other devices have letters that can be selected by various means for the children who have the ability to read and write. Such letters can be selected by using the eyes to look in varying directions in a sort of code, by using limited head control to point to letters with a head stick, by using a gross movement to stop an electrically operated scanning device when a desired letter appears, and by a gross hand movement over a surface with pictures, letters, or words of common use, resulting in the chosen symbol appearing on a television screen or on a printout tape for the reader to see.

The Bureau of Education for the Handicapped has funded a project designed to produce a compilation of communication devices that are presently available (Vanderheiden and Grilley, 1976; Vanderheiden and Harris-Vanderheiden, 1976). Currently, the primary need is not for development of more equipment, but rather to disseminate information regarding the many things that are available and to obtain the often large amounts of money needed for their purchase.

There is a much greater market for adaptive equipment than ever before, and many have entered the business of adaptive equipment production. There are currently so many sources that merely locating them can be a major task. The Bureau of Education for the Handicapped has funded a project to develop methods for cataloging and indexing adaptive and assistive equipment. The result of that project is a file of catalogs, an index-glossary, and a locator which links the functional need to the manufacturers of the equipment. The system includes 666 items made by 237 manufacturers, producing 32,080 cross references (ISAARE, 1976). The catalogs available through this source require a two-drawer filing cabinet for storage. As the interest in this area grows, there undoubtedly will be even greater numbers of items as well as manufacturers.

There is also a great deal of information available concerning other types of media, materials, and resources available to the teacher of the handicapped learner. Although established for all types of exceptional learners, they particularly apply to crippled children because of the multiplicity of problems exhibited. A teacher may have all of the types of handicapping conditions exhibited within one classroom, necessitating great imagination and intelligence in programming for them. Although the needs of some children can be met by such simple efforts as taping down their papers or placing some insulation tape around the edges of a desk to prevent objects from being knocked off by extraneous movements, others may need extensive adaptive equipment as well as specially adapted materials to meet their perceptual, motor, and language problems. The needs of crippled children cannot be met merely by medical intervention and prosthetic devices, but these factors must be taken into account, adapting the total environment with skillful application of the principles of learning.

EARLY INTERVENTION

The past ten years have seen an increased emphasis on early education of handicapped children. At first there was the belief that only children of school age could benefit from an education. Early education, for both normal and exceptional children, was felt to be a province of the home. School age was then lowered to three in a number of states. Many professionals thought that three years of age would be the minimum age at which children with orthopedic handicaps could be clearly identified. Although abnormalities and differences often were observed from birth, medical people in particular thought that a clear diagnosis should not be made until the abnormal motor patterns that resulted from brain damage clearly appeared. It was not unusual for children to be diagnosed after three years of age, because some types of cerebral palsy do not manifest clearly identifiable motor problems until that time.

Physicians no longer wait for the appearance of inadequate or maladaptive motor responses to diagnose orthopedic conditions, but look at signs such as hyper- or hypotonicity, delayed motor milestones and hyper- or absent deep tendon reflexes, as well as the presence of abnormal reflex patterns to make a diagnosis of motor problems in need of early intervention. The de-emphasis of some traditional special education labels has contributed to an earlier referral for special education purposes. When children previously had to be labeled as "brain-damaged," "cerebral palsied," or "epileptic," the doctor was unsure if the child would actually develop into the more severe case where special education would be required. Since "high risk" children and those in potential danger of developing handicapping conditions are now included in early intervention classes, doctors and other medical personnel are referring more children and at younger ages. Cases of spina bifida are now being referred to educators from the newborn nursery because medical personnel have seen the advantages of early intervention, not only for the children but also for the parents in terms of their expectations, ability to physically manage the children, and lack of interest in institutionalization (Rembalt and Roth, 1977).

Two distinct federal programs have been particularly effective in promoting earlier referral and treatment of physically handicapping conditions: The Handicapped Children's Early Education Program and the Developmental Disabilities Act. The former, founded under the auspices of the Bureau of Education for the Handicapped, first began in 1969. The purpose of the program was to create a number of model demonstration programs throughout the country that could be used by others desiring to set up similar programs. The demonstration centers were funded for a three-year period. Federal money was then available for the staff who had set up the original program to meet with others interested in adopting the model, to advise and guide them in implementation. Hundreds of programs have been established because of this funding source. The success of the program is evidenced by the fact that seven early intervention projects were among the first projects validated by the Joint Effectiveness Review Panel within the U. S. Office of Education as making a demonstrable difference in the growth of the children served. Clearly, the program has alerted professionals and parents to the effectiveness of early education for handicapped children.

The Developmental Disabilities Act is funded through the Office of Human Development, Department of Health, Education and Welfare. Developmental disabilities (DD) include: mental retardation, cerebral palsy, epilepsy, and in the 1975 law, autism. The disability must originate before the age of eighteen for children to be eligible. The law is funded for those in whom a handicap is substantial enough that the ability to function normally in society is threatened (Schloss, 1975). Funding for university-affiliated facilities, which provide demonstration services to the developmentally disabled, and for interdisciplinary training programs has been particularly effective in helping all professions become aware of the problems of handicapped children. The 1975 version of the DD law requires states to develop deinstitutionalization and institutional reform programs, with 10 percent of the state's allotment used for this purpose in 1976 and 30 percent in the following years. This undoubtedly will continue to affect the lives of young developmentally disabled children for years to come. It has resulted in state and private agencies exerting efforts to aid the child in the home with early intervention, as well as providing other services such as respite care to families who might otherwise be overwhelmed by the birth of an exceptional child and move to place that child in an institutional setting. Advocacy and protection of the rights of the developmentally disabled are also parts of the legislation, as well as the requirement that all organizations receiving DD grants practice affirmative action regarding employment and advancement of qualified handicapped individuals. *Amicus,* 1977; *National Spokesman,* 1975). The DD legislation has also resulted in the awarding of grants involving participation of all four national voluntary agencies serving developmentally disabled people: The Epilepsy Foundation of America, the National Association for Retarded Citizens, The National Society for Autistic Children, and United Cerebral Palsy (*National Spokesman,* 1977). The cooperative efforts of these voluntary agencies that have involved themselves in the cause of DD children should contribute much to future development of services in this area.

ADULT SERVICES

While legislation has resulted in many improvements for preschool and school-age handicapped children, there has also been recent legislation that should affect the children positively as they grow into adulthood. Section 504 of the Vocational Rehabilitation Act was passed in 1973 but no regulations were provided regarding how the law would be implemented. The regulations finally were published in 1977 after months of hearings, commentary, review, and pressure from many groups sympathetic to the handicapped population.

Section 504 includes such provisions as: (1) every child is entitled to a free public education; (2) handicapped children are to be educated with the nonhandicapped to the maximum extent; (3) the cost of residential placement because of handicapping conditions must be met by public authorities; and (4) facilities offering services must be modified to provide access to handicapped people (*National Spokesman,* 1977). The latter point has generated much discussion and excitement since it implies that access to services cannot be denied because facilities are not modified to handle nonambulatory or other handicapped persons. Barrier-free architecture is now mandated and tax incentives are available for qualified agencies which comply. Although in effect for some time as applied to building and construction with federal funds, the current law means that standing buildings must be modified so as to be barrier free. Instruction in independent travel and use of community resources, as well as other supportive services, must follow.

These changes should allow older physically handicapped people to take a greater part in the world around them. In the past, too often children were active during the school years when transportation and special facilities were provided. Upon formal completion of schooling, it often meant that the individual was relegated to a home situation from which there could be little movement. Adults who had good socialization and mobility skills were often left in their homes for great periods of time because there were few places to go and no ways to get there. Their worlds thus became smaller and smaller, with extremely limited communication with the outside world. Institutionalization often resulted.

Now more jobs will open for the physically handicapped, and there will be more people and more money to train them. Architectural and transportation barriers will be removed so they can get to and from work.

Many architectural barriers are simple to eliminate, others are more difficult. The author remembers one very involved discussion with some school architects who couldn't understand why it was necessary to have lavatories placed adjacent to the classrooms when such placement would greatly increase the cost of the building. Only after watching the time consumed as a child laboriously traveled the length of the hall, and watching the same child encounter the many restrictions placed in the regular school toileting facilities, was the point made clear. Inaccessibility of phones, drinking fountains, cafeteria tray holders, revolving doors, as well as uncountable other necessities has done much to inadvertently discriminate against the handicapped. Now that architectural barriers are to be removed, it means that more nonambulatory adults will be able to attend social events, as well as obtain and keep employment. Removal of physical barriers, including those in public transportation, and inclusion of handicapping conditions as a condition of employment should do much to widen the horizons of handicapped children and adults whose future prior to this time looked very bleak.

CONCLUSION

The crippled population has changed considerably during the past twenty years. With continuing medical and surgical research, further development of intervention treatments such as biofeedback, and new uses of older established therapy for those who are currently classified as crippled, the population should continue to change as should the accessibility and receptivity of the world around them. For those who are born today with handicapping conditions, the future has never been so bright. With all the many different agencies, organizations, bureaus, and individuals involved in helping to normalize life for those born with physical limitations, there is nowhere to go but up.

REFERENCES

Apgar, Virginia, and Beck, Joan. *Is My Baby All Right?* New York: Pocket Books, 1974.

Apropos. A publication of the National Center on Educational Media and Materials for the Handicapped. Columbus, OH: Ohio State University, Spring-Summer, 1976.

Campbell, P.; Green, K.; and Carlson, L. Approximating the norm through environmental and child-centered prosthetics and adaptive equipment, in E. Sontag (ed.), *Educational Programming for the Severely and Profoundly Handicapped.* Reston, VA: Council for Exceptional Children, 1977.

Carter, S. Assessing prognosis after a child's first febrile seizure. *National Spokesman*, April 1975, p. 5.

CEC receives child abuse project. *Insight*, July 30, 1976.

Center for Disease Control. *Rh Hemolytic Disease Surveillance.* Annual Report, June 1975.

Cooperative efforts between agencies create programs. *National Spokesman*, April 1977, p. 9.

Epilepsy Foundation of America. *Current information*, October 1971.

Haessermann, E. *Developmental Potential of Preschool Children*. New York: Grune & Stratton, Inc., 1958.

Hart, V. The use of many disciplines with the severely and profoundly handicapped, in E. Sontag (ed.), *Educational Programming for the Severely and Profoundly Handicapped*. Reston, VA: Council for Exceptional Children, 1977.

Haynes, U. *The First Three Years—Programming for Atypical Infants and their Families*. A United Cerebral Palsy Nationally Organized Collaborative Project to Provide Comprehensive Services. New York: United Cerebral Palsy Association, Inc., 1974.

HEW issues interim DD advocacy guidelines. National Center for Law and the Handicapped, *Americus*, February 1977, pp. 11–12.

Highlights of 1975 national data. National Study on Child Neglect and Abuse Reporting. Englewood, CO: Children's Division, American Humane Association, 1976.

ISAARE (Information System for Adaptive, Assistive, and Recreational Equipment). Portland, OR: United Cerebral Palsy Association of Oregon, 1976.

Jedrysek, E. *Psychoeducational Evaluation of the Preschool Children—A Manual using the Haessermann Approach*. New York: Grune & Stratton, Inc., 1972.

Johnston, R., and Harryman, S. Postural reflexes—identification and clinical significance. *Syllabus of Instructional Courses*, Twenty-ninth annual meeting. New Orleans: American Academy for Cerebral Palsy, September 24–28, 1975.

Joseph Califano signs S.504 regulations. *National Spokesman*, June 1977, pp. 1–6.

Kappelman, M. Prenatal and perinatal factors which influence learning, in J. Hellmuth (ed.), *Exceptional Infant*, vol. 2, Seattle, WA: Special Child Publications, 1972.

Lowman, E., and Klinger, J. *Aids to Independent Living*. New York: McGraw-Hill, Inc., 1969.

Pearson, P., and Williams, C. *Physical Therapy: Services in the Developmental Disabilities*. Springfield, IL: Charles C Thomas, Publisher, 1972.

President Ford signs DD act. *National Spokesman*, Nov.–Dec. 1975, p. 1.

Rembalt, R., and Roth, B. *Cerebral Palsy and Related Developmental Abilities—Prevention and Early Care: An Annotated Bibliography*. (4 vols.), Columbus, OH: Ohio State University Press, 1975–1977.

Robinault, I. (ed.). *Functional Aids for the Multiply Handicapped*. New York: Harper & Row, Publishers, 1973.

Schemeller, K. Attending college when you're home-bound. *Community and Junior College Journal*, April 1975, pp. 28–29.

Scherzer, A., and Gullo, S. *Diagnosis, Management and Treatment of the Infant with Cerebral Palsy*. Instructional course #5, Twenty-ninth meeting, New Orleans: American Academy for Cerebral Palsy, September 24–28, 1975.

Schloss, I. *Washington Report,* December 1975.

———. General revenue sharing, *Washington Report,* February 1977.

Slominski, A. *Please Help Us Help Ourselves—Inexpensive Adapted Equipment for the Handicapped.* Indianapolis, IN: Cerebral Palsy Center, Indiana University Medical Center, 1970.

Soeffing, M. Abused children are exceptional children. *Exceptional Children,* November 1975, pp. 126–133.

Sternfeld, Leon. *Report of the Medical Director to the Members of the Corporation.* Annual conference, Washington, DC: United Cerebral Palsy Associations, Inc., April 22, 1977.

Sternat, J., Messina, R. et al. Occupational and physical therapy services for severely handicapped students: Toward a naturalized public school service delivery model, in E. Sontag (ed.), *Educational Programming for the Severely and Profoundly Handicapped.* Reston, VA: Council for Exceptional Children, 1977.

Swingard, C. *The Child with Spina Bifida.* Patient publication series No. 6. New York: Institute of Rehabilitation Medicine, New York University Medical Center, 1975.

———. Time trends in anencephaly and spina bifida birth defects monitoring data. *Congenital Malformations Surveillance.* July 1974–June 1975 issued December 1975.

Utley, B.; Holvoet, J.; and Barnes, K. Handling, positioning, and feeding the physically handicapped, in E. Sontag (ed.), *Educational Programming for the Severely and Profoundly Handicapped.* Reston, VA: Council for Exceptional Children, 1977.

Vanderheiden, G., and Grilley, K. *Non-Vocal Communication Techniques and Aids for the Severely Physically Handicapped.* Baltimore, MD: University Park Press, 1976.

———, and Harris-Vanderheiden, D. Communication techniques and aids for the non-vocal severely handicapped, in L. Lloyd (ed.), *Communication Assessment and Intervention Strategies.* Baltimore, MD: University Park Press, 1976.

CHAPTER 8

ORAL COMMUNICATION DISORDERS

JOHN HATTEN

INTRODUCTION

Development of speech and language is one of the most demanding of man's activities. It calls for intricate movements of the tongue, lips, jaw, and soft palate; coordination of respiration, phonation, resonation, and articulation; complex interplay of the auditory, visual, and tactile/kinesthetic systems to provide feedback to the brain; and most importantly, the construction of word sequences which satisfy all the rules of syntax, semantics, morphology, phonology, and pragmatics of a given language. Luckily, the newborn infant has not been told how complex this task is and so proceeds to conquer the complexities of the language and the speech production process in a few short years. Indeed, it would be difficult to convince the mother of a typical three-year-old of the enormity of the task of learning speech and language. Although speech and language are learned behavior, they are not taught. No one is able to teach a child how to talk, in the formal sense of the word, primarily because in order to teach we would have to know what we do when we talk. The most profound of experts could not satisfactorily explain all of the parameters of language competence and performance, much less put such an explanation into a form understandable by an infant.

The primary parameters of speech include phonation, articulation, and resonation. Phonation is technically the end product of the valving of the airstream as it is being expelled from the lungs, producing a sound which has a distinguishable pitch, loudness, and quality. However, the product of phonation does not resemble any of the speech sounds until it passes through the throat, oral, and nasal cavities. Pitch, loudness, and quality are the perceived characteristics of a person's speaking voice which result from the physical characteristics of the signal. Pitch refers to the highness or lowness of a tone relative to the musical scale, loudness refers to the prominence of the sound, and quality refers to both the degree of pleasantness of the voice and those unique tonal characteristics which distinguish one speaker from another. When you hear a person over the telephone, you identify the speaker partially on word selection, pitch, and loudness, but primarily on the quality of the speaking voice.

The terms articulation and resonation refer to the alteration of the sound in the vocal tract once it has been produced or phonated in the larynx. Articulation involves the constriction of the air stream resulting in the modification of the phonated tone, thus producing the specific sounds or phones of a language. McDonald's (1964a) definition of articulation emphasizes the dynamic nature of the process and stresses the influence that sounds have on the production of sounds adjoining them.

> Articulation is a process consisting of a series of overlapping, ballistic movements which place varying degrees of obstruction in the way of the outgoing air stream and simultaneously modify the size, shape, and coupling of resonating cavities (p. 87).

Resonation influences the production of vowel sounds. The cavities above the vocal folds resonate (enhance) or damp (decrease) various components of the sound produced in the larynx. The shape and size of the cavities are the primary determinants of which frequency levels of the complex vocal tone are altered. Articulation movements causing greater constriction of the air stream are responsible for consonant sounds, while resonation alters the vocal tone to produce vowels and influence the quality of the voice.

Speech is an overt neuromuscular activity, but language is an internalized system. Language could be defined as a *socially acquired, primarily aural, inductively acquired symbol system used to communicate between and within individuals.*

The concept that language is *social acquired* is intended to underscore the importance of language stimulation in the natural setting. The most efficient environment for language learning is the social setting wherein children can become active agents who not only receive stimulation from their surroundings, but act upon such stimulation as well. The child is no longer seen as a passive learner in the language process, but rather as an active agent for change.

Language is *primarily oral/aural* in nature, although this is certainly not the exclusive channel of reception and expression. The learning of language is most efficient when hearing, the aural modality of reception, is intact and when the samples of language from which the child learns are presented orally. Similarly, the most efficient early means of expression of language is through speech.

The child learns the rules and complexities of language from samples of those rules presented individually. In other words, *inductive learning* is exemplified when generalized rules are learned from examples governed by those rules. Although we have no direct proof of how one learns the rules of a language, we can surmise that learning has taken place when one begins to behave as if one knows the rules (Slobin, 1971). Inductive learning, akin to generalization, is a key concept in language learning because the samples of any one particular language rule may be presented to a child only infrequently and in varying contexts.

Symbolic behavior implies a system of substitutions. The symbols of a language represent things, feelings, actions, and so on, and as such they serve as substitutes. The symbols of a language vary in many dimensions, such as degree of abstractness, clarity of referent, connotative implications, and others.

In the definition of language the word *system* is used to convey the rule-governed nature of language. Learning a language means learning rules. Five rule systems are usually described: phonology, semantics, syntax, morphology, and pragmatics. Space limitations do not permit elaboration on each of these categories; however, it is important to realize that there are rules that govern the acquisition of the sounds of a language (phonology), the meaning units of a language (semantics), the phrase structure and word ordering of a language (syntax), the meaning markers of a language (morphology), and the communicative values of language (pragmatics). Since the mid-1950s the study of language has been dominated by the investigation of syntax while current emphasis is on semantic and pragmatic rules.

Language is an abstract system which exists in the central nervous system of the individual. It is not, as such, an overt behavior nor is it directly observable, measurable, or testable. Speech is an overt and observable behavior which uses the language system as a prerequisite. Oral communicative disorders involve imperfections in one or both of these facets of behavior.

ISSUES IN DEFINITION OF COMMUNICATION DISORDERS

In order to present a satisfactory definition of a disordering condition in any domain, it is necessary to be able to satisfactorily define the normal state. As with so many human characteristics, it is difficult to identify such a "normal" condition regarding speech and language performance. Each individual can be placed on a continuum regarding accuracy of the various sounds of speech, pitch of the voice, pleasantness of the speaking voice, number of hesitations, and repetitions in speech, syntax, and so on. There is no universally accepted standard against which we can judge the various characteristics of a person's communication performance. We must trust our listening skills, scant and sometimes insufficient objective testing instruments, and environmental input in order to determine when a speech or language pattern constitutes a disorder.

Van Riper (1978) defined a speech disorder incorporating three major concepts: "Speech is abnormal when it deviates so far from the speech of other people that it calls attention to itself, interferes with communication, or causes the speaker or his listeners to be distressed" (p. 43). Generally, it is assumed that the first portion of the definition refers to negative attention. In many instances attention may be called to a person's manner of speech or vocal quality, but the listener response is positive or desirable. Many noted actors and actresses use their distinctive vocal quality as a tool, and although the speech pattern may call attention to itself, the attention is positive, desired, and useful in conveying some total message or portraying some image.

The question of how much of a speech or language difference is necessary to interfere with communication is obviously of paramount concern to speech clinicians. Unfortunately, however, the definitive answers are unavailable regarding even the most common of speech disorders. If an individual is unable to articulate the /r/ sound, for example, the profession of speech pathology cannot give an absolute answer to the question of how significantly that inability will interfere with communication. An early study (Adkins, 1959) done with rather small numbers of listeners has indicated that communication of information is not altered with single sound articulation errors; however, this writer has been involved with several pilot studies which indicate that single sound errors do significantly decrease the listener's acquisition of information. These studies have also indicated that listeners tend to rate speakers with articulation errors lower on scales of desirability and influence.

An added factor, not present in the Van Riper definition of communication disorders, must be the potential abusive power of certain types of speech patterns. Certain voice disorders, vocal strain for example, have the potential of actually causing physical change and damage to the vocal folds. Although the resultant acoustic speech pattern may not be attention gaining, nor interfere with communication nor be even noticeable to the speaker, it may constitute a speech disorder if it has a deleterious effect upon the speech-producing mechanism.

It is incumbent upon any definition of communication disorder to speak to the question of societal variations. Regional, cultural, or ethnic variations in speech and language performance do not, in themselves, constitute a communication disorder. Communication variations of individuals within a particular population must be measured and held up to the standards of that population rather than compared to the total population. The speech and language patterns of Black English, for example, are just as rule governed and just as elaborate as standard English.* Speakers of such a dialect should be considered candidates for remediation only if their speech and language pattern is outside of the norm for that culture. The option of learning standard English and standard speech patterns for added flexibility is looked upon as providing an alternative form of communication rather than correcting existing errors.

The definition of defective oral communication must include three dimensions: (1) variation of the speech and language signal relative to some standard, (2) influence of that acoustic and linguistic variation upon the intelligibility and information-bearing capability of the message, and (3) any impact or handicapping condition that results from the first two aspects (Emerick and Hatten, 1974). The profession of speech pathology has made significant progress, as noted earlier, in determining the degree of acoustic variation of a speech signal. However, there has been only limited progress in determining the influence of variations upon communication, and almost no progress in determining impact of communication variations upon the communicants.

PREVALENCE OF SPEECH DISORDERS

An operational method for determining how a profession defines its boundaries is to look at the prevalence figures promulgated throughout that profession. The incidence of oral communication disorders directly reflects how the profession defines disorder, since a high incidence would indicate rigid standards of correctness and a lower incidence would indicate greater permissible variation in speech and language patterns.

In a very real sense prevalence figures are self-fulfilling prophesies. If the major textbooks in a profession indicate that the competent practitioner of that profession will find a given percentage of the general population to exhibit a given characteristic, most dutiful individuals will make certain to come close to the expected norm.

Early prevalence figures in communicative disorders ranged as high as 15 to 20 percent. Young professions, reflecting a missionary zeal, tend to present spuriously high prevalence figures. More recent studies indicate a prevalence of 2 to 4 percent in the total school age population.

Another interesting phenomenon regarding prevalence of communicative disorders is the tendency to show higher prevalence for younger children and a decreasing prevalence for high school and adult populations. If 10 percent of a younger population are thought to have speech disorders and only 2 percent of an adult population, 8 percent of that younger pop-

---

*The term "Standard English" is not intended to imply correctness or a "standard to be achieved" but rather to indicate the speech and language pattern of the majority of the population. Variations of this pattern exist in all parts of the country and in many cultural and ethnic groups.

ulation must have developmental differences which will disappear with maturation. So long as there is no intervening clinical speech service the percentage of communicatively handicapped individuals should remain constant. Obviously what is needed is a tool for predicting those from the younger population who will maintain their communicative disorder through to adulthood and those who will correct this difference during maturation. The profession has made valid attempts to accomplish this task (Van Riper and Erickson, 1968). In general the prevalence of handicapping nondevelopmental oral communication differences in the school population, regardless of age, is probably no more than 4 percent.

CLASSIFICATION SYSTEMS

It is possible to tell a good bit about a discipline by studying the method of classification it uses. Communicative disorders has had a colorful if erratic history regarding the use of titles. The discipline itself is variously called speech pathology, speech correction, speech and hearing science, communicative disorders, communicology, and so forth. The titles used for the practitioners of the field are equally as varied, witness the use of the titles speech pathologist, speech clinician, speech therapist, speech correctionist, and even communicologist. All of these titles are being used and refer to people who conduct essentially the same function, although setting and clientele may vary. One might wonder if we are in the business of communication disorders or disordered communication. The discipline has yet to adopt a universally accepted nomenclature system, and this lack of uniformity extends to the classification system used to identify both the professional workers and the population served.

Two major methods of classification can be identified in the literature. One method classifies communicative disorders primarily on the basis of etiology (cause), and the other classifies primarily on the basis of symptom.

Classification systems based upon the etiology of the disorder imply that similar speech patterns tend to result from a given causal condition. Speech clinicians may indicate that one is working with a "cleft palate" child and assume that the listener will know something of the nature of the speech pattern because of the "universal" typical characteristics associated with that problem.

The term "organic" refers to a disorder whose underlying cause is a physical difference of the structures important to speech production. This physical difference could involve any of the major systems of the body (respiratory, nervous system, and so on) and could range from being life-threatening to having no medical implications. Organic disorders would include such problems as cerebral palsy, cleft palate, aphasia, and laryngectomy.

The term "functional" is used to imply a disorder whose causal factor is not directly related to *physical* difference in the organism. Essentially the problem lies in the aberrant functioning of a normal organism. Faulty learning, improper speech models, and emotional problems could be considered functional factors.

The dichotomy between organic and functional causes of speech problems becomes less distinct when one realizes that certain organic problems lead directly to psychological differences which in and of themselves could contribute to a speech disorder. For example, consider the problems of a cleft palate child whose organic difference leads to parental rejection which in turn results in emotional problems for the child. Conversely, it is quite possible for a child with a functional speech problem, such as abusive use of the voice, to develop growths on the vocal folds constituting an organic difference. The organic/functional classification scheme appears to be more a convenience of the classifier than a reality of conditions.

A more satisfactory method for classifying communication disorders is to label them according to the communicative pattern. This system labels according to symptoms and generally includes four types of disorders: language, articulation-resonance, voice, and rhythm.

Language Disorders in Children

Although language skills have long been realized as integral to school success, it has only been within the past twenty years that language disorders have been studied with any degree of scientific rigor. The current knowledge of language disorders is the result of a rather stormy mixture of psychology, linguistics, speech pathology, and learning disabilities.

Definition

Language was defined previously as a socially acquired, primarily aural, inductively acquired symbol system used to communicate between and within individuals. Since many definitions of language are available in the literature, it is important to put this definition into a schema that will set the stage for further discussions. Figure 8.1 differentiates three primary concepts which are central to the writer's definition of language. Pre-expressive and sublanguage behaviors are those factors which are necessary for the development of the language system but are not a part of the system itself. The language system of rules is a central nervous system capacity. Language dependent behaviors are those human activities such as speaking or reading which are dependent upon the language system, but not thought of as a part of the system as such.

The focus of this discussion is language as a symbolic process. Consequently, *a language disorder could be defined as an inability to learn and/ or use the rules of language appropriately to the intellectual ability of the individual.* Classically, there has been a distinction made between language delay and language disorder, but recent research (Morehead and

Fig. 8-1: Sublanguage, Language, and Language Dependent Areas of Behavior.

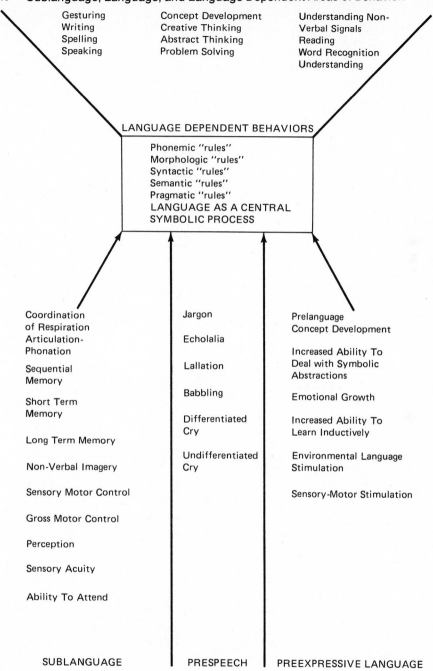

Gesturing
Writing
Spelling
Speaking

Concept Development
Creative Thinking
Abstract Thinking
Problem Solving

Understanding Non-
Verbal Signals
Reading
Word Recognition
Understanding

LANGUAGE DEPENDENT BEHAVIORS

Phonemic "rules"
Morphologic "rules"
Syntactic "rules"
Semantic "rules"
Pragmatic "rules"
LANGUAGE AS A CENTRAL
SYMBOLIC PROCESS

Coordination
of Respiration
Articulation-
Phonation

Sequential
Memory

Short Term
Memory

Long Term Memory

Non-Verbal Imagery

Sensory Motor Control

Gross Motor Control

Perception

Sensory Acuity

Ability To Attend

Jargon

Echolalia

Lallation

Babbling

Differentiated
Cry

Undifferentiated
Cry

Prelanguage
Concept Development

Increased Ability To
Deal with Symbolic
Abstractions

Emotional Growth

Increased Ability To
Learn Inductively

Environmental Language
Stimulation

Sensory-Motor Stimulation

SUBLANGUAGE   PRESPEECH   PREEXPRESSIVE LANGUAGE

Emerick, L., and Hatten, J., *Diagnosis and Evaluation in Speech Pathology,* 2d.
ed. Englewood Cliffs, N.J.: Prentice Hall, Inc. (In press, 1979 edition).

Ingram, 1973) indicates that the distinction is much clearer on paper than in reality. A language delay would be manifest by slower rate of development but normal sequence and structure. A child with disordered language would display not only a delay in language acquisition, but also aberrant patterns of development. Such a child would follow neither the rate nor the sequence of normal language development. This is conceptually very convenient, but further study is needed to determine its validity.

Prevalence

There are no satisfactory figures on the prevalence of language disorders in children. The primary reasons for the lack of consistent information are the widely varying definitions used for language disorder, and the fact that most language disordered children also have multiple articulation disorders, resulting in an overlapping of categories in incidence studies. Most professionals would probably agree that language disorders are the second most frequent oral communication disorder. Depending on the stringency of the definition used, probably from 1 to 2 percent of the school population can be said to have language disorders which cause significant communication and educational problems.

Etiology

Five primary factors are thought to be responsible for language disorders in children. These include environmental factors, mental retardation, emotional disturbance, minimal brain disorders, and hearing loss.

Early literature (Berry and Eisenson, 1956) cited numerous environmental factors as being important in language development. Such things as number of siblings, sex of the child, birth order, socioeconomic status of the family, and bilingualism were mentioned as influential. In the 1960s, however, there was a swing in emphasis away from factors external to the child, and most literature began placing less importance on the environment and more on the developmental characteristics of the child (Lenneberg, 1967). Recently many investigators have returned to studies of the impact of environmental factors on language development. Broen (1972) summarized a number of studies on parent-child interaction and concluded that parents of normally developing children do present language stimuli to the child in a manner designed to maximize learning. Contrary to some theorists' claims that children are "born" language learners, it is possible to conclude from current research that parents (environments) are natural language facilitators. If this current trend continues to prove fruitful in documenting the importance of parental interaction in language learning, it is evident that some language disorders may well be related to environmental deviations. In a sense we have come full circle in returning to a stress on environmental factors in language development, with present claims of environmental importance being based on empirical research.

The relationship between intellectual ability and language is primarily one of dependence of language upon cognition. Children seek to learn the linguistic structures which code their knowledge. In other words children's knowledge of the world motivates them to seek linguistic structures to symbolize this knowledge, and eventually the link between experience and language is made.

Mental retardation is thought to be a cause of language disorders since, in most instances, the language development of the moderately or severely retarded child is significantly behind that of normal children of similar age. This fact alone, however, should not constitute inclusion of mental retardation as an etiological category, since the child's language development should properly be compared with that of children of comparable *mental age*. In addition to the delay in language development observed in mentally retarded children, there are also often aberrant patterns of development, thus justifying the inclusion of the syndrome as a cause of language disorders.

Certain types of emotional disturbance may so severely interfere with children's interaction with their environment that normal language learning is impossible. A child may be so effectively "removed" from the surrounding environment that the normal stimulation of interaction is rendered ineffective, and language growth suffers. The language of severely disturbed children is often abnormal in structure as well as use.

The term "childhood aphasia" is used by some workers (Eisenson, 1972) to identify children whose language development is deviant due to some central nervous system difference which makes symbolic behavior difficult. Primary to this disorder are disabilities in auditory perception, inability to learn inductively, and lack of insight into the relationship of verbal stimuli with environmental events. Aphasic children are often mistakenly identified as deaf, and their behavior often resembles that of deaf children. The significant difference, however, is that the deaf child's disability is peripheral to the central nervous system (in most instances), and the child will, therefore, learn language if the ineffective pathway is circumvented.

Unless early and extreme measures are taken, children with profound hearing loss will not develop language at the normal age and rate (see chapter 9). Language is most naturally and easily learned through the aural channel. Obviously, in order for language to be learned, incoming stimuli must reach the central nervous system, and deafness will effectively block such transmission. Since all aspects of language must be taught directly and systematically to deaf children, their language is often incomplete and inaccurate.

Diagnostic Methods

The diagnosis of language disorders could easily be the topic for an entire volume. A multitude of tests and diagnostic formats have been published within the past fifteen years, and no volume could do justice to the amount of progress which is currently being made in the refinement of

Courtesy of the Lexington School for the Deaf.

diagnostic techniques.

Assessment of sublanguage skills would include investigation into such factors as ability to attend, sensory acuity, perception, perceptual-motor skills, gross motor skills, memory, and cognitive functioning. Obviously, there is no single test that will adequately evaluate such a wide variety of skills, and very often such an assessment must call for interdisciplinary investigation since no single professional will have the skills necessary to measure all areas. Similarly, measurement of language dependent behaviors includes the investigation into numerous skills such as spelling, reading, speaking, and math.

A logical outcome of diagnosis would be determination of the cause of the disorder. In the case of a language disorder, this determination may be of somewhat more importance than in other communicative disorders, since ultimate clinical intervention may be significantly shaped by the nature of the cause. The clinical approach to a deaf child is not identical to the clinical approach to an "autistic," or severely disturbed child, although their language performances may be quite similar on certain objective tests. Determination of the cause of language disorders is often a comprehensive and time-consuming task involving careful case history, parent interviews, psychological testing, and neurological examination, in conjunction with a total examination of the language skills of the child.

The examination of greatest relevance to this discussion is the measurement of the language system itself. Since language is an internal system rather than an overt behavior, there is no *direct* test of language. All tests measure some aspect of behavior and make hypotheses regarding the integrity of the language system itself. Such indirect methods have inherent weaknesses and in most instances, what is being measured is probably a low estimate of the child's actual language capacity. Testing the language system involves measurement of the comprehension and expression abilities of the individual across the various language components: phonemics, semantics, morphology, syntax, and pragmatics. These components are defined as follows:

Phonemics refers to the sound system of a language. The smallest units of any language which distinguish meaning are called phonemes.

Semantics refers to the meaning of a statement, the correlation between words and word groupings and the things and ideas to which they refer.

Morphology relates to the minimal units of a language which contain meaning— the morpheme. Morphemes are the meaning units of a language.

Syntax refers to the arrangements of words and word groupings in relation to one another.

Pragmatics may be broadly defined as the relationship between language and the language users. It has come to refer to the uses people make of language, such as to inform, control, question, and so on.

Phonemes are the smallest units which distinguish meaning; therefore, measurement of a child's comprehension ability at the phoneme level could involve auditory discrimination testing of minimally paired words. In such a task the child differentiates between such word pairs as cat/cap, sit/hit, and so on, displaying the ability to hear sound differences and knowledge that those differences influence meaning.

Comprehension of semantic units is measured through tests of understanding vocabulary. Tests such as the Peabody Picture Vocabulary Test (Dunn, 1965) and the Vocabulary Comprehension Scale (Bangs, 1975) are popular. The former assesses comprehension vocabulary using picture stimuli, while the Bangs test uses interactive play and cardboard objects.

Comprehension of morphological units and syntax are also measured by presenting various spoken stimuli and requesting the child to point to the picture named. The Test for Auditory Comprehension of Language (Carrow, 1970) is probably the most widely used measure of vocabulary, morphology, and syntax.

Two methods are employed as primary vehicles to assess expressive language: elicited imitation and spontaneous language sampling. Both procedures have advantages and disadvantages, and most language clinicians employ both when undertaking a complete diagnosis.

Elicited imitation involves sentence or sentence-part repetition, and has the advantage of being controlled, efficient, and stable. In typical elicited imitation tasks, sentences containing various grammatical structures are presented to the child for repetition. The premise upon which such procedures are based is that children will not include in their expressive language any grammatical construction which is not present in their basic store of linguistic knowledge. During imitation children will reduce the stimulus to conform to their own set of rules (McNeill, 1970). For example, if a child does not yet include a given rule of language in conversational speech, it will not be included in the child's imitation of a sentence. Length of the stimulus sentence, however, is a relevant factor. Statements that are too long or too short fail to achieve the desired result, since in long sentences the factor measured involves memory as well as rule knowledge, and in short statements the stimulus may be echoed without comparison to the rule system. Slobin and Welsh (1973) indicate that imitation tasks are most revealing when they put some stress on immediate memory.

The Carrow Elicited Language Inventory (1974) provides a standardized and comprehensive test of elicited imitation. Its comprehensive scoring procedure and inclusion of a number of grammatical elements has made it a popular procedure among language clinicians.

In order for an evaluation of expressive language to be considered complete, it must include a spontaneous language sample. Numerous systems have been developed to systematize the analysis of children's language, beginning with methods devised by McCarthy (1930). Such factors as mean length of utterance, grammatical complexity, and presence of specified grammatical constructions are measured in the analysis in order to form judgments regarding the child's expressive language.

Lee (1974) developed techniques to measure children's expressive language at both the presentence and sentence levels. The Developmental Sentence Types and Developmental Sentence Scoring (D.S.S.) procedures provide the clinician with an objective and easily administered procedure. The D.S.S. procedures provide weighted scoring for various grammatical elements based upon developmental norms. The procedure provides a basis for objectifying this heretofore subjective process.

Measurement of phonology of expression is accomplished through the traditional articulation test with a follow-up analysis of the phonological rules being employed. Such an assessment is generally completed through distinctive feature analysis, a procedure to be dealt with in detail later in the chapter.

The language diagnosis should provide the clinician with an objective evaluation of the child's receptive and expressive language. The information obtained is important in part in determining if the language pattern is significantly deficient; however, the primary purpose is to provide the clinician with a clear picture of what grammatical elements need to be developed relative to the known normal process of language development.

Clinical Procedures

An array of procedures are currently being employed in the name of language training. Children are drawing lines between points on a piece of paper, walking a balance beam, placing pictures in their proper sequence, learning the final "e" rule, and thousands of equally disparate activities. Differentiating among sublanguage, language dependent, and actual language behaviors may clarify some of the confusion. Work on sub-language tasks such as attending behaviors and various other "psycholinguistic" skills has been particularly popular in the past fifteen years. The development of the Illinois Test of Psycholinguistic Abilities (Kirk, McCarthy, and Kirk, 1968) and subsequent training programs was met with uncritical acceptance on the part of many language clinicians, and it has only been recently that serious question as to the efficacy of such procedures has been presented (Newcomer & Hammill, 1976). Programs for language-dependent skills such as reading and writing are discussed elsewhere in this text.

Rather than reviewing the multiplicity of language programs currently available, ten axioms of language intervention will be presented. These ten postulates represent the author's guidelines which are used in the development of each language program. Some are well-accepted "facts" of language intervention, while others are somewhat controversial.

1. *Language is not taught.* Although language is a set of rules which a child learns, it is not efficiently taught as a teacher would teach didactic information to a class. Language is best and most naturally learned in the give-and-take interaction of spontaneous conversation, rather than in the formality of a teacher-learner format.

2. *The child must be an active participant.* Children learn language best when they are doing and acting upon their environment. Language learners are not passive recipients but active hypothesis testers trying out their skills on an interactive environment. Children must learn that their activities have an impact upon the environment. Language makes the world "shake a bit." This premise must be built into clinical activities.

3. *Language work starts from the basis of what the child knows.* Basic to language work is the assumption that children are searching for the links between what they know and the linguistic forms which describe what they know. An attempt is made to systematically match language with what the child knows and is currently perceiving.

4. *Language intervention should follow what is known of the normal sequence.* The normal sequence of language development is a more reliable guideline for the sequence of language intervention than any other format.

5. *Parents are active participants.* It is an unspoken truth of language intervention that if the parents are not integrally involved in the clinical process, the progress which is made is primarily from maturation, with the clinical effort being given credit for an assist.

6. *Meaningful and manipulable stimuli should be used.* Although pictures are convenient and thus frequently used in language intervention, real objects have numerous advantages and should be used whenever feasible. Real objects can be manipulated by the child, they increase carry-

over potential, and they demand fewer mental operations to use and understand than pictures. The objects used must be representative of the child's everyday life. It appears more logical to center a clinical session around a child's shoes and socks than a set of pictures of farm animals.

7. *Language intervention should isolate a linguistic structure as a goal, and bombard the child with examples of that structure.* The essence of clinical language work is to present the child with so many examples of a particular language structure that the inductive learning task is greatly facilitated. No longer will children have to attempt to appropriately group language stimuli into similar units, since they are being presented with samples already grouped. This is in sharp contrast with natural language stimulation where various structures are presented in a haphazard fashion.

8. *Language intervention should build several modes of interaction into the spontaneous interaction with the child.* Most language clinicians, in their general conversation with the child, attempt to automatize such behaviors as language modeling, grammatical expansion, imitation, and rephrasing using alternative grammatical forms.

9. *Interaction should be structured around the known reasons why children talk.* The study of pragmatics has revealed that children use communication to function in a number of ways. Such functions as regulatory, interactional, information seeking, imaginative, giving information, and requesting assistance constitute the bulk of children's utterances. Language clinicians use this knowledge to structure situations in which the child is cued to use language for one of the major pragmatic functions.

10. *Skill generalization should be continuously targeted and tested.* As with all speech disorders, carryover into everyday speech is a major problem with language disordered children. Early clinical procedures should be planned so that ultimate carryover is accomplished and continuous efforts are made to see that this is occurring with those language structures being taught.

Language intervention must be tailored to the child's needs and disabilities. The immediate goal is not articulate speech, but communication in whatever manner is feasible for the child. In order to be effective, intervention should be intensive and should begin early. Language disordered children demand the utmost of clinical skill and knowledge.

Articulation-Resonance Disorders

Definition
Defective articulation involves the faulty production of speech sounds resulting in an acoustic pattern which is readily identified by the listener as aberrant. Since the sounds of a language are used to distinguish meaning, articulation errors are among the most damaging with regard to message distortion.

Articulation disorders are of three primary types: substitutions, omissions, and distortions. *Substitutions* involve the "substitution" of one standard speech sound for another. In this case the individual is producing a sound which is a part of the language but using it in place of another sound. An example would be the classic th/s substitution popularly called a lisp.

An *omission* is exactly what the name implies, the leaving out of a speech sound where one should be. Such productions as, *oup* for *soup* or *di* for *dish* are examples of omission of a speech sound.

A *distortion* is the substitution of a nonstandard speech sound for a standard speech sound. In this case the individual produces sounds which are not traditional speech sounds of the language in an attempt to produce the target sound.

Although individual differences make it impossible to identify an exact relationship between acoustic product and degree of severity of the problem, several factors have a bearing on the degree of handicap incurred by articulation differences. The frequency of the errored sound in the language has a direct and obvious impact on the severity. Misarticulation of a sound which occurs more frequently will generally result in greater interference than a less frequently occurring sound.

The acoustic difference between the target sound and the sound produced has substantial effect upon intelligibility. Obviously, the omission of a sound leaves the listener with the fewest clues as to the sounds being attempted, while a slight acoustical distortion of the sound may have little or no impact on the communication. It is generally assumed that sound omissions constitute the most severe handicaps, followed by substitutions and distortions.

The degree of severity of the articulation difference must also be judged in relation to certain personal factors, such as age. The term developmental implies that there is a gradual and orderly development of the skill over time and that children's production of speech sounds becomes more accurate and complete with time. Sanders (1972) presents an excellent review of developmental studies of sound acquisition. It is important to realize that no child has read the developmental charts prior to learning to articulate, and there is a great deal of variation in the order of acquisition of sounds from child to child. Speech clinicians do not work directly from developmental charts in order to determine if a sound difference constitutes a disorder, because there are a myriad of coinfluencing factors which must be taken into account.

Factors such as the individual's vocational goals, intellectual level, and socioeconomic status may also need to be taken into account when determining the impact or severity of the articulation disorder. Once again it becomes apparent that there is not a direct one-to-one relationship of severity of disorder to acoustic signal, and several related factors play an important part in the total picture.

Certain articulation disorders have greater impact upon their possessor because of the cosmetic effect they have. Some sound productions simply look worse than others. The frontal lisp, sometimes classified as a th–s substitution can have a significant visual impact, and indeed it is possible for some speakers to produce an acoustically accurate /s/ sound with the tongue between the teeth and yet be judged to have an articulation error because of the appearance.

Prevalence

Articulation errors constitute the single most prevalent speech disorder. Approximately 75 percent of all speech handicaps which demand clinical intervention are articulation disorders (Perkins, 1977). This figure is somewhat misleading since the classifications are not mutually exclusive. Most youngsters who have language disorders, for example, also have difficulty with the articulation of speech sounds. Nonetheless, articulation errors constitute the majority of most speech clinicians' caseloads.

Etiology

Organic causes of articulation errors may be identified as sensory, neuromotor, or faciodental. Functional etiologies include learning and psychological factors.

In order to learn to correctly articulate the sounds of speech, one must first be able to hear and perceive those sounds. The adequacy of the auditory-sensory system to process the speech stimuli has profound impact on the articulation of speech sounds for two primary reasons. First, in order for the child to have a clear perception of sounds it is necessary to hear others using those sounds. Second, in order to determine the accuracy of a child's articulation it is necessary to compare those attempts with other's speech patterns. Although the sense of hearing is not the exclusive channel through which the individual receives speech input, it is probably the primary channel.*

Beginning with the writings of Travis and Rasmus (1931) and continuing to current researchers, the belief has long been held that articulation accuracy is in some way related to auditory discrimination. Auditory discrimination is the skill of perceiving the differences among sounds, and with regard to the current topic, differences among speech sounds. Although there is not total agreement in the literature regarding the inferiority of auditory discrimination of individuals with articulation errors, many clinicians make the assumption that auditory discrimination weaknesses influence articulation.

Other auditory skills such as auditory memory span, auditory closure, auditory synthesis, and auditory analysis have been hypothesized to cause articulation errors; however, research findings tend to be inconsistent and inconclusive.

A major organic cause of articulation disorders is neuromotor impairment. The two primary types of neuromotor impairments are called dys-

---

*There is substantial literature to indicate, however, that the tactile, proprioceptive channel of feedback is of extreme importance in articulation production (Locke, 1968).

arthria and dyspraxia. Dysarthria is a group of disorders of articulation resulting from impairment of the nerve innervation of the muscles of articulation, and resulting in paralysis, weakness, or incoordination (Perkins, 1977). Although several dysarthric speech patterns exist, the primary dysarthric syndrome is slow, labored articulation which lacks precision, has poor breath support, and contains many errors that are consistent in all positions in words. Dyspraxia is a disorder of articulation involving planning and carrying out volitional movements, and results in a speech pattern characterized by inconsistency and unpredictability.

The importance of faciodental anomalies for articulation precision has long been a heated topic in speech pathology literature. Clearly, in cases of major structural deviations (such as cleft palate) there is a detrimental effect on articulation accuracy; however, it is evident that many individuals are capable of perfectly adequate articulation with structural differences of rather sizable proportions. Indeed there are cases of adequate, if not perfect articulation following the excision of a significant portion of the tongue, as well as with all of the teeth missing. Compensatory abilities for speech articulation are significant.

Cleft palate is a disorder in which the roof of the mouth has failed to close, leaving a space or opening between the oral and nasal cavities. The resultant gap may include only a portion of the roof of the mouth or be so complete as to include the gum ridge and the upper lip. As would be expected, such individuals have significant difficulties with precise articulation of speech sounds. Interestingly, the problem in articulation does not simply relate to the change in oral geography for purposes of making contact and altering the airstream. Equally significant is the inability of the person to build up adequate intraoral breath pressure for articulation. Many children with cleft palate have difficulty producing the /s/, /z/, /p/, and other "high pressure" sounds.

The tongue is obviously the most mobile and important articulator. Most people, when asked about the causes of articulation disorders, would probably be inclined to blame the tongue for being too large, too small, or even "tied." There is very little evidence, however, which would indicate that the size of the tongue has much of an impact upon articulation. Current thinking indicates that the tongue mobility may contribute to articulation disorders in certain cases (Fletcher and Meldrum, 1968). Research in the past fifteen years underscores the need for caution in inferring a direct relationship between physical differences in the oral mechanism and articulation disorders. The impact of a given physical difference cannot be precisely predicted for any individual.

Perception of the accuracy of one's own speech signal is in part dependent upon auditory feedback and in part dependent upon tactile-kinesthetic feedback from the articulators. We judge the adequacy of our articulation based not only on how it sounds, but also on how it feels. Recent investigations into oral stereognosis, or the ability to discriminate differences in stimuli in the oral cavity, have postulated a correlation between poor oral discrimination and articulation errors (McNutt, 1977). Although a clear cause-effect relationship has not been established through research, most speech clinicians acknowledge the importance of oral discrimination as a feedback channel for articulation.

Probably the most frequent functional cause of articulation errors is related to some form of learning difference. Two types of mislearning are involved. First, some cases of misarticulation are caused by actual imitation of faulty articulation patterns of peers, siblings, or parent models. Other, and more frequent incidents involve the accidental learning of a faulty pattern through errored progressive approximations of the target sound. Possibly, in this second type of learning, parents have reinforced errors because of some internal needs of their own, but more probably the reinforcement procedures are accidental and inadvertent.

Many writers identify minimal sensory, motor, or perceptual differences as being etiologically linked with articulation errors. This relationship, because of the minimal and often undetectable nature of the physical differences, is usually determined to be "functional" in nature. It is evident that minimal physical differences may have important impact upon articulation skills.

Attempts to establish psychological factors as causes of articulation difficulties have, in general, proven unproductive. Much of the findings is probably due to poor research design, small numbers of subjects, and contradictions in data. One study of significance was that of Rousey and Moriarty (1965). These authors, working from a basic premise that consonant acquisition reflects psychosexual development, developed a set of assumptions relating type of articulation error and personal adjustment as measured through psychiatric evaluation. As an example they proposed that a lateral lisp is associated with excessive narcissism. In their experimental study they found that in 83 percent of the cases the expected diagnosis (based upon articulation pattern) was corroborated by psychiatric evaluation. Although many clinicians suspect there to be a relationship between articulation difficulties and personality, current research is inconclusive.

No discussion of the etiologies of articulation disorders would be complete without acknowledging an existing *theory* of articulation behavior based upon linguistic percepts. Recently speech pathologists and linguists have presented a provocative theory which postulates that articulation differences in some children are related to the child's ability to learn the linguistic rules for phoneme production (McReynolds & Engmann, 1975). Speech sounds, it is hypothesized, are learned not as isolated units but rather as the result of learning a set of contrasts which are necessary to produce the sounds. Contrasts such as vowel versus consonant, voiced versus voiceless, continuant versus stop, are gradually acquired and allow the child to produce the sounds which imply one or the other of the features. Every speech sound is in actuality a bundle of features rather than an isolated production. This theory provides a more efficient explanation of articulation learning, since the child is required to learn a rather small number of features rather than each phoneme independently. The implication of this theory is that some, and possibly many, articulation errors are not directly caused by an inability to move the articulators to produce the sound, but rather by an inability to learn the linguistic rules (distinctive features) that govern articulation production.

Diagnostic Methods for Articulation

Diagnostic procedures in speech pathology are generally aimed at answering three basic questions: does a problem exist, what is the etiology of the problem, and what are the most efficient procedures for directing the remedial effort (Emerick and Hatten, 1974). Although knowing whether a problem exists and knowing the most efficient remedial procedures are uncontested concepts in diagnosis, there is substantial controversy concerning the value of extensive testing to find the cause of a speech disorder. Traditionally speech pathology has been very concerned with this facet of diagnosis for three primary reasons. First, the parents have a right to know what causes their child's problems. Second, knowing the cause may have direct research or long-range effect upon the discipline in matters of prevention and general expansion of knowledge. Third, knowledge of the cause may have a direct impact upon the remedial effort.

PHONETIC ANALYSIS. The first step in articulation testing is to make an analysis of the speech sounds of the person. This is generally accomplished through the use of an articulation test. Articulation tests organize the child's spoken responses to stimuli (either pictures or printed materials) in such a manner that every major speech sound is sampled in various positions in words. There are numerous commercial articulation tests available. Several tests attempt to provide the speech sounds in an orderly manner so that the examiner can immediately know the developmental age for each sound and the frequency of the sound in the language. Such a test is the Arizona Articulation Proficiency Scale (Fundula, 1970.) This particular test results in an articulation score which has obvious value for accountability purposes, since the clinician is able to conclude the test with a score rather than a subjective description of severity.

Once the basic phonetic analysis has been completed for an individual child, the examiner has knowledge of which sounds are in error, where the errors occur in words, and what types of errors (substitutions, omissions, distortions) exist. Obviously, this is only a partial picture of articulation behavior, since the more important skill is to be able to articulate sounds in contextual speech. For this reason most articulation tests have some procedure for eliciting spontaneous speech samples. The Goldman-Fristoe Test of Articulation (1969) contains a unique "sounds in sentences" subtest which is of value in obtaining a running speech sample.

STIMULABILITY.   Once it has been determined which sounds are produced incorrectly, the examiner attempts to determine whether the individual is capable of producing the sound correctly under optimal circumstances. In other words, is the sound stimulable? The examiner provides auditory, visual, and tactile-kinesthetic stimulation in an attempt to elicit the correct sound. If the individual is able to produce the sound correctly under stimulation, this is thought to be a sign of favorable prognosis.

VARIABILITY.   Seldom is an articulation error totally consistent. Since an individual sound influences how the sounds around it are produced, it appears logical that some sounds may facilitate the correct production of others. This thesis has been formalized by McDonald through the development of his Deep Test of Articulation (1966), which systematically presents each speech sound juxtaposed with every other speech sound in an attempt to find key phonetic contexts that facilitate the correct production of the target sound. McDonald uses twenty-five consonants and ten vowels in an attempt to observe the influence of these sounds on the target sound.

MOTOR ABILITY.   Since articulation is a coordinated motor skill, it is logical that most speech clinicians make some analysis of the general and specific motor skills of the individual. Evaluation of gross motor skills would involve such behaviors as balance, locomotion, manual dexterity, and laterality. This information may be of value in establishing the general maturation of the child and his or her readiness for articulation development. Fine motor skills tested include speed, accuracy, and coordination of movements of the tongue, lips, and jaws. Evaluation of the oral mechanism generally involves a careful examination of the structural and functional integrity of the mechanism.

ORAL DISCRIMINATION.   A variety of techniques are available for the speech clinician to evaluate the ability to discriminate differences in stimuli in the oral cavity, or "oral stereognosis." One of the more common testing procedures involves having the individual place plastic shapes in the mouth and identify the shapes through oral contact.

AUDITORY ACUITY.   The evaluation of auditory acuity usually takes the form of a pure tone hearing test. The relationship between hearing acuity and articulation accuracy has been well established.

AUDITORY DISCRIMINATION.   Most speech clinicians assess the individual's auditory discrimination skills using any one of a number of tests of auditory discrimination. Several obvious difficulties exist with regard to auditory discrimination testing. First, the actual skill required during speech is an instantaneous determination of the accuracy of one's own speech.

Most tests of auditory discrimination, in contrast, allow the listener time to reflect upon the quality of the sounds and involve auditory stimuli presented by another speaker. Nevertheless, auditory discrimination testing is popular among speech clinicians.

AUDITORY MEMORY SPAN.   Although the research is inconclusive regarding the link between auditory memory and articulation (Winitz, 1969), most speech clinicians use tests of digit recall, speech sound, or syllable recall to assess this short-term memory skill.

PREDICTION TESTING.   The concept of prediction is an attractive one for speech clinicians. With accurate and reliable instruments to indicate which youngsters will spontaneously correct their speech differences with maturation, speech clinicians are able to concentrate their efforts on those who have less probability of spontaneous correction. Stimulability, consistency of error, auditory discrimination, and tongue mobility have all been postulated to have prediction value with regard to spontaneous correction of articulation problems. The Predictive Screening Test of Articulation (Van Riper & Erickson, 1968) has proven to be a valuable tool for articulation prediction.

DISTINCTIVE FEATURE ASSESSMENT.   According to distinctive feature theory, children's acquisition of articulation accuracy is related to the learning of sets of features which go into the makeup of each speech sound. Each sound may be identified by the set of features which constitute it. For example, a partial description of the constituents of the /t/ sound would include:

+   consonantal
+   anterior
+   coronal
–   nasal
–   voice
–   continuant

Use of distinctive feature theory for remedial purposes is rapidly developing and procedures have been developed (McReynolds and Engmann, 1975) to evaluate articulatory patterns in order to determine if a particular feature is at the root of the errors.

Clinical Approaches

Speech clinicians have traditionally worked from the premise that diagnostic information dictates the method of remediation. A number of clinical approaches for problems of articulation have been described in the literature, and this discussion will overview only the major ones.

SOUND STIMULATION APPROACH.   Charles Van Riper's (1978) writings have probably had as profound an impact upon the activities of the speech clinician as any other single author. His format for articulation correction is still popular and involves a carefully controlled series of steps beginning with auditory discrimination training and working through stages of sound production. The premise of Van Riper's approach is that the child must be able to discriminate and identify the sound prior to being able to produce it. Initially the goal is to improve the child's listening and auditory discrimination skills. The ensuing work on production of the sound moves from sound production in isolation to work in nonsense syllables, words, sentences, contextual speech, and carryover. The Van Riper approach to articulation therapy has stood the test of time.

PHONETIC PLACEMENT APPROACH.   The phonetic placement approach to articulation stresses the physical postures which the articulators must assume in order to produce the various speech sounds. The procedure may or may not be preceded by auditory training work and incorporates a wide variety of methods for eliciting the target sound. Oral instruction, diagrams, physical manipulation of the articulators, visual cueing, and modeling are all used in an attempt to obtain correct production. Although it is intuitively obvious that it would be advantageous for the speaker to know the proper "place" to produce each speech sound, research on the dynamics of speech production has raised serious doubts as to the validity of an approach which teaches one articulatory posture for any given sound (McDonald, 1964a).

BEHAVIOR MODIFICATION.   Since articulation appears to be somewhat free from psychodynamic factors and highly linked to motor behavior and habit strength, it is little wonder that the procedures of behavior modification have been found very useful in articulation therapy. Mowrer, Baker, and Schultz (1968) developed procedures that emphasize the production aspects of articulation and teach sound production in a step-by-step manner using control of stimuli, responses anticipated, and reinforcements. This approach primarily disregards such factors as auditory skills and other underlying etiological factors, and emphasizes sequential practice in the production of the sound at increasingly difficult levels of context complexity.

SENSORY-MOTOR APPROACH.   McDonald's sensory-motor approach (1964b) to articulation intervention is based on the premise that most children have a few phonetic contexts in which the problem sounds are produced correctly. Determination of these key phonetic contexts is made through use of the McDonald Deep Test of Articulation described earlier. The aim of articulation work then becomes helping the individual increase the number of phonetic contexts in which the sound is produced correctly. McDonald (1964b) spells out his goals as follows:

1. Heightening (the child's) responsiveness to the patterns of auditory, proprioceptive, and tactile sensations associated with the overlapping ballistic movements of articulation.
2. Reinforcing the child's correct articulation of his error sound.
3. Facilitating the correct articulation of the error sound in systematically varied phonetic contexts (pp. 134–135).

PAIRED STIMULI TECHNIQUE. Irwin and Weston (1971) have devised a procedure that utilizes key words (words in which the errored sound is produced correctly) to elicit correct production. In this approach the correct production of the sound is paired with the incorrect production in a series of paired words. Irwin and Weston (1971) have discovered that transfer from the correct to the incorrect does take place, and individuals are able to increase their repertoire of words in which the target sound is produced correctly. As Winitz (1975) points out, this particular approach emphasizes retrieval from memory or self-retrieval, as opposed to auditory stimulation which is an important element of so many other approaches.

DISTINCTIVE FEATURES. As mentioned earlier, distinctive features are the articulatory, acoustic, or perceptual features which constitute each phoneme. A phoneme is the end product of a simultaneous production of its unique set of features, and every sound is differentiated from other sounds by at least one feature difference. Distinctive feature analysis of a child's articulation errors could result in the discovery of a pattern of feature characteristics which underlie the articulation errors. This discovery could lead to a more efficient procedure for correction based upon errored features which may impact upon several speech sounds, rather than working on each specific sound as an autonomous unit. This procedure is still in the developmental stages. (McReynolds & Engmann, 1975; Winitz, 1975.)

Summary

Very probably an eclectic approach to articulation intervention remains the most popular perspective of most speech clinicians. The following elements are common to most approaches.

1. Attention to order and sequence is important so that the individual is presented with small incremental steps which are reasonably attainable.
2. The child needs to have the sound firmly established as a perceptual unit, either auditorially, tactually, or kinesthetically prior to attempts to produce it. Self monitoring and feedback are emphasized.
3. Production generally moves from part to whole. Although this is less universal than the others, it is generally accepted that production begins with the sound in isolation and progresses to varying phonetic contexts.
4. Progressive approximations of the target sound are useful in working toward final production.

5. Key phonetic contexts are usually possible to detect and use as aids in the clinical process.
6. Control of the stimuli, responses, and reinforcements is crucial.
7. Carryover is an important part of the process and demands procedures to stabilize the sound production under varying conditions of communication stress and contextual characteristics.
8. No single clinical approach will be effective with every child, and the clinician must have several alternatives available in response to child need.

Voice Disorders

Definition

Deviations of pitch, loudness, or quality are said to constitute voice disorders. The pitch of the speaking voice must be appropriate for the age, sex, and general personality of the speaker. Pitch levels that are too high usually present more of a problem for men than women, and conversely pitch levels that are too low usually are more deleterious for women. Diminished pitch variation and lack of control of pitch variation constitute types of voice disorders.

Loudness disorders must be judged relative to the setting and communicative purpose of the speaker. As with pitch problems, loudness which lacks variation or varies independent of meaning constitutes a disorder. A good deal of professional judgment is involved in determining the appropriateness of varying degrees of pitch and loudness in an individual's speaking voice.

The term "quality" refers to the "pleasantness" of one's voice. This assessment is highly subjective, as is evidenced by the plethora of terms used to describe various vocal quality disorders; hoarseness, harshness, breathiness, huskiness, metallic, stridency, thin, and so on. Murphy (1964) found that over fifty terms have been used to describe various vocal qualities, and numerous authors have noted inconsistencies in the professional literature with regard to definition of the terms. The publication of audiotapes for voice training purposes has been a significant help in standardizing the nomenclature (Wilson and Rice, 1977).

Some literature distinguishes between phonatory and resonatory voice disorders. Phonatory disorders result from improper function of the vocal folds during sound production. Organic differences, such as growths or ulcerations on the folds, or functional deviations may result in phonatory disorders. Differences in pitch, loudness, and most differences in vocal quality are directly related to phonation. Nasality, however, is not caused by faulty phonation but rather from improper resonation of the sound in the oral tract. There are a number of different types of nasality (hyper, hypo, and so on) resulting from too much or too little nasal resonance or a combination thereof. Since it is technically accurate that resonatory voice disorders such as the nasalities are caused by malfunctioning of the articulators, some prefer to consider resonatory problems along with articulation errors.

Prevalence

Milisen (1971) summarized his review of prevalence figures by concluding that approximately one percent of the total population suffers from voice disorders. However, figures vary greatly with regard to this particular communication disorder, and figures range from less than 0.5 percent to 6 percent (Senturia and Wilson, 1968). Apparently the identification of voice disorders is dependent upon the listener to a degree somewhat greater than it is for other communicative disorders.

Voice disorders are not readily identified by parents, peers, or classroom teachers to the extent that some other communication problems are (Diehl and Stinnett, 1959; James and Cooper, 1966). There is a tendency for people to perceive deviations in voice as being unmodifiable, and there is little general awareness that voice characteristics are the end product of physical, personality, and behavioral patterns which can be altered.

Etiology

Voice disorders are caused by structural differences of the larynx or neural innervating system, misuse and abuse of the vocal mechanism, and psychodynamic factors. A wide variety of structural differences are possible. Some have life-threatening potential, such as carcinoma, while others are temporary, such as inflammation resulting from laryngitis. A frequent problem noted in the school-age population is vocal nodules, small callous-like growths that appear on the vocal folds and which result from general tension, misuse, and abuse of the voice. Vocal nodules are sometimes called screamer's nodules, indicating the probable cause.

The voice is said to be a barometer of the personality, and as such it is strongly influenced by major personal adjustment problems. Too much tension, either muscular or mental, can find its way to the muscles of the larynx, causing hyperfunction of the structure, abuse of the vocal folds, and potentially aberrant vocal quality. Aphonia, or total loss of voice without medical explanation, is generally functional in nature resulting from significant personal problems.

Diagnostic Methods

Because of the diversity of voice disorders there is no single format of evaluation which is uniformly satisfactory. The following six areas constitute the general voice evaluation:

1. *Listening to the speech sample:* The first task of the speech clinician is to listen to the voice, determine if a voice disorder exists, and make a judgment as to the type of voice disorder. This judgment will culminate in a label and generally will also provide an estimate of the severity of the problem. At this time the clinician makes some judgment of the degree of laryngeal tension associated with voice production, since voice disorders are generally associated with some degree of hyper- or hypofunctioning of the laryngeal structure.

2. *Case history:* Although a careful case history is thought to be a routine part of all speech and language evaluations, it is particularly important in the case of voice disorders since duration of the symptom, time of onset, health characteristics, and general family relationships and tensions can have direct influence on clinical decisions.

3. *Personal adjustment evaluation:* Some evaluation of personal adjustment is necessary for many voice cases. Even in instances where the apparent culprit is vocal abuse, there is now ample evidence to indicate that personality characteristics are often allied factors in perpetuating the problem.

4. *Respiration functioning:* Since the process of respiration provides the raw material for voice production, it has direct influence upon the end product. Evaluation of respiratory functioning generally attempts to determine if adequate breath support is being provided for speech purposes, and if that support is being provided without undue tension. The coordination of respiration and phonation is crucial for speech production. Evaluation of the coordination of breathing and phonation must be accompanied by careful assessment of the type of breathing patterns of the speaker during various speech acts.

5. *Assessment of voice components:* One of the major elements of the diagnostic process is determination of the optimal functioning level of the voice. The concept of optimal functioning refers to the theoretical pitch and loudness level of the voice at which the structure is producing the best voice with the least amount of tension. It is assumed that there is an optimal or most efficient pitch level for every voice mechanism, and if a speaker is not using that level in everyday speech, undue tension may result. Although a number of techniques have been devised to determine this optimal level of pitch, no technique has met with complete acceptance.

A variety of procedures are used to determine the effect of various alterations in voice production upon the disordered component. Changes in sound onset, tension, pitch level, loudness level, and head positioning, are made in an attempt to modify the voice. A careful cataloguing of the effects is made to determine if a pattern emerges.

6. *Auditory skills:* Hearing testing and tests of ability to perceive differences in pitch, loudness, and quality are undertaken. Voice disorders may be related to hearing loss or auditory perceptual problems.

Clinical Approaches

Voice production is the direct result of physical adjustments made by a speaker. Even though these muscular coordinations are not directly observable as with articulation production, they are nonetheless able to be controlled.

Generally, speech clinicians take a somewhat symptomatic attack on voice disorders following Boone's (1977) suggestion that work on the symptoms will result in improved voice production. Often the decision as to whether voice therapy or surgery should be selected is made by the physician and the speech clinician. When the voice misuse is resulting in vocal nodules, it is obvious that surgery alone will not alter the long-range prognosis, since the growths will reappear once faulty voice habits are reinstated. For this reason physicians and speech clinicians work cooperatively with many voice cases.

An early goal of voice therapy is achievement of optimal voice production. This may infer alteration of the pitch and/or loudness level of the voice to bring it more in line with the most efficient level for the vocal mechanism. Altering vocal production to bring the proper degree of tension is not an easy task. Whereas relaxation techniques may be needed for those with too much tension, others may need exercises to increase tension and increase vocal efficiency.

Coordination of respiration and phonation and the development of adequate breath support are clinical goals in some instances. Similarly, many clinicians spend considerable time increasing oral resonance in those cases where undue tension has decreased the efficiency of the oral mechanism.

Since vocal abuse and misuse are most common causes of voice disorders in children, a logical goal may be the elimination of such abuses. This work often culminates in parents and peers working on assisting children to identify when abuse is taking place, as well as providing support for their efforts to curtail abuse. Many speech clinicians have found that family and group work is most efficient with young children with vocal-abuse problems, since abuses are generally related to patterns of interaction in the home.

Stuttering

Definition
Everyone knows what stuttering is except the experts. Stuttering is easy to define until one studies all of its complexities and appreciates the enormity of the disorder. Most people would define the term primarily taking into account the actual moment of stuttering and little else. Although the stuttering episode is an important aspect of stuttering, it is not the entirety of the problem. What is seen and heard is little more than the tip of the stuttering iceberg.

The overt characteristics of stuttering are observable and have been described in detail in a number of sources (Bloodstein, 1975). Repetitions of sounds, syllables, and words, prolongations of sounds, and unusual silence periods punctuate the speech of a stutterer. These audible signals are often accompanied by facial and general body movements, eye blinks, breathing pattern changes, pitch changes, and numerous other characteristics which are secondary to the change in speech fluency. Stuttering is notoriously episodic. Most stutterers will not stutter while singing, speaking to an infant, or involved in choral speaking. No objective count of such dysfluencies and secondary characteristics is adequate to define stuttering, since stuttering also involves a distinct self-concept. Stuttering is not only a speech pattern; it is also a personal outlook and related self-image. Stutterers perceive themselves as stutterers and, possibly as a result of that, anticipate difficulty with speech, postpone and avoid certain speech attempts, and engage in tension-producing struggle behavior in an attempt to avoid the expected stuttering incident. As Johnson (1944) has indicated, stuttering is to some degree the result of what a person does while trying not to stutter.

Stuttering is an insidious problem that usually begins in childhood. Somewhat like an ever increasingly tangled web, stuttering becomes more and more complex with time. Bloodstein (1975) describes four stages of stuttering which reflect increasing frequency, fear, and frustration as stuttering progresses from an episodic and easy repetition to a chronic and painful struggle.

Prevalence

As with most speech and language disorders stuttering affects more males than females. The estimates range from a ratio of 1.5 to 1 (Glasner and Rosenthal, 1957) to 9 to 1 (Milisen, 1971). Most studies of the prevalence of stuttering indicate that somewhere between 0.5 and 1 percent of the population stutter. There is some clinical evidence that the prevalence may be decreasing, and an estimate of 0.7 percent of the school-age population is probably accurate. (Young, 1975).

Etiology

No communication disorder is associated with greater controversy than stuttering. Theories of cause and remedial approaches have been de-

Courtesy of the Lexington School for the Deaf.

veloped and defended for hundreds of years, with the battles continuing to this day. As Bloodstein (1975) points out, there are two general theories on the cause of stuttering. One set of hypotheses attempts to explain the etiology of the onset of stuttering, while another set of theories is attempting to explain the cause of the moment of stuttering. The second theory is related to factors such as anticipation, struggle, and approach-avoidance, which are explanations of the actual stuttering pattern.

There is substantial danger in attempting to summarize the theories of the cause of stuttering. Entire texts have been devoted to just that topic with limited success. Nevertheless a brief review of theories of stuttering will be presented using the classification system suggested by Emerick and Hamre (1972).

Biogenic or organic theories of stuttering have waxed and waned for years. There is appeal in the concept that stuttering is caused by some uncontrollable organic difference, since the disorder itself has been somewhat uncontrollable. The most classic of the organic theories claims that there is a confusion of cerebral dominance in stutterers which results in confused signals leaving the brain.

Bryngelson (1942) termed the condition "dysphemia," which he defines as: "an irregularity of neural integration in that portion of the central nervous system responsible for the flow of nerve impulses to the speech mechanism" (p. 15). A confusion of cerebral dominance is thus proposed by Bryngelson as the cause of stuttering.

Robert West (1958) advocated a metabolic and chemical difference as an explanation of stuttering, with emotional and interpersonal pressures possibly triggering the chemical reaction. Such an explanation links the known and observable interpersonal characteristics of stuttering to a potential etiological factor.

Eisenson (1976) suggested that stuttering is caused in the majority of instances by a predisposition to motor and sensory perseveration. Perseveration, the continuation of an activity beyond its usefulness, exemplifies stuttering in its repetitive nature.

Other theories have been postulated linking motor coordination, auditory skill differences, and a multitude of other potential physical abnormalities with stuttering. There is no conclusive evidence, however, that stutterers, as a population, vary systematically on any single physical parameter.

A number of theories have been proposed that link stuttering with psychoemotional factors. These psychogenic theories include psychoanalytic explanations which imply that stuttering fulfills repressed needs. According to classical Freudian theory, stuttering stems from fixations at various psychosexual levels of development. Interestingly, psychoanalytic theory suggests that stuttering not only constitutes a problem for its possessor but concomitantly represents the stutterer's attempt to resolve a problem.

The "developmental" theories of stuttering probably enjoy the widest acceptance by speech clinicians. Wendell Johnson's theory of stuttering has had a profound impact upon clinical approaches. Johnson's "diagnosogenic" (the onset is caused by the diagnosis) theory indicates that the child who stutters was once a normally developing child whose environment misidentified normally dysfluent speech as a disorder, labeled it as such, and thus prompted the child to work to overcome it. In this theory the stuttering is initially a function of increased sensitivity of the listener, although the end result is a child who struggles to prevent a problem that is only exacerbated by the child's attempts to solve it. Three postulates summarize Johnson's theory:

1. Stuttering is initially diagnosed by a layman (usually a parent) rather than a speech clinician.
2. What has been diagnosed as stuttering is essentially normal hesitations and repetitions which characterize a large number of children in the two- to six-year age group.
3. Stuttering becomes a genuine disorder after it has been diagnosed (identified) rather than before. (Johnson, 1944.)

Many speech clinicians broaden Johnson's theory to include the possibility that one may diagnose oneself as a stutterer. Any factors, such as articulation or language difficulties, which work to convince the child that speech is a difficult task requiring preparation, force, and struggle could result in stuttering (Bloodstein, 1975).

According to some, stuttering is operant behavior (Shames & Sherrick, 1963). The stuttering episode may be followed by positive reinforcements such as greater attentiveness on the part of listeners. Punishing responses such as reprimanding may result in the child's alteration of behavior through silence or struggle. The very fact that the word is ultimately uttered is a type of reward for the struggling which precedes it. Stuttering could be a learned behavior resulting from a complex of self-imposed and external reinforcements and punishments.

Stuttering is a complex behavior which very probably results from several factors and which may result from different constellations of factors in different people. The ultimate answers to the riddle of the cause of stuttering will be found by those researchers capable of finding a pattern in the complex and varied behaviors of stutterers.

Diagnostic Methods

Two primary questions are being answered through the diagnostic process. First, the clinician wishes to know how advanced the stuttering is or, more specifically, what stage of stuttering is being presented. Secondly, it is important to have specific and detailed information regarding the stutterer as a person.

In order to determine the severity of the stuttering, it is necessary to obtain an extensive sample of the individual's spontaneous speech. From the sample, the speech clinician determines such factors as the number of stuttering episodes per speech sample, type of stuttering block, avoid-ances, struggle pattern, postponing devices, feared sounds and words, du-ration of fluent periods, and consistency of stuttering over repeated readings of the same passage. These factors provide a picture that allows the clinician to place the stutterer along a continuum of severity.

Investigation of the stutterer as a person leads to information about the importance of the disorder to the possessor, the impact of personality on speech and vice versa, and the influence of important people in the individual's life and their reaction to the stuttering. In no other speech disorder is the concept that we treat the whole person more important. Every factor that may have an influence upon the individual's speech pat-tern must be examined.

Clinical Approaches

There is a high degree of insecurity among speech clinicians regarding stuttering management. Partially this is the result of the conflicting theories of cause and cure, and partially it is because it appears that nearly anything will work with some stutterers, while no one thing will work for all stutterers. Clinical successes with stutterers serve to reinforce beliefs, and it is not uncommon for speech clinicians to explain away fail-ures on the basis of environmental, motivational, or other external factors.

The nature of clinical intervention with stutterers is based to some de-gree upon the stage of development of the stuttering pattern. With the very young child in the first stage of stuttering, there is a strong inclination to work exclusively with the parents. The clinician provides the parent with guidelines designed to maximize the chances of fluent speech devel-oping. Suggestions presented to the parents traditionally include the following:

1. Remove all unnecessary pressures from the child.
2. Do not tolerate competition for speaking among the siblings in the family.
3. Provide the child with as much success and reward for success as is possible.
4. Encourage the child to talk during fluent times and gently discourage talking when there is great difficulty or pressure.
5. Do not ask the child to perform for others.
6. Convey confidence in your child's ability to talk easily. Guard against show-ing panic, fear, or remorse over moments of dysfluent speech.
7. Slow the pace of your life and spend more time in relaxed conversation with your child.

Such lists of suggestions do not constitute the entirety of work with parents, since there is substantial need for counseling and support during these trying months. Most parents find it difficult to keep from conveying their panic over the child's speech, and quite possibly this is the most im-portant of all factors. An extremely high percentage of young stutterers "outgrow" their problem. Martyn and Sheehan (1968) found that as many as 80 percent of such children do not stutter as adults, and this information alone can be used by the clinician to allay parental fears and improve the possibility of adequate progression toward normal speech.

When speech clinicians are confronted with stuttering of somewhat greater severity, they must determine when to work directly with the child. The question becomes, should we work with the child and risk heightening the child's awareness of the difficulty thus causing greater tension and struggle? The speech clinician runs the risk of convincing the child that there is a problem, and this knowledge may serve only to increase the severity of the problem.

Although there are many approaches to treatment in older stutterers, only two major methods will be discussed here. Van Riper (1971) is most closely associated with a method of stuttering management called desensitization therapy. There are two major elements of this approach. The first involves an attempt to desensitize the individual to stuttering. The goal is to produce an individual who has directly confronted the stuttering problem and is willing to talk about it, purposefully alter it, and generally become adjusted to it. The reasoning behind this first stage is that if the stuttering is due to the child's desperate effort *not* to stutter (the struggle philosophy), then desensitization to the speech problem may decrease the need to stop stuttering. In a sense the goal is a rather unrealistic one ... get the stutterer to the point of saying, "I stutter—so what?"

The second part of the Van Riper approach is to provide the individual with specific techniques for control of the stuttering moment. Such methods provide the stutterer with ways to bring under conscious control a facet of life that is felt to be totally out of control. Devices are introduced gradually and systematically in an attempt to provide the stutterer with a means for control.

In contrast to the Van Riper approach, many variations of behavior modification procedures have been used. Martin and Haroldson (1969) and their co-workers reported clinical success using time-out, a form of punishment for stuttering episodes. Other workers have worked primarily on reinforcement of fluency, under the supposition that if the duration of fluent speech can be increased, stuttering will automatically decrease. Goldiamond (1965) was a pioneer in the use of reward for fluent speech. Generally the technique involves devising some procedure for artificially increasing the fluency of the person's speech and systematically reinforcing that fluency. Then, under controlled conditions the procedures used to induce the fluency in the first place are removed. Procedures that have proved effective in increasing fluency include control of the rate of speech, delayed auditory feedback, auditory masking of feedback, and superimposed rhythms.

Although stuttering has intrigued and frustrated workers for centuries it is only within the recent past that a scientific approach to its study has been initiated. The final answers as to its onset and correction are still a distant goal. While many documented cases of clinical success are available, much is still to be learned about this perplexing human condition.

Courtesy of the Lexington School for the Deaf.

CLINICAL SPEECH SETTING

The speech clinician finds employment in a number of settings. Although the basic precepts upon which speech intervention is founded are similar, there are differences among settings with regard to type of client, scheduling pattern, and a host of other related factors.

Clinical Speech Services in the Schools

The majority of speech clinicians are employed within the schools. Providing services to children throughout the grades, the speech clinician is generally expected to serve more than one school, depending upon the size and nature of the school. Responsibilities include case detection, diagnostic testing, clinical management, in-service education of the teaching faculty, and parent programming for speech improvement. The responsibilities of the speech clinician have significantly changed in the past ten years, and the following major issues have had an impact upon these changes. (Hatten and LaRoque, 1972)

CLINICAL APPROACH WITHIN THE PUBLIC SCHOOLS. Although the term *clinical approach* is not always descriptive, it has come to imply greater concern for individual needs, in-depth diagnosis, integral one-to-one intervention, and in general a more intense method of interaction with the communication disordered child. During the major growth period of speech pathology, the profession developed an image of superficiality. Speech pathology in the schools was primarily "articulation" work geared to minimal speech differences dealt with on a twice a week schedule in large groups. It was common to see a speech clinician working with 150 to 200 children in a week, in groups of as many as 15 to 20 children. Many of the children's speech differences constituted no real handicap and were developmental in nature. In many settings the clinicians were more technique-oriented than child- or disorder-oriented, and it is accurate to describe the state of the profession as being primarily mechanical and technical rather than scientific. With pressures both from within and without the profession, speech clinicians began to differentiate between speech differences and speech handicaps and set about changing their image from "s" and "r" mechanics to professionals interested in altering significant communication disorders. Many states now set maximum case-load limits (some as low as forty), and speech clinicians work with as few as fifteen children per week on a total involvement basis. Speech pathology has at long last realized that not every speech difference constitutes a handicap, and those with significant communication disorders deserve maximum service to ensure progress. The clinical approach involves the following factors:

1. Small caseload of speech *handicapped* children.
2. Scheduling based upon child need rather than school convenience.
3. Careful and complete diagnosis of each child's communication.
4. Individual service plans for each child.
5. Small group and individual scheduling with group size determined by the child's needs rather than the clinician's need for a larger caseload.
6. Data-based intervention patterns that rely upon careful evaluation of the child's skills and knowledge of the steps necessary to move the child toward correction.
7. Maximal environmental involvement.
8. Theory-based rather than technique-based interaction modes.

CASE DETECTION. Procedures for case detection have significantly changed in the past few years. Public school speech clinicians previously identified children with speech handicaps through individual screening procedures; however, many school districts have recently discovered that the lengthy screening process is inefficient. The current trend is toward increased reliance upon teacher, parent, and community referral. Central to this development is the idea that if children's communication skills are significantly handicapping, they will surely be identified by those with whom they have frequent contact. In part this change reflects the philosophy that if the communication difference is not handicapping in everyday speech, it should not be identified as handicapping by the speech clinician.

EARLY INTERVENTION. Many state laws mandate service to communicatively handicapped preschool children. This nationwide trend reflects the assumption that early intervention may have greater impact and efficiency in some instances, since language development appears to have a prime readiness period in the early years. The efficacy of such programs has yet to be determined through empirical research.

SERVICE TO THE PROFOUNDLY HANDICAPPED. For many years speech pathology largely ignored the communication needs of the severely and profoundly handicapped. Partially because of a lack of adequate intervention techniques and partially because of a manpower shortage, the profession simply ignored this population. Current programs in clinical management for the severely and profoundly handicapped emphasize the need for functional communication tools, whereas earlier programs emphasized the need for speech as the only tool for communication. The rapid growth of non-oral alternatives to communication for several populations attests to the fact that speech pathology has grown to accept the importance of communication among all people.

MAINSTREAMING PRESSURES. Speech clinicians have historically worked on the tutorial model in dealing with children in the schools. Communicatively handicapped children were removed from the classroom for short periods several times each week and dealt with on an individual or a small group basis. Although there has been acknowledgement of the desirability to provide most special services to handicapped children within the classroom, no universally acceptable approach to total mainstreaming of communicatively handicapped children has yet been devised. In partial response to this trend, however, several states have developed clear statements of "levels of service" provided the communicatively handicapped child. Examples might be: (1) Direct service—child is seen individually in the traditional tutorial fashion, (2) Indirect service—speech clinician serves as a consultant or program manager for a child but does not work directly with the child, (3) Observation and carryover—child is seen on an intermittent basis to check carryover of learned skills, (4) Dismissal—child has completed work and has no further need for direct contact.

ACCOUNTABILITY. Although there is ample evidence that the emphasis on accountability has exacted a substantial toll on all areas of education, the ultimate value of the concept is indisputable. Clinical speech, as all other areas of education, has moved timidly toward a posture of more careful data collection and measurement of student growth. At this point the end product is sometimes rather stilted statements of goals and objectives, and contrived methods for measurement of variables which do not easily lend themselves to measurement. Historically, however, speech clinicians have prided themselves on careful assessment, orderly and sequential intervention programs, and continuous progress evaluation. These qualities appear to be of extreme value in developing programs for accountability.

DUE PROCESS.   Although the full impact of due process laws has yet to be felt in education, certain elements of these laws are having significant effects upon the school clinician. Parent involvement in the decision-making process in education has dictated changes in speech programming. Although an initial effect has been to slow down the case detection, diagnosis, and program development, in the long run the need to inform and solicit permission from parents will produce healthy effects in terms of increased parent cooperation and involvement.

PRIVATE PRACTICE.   Private practice in speech pathology has grown rapidly in the past fifteen years. With a significant increase in the available work force and a shrinking job market, many clinicians have developed thriving private practices. The caseloads of most of these clinicians consist of preschool children and adults.

Although the clinical skills required in private practice are quite similar to those required in other work settings, there are a number of added skills which speech clinicians have been required to develop. Knowledge of cost accounting, the development of relative value indexes, billing procedures, and knowledge of third-party paying sources have become a part of the everyday work skills of clinicians in private practice.

HOSPITAL CLINICS.   Most major hospitals now employ a speech clinician to provide both in-patient and out-patient services to the communicatively handicapped. The nature of the caseload is in part determined by the type of facility, but in most instances stroke patients, laryngectomees, patients with neurological disorders, and accident victims constitute the majority of the caseload.

The autonomy of the speech and hearing profession in medical settings is of great concern to working clinicians. A recent resolution passed by the American Medical Association's House of Delegates stated that the best interests of patients with speech, hearing, or balance disorders are served by diagnosis, treatment, and rehabilitation under physician supervision. A careful review of the curricula of most medical schools would reveal scant information concerning communicative disorders, their diagnosis and treatment.

PRESCHOOL SETTINGS.   Nursery schools, day-activity centers, day-care centers, and Headstart programs often employ speech clinicians either to provide direct services or to serve as consultants in the development of speech and language stimulation programs. Such centers provide an ideal setting for language stimulation, since early intervention is deemed essential for youngsters with a high risk of disordered language development.

NURSING HOMES AND EXTENDED CARE FACILITIES.   With society's realization that the need to communicate is a basic human characteristic and the right of every individual, speech and hearing clinicians have become a part of the professional staff of many nursing homes throughout the country. Except in instances of exceptionally large facilities, there is often not a great enough demand for services in a single nursing home. Thus, speech clinicians often contract their services to a number of nursing homes, in actuality conducting a private practice within a specialized environment.

The services provided in nursing homes include hearing evaluation, orientation to the use of a hearing aid, and speech and language work with dysphasic patients as well as others with the full range of communicative disabilities. In-service education for the primary care personnel is an extremely important function as well.

SUMMARY

Speech pathology is a profession with a bright future. While the information base is expanding rapidly, a multitude of questions remain unanswered to provoke and motivate researchers in the field. There appears to be a vigorous attempt to improve the quality of service to the handicapped through increased reliance upon scientifically gathered data.

The following will hallmark the profession in the next decade: (1) Increased service to the severely and profoundly handicapped, with emphasis upon communication rather than speech, (2) Increased concern for the communication problems of the aged, (3) Growth in interdisciplinary cooperation with all other areas of special education, and (4) Increased availability of speech service in settings other than the public schools.

REFERENCES

Adkins, L. G. The effect of recorded lateral lisping on listener comprehension. Unpublished thesis. Kalamazoo, MI: Western Michigan University, 1959.

Bangs, T. E. *Vocabulary Comprehension Scale.* Austin, TX: Learning Concepts, 1975.

Berry, M. F., and Eisenson, J. *Speech Disorders.* New York: Appleton-Century-Crofts, 1956.

Bloodstein, O. *A Handbook on Stuttering.* Chicago: National Easter Seal Society for Crippled Children and Adults, 1975.

Boone, D. R. *The Voice and Voice Therapy.* (2nd ed.) Englewood Cliffs, NJ: Prentice-Hall, Inc., 1977.

Broen, P. The verbal environment of the language learning child. *American Speech and Hearing Association Monograph,* 1972, *17.*

Bryngelson, B. Investigations in the etiology and nature of dysphemia and its symptom, stuttering. *Journal of Speech Disorders,* 1942, *7,* 15–27.

Carrow, E. *Test for Auditory Comprehension of Language.* Austin, TX: Learning Concepts, 1970.

————, *Carrow Elicited Language Inventory.* Austin, TX: Learning Concepts, 1974.

Diehl, D., and Stinnet, C. Efficiency of teacher referrals in a school speech testing program. *Journal of Speech and Hearing Disorders,* 1959, *24,* 34–36.

Dunn, L. M. *Peabody Picture Vocabulary Test.* Circle Pines, MN: American Guidance Service, Inc., 1965.

Eisenson, J. Stuttering as a perseverative behavior. In J. Eisenson (ed.), *Stuttering: A Second Symposium.* New York: Harper & Row, Publishers, 1975.

————. *Aphasia in Children.* New York: Harper & Row, Publishers, 1972.

Emerick, L., and Hamre, C. *An Analysis of Stuttering: Selected Readings.* Danville, IL: The Interstate Printers & Publishers, Inc., 1972.

————, and Hatten, J. *Diagnosis and Evaluation in Speech Pathology.* Englewood Cliffs, NJ: Prentice-Hall, Inc., 1974.

Fletcher, S., and Meldrum, J. Lingual function and relative length of the lingual frenulum. *Journal of Speech and Hearing Research,* 1968, *11,* 382–390.

Fundula, J. *The Arizona Articulation Proficiency Scale.* Beverly Hills, CA: Western Psychological Services, 1970.

Glasner, P., and Rosenthal, D. Parental diagnosis of stuttering in young children. *Journal of Speech and Hearing Disorders,* 1957, *22,* 288–295.

Goldiamond, I. Stuttering and fluency as manipulatable operant response classes. In L. Krasner and L. Ullman (ed.), *Research in Behavior Modification.* New York: Holt, Rinehart and Winston, 1965.

Goldman, R., and Fristoe, M. *Goldman-Fristoe Test of Articulation.* Circle Pines, MN: American Guidance Service, 1969.

Hatten, J., and LaRoque, D. Changing directions in public school speech therapy. *Ohio Journal of Speech and Hearing,* 1972, *7,* 15–22.

Irwin, J., and Weston, A. *A Manual for the Clinical Utilization of the Paired Stimuli Technique for Articulation Modification.* Memphis, TN: National Educator Service, 1971.

James, H., and Cooper, E. Accuracy of teacher referral of speech-handicapped children. *Exceptional Children,* 1966, *30,* 29–33.

Johnson, W. The Indians have no word for it. I. Stuttering in children. *Quarterly Journal of Speech,* 1944, *30,* 330–337.

Kirk, S., McCarthy, J., and Kirk, W. *Illinois Test of Psycholinguistic Abilities.* (rev. ed.) Urbana, IL: University of Illinois Press, 1968.

Lee, L. *Developmental Sentence Analysis.* Evanston, IL: Northwestern University Press, 1974.

Lenneberg, E. *Biological Foundations of Language.* New York: John Wiley & Sons, Inc., 1967.

Locke, J. Oral perception and articulation learning. *Perceptual and Motor Skills,* 1968, *26,* 1259–1264.

Martin, R., and Haroldson, S. Time-out as a punishment for stuttering during conversation. *Journal of Communication Disorders,* 1971, *4,* 15–19.

Martyn, M., and Sheehan, J. Onset of stuttering and recovery. *Behavioral*

Research and Therapy, 1968, *6,* 295–307.

McCarthy, D. The language development of the preschool child. *Child Welfare Monograph,* 1930, *4.*

McDonald, E. *Articulation Testing and Treatment: A Sensory-Motor Approach.* Pittsburgh, PA: Stanwix House, Inc., 1964a.

———. *A Deep Test of Articulation.* Pittsburgh, PA: Stanwix House, Inc., 1964b.

McNeill, D. *The Acquisition of Language.* New York: Harper & Row, Publishers, 1970.

McNutt, J. Oral sensory and motor behaviors of children with /s/ or /r/ misarticulations. *Journal of Speech and Hearing Research.* 1977, *20,* 694–703.

McReynolds, L., and Engmann, D. *Distinctive Feature Analysis of Misarticulations.* Baltimore: University Park Press, 1975.

Milisen, R. The incidence of speech disorders, In L. E. Travis (ed.), *Handbook of Speech Pathology and Audiology.* New York: Appleton-Century-Crofts, 1971.

Morehead, D., and Ingram, D. The development of base syntax in normal and linguistically deviant children. *Journal of Speech and Hearing Research,* 1973, *16,* 330–352.

Mowrer, D.; Baker, R.; and Schultz, R. *Modification of the Frontal Lisp: Programmed Articulation Control Kit.* Tempe, AZ: Educational Psychological Research Associates, 1968.

Murphy, E. *Functional Voice Disorders.* Englewood Cliffs, NJ: Prentice-Hall Inc., 1964.

Newcomer, P., and Hammill, D. *Psycholinguistics in the Schools.* Columbus, OH: Charles E. Merrill Publishing Co., 1976.

Perkins, W. *Speech Pathology: An Applied Behavioral Science.* St. Louis: The C. V. Mosby Co., 1977.

Rousey, D.C., and Moriarty, A. *Diagnostic Implications of Speech Sounds.* Springfield, IL: Charles C Thomas, 1965.

Sanders, E. When are speech sounds learned? *Journal of Speech and Hearing Disorders,* 1972, *37,* 64–74.

Senturia, B., and Wilson, F. Otorhinolaryngic findings in children with voice disorders. *Annals of Otology, Rhinology, and Laryngology,* 1968, *77,* 1027–1045.

Shames, G., and Sherrick, C., Jr. A discussion of nonfluency and stuttering as operant behavior. *Journal of Speech and Hearing Disorders,* 1963, *28,* 3–18.

Sheehan, J. *Stuttering Research and Therapy.* New York: Harper & Row, Publishers, 1970.

Slobin, D. *Psycholinguistics.* Glenview, IL: Scott, Foresman and Company, 1971.

———, and Welsh, C. Elicited imitation as a research tool in developmental psycholinguistics. In C. Ferguson and D. Slobin (ed.), *Studies in Child Language Development.* New York: Holt, Rinehart and Winston, 1972.

Travis, L., and Rasmus, B. The speech sound discrimination ability of cases with functional disorders of articulation. *Quarterly Journal of Speech*, 1931, *17*, 217–226.

Van Riper, C. *The Nature of Stuttering*. Englewood Cliffs, NJ: Prentice-Hall, Inc., 1971.

————. *Speech Correction: Principles and Methods*. (6th ed.), Englewood Cliffs, NJ: Prentice-Hall, Inc., 1978.

————, and Erickson, R. *Predictive Screening Test of Articulation*. Kalamazoo, MI: Western Michigan University Press, 1968.

West, R. An agnostic's speculations about stuttering. In Eisenson, J. (ed.), *Stuttering: A Symposium*. New York: Harper & Row, Publishers, 1958.

Wilson, F. and Rice, M. *Voice Disorders*. Austin, TX: Learning Concepts, 1977.

Winitz, H. *Articulatory Acquisition and Behavior*. New York: Appleton-Century-Crofts, 1969.

————. *From Syllable to Conversation*. Baltimore: University Park Press, 1975.

Young, M. Onset, prevalence, and recovery from stuttering. *Journal of Speech and Hearing Disorders*, 1975, *40*, 49–58.

CHAPTER **9**

HEARING IMPAIRMENTS

DONALD MOORES

The education of individuals with hearing impairments presents unique challenges to special education because the loss of hearing prevents or hinders the development of language and communication ability through its normal channel—the auditory-vocal. The more severe the hearing loss, the greater the reliance on the visual-motor sphere in the acquisition of knowledge. Because severe hearing loss among children is relatively rare, there is a common misunderstanding of the essential difficulties it involves, as well as techniques necessary to allow children to develop to the full extent of their capabilities. Although special education began more than four-hundred years ago with the establishment of an educational program for deaf children in Spain, the education of hearing-impaired children is considered by most educators to be an esoteric area, somehow removed from general education and even other areas of special education. Perhaps the major reason for this misconception is related to the fact that most severely hearing-impaired individuals are normal physically, intellectually, and emotionally, but deviate from the general population greatly in terms of speech and mastery of English. The widely divergent patterns of functioning have caused serious misconceptions throughout history concerning the effects of severe hearing loss on the intellectual and psychological development of human beings. Only in the last few years have some traditional stereotypes been refuted, but it will be generations before their harmful effects are erased.

This chapter will deal with the education of children with severe hearing impairments from a number of perspectives. It is designed with the intention that the reader will achieve both a sensitivity toward the unique characteristics and needs of individuals with severe hearing impairments, and knowledge of trends in education, psychology, and linguistics designed to capitalize on these characteristics and meet these needs. Issues will be developed and presented from three perspectives: (a) historical trends; (b) education of hearing impaired individuals as it relates to general education; and (c) education of hearing impaired individuals as it relates to special education.

DEFINITION OF TERMS

Because so much confusion has existed over the use of terms such as deafness, hard of hearing, hearing impaired, acoustically impaired, and so forth, the Conference of Executives of American Schools for the Deaf has developed a set of definitions which would be useful for educational purposes (Frisina, 1974). It was first recommended that there be a conscious effort to emphasize distinctions between the terms *impairment, disability,* and *handicap,* rather than use them interchangeably. Briefly, *impairment* refers to the physical condition of the auditory mechanism. *Disability* is measured by reception of speech or other sounds calibrated for frequency and intensity. *Handicap* refers to the extent to which an individual's functioning is limited by the disability of deafness. The Conference of Executives of American Schools for the Deaf accepted the following definitions (Frisina, 1974):

> A Definition for Educational Placement and Research:
> *Deafness* refers to the condition of individuals whose hearing is disabled and is expressed in terms of speech or other sounds calibrated for frequency and intensity. Those individuals are classified according to the following categories of deafness. The stated requirements in communication and education associated with these levels are to be assumed necessary in each infant/child/adult until proved otherwise:
>
> 1. Level I, 35 to 54 dB.* Individuals in this category routinely do not require special class/school placement; they routinely do require special speech and hearing assistance.
> 2. Level II, 55 to 69 dB. These individuals occasionally require special class/school placement; they routinely require special speech, hearing and language assistance.
> 3. Level III, 70 to 89 dB. Those in this category of deafness occasionally

---

*The symbol dB refers to decibel, the standard unit for measurement of intensity of a sound. Zero decibels represents about the least intensity of sound that can be heard by the normal ear.

require special class/school placement; they routinely require special
speech, hearing, language, and educational assistance.

4. Level IV, 90 dB and beyond. These individuals routinely require special
   class/school placement; they routinely require special speech, hearing,
   language, and educational assistance.

Definitions Related to Age at Onset of Deafness:

Prelingual deafness refers to the condition of persons whose deafness was
present at birth or occurred at an age prior to the development of speech and
language.

Postlingual deafness refers to the condition of persons whose deafness occurred at an age following the spontaneous acquisition of speech and language.

As might be expected, mild hearing loss is relatively common in the
general population. For most individuals, the maturation and aging process
involves some diminution of hearing acuity. The present chapter, however,
is concerned with severe and profound hearing loss present at birth or
acquired at an early age. This is a very small subset of the hearing impaired
population. In a National Census of the Deaf Population, Schein and Delk
(1974) estimated that 13,400,000 Americans had an impairment of hearing.
This represents more than 6 percent of the population of the United States.
Of this number only 201,000 were prelingually deaf. Roughly, then, the rate
of hearing impairments at all ages in the United States is sixty-six per thousand; the rate of prelingual deafness is one per thousand.

HISTORICAL TRENDS*

Although obviously no direct evidence exists, it is possible that severe
hearing impairment has been part of the human condition since the origin
of the species. Evidence suggests that all existing human races or ethnic
groups possess genes for deafness. There is no reason to doubt that this
has always been the case. Throughout history, human beings probably
have been susceptible to diseases that could cause hearing losses such as
present day maternal rubella and meningitis. Untreated otitis media, or
middle ear infection, can also cause substantial hearing losses. It is logical
to assume that otitis media has always been relatively common.

Although hearing-impaired individuals would probably be at a disadvantage in most societies, there is no reason to believe they did not and
could not function effectively under most circumstances. It has been suggested (Moores, 1978) that perhaps the handicap of severe hearing impairment is greatest in highly industrialized, technical societies which put a
premium on oral communication skills. Evidence from an isolated tribe,
the Tasady of the Philippine Islands, would tend to support this. Nance

---

*This section will deal primarily with trends specifically related to later development of
programs in the United States. For a more complete treatment the reader is referred to
Moores (1978).

(1975) reported that two adults in the total community of approximately twenty-five people were deaf. The man was a member of the tribe, his wife was a deaf woman from another tribe. The couple took part in the procurement of food and social activities. According to Nance a sign language of great subtlety was employed in which plans could be made and communicated concerning such things as overnight trips and division of labor in food gathering and fishing. In his study of American Indian sign languages, Mallery (1880) reported on the case of a three-year-old deaf girl who communicated easily and efficiently by means of sign language with other members of the tribe.

Although one cannot generalize from a relatively few references to the presence of deafness in nonindustrialized societies, it is interesting to note that under such diverse environments as the Philippine forests and the American plains, deaf individuals existed, were accepted, and communicated effectively with other members of the community.

Ancient and Medieval Times

There are, of course, written references to deafness in the Bible, and Hebrew law specified the rights of deaf individuals. In classical Rome and Greece references to deafness and deaf individuals are common. For example, Socrates referred to the sign language of deaf (Levinson, 1967) and St. Augustine treated the issue of immortality as it related to hearing, speech, and the communication of deaf people (Fay, 1912).

In 530 A.D. the Justinian Code defined the rights of hearing-impaired individuals under the Roman Empire. The Code is quite sophisticated in that it differentiated between those born deaf and those with acquired deafness. It also addressed issues of residual hearing, speech ability, and literacy. Rights were bestowed on those with acquired deafness, speech, and/or literacy. However, despite enlightened treatment of those who had lost their hearing after acquiring speech and those with residual hearing, it should be pointed out that those who were deaf from birth typically had no rights. There is no evidence of any attempts to teach congenitally deaf children who, as a result of educational neglect, would grow up mute and illiterate, thus devoid of the benefit of the Code.

The position of deaf people in medieval times was probably even worse than in classical times. Many countries placed restrictions on civil rights of deaf individuals. Limitations frequently were placed on the right to marry, receive inheritances, and celebrate the Mass (H. Peet, 1851). It was not until near the end of the medieval period that serious consideration was first given to the possibility of educating deaf individuals.

The Beginning of Special Education: Spain

The first teacher of the deaf and the father of special education was a Spanish Benedictine monk, Pablo Ponce de Leon (1520–1584), who established a school at a monastery and utilized techniques which may have influenced later procedures used in education of deaf children, as well as indirectly providing the basic foundations for the work of Itard, Seguin, and Montessori with retarded populations.

Ponce de Leon was motivated to begin his work by the presence of two deaf brothers, Francisco and Pedro de Velasco, in the Monastery of San Salvador de Ona in North Central Spain (Chaves and Solar, 1974). The brothers were members of the wealthy and influential Velasco family which, for financial reasons, had a tradition of consanguineous marriages. The presence of recessive genes for deafness resulted in a large number of deaf children. Francisco and Pedro Velasco, for example, were from a family in which five of eight children were deaf. The three deaf sisters were sent to convents.

Ponce de Leon understood the task of teaching Francisco and Pedro Velasco to read, write, and speak. His efforts met with astonishing success. Francisco learned to speak and write and thus was able to obtain his legal inheritance (Peet, 1851). Pedro's success was even more spectacular. He became proficient in Spanish and Latin, studied history and was granted a special papal dispensation which allowed him to be ordained to the priesthood (Chaves and Solar, 1974). Ponce also taught two of the Velasco sisters and at least twelve other deaf individuals, most of whom were members of the Spanish aristocracy (Chaves and Solar, 1974; Moores, 1978).

Unfortunately Ponce de Leon did not train any successors to carry on his work, and efforts to educate the deaf stopped upon his death in 1584 and were not resumed until approximately thirty years later, again with members of the Velasco family. Some time around 1615 Juan Pablo Bonet undertook the instruction of Luis Velasco, whose grandfather, Inigo, was the brother of Francisco and Pedro Velasco (Chaves and Solar, 1974; Moores, 1978).

In 1620, Bonet produced the first book ever published on education of the deaf, *The Reduction of Letters and the Art of Teaching the Mute To Speak*. In his work Bonet claimed to have studied the matter himself and originated the methods completely. He never referred to the work of Ponce. Although Bonet must have been aware of the work of Ponce with the great uncles and aunts of young Luis, it is unclear whether he relied on techniques developed by Ponce or in fact generated his own methods independently. It is probable that he was influenced at least to some extent by Ponce. For example, Bonet advocated the use of a one-handed manual alphabet, which apparently was used by Ponce. Bonet's manual alphabet, incidentally, was taken to France by the Spanish educator, Pereire, and was later exported to the United States as the French Manual Alphabet. The present American Manual Alphabet is almost identical to Bonet's alphabet as illustrated in 1620.

Bonet emphasized the benefits of a consistent environment and urged all members of the family to use the manual alphabet. He emphasized early speech training and stressed a coordinated reliance on the integration of speech, writing, and finger spelling.

France

The beginnings of education of the deaf in France may be traced to the work of the Spanish born Jacob Rodriguez Pereire (1715–1780) whose family migrated to Portugal and finally France to escape religious persecution. Pereire utilized the one-handed alphabet and employed techniques of sense training that apparently were based on the work of Bonet. Although Pereire himself did not work directly with retarded individuals, his work heavily influenced techniques employed by later educators of the retarded. In his work with Victor, *The Wild Boy of Aveyron*, the physician Itard utilized sensory training procedures which can be traced to Pereire. Seguin, perhaps the leading early educator of the retarded in Europe and later in the United States, expressed his indebtedness to Pereire on many occasions (Seguin, 1860; Kanner, 1964). Montessori, in turn, based much of her work on the pioneering endeavors of Itard and Seguin. Thus, a straight line progression can be traced from Bonet—and possibly Ponce de Leon—in Spain through Pereire in France on to Itard, Seguin, and Montessori.

Although Pereire was the first documented educator of the deaf in France, the Abbé de l'Epée (1712–1789) is widely acclaimed as the father of education of the deaf in France. Many educators, unaware that de l'Epée's techniques were largely based on the pioneering work of Spanish predecessors, tend to view him as the dominant figure in early education of the deaf.

De l'Epée's major contribution was the establishment around 1755 of the first permanent school for the deaf in the world in Paris, a school that was the model for later schools for the deaf in the United States. De l'Epée was the catalyst for the establishment of additional schools in France and other countries, although he was severely criticized for his emphasis on sign language alone and his neglect of speechreading and articulation. His most vocal critics were Pereire and the German educator Heinicke (Garnett, 1968).

Establishment of Schools in the United States

The first United States school for the deaf, the American Asylum for the Education of the Deaf and Dumb, was established in 1817 in Hartford, Connecticut, by Thomas Hopkins Gallaudet. In hopes of combining elements of both oral and manual systems of instruction, Gallaudet had planned to study oral techniques in England and manual techniques in France. Rebuffed by British educators, he went on to France and observed the programs at the Paris school. He was able to obtain the services of Laurent Clerc, a deaf teacher at the school, who agreed to accompany Gallaudet to the United States and became the first teacher of the deaf at the American school.

At first it was thought that one school for the deaf would be sufficient to serve the needs of the entire country. However, as the existence of the school became advertised a large number of previously unknown deaf individuals were identified. Within three years, two more schools for the deaf were established, one in New York and one in Philadelphia. By the time of the Civil War there were schools in most states of the United States.

Contrary to popular opinion, not all of the earliest schools were residential institutions. The first schools usually were situated in metropolitan areas and many were originally day schools or combined day/residential schools. For example, two of the first three schools, New York and Philadelphia, started as day school programs. Residential components were added later when the schools began serving children from a wider geographic area. It was not until later that schools were built away from centers of population. Thus we find, in the North and East, that state schools for the deaf tend to be situated in metropolitan areas such as New York, Buffalo, Hartford, Philadelphia, and Pittsburgh. In the Midwest they are in towns such as Delavan, Wisconsin; Fulton, Missouri; Faribault, Minnesota; and Jacksonville, Illinois.

As in Europe, the establishment of schools for the deaf in the United States marked the beginnings of special education and provided the model for the later establishment of schools for the blind and the retarded. As the number of schools and programs for the deaf expanded and as the quality of instruction improved, progress was often hindered by the highly emotional and often personal arguments between proponents of oral-only, manual-only, and combined oral-manual systems. The often bitter hostility between the various camps has been continued until the present day. Only in recent years has there been discernible progress toward resolution of the problems.

SPEECH, SOUND AND THE PROCESS OF HEARING

An exposition of the physics of sound and the anatomy and physiology of the speech and hearing mechanisms is beyond the scope of this chapter. Readers interested in comprehensive treatment of these subjects should refer to Wever (1949), *Theory of Hearing;* Ladefoged (1962), *Elements of Acoustic Phonetics;* and Zemlin (1968), *Speech and Hearing Sciences, Anatomy and Physiology.* Two useful introductory texts would be Northern (1976), *Hearing Disorders;* and Durant and Lovronic (1977), *Bases of Hearing Science.* A nontechnical presentation of the use of hearing aids is presented by Berger (1970), *The Hearing Aid.*

Sound is a physical entity and the study of sound, *acoustics,* is a discipline in the field of physics. Vibration is the source of all sounds, and in the human voice the vibrations are produced through articulatory mechanisms. Human speech itself involves a variety of complex processes. Articulation, one of the major processes, is concerned with the production of speech sounds through modifications of the vocal tract. The primary articulators for human speech are the lips, teeth, tongue, palate, and pharynx. Changes in placement and manner of these articulators produce changes in human speech sounds. The power sources for speech are the lungs and various muscular and skeletal elements. Respiration provides the basic air stream for speech. The larynx produces a vibrating air stream and provides phonation which deals with vocal tone production.

The major mechanisms involved in human speech production all represent secondary adaptations. Their primary biological functions are closely related to eating and breathing.

Sound, then, is the physical stimulus that triggers the process of hearing. During this process sound undergoes three basic transformations as it is conducted to and processed by the human brain. The ear may be viewed as consisting of three major parts; the inner ear, the middle ear, and the outer ear (Figure 9–1). Sound reaches the outer ear in the form of acoustic energy. Upon hitting the eardrum it is converted to mechanical energy and carried across the middle ear. Between the middle and inner ear boundaries, the mechanical energy is transformed to hydraulic energy and conducted through the fluid of the cochlear and vestibular structures. The hydraulic energy finally is converted to neuroelectric impulses which are transmitted to the brain.

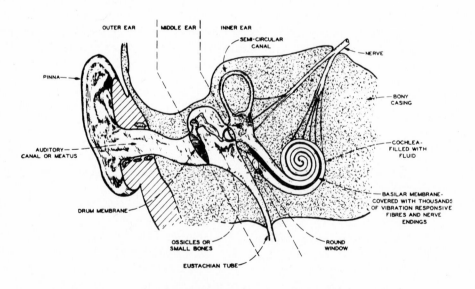

DIAGRAM OF THE EAR

FIG. 9–1   Anatomy of the ear. Drawing of the outer, middle, and inner ear based upon frontal section of the head. (Adapted from Brodel, M. (1946). *Three Unpublished Drawings of the Anatomy of the Human Ear*, W. B. Saunders Co., Philadelphia.)

The outer and middle ears serve to collect and transform sound preparatory to hearing. They may be considered basically the conducting apparatus. The outer ear consists not only of the auricle, the external flap which lay persons think of as the ear, but also the external auditory meatus, or ear canal, leading to the tympanic membrane (eardrum).

The middle ear is an extremely small cavity. Although small, the middle ear is complex and contains, or is attached to, a number of important structures, including the tympanic membrane and the Eustachian tube. Within the middle ear is the ossicular chain, consisting of the three hardest bones in the human body, the malleus, incus, and stapes, also known as the hammer, anvil, and stirrup (Figure 9–2). The malleus is attached to the tympanic membrane and mechanical energy is carried across the middle ear through the interaction of the malleus, incus, and stapes. The inner ear, located deep in the skull, contains both the cochlear system, the sensory organs for hearing, and the vestibular system, the sensory organs for balance. The inner ear consists of a series of interconnecting canals within the exceptionally hard and dense portion of the temporal bone. The three major portions of the inner ear are the semicircular canals, the vestibule, and the cochlea.

The external, middle, and inner ear comprise the peripheral auditory system. Connection between the peripheral auditory system and the central nervous system is provided by the VIIIth cranial nerve, the acoustic nerve. Neurons carry acoustic energy to the brain through the acoustic nerve, which passes through a canal called the internal auditory nectus and opens into the cranial cavity.

Given the complexity of the hearing process, it is not surprising that

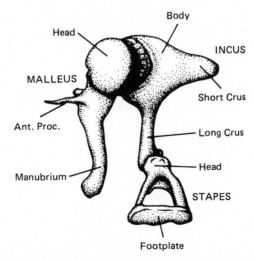

FIG. 9–2 The Ossicular chain. (Based on drawing by Anson, B. J., and Donaldson, J. A. [1973.] *Surgical Anatomy of the Temporal Bone and Ear.* W. B. Saunders Co., Philadelphia.)

there are breakdowns in the system. In fact, it is somewhat surprising that the incidence of hearing loss is relatively low in human populations.

Children exhibiting severe to profound hearing losses and in need of intensive remediation typically do not have hearing losses caused by malfunctions in the conductive systems in the outer and middle ear. Such problems frequently can be treated either surgically or by bypassing part of the conductive system. The major causes of prelingual childhood deafness—for example, recessive genetic inheritance, maternal rubella, meningitis—tend to be sensorineural in nature. They tend to disrupt inner ear functioning or the processing of acoustic information. Despite some progress, there is little optimism about dramatic medical breakthroughs to cure such deafness in the foreseeable future.

ETIOLOGICAL CONSIDERATIONS

Although many people tend to think of deafness and deaf individuals as encompassing a general category, the cause of deafness can have considerable implications for the child's development and functioning. It is especially important that etiological factors be taken into account because many of the causes of deafness are related to other handicapping conditions. It should be pointed out that frequently there is great difficulty in pinpointing the cause of deafness. The process is usually retrospective. Parents typically may have had no prior experience with deafness and the final diagnosis may not be made until the child is two, three, or four years of age. Tracing the cause can be difficult under these circumstances. It is not surprising to find that even in recent surveys, the cause is listed as unknown for approximately 30 percent of the deaf school-age population (Moores, 1978).

Major Causes of Deafness

Major causes of deafness have been an object of investigation in the United States and Europe since the nineteenth century. Attention was especially devoted to the relationship between deafness and consanguinity, marriage between close relatives. In the United States Bemiss (1858), Peet (1856), and Turner (1848) all expressed concern over the fact that marriage of relatives tended to produce a much higher proportion of handicapped children than marriage of nonrelated people. In Europe the reported rates of deafness in the middle of the nineteenth century ranged from one per two hundred in isolated areas of Switzerland with frequent consanguineous marriage, to less than one per two thousand in parts of Germany with more heterogeneous populations (H. Peet, 1854). Although there was probably a large number of unreported deaf children in Germany at that time, the differences are still significant. Other investigators throughout Europe (Buxton, 1858; Morris, 1861) consistently reported that the proportion of children born deaf was highest in those areas of stable

homogeneous populations and lowest where the populations were heterogeneous. As late as 1963 in the United States, Sank and Kallman (1963)
reported that 12 percent of a sample of the deaf population of New York
State were children of marriages of near relatives.

Although deafness is related to a number of factors and conditions
such as prematurity and mother-child blood incompatibility, there are
three major commonly accepted etiologies: rubella, meningitis, and hereditary deafness.

RUBELLA. Although maternal rubella is the most widely known and
most common nongenetic congenital (present at birth) cause of deafness,
its relationship to deafness was not established until 1944 (Bordley,
Brookhauser, Hardy, and Hardy, 1967). Rubella is a common virus disease
that frequently is quite mild in effect and often difficult to diagnose. The
danger occurs if a woman is in the first three months of pregnancy. The
virus is capable of killing growing cells, with the developing tissues of the
eye and ear particularly vulnerable in the sixth and thirteenth weeks of
pregnancy. In addition to severe hearing loss, effects of rubella might include vision problems, heart defects, and inadequate skeletal development, among others.

Rubella is cyclical with the greatest known effect occurring in the early
1960s in the United States, accounting for a great increase in the deaf population for that period and tremendously increasing the number of deaf-
blind children. This "rubella bulge" is passing through our educational
system. Although no comparable epidemic has occurred to date, the effects of the 1960s epidemic will be felt for years to come.

It is possible that immunizations and therapeutic abortions have reduced deafness due to rubella. Eventually rubella will be eliminated as a
cause of deafness but technical problems must be solved first. Some of
the dangers, as expressed by Chenoweth (1969) are: (1) Rubella babies
may excrete the virus for three years and endanger fetuses; (2) Vaccination of pregnant women is dangerous to the fetus; (3) Vaccination of a
woman who becomes pregnant within two months of vaccination is dangerous to the fetus.

MENINGITIS. Meningitis has long been recognized as the most common
cause of adventitious deafness, that is, deafness acquired after birth. It
was estimated to account for almost 30 percent of the cases of deafness in
the late nineteenth century, dropping to 15 percent by 1920 (Best, 1943).
Incidence figures have steadily declined since that time due to the development of antibiotics and chemotherapy.

Meningitis involves a bacterial invasion of the labyrinths and is accompanied by a high fever. Improved medical treatment has reduced the
number of children who are deaf as an aftermath of meningitis. However
there is some indication that children—especially very young children—
who previously might have died are now living, but survive with not only
severe hearing losses but also other handicaps in addition to deafness.

Recent estimates of prevalence suggest that meningitis accounts for 5 percent to 7 percent of the total school-age deaf population (Hudgins, 1973; Ries, 1973). One exception to this is the black deaf population, in which as much as 18 percent of the school-age deaf may have an etiology of meningitis. The higher prevalence probably reflects less adequate medical care.

HEREDITARY DEAFNESS. Although estimates of the prevalence of hereditary deafness vary widely, it is the most common cause of early childhood deafness, possibly accounting for half of all cases. Although deafness can be transmitted through dominant inheritance and there are some cases of sex-linked deafness, probably more than 90 percent of inherited deafness involves transmission of recessive genes. Typically, each parent has normal hearing but is a "carrier" for deafness. A child who receives a recessive gene for deafness from each parent, an event which occurs in 25 percent of such cases, would be deaf. Frequently deafness has not occurred within the memory of members of either side of the family. In many cases there is a tendency to search for other causes; in an unknown number of cases, rubella may incorrectly be identified as the cause.

Of the major causes, only hereditary deafness is not related to a high incidence of other handicapping conditions. Although syndromes exist with a number of characteristics, most children who are deaf because of hereditary factors are normal physically and mentally. A larger proportion of deaf children with histories of rubella or meningitis suffer from additional handicaps.

EDUCATIONAL PROGRAMS

Somewhat less than 60,000 hearing-impaired children in the United States presently receive some kind of special education services, a figure consistent with estimates that the prevalence of prelingual deafness in the population is approximately one per one thousand (Carhart, 1969; Schein and Delk, 1974). Most of the children currently in programs would have severe to profound hearing losses, Levels III and IV in the previously presented definitions. A larger number of children with milder hearing losses exist who may or may not be receiving appropriate services. Many are probably receiving speech and hearing services. Unfortunately, it is quite possible that many others have been misdiagnosed as learning disabled or retarded. It is to be hoped that the needs of children with mild and moderate hearing losses will be addressed more efficiently as school programs move toward more individualized models of instruction.

As of October 1976, a total of 58,468 hearing-impaired children were identified as enrolled in special programs for the hearing impaired (Craig and Craig, 1977). Table 9–1 presents both program and student information. Although traditionally the majority of students have been educated in residential schools, most children now are enrolled in public school programs. Also, as may be seen in Table 9–1, approximately 25 percent of

Table 9-1   Summary of Schools and Classes in the United States, October 1, 1976

SCHOOLS	PUBLIC RESIDENTIAL SCHOOLS (65)	PRIVATE RESIDENTIAL SCHOOLS (9)	PUBLIC DAY SCHOOLS (63)	PRIVATE DAY CLASSES (29)	PUBLIC DAY CLASSES (103)	PRIVATE DAY CLASSES (25)	MULTI-HANDICAPPED ONLY (30)	SPECIAL HANDICAP FACILITIES (47)	TOTAL SCHOOLS AND CLASSES (671)
Program Data (classes)									
Preschool	43	7	52	13	262	17	15	16	425
Multihandicapped Program	46	3	36	5	148	10	0	0	248
High School	52	1	25	1	130	3	0	0	212
Total Enrollment	18,884	605	7,909	656	27,729	513	709	1,503	58,468
Student Enrollment									
Residential	13,378	310	4	0	113	0	213	1,025	15,043
Day	4,855	252	6,090	554	17,007	431	425	292	29,906
Mainstreamed	64	40	731	62	4,980	57	21	53	6,008
Partially Mainstreamed	547	3	1,084	40	5,629	25	50	133	7,511
Total									
Multihandicapped	4,479	19	1,600	146	2,811	97	403	1,304	10,859
Deaf-Blind	112	0	92	8	167	7	105	480	971
Deaf-Mentally Retarded	793	2	265	3	799	19	91	637	2,609
Learning Disabled, incl. Aphasic	1,435	10	781	68	791	30	52	45	3,212
Socially-Emotionally Disturbed	747	0	189	4	272	8	11	22	1,253
Other Multi-handicapped	791	1	112	11	376	20	14	18	1,343
Combination	601	6	161	52	406	13	130	102	1,471

Source: Adapted from W. Craig and H. Craig (ed.) Directory of Services, **American Annals of the Deaf**, 1977, 122, p. 138.

students in residential schools commute daily. Therefore less than 50 percent of students in programs for the deaf are now residential students.

The number of children in programs for the deaf approximately doubled over a fifteen-year period beginning in 1961, when 28,529 children were enrolled (Doctor, 1962). The increase has been even greater than the general population growth, but there is no real evidence of an increase in the incidence of deafness itself. In addition to the population increase, a number of other factors may be identified. First, a severe rubella epidemic in the early 1960s caused an unusually high incidence of deafness over a two-year period. These children are still moving through the educational system. In addition, preschool and postsecondary opportunities have expanded significantly. Also, under the impact of federal and state legislation, growing numbers of children with less severe hearing losses are now being served. Finally, there are the beginnings of a commitment to serve severely multiply handicapped deaf individuals.

Early Intervention Programs

Data presented by the *Annual Directory of Programs and Services for the Deaf* reveal a tremendous increase over a fifteen-year period in the number of young children receiving services (Craig and Craig, 1977; Doctor, 1962). Impetus developed in the mid-1960s to meet the needs of children affected by the rubella epidemic of 1962–1963. At present it appears that a majority of severely hearing-impaired children are identified and receive some educational services prior to beginning school at the traditional kindergarten or first-grade level.

Many programs were first established in clinics or speech and hearing centers. In recent years public school districts increasingly have assumed responsibility for providing services to severely hearing-impaired children at the time of identification. The process has been facilitated by both mandatory and permissive legislation at federal and state levels.

As might be expected during a period of rapid program growth, preschool programs for the deaf in the 1960s followed a variety of models. Evaluation of the effectiveness of such programs was of limited usefulness in that evaluations were typically limited to one program and were conducted with individuals affiliated with the program being assessed (Craig, Craig, and DiJohnson, 1972; Hester, 1963; McConnell and Horton, 1970; McCroskey, 1968; Simmons, 1967).

Moores and associates (Moores, Weiss, and Goodwin, 1976, 1978; Weiss, Goodwin, and Moores, 1976), conducted a longitudinal evaluation of seven public and residential preschool programs for the deaf over a five-year period. Among the major results were:

1. The children functioned in the normal range intellectually, measured by the WISC Performance Scale and Piagetian measures of classification, conservation and seriation.

2. The children scored at age norms for children with normal hearing on four of the five visual motor subtests of the Illinois Test of Psycholinguistic Abilities (ITPA). (On the fifth subtest, Manual Expression, they were significantly higher than the learning norms.)
3. At age seven, the children possessed decoding skills for reading readiness equivalent to hearing children. However, they exhibited difficulty in processing complex linguistic structures such as passives and negatives.
4. At age seven, the children were below norms for hearing children in arithmetic.
5. It was possible to incorporate strong programs in auditory training, speech, and manual communication at very early ages. The different components seemed to facilitate each other.
6. The single most effective means of communication was simultaneous use of speech and manual communication.
7. The most effective programs had both cognitive-academic and social elements from the beginning; children in programs introducing cognitive-academic training after age four fell steadily behind in all academic measures.

The results here served as the basis for recommended policies and procedures for early intervention programs (Moores, Weiss, & Goodwin, 1976). Complete details of the study, extending from 1969 to 1975, may be found in Moores, Weiss, and Goodwin, 1978.

Postsecondary Education

Special note should be made of what amounts to a revolution in education for the deaf, the amazing explosion of programs available at the postsecondary level. In 1864, Gallaudet College was established in Washington, D.C. (M. Boatner, 1959). It remains today the only liberal arts college for the deaf in the world. Incredibly, from 1864 to 1964, while postsecondary opportunities for the general population were rapidly expanding, essentially no new programs were established for the deaf. Deaf individuals had a very restricted choice: they could either attend Gallaudet College or attempt to succeed at other colleges with little or no support services. The difficulties inherent in the second choice are illustrated by the results of a study of deaf graduates of hearing colleges involving the University of Illinois Institute for Research on Exceptional Children, the Alexander Graham Bell Association for the Deaf, the National Association of the Deaf, and the United States Vocational Rehabilitation Administration (Quigley, Jenne, and Phillips, 1968). The investigators were able to identify only 113 prelingually deaf individuals who had graduated from regular colleges and universities from 1910 to 1965.

In 1965, more than one hundred years after the establishment of Gallaudet College, the United States Congress authorized the establishment of the National Technical Institute for the Deaf (NTID), which was designed to serve as a technical school alternate to the liberal arts offerings of Gallaudet. NTID was based on a different administrative model in that

Courtesy of the Bell & Howell Company.

it is a part of the Rochester (New York) Institute of Technology, and the program is coordinated with that originally designed for students with normal hearing. The range of offerings vary from self-contained programs entirely for deaf students to attendance in integrated classes with students with normal hearing. Counseling, tutoring, speech training, note-taking services, and manual communication interpreters are provided according to a student's needs. NTID is viewed as a national program serving highly qualified deaf students.

Shortly after the establishment of NTID, federal legislation also facilitated the establishment of three regional vocational-technical programs for deaf students at the postsecondary level. Like NTID the programs were established at already existing institutions for students with normal hearing and were designed to provide additional services in the form of tutoring, counseling, interpreter services, note-taking, and so on. The programs were located at Delgado Vocational Technical Junior College in New Orleans (Louisiana), Seattle (Washington) Community College, and St. Paul (Minnesota) Technical Vocational Institute.

In 1964, California State University at Northridge (CSUN) first accepted deaf graduate students into its National Leadership Training Program in the Area of Deafness. Given note-taking and interpreter services the students proved that they were capable of competing with hearing students on an equal basis and met the requirements for the M.A. degree. Since that time deaf students have been accepted into the program on a regular basis (R. Jones, 1972).

When CSUN established a graduate program to train teachers of the deaf in 1969, a special effort was made to attract deaf students. Shortly after this, services were expanded to enable deaf students to enroll in all programs at the university. By 1975, more than 150 deaf individuals had earned graduate degrees from CSUN.* The results are amazing in comparison to the figures reported by Quigley, Jenne, and Phillips on the number of deaf individuals graduating from regular colleges in the United States from 1910 to 1965. The results indicate that a modest commitment in terms of counseling, interpreter services, and note-taking can have tremendous impact on educational opportunities available to deaf individuals.

Several programs have also been developed since 1969 based on legislation mandating that federal funds committed to vocational education should be utilized to a significant degree to train handicapped individuals. Many states developed programs for the deaf, again in facilities originally designed for students with normal hearing. The programs generally followed the same model as NTID, CSUN, and the three regional vocational technical programs. Most provided manual interpreters, counseling, note-taking, and tutoring services. By 1972, there were twenty-seven postsecondary programs for the deaf (Stuckless and Delgado, 1973), and by 1975 the number had expanded to more than 40 programs (Rawlings, Trybus, Delgado and Stuckless, 1975).

To put the growth of opportunities in proper perspective, it should be repeated that from 1864 to 1964 only one postsecondary program available exclusively to deaf students was in existence—Gallaudet College. From 1965 to 1975 more than forty new postsecondary programs were established, offering training at the vocational, technical, and collegiate levels.

Racial and Ethnic Minorities

It is not surprising to find that deaf individuals from ethnic and racial minorities have not received full benefits from existing educational programs. The problems faced by groups today seem to be similar to those documented from the 1830 U.S. Census, the first census in which an attempt was made to enumerate the deaf population of the United States. Census findings were intriguing to educators and legislators alike and caused a large amount of controversy and speculation. Some of the major

*Personal communication, Dr. Ray Jones, Director of CSUN Programs in Deafness.

findings indicated that the incidence of deafness was lower in the United States than in Europe. Within the United States deafness appeared to be much less common among blacks than in the Caucasian population. Each census also resulted in a far higher incidence of deafness in rural areas as opposed to the cities. Finally, the incidence of deafness appeared to be declining in some states, notably in southern New England, and remaining stable or increasing in other states, particularly in the Southeast.

The reasons for such findings obviously must have been complex, but they do have some bearing to the unique nature of the nineteenth-century American population, as well as implications for the present situation. The results of the four censuses from 1830 to 1860 in regard to the deaf were addressed in great detail by the Superintendent of the Census Bureau (Kennedy, 1862, 1864). In regard to reported differences between the United States and Europe, it is quite possible that there was a higher incidence in Europe. In many areas of Europe the population is stable and homogeneous; in most of the United States at that time the population tended to be mobile and heterogeneous. In fact it was argued that the parts of the United States in which deafness was declining had heterogeneous populations, and where deafness was increasing, the population was homogeneous. It was also documented that very few deaf people were immigrants to the United States. On the other hand it was acknowledged that perhaps the European census figures were more accurate than the American in identifying deaf individuals, and that perhaps the differences were negligible (Kennedy, 1862). By virtue of their more stable populations with less linguistic and cultural diversity within any one area, it is probable that the figures obtained in Europe were more accurate. In the United States spot checks on children enrolled at schools for the deaf indicated that as many as one half were not identified by the census (Kennedy, 1864). Deaf children under ten years of age were seldom identified.

The differential rates of deafness reported in cities and country areas were explained by other factors, especially since enrollment in schools for the deaf in large part consisted of children from cities. As in recent census efforts, reports on city dwellers, the poor, and speakers of foreign languages yielded inaccurate results. In commenting on the findings Kennedy (1864) stated:

> There is no reason to suppose that the proportion of deaf mutes found in cities is really smaller than in the country. The small proportion returned from the city is to be ascribed to the greater haste and carelessness of assistant marshalls hurrying from door to door in a populous city, among families most of whom are strangers to him, while the marshall who takes the census of a small district in the country generally knows all of the deaf mutes in his district and hence is much less likely to overlook them.
>
> ...we find that, first, children under ten; second, large cities; third, emigrants, especially foreigners, each present a very small proportion of deaf mutes. Hence, a district where the proportion of children is large, and where

a large proportion of the population live in cities, and are where there is a large immigrant population, will respectively return small proportion of deaf mutes (p. 58).

Although the situation has improved somewhat in the more than one hundred years since Kennedy drew his conclusions, many of his general comments are relevant today for minority populations of the United States who tend to live in large cities, have difficulty or are reluctant to provide information to outsiders, and have a greater proportion of their children under ten than the general population. Although the situation is probably similar for all minority groups, information exists for only the two largest groups; the Spanish-surnamed and the black.

SPANISH-SURNAMED. The three largest sources of the present Spanish-surnamed population of the United States are Mexico, Puerto Rico, and Cuba. The Mexican-American, or Chicano, population can be traced not only to Mexico but to southwestern states taken from Mexico in 1848 following the Mexican-American War. Puerto Rico, of course, has commonwealth status and has been part of the United States since the Spanish-American War in 1898. The greatest impetus for Cuban migration was the takeover of Cuba by the Castro regime. Obviously there is great ethnic and cultural diversity in the Spanish-surnamed population of the United States. What is shared is the Spanish language, the heritage of the Spanish colonial system, and a surprising number of traditions which have endured for generations over different environments.

For the most part the needs of Spanish-surnamed deaf individuals have been ignored by educators. There has been an unfortunate assumption that the Spanish-surnamed population is small. For example, in the most recent national census of the deaf (Schein and Delk, 1974), enumeration of the Spanish-surnamed population was ignored.

The extent of the deaf Spanish-surnamed population was first shown by a survey of programs for the deaf by Gentile and McCarthy (1973), which found that of those deaf children in programs in 1971 for whom ethnic information was available, 7 percent were Spanish surnamed.

The present Spanish-surnamed population of the United States, as related to deafness, seems to have many characteristics in common with immigrant populations as observed by Kennedy in 1862 and 1864. First, the population is predominantly urban, making enumeration of all individuals, hearing and deaf, difficult. Secondly, many of the adults are not proficient in English, restricting communication with census takers. Third, there is a suspicion of government workers, which is exacerbated when a proportion of the population may not have entered the country legally. Just as in the nineteenth century a large number of Irish migrated to Canada and then illegally crossed the St. Lawrence River, in the twentieth century a large number of Chicanos, or their parents, have illegally crossed the Rio Grande. In both cases there has been a noticeable lack of enthusiasm about volunteering information.

The figure of 7 percent of the school-age population for 1971 must be seen as a minimum. It is probably much larger and increasing. The Spanish-surnamed population has the highest birth rate of any group in the United States. Undoubtedly there are illegal aliens who fear to request services for their deaf children, and there are probably many children receiving no educational services because of the lack of programs or discrimination, either covert or overt (Maestas y Moores and Moores, in preparation).

There is a surprising lack of sensitivity toward cultural differences and needs of Spanish-surnamed deaf children. There has been no attention, for example, given to phonemic, syntactic, and semantic properties of English as they relate to different dialects of Spanish spoken in the United States.

At present there are very few Spanish-surnamed teachers of the deaf or administrators. Those working with Spanish-surnamed deaf children frequently have little understanding of the social/cultural background of the children and have difficulty communicating with parents.

BLACK.   Black deaf individuals have received more attention than their Spanish-speaking counterparts, probably because blacks have constituted a significant portion of the population of the United States since its inception. However, the extent of deafness and the needs of black deaf individuals consistently have been underestimated. From 1830 to 1930, when information on deafness was gathered, each census reported a much lower incidence of deafness in blacks than in the rest of the population (Best, 1943). Every investigation since World War II also has identified a smaller number of black deaf individuals than would be expected. The numbers have been so low that there has been a consensus that deafness is relatively more rare in the American black population (Schein and Delk, 1974).

Recent evidence summarized by Moores and Oden (1977) indicates that approximately 15 percent of the school-age deaf population is black, a figure consistent with or even somewhat higher than the black proportion of the general school-age population. There is evidence that the incidence of deafness due to meningitis, for example, is higher for the black population (Gentile and McCarthy, 1973), which can be explained by less adequate medical care.

Black deaf individuals only now are beginning to receive minimal services. As recently as 1963, eight states maintained separate facilities for black deaf students (Babbidge, 1965). Gallaudet College, the only liberal arts college for the deaf in the world, did not accept black students until after World War II (Bowe, 1971). The economic status of black deaf adults is below that of white deaf adults (Best, 1943; Furfey and Harte, 1968; Lunde and Bigman, 1959). Black deaf adults frequently face discrimination from social clubs consisting of white deaf members (Anderson and Bowe, 1972).

In terms of educational programs, black deaf children are unlikely to be diagnosed and receive training in preschool years. Deaf black children are also more likely to be classified as retarded by the school systems (Moores and Oden, 1977).

As is the case with the Spanish-surnamed population, the size of the deaf black population has been seriously underestimated. As such, the needs have been minimized and no systematic attempts have been made to address the major problems.

SPECIAL NEEDS AND LOW INCIDENCE: THE PROVISION OF SERVICES

One of the dilemmas facing educators of the deaf is the question of how to provide adequate services to children who require instruction from highly trained specialized professionals, but who constitute a very small proportion of the population. At present, heavily populated large metropolitan areas may handle the situation adequately because their population base enables them to concentrate resources and to provide children with a range of options. In terms of educational placement the options could range from self-contained classrooms, to a resource room model, to provision of services on an itinerant basis, to mixed classes of deaf and hearing students team taught by a teacher of the deaf and a teacher of the hearing. Any comprehensive program should have all of these options available to meet the needs of individual children. In the past only children with relatively moderate hearing losses and/or well-developed oral skills were candidates for integrated settings and resource rooms. In recent years more profoundly deaf children have been placed in such settings with special provisions such as interpreters and individual tutoring provided.

The problem is much more complex in more sparsely populated regions. Given an incidence of severe hearing impairment of one per one thousand, it is difficult for school districts of low or moderate density to provide the trained personnel and equipment necessary for appropriate parent counseling, language and speech therapy, sound treatment of rooms, and curriculum modification. Many parents face an age-old problem: they want to keep their children at home, yet they are not sure if the local educational systems can meet the needs of their children. Sending a child away to school can cause enormous strains. So can keeping a child at home if parents feel this retards academic and social development.

Trends at the present time are not clear. There is a movement toward regionalization of services or multidistrict cooperation. Although for many regions the geographical area is great and teachers may spend a great amount of time driving, the model has worked in some cases. One variation of this model has been to establish a number of self-contained classrooms and resource rooms in centralized facilities and to have children with more profound hearing losses stay in foster homes four days a week.

In spite of the success of some regional programs, many areas of the country simply do not have the population base to provide adequate education for all hearing-impaired children. For many of these children the least restrictive environment is not the regular classroom or resource room, but a highly specialized program.

Regions throughout the United States are experimenting with various systems to try to meet the needs of as many hearing-impaired children as possible. Perhaps the most common model is to serve all children at the preschool and elementary school ages. By the time children reach junior high school age, there is greater educational complexity. For example, in most school districts in the United States, many elementary schools provide the students for one junior high school. Two or three junior high schools, in turn, provide the students for one senior high school. As students mature and as the range of curricular materials widens, there is a need for a larger critical mass of students. By the same token, it is possible that the same situation exists for hearing-impaired students. Perhaps many who can be served in local programs through the elementary years need more specialized programs from junior high school and beyond. At present, many residential schools for the deaf have relatively high enrollments of junior and senior high school students because of transfers of

Courtesy of the Lexington School for the Deaf.

students from local districts. Whether or not the pattern of educating young hearing-impaired children in local districts, and older students in regional centers or residential schools, is an effective model is not known. There are no data to either support or refute it. However, it does seem to be a policy, either implicit or explicit, in many states.

Another approach has been to serve all hearing-impaired children in local or regional programs, but to provide no local services to severely multiply handicapped children. This approach can be challenged on the basis of recent legislative and judicial developments, but many school districts simply do not have the capability to meet the needs of such children at present. Whether the capabilities will be developed is not clear.

A third alternative is for local and regional programs to provide for children with moderate hearing losses and to refer those with more severe and profound losses to residential schools. In the past, this has been the most common practice for low- and medium-density areas, but this is changing as more school districts make good faith efforts to educate children near the home environment.

Given the obvious state of flux and uncertainties at present, it should be constructive to realize that educators and parents have been facing the same issues over almost two hundred years in the United States and in Europe with wide fluctuations in policy. An examination of policies and practices in other times might help to put the present situation in proper perspective.

National Mainstream Movements

For some reason most educators seem to believe that interest in educating deaf children contiguous to hearing peers is a recent phenomenon. In reality, educators of the deaf historically have been interested in educating deaf children at home, in interaction with hearing children. One reason why most schools in the nineteenth century did not accept students until relatively late ages was a reluctance to separate young children from their families. In fact a large number of articles in early issues of the *American Annals of the Deaf* related to early instructions and directions for parents of young deaf children (Ayers, 1849; Crouter, 1885; Gordon, 1885a; Hirsch, 1887; H. Peet, 1886; Ray, 1852; Waldo, 1859). In many cases the advantages of living at home were emphasized (Gordon, 1885b; Pettengill, 1874), and in fact the first preschool program for the deaf in the United States integrated deaf and hearing children into a school with all children learning signs and manual alphabet. The school was modeled along the lines of a family unit (Bartlett, 1952).

There were attempts to educate deaf children in regular classes in Germany and in England at the beginning of the nineteenth century (Gordon, 1885b). In fact there were national mainstreaming movements in Germany and France in the nineteenth century and in the Soviet Union in the twentieth century. In each case the movement was abandoned. A brief examination of these movements, as well as activity in the United States, should be instructive. The interested reader might wish to pursue the subject in greater detail (Moores, 1978). Awareness of the failures of the past might help to avoid at least some of the more obvious pitfalls.

Germany

The sources of the mainstream movement for handicapped children may be traced to the work of German educators of the deaf in the early nineteenth century. As early as 1815, opposition to residential schools for the deaf was expressed. Criticism centered on cost of residential facilities, separation from families, and isolation from children with normal hearing. An experimental school was established in Bavaria in 1821 in which deaf and hearing children were taught together for much of the day, with the deaf children receiving additional special tutoring. Within two years six programs based on this model were established in public schools. In 1828 the German Ministry of Education predicted that within ten years all deaf children would be served by the schools. The predicted results did not come to pass and the program was abandoned in Bavaria. Gordon (1885b) quoted the German educator Moritz Hill, as stating that school authorities and parents of hearing children opposed the integration of deaf children because they were always a detriment to academic progress of hearing children.

A similar mainstream movement started somewhat later in Prussia. In 1871 only 60 percent of deaf children were enrolled in residential schools and 40 percent in common schools. Within ten years not one deaf child was left in the common schools (Gordon, 1885b).

France

Beginning in the 1830s, movements in support of integrated education of deaf and hearing children and closing of institutions for deaf began to gather strength. By the 1850s ten integrated schools were in operation, the French Council of Public Education enthusiastically supported integration, and the French Ministry of Education officially endorsed the system. When the results did not meet the promises of the more enthusiastic supporters of integration, the official endorsement of the Ministry was withdrawn and within a generation no more than thirty deaf children were receiving training in integrated settings (Gordon, 1885b).

The Soviet Union

Following the revolution, an effort was made to educate deaf children in the same environments as hearing children. The results were negligible and it was decided that deaf children possess unique characteristics. Appropriate education, therefore, can meet the potential for such children in specialized environments involving highly trained personnel and curricula specifically designed for deaf children. For the past several decades, the Soviet system has been based on segregated residential facilities and a minimum of contact with hearing children for educational purposes (Gallagher and Martin, 1974).

Implications

Most educators of the deaf are not aware of the existence of the previously mentioned national mainstream movements. In fact, most educators are not aware of similar trends in other areas of special education. Although the movement in each of the three countries had unique characteristics, a number of common trends may be identified. The most obvious commonality is that, despite enthusiastic early support and projections of success, each movement failed and was abandoned. No lasting benefit could be perceived. Obviously, the reasons for failure were complex, many of them not related to the realities of today's world. There were a number of beliefs—implicit and explicit—about mainstreaming that were false. To some extent many of the same assumptions are in existence today. In the author's opinion they are as potentially harmful now as they have been in the past. Probably the greatest danger has been assuming an "all or none" approach. Many of the early supporters of mainstreaming were primarily motivated by a desire to eliminate residential schools and replace them with one model which they favored. In other words, rather than expanding the options available to deaf children, one restrictive system was substituted for another. In either system some children would suffer. A second mistake was the belief that merely placing deaf children with hearing children would be beneficial. There was—and is—ignorance of the fact that deaf children do in fact have special needs, especially in the area of communication. A "normalized" environment will not produce "normal" academic achievement in a deaf child; special techniques are necessary. Without special services the failures of the German, French, and Soviet experiments will be reenacted in the United States. Related to the above failings has been the tendency to establish unrealistic expectations which could only lead to disillusionment. Thus, rather than identify and incorporate successful elements of previous attempts, in each case the movement was rejected in total. Finally, it has been assumed that public school education would be far less expensive than education in residential facilities. It is usually a shock for educators to discover that provision of truly adequate resources for deaf children is an expensive proposition regardless of school setting.

School Placement in the United States

Although there has been no previous national mainstream movement in the United States, educators of the deaf, as previously noted, have been aware of the importance of the family environment and they have always expressed concern over early separation of deaf children and their families. Until recent times there has been an unfortunate tendency to confuse the issues of school placement with the controversy over oral and manual methods of instruction which has raged for so long.

In a report entitled *Memoir upon the Formation of a Deaf Variety of the Human Race,* Alexander Graham Bell (1883) intricately tied together issues of genetic inheritance, sign language, and school placement. Noting that graduates of schools for the deaf tended to marry other deaf people, Bell expressed the fear that such marriages would increase the incidence of deafness substantially. He argued that education of the deaf should be altered in such a way as to discourage the intermarriage of deaf people. Among his proposals were: (1) deaf teachers should not be employed; (2) organizations and publications predominantly representing deaf individuals should be discouraged; (3) deaf children should be educated in integrated settings; and (4) the sign language should be abolished.

In an extended study of marriage patterns of deaf individuals in the United States and relying heavily on material provided to him by Bell, Fay (1898) was able to disprove some of Bell's statements. First, deaf individuals have a preference for deaf marriage partners regardless of educational placement. Those who are educated in completely integrated settings tend to seek out other deaf individuals for spouses. Second, in direct refutation of the fears of Bell over the formation of a deaf variety of the human race, the evidence was indisputable that the vast majority of deaf children have parents with normal hearing, a situation that holds true today. In fact, most deaf people themselves have children with normal hearing. The incidence of deafness can be reduced more easily by concentrating on diseases such as rubella and meningitis than by unnecessary violations of the civil rights of deaf individuals.

Although Fay's results were acceptable to Bell, the effects of Bell's original treatise have continued to the present time. Many deaf individuals have viewed public school programs with suspicion because of past discrimination against deaf teachers and refusal to allow manual communication. It was not until the 1970s that public schools began to have deaf teachers in any substantial numbers.

As in other areas of special education the reactions of educators of the deaf have been mixed. Speaking from the perspective of a superintendent of a large residential school, Brill (1975) argued that in order to assure homogeneity of grouping of deaf children by age and academic level, a large population base is needed, and that most small school districts have neither adequate populations nor facilities to meet the needs of profoundly hearing-impaired children. On the other hand, Biklen (1975) noted that in a metropolitan area the size of Syracuse, New York, more than one-hundred deaf children were sent to residential schools in different cities. No local services were provided until the initiation of a legal complaint.

Most discussion has centered on the adequate provision of services to deaf children. Sparsely populated areas cannot be expected to provide comprehensive education for all severely hearing-impaired children. On the other hand, large metropolitan areas will no longer be able to ignore the needs of deaf children. The major concern, in reality, deals with inadequate past practices in integrating deaf and hearing children. Vernon and Prickett (1976) for example, have argued that the most common form of mainstreaming currently employed involves placement of deaf children in physical contiguity with hearing children. Except for occasional contact with a speech therapist or resource teacher, there is no attention paid to curriculum modification or social-emotional needs. In other words, the procedures reflect the worst features of previous unsuccessful national mainstream movements. Vernon and Prickett conclude that such an approach has been of little or no benefit. It is important to note that they do not attack the concept itself, but rather the inefficient, unsystematic way in which it has been approached.

The author is aware of programs in Illinois and Minnesota in which children from rural areas are placed in foster homes in cities in which there are programs for the hearing impaired. Typically, the children stay in the foster home from Monday through Friday and return home for the weekend. Although no systematic evaluations have been conducted, subjective evaluations appear to be favorable.

Research related to the question of placement is of quite limited generalizability. One notable exception is the demonstrated success of postsecondary programs, which have developed since the middle and late 1960s and have been housed within already existing programs designed for individuals with normal hearing. In the author's opinion, deaf children and their families are being presented with a growing number of alternatives. Despite obvious difficulties in program development, diagnosis, and remediation, the trends can be viewed as beneficial.

SPECIAL TECHNIQUES

The education of severely hearing-impaired children has benefited from significant technical advances in recent years. In general, children are identified and receive training at an early age. The fitting of hearing aids is becoming more and more efficient and many children are able to utilize residual hearing much more effectively than was the case twenty years ago.

Special techniques and specific curriculum modifications still are necessary for children with severe hearing losses. Greatest attention generally is directed to the two areas in which deaf children have differed most markedly from the hearing population—speech and language. In both areas, attempts have been made to teach deaf children for many centuries with limited success. In each area two rather separate approaches have been developed. One may be considered an analytical or formal approach, and the other a natural or informal approach. An analytical approach would be designed to teach children specific skills necessary for communication, usually by building clinically from basic elements of speech or grammar. A natural approach tends more toward recapitulation of normal processes of speech and language acquisition in natural settings. Both will be mentioned briefly here in relation to speech and language development of deaf children. For a more complete treatment of language acquisition of deaf children, the reader is referred to Moores (1978), and for an overview of speech training to Calvert and Silverman (1975).

Speech

Bonet's (1620) original treatise dealt with the development of both speech and language skills and reflected an analytical orientation. Through the years various systems, both analytical and natural, were developed in the United States and in Europe. The analytical system that has had the greatest impact on teaching of speech to the deaf in the United States was Visible Speech, developed by the British phonetician, Alexander Melville Bell. Visible Speech was designed to convey any and all sounds produced by human beings. This was accomplished by a detailed analysis of the articulatory mechanisms necessary to produce human speech. The system was based not upon sounds per se, but upon the process of vocalization itself.

The system was used with deaf children in London in 1869 by Alexander Graham Bell, the son of Alexander Melville Bell. Shortly thereafter the younger Bell migrated to America where he trained teachers of the deaf in the use of Visible Speech, and where he himself utilized it as a teacher of the deaf. Bell claimed that Visible Speech could produce perfect articulation in deaf students although he made no claims for its usefulness in developing speech rhythm and modulation (Bell, 1872).

The work of Alexander Melville Bell and Alexander Graham Bell still influences the teaching of speech in the United States. Much of the influence can be traced to the relation of A.G. Bell to the Clarke School for the Deaf in Northampton, Massachusetts, which has played a leadership role in developing methods of teaching speech to the deaf. Yale (1939), working on the foundation provided by Visible Speech, developed the most commonly employed elemental system. The Northampton (or Yale) charts, illustrating English sounds and consonants, are in common use today.

A contrast to the relatively formal approach presented above is provided by the reliance on a "natural" approach, as exemplified by work pioneered at the Lexington School for the Deaf in New York City. The emphasis in a natural approach is on meaningful, interesting communication. Where an analytical approach is microscopic, a natural approach is macroscopic. The first starts with elemental building blocks—individual sounds—and constructs larger and larger units. The second concentrates on

Courtesy of the Lexington School for the Deaf.

larger units to begin with and only later returns to an analysis of elements.

To illustrate the difference, an analytical approach might begin with drill in one phoneme, for example, /b/. The child would practice again and again all of the essential elements to produce the sound: place and manner of articulation, respiration, and so on. Following this might be drill in the phoneme /a/. When completed this might be followed by /t/. Finally all of the elements would be joined to produce *bat*. The approach is slow, useful, and elemental. A natural approach, on the other hand, may try to elicit *the bat flew out of the belfry!* The emphasis would be on spontaneity and communicative effectiveness. The production of the word *bat* might not be perfect—the /b/ may sound like an /m/ and the /t/ like a /d/, but the overall emphasis is not originally on perfect articulation. Specific drills come later.

Although the use of technical speech aids has received a great amount of attention, results to date have been minimal. Bell himself used an aid, a lettered glove with the letters of the alphabet on it, to teach speech (Bell, 1883), an idea he copied from the philosopher, Dalgarno (1680). In an analysis of speech training and speech reception aids with the deaf, including auditory, visual, and tactile aids, Nickerson (1975) concluded that developments have had little demonstrable effect on the speech of the deaf.

Language

Although human language typically is manifested in speech, it should be emphasized that speech and language, although related, are different. Speech may be perceived as a manifestation of language. Perhaps the biggest failure of many educators of the deaf has been the tendency to treat speech and language as interchangeable, leading to a misguided preoccupation with the development of articulation skills as the major goal in education of the deaf. Such a preoccupation has not only inhibited the development of academic, language, and social skills but also, by concentrating on speech in isolation, has even had negative effects on the development of satisfactory speech skills. For the acquisition of language skills, the child must have mastery over not only the sound system but also grammar, including word order, word changes, and semantics (Moores, 1970).

As in the teaching of speech there have been two types of approaches to the teaching of language, one using formal analytic procedures and the other informal and natural techniques. Formal systems were brought to the United States from France with the establishment of the American School for the Deaf and can be traced back to the work of Ponce de Leon and Bonet (Moores, 1978). At present the most widely used analytic method is the Fitzgerald Key developed by a deaf teacher, Edith Fitzgerald, in 1929. The Key begins with simple presentation of words under headings such as *Who, What, Why*, and so on, and children practice classification and word order. Complexity is increased gradually to include phrases, transitive verbs, clauses, and all elements of English. The Key is designed to help children both to generate appropriate sentences and to examine sentences for correctness.

The natural methods in use today may be traced to the work of the nineteenth-century German educator of the deaf Hill (Nelson, 1949), who believed that language could be developed in a natural way in deaf children. In the United States leadership in a natural approach to language has come from work begun at the Lexington School for the Deaf by Greenberger (1879). Emphasis is not in building up "correct" English on the basis of elements, but rather on generating rich spontaneous language with attention to correctness coming later. To overgeneralize somewhat, it may be stated that analytic approaches tend to generate correct but stilted language, and natural approaches generate a richness of expression at the expense of grammatical correctness.

MANUAL COMMUNICATION AND AMERICAN SIGN LANGUAGE

There probably has been more confusion generated over the use of manual communication than on any subject related to education of the deaf. The confusion has been compounded by the emotional way in which the question of the appropriateness of manual communication for the deaf has been approached. Educators of the deaf traditionally have split into two hostile camps, one strongly supporting the use of manual communication as an educational tool and the other strongly opposed to it.

Educators of the deaf are aware that the majority of deaf adults in the United States and Canada use a form of communication referred to as American Sign Language. (For a treatment of functional and structural characteristics of sign languages, see Moores, 1974.) Depending on the situation and the user's predispositions, the signing may or may not be accompanied by speech and may or may not follow spoken English word order. For most educators, the personal communication styles of adults is not an issue. The concern and controversy has centered on whether the influence of manual communication on the development of speech and English language skills is positive, negative, or neutral for young deaf children.

In essence, manual communication involves two elements: fingerspelling and signs. It is possible to spell every letter of every word utilizing the American Manual Alphabet (Figure 9–3). In the United States the system known as the Rochester Method utilizes fingerspelling and speech simultaneously. The system is known as Neo-Oralism in the Soviet Union. In the Rochester Method and Neo-Oralism, no signs are used. Total Communication involves the use of signs, fingerspelling, and speech. Rather than completely spelling a word such as *DOG, ROOM, EXERCISE, SITUATION*, and so on, in each case a sign might be employed. Again, the manual communication is coordinated with speed. When signing, some

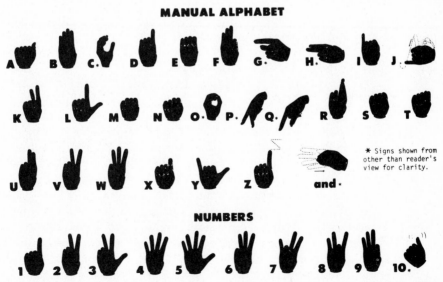

FIG. 9–3 The American Manual Alphabet. (Used by permission. Copyright © 1976, Kathryn A. Licht.)

elements such as bound morphemes (*LY, MENT*) or function words (*OF, BY*) may be added through fingerspelling.

When Thomas Hopkins Gallaudet established the first school for the deaf in the United States, he had hoped to avoid the bitter controversies dividing European educators by combining the best elements of the oral and manual methods. Because leading educators in Great Britain refused to teach him their techniques—a relative was attempting to start a school in Virginia—Gallaudet brought back only a knowledge of the French manual method, thus laying the groundwork for future strife.

Although the "manual" schools did provide articulation training and training in use of residual hearing to hard of hearing and adventitiously deaf students, many students received no training whatsoever in oral skills (Moores, 1978). Oral-only schools were developed in opposition to the overemphasis on manual communications. Evaluation by the author of nineteenth-century school reports, articles, and other publications lead to the subjective conclusion that the oral schools provided adequately for hard of hearing and adventitiously deaf children, but were ineffective generally with those students who were congenitally deaf. The manual schools seemed more adequate for the congenitally deaf, but did not meet the needs of those who had significant residual hearing or who lost their hearing after acquiring speech and language skills. By the end of the nineteenth century, the oral-only proponents had gained a clear-cut advantage which was increased through the first half of the twentieth century. By that time, manual-only schools were a thing of the past. Even those schools that had previously been classified as manual would start all children in oral-only instruction. Manual communication would be used in the classroom only after twelve years of age in most schools. The signs were presented by means of the simultaneous method, that is, words were signed and spoken simultaneously. In 1960, according to all available information, manual communication was not allowed in any preschool program for the deaf in the United States.

The situation began to change in the United States in the 1960s. First, there was general dissatisfaction with the results of educational programs for the deaf in terms of speech, language, social-emotional development, and academic achievement (Babbidge, 1965). Despite a large amount of publicity, newly developed oral-only preschool programs for the deaf seemed to have little or no lasting value (Craig, 1964; McCroskey, 1967; Phillips, 1963). In fact a series of studies reported that deaf children who were exposed to manual communication from birth by their deaf parents were superior to deaf children of hearing parents in academic achievement, English, written expression, reading, and social maturity, with no differences in speech (Meadow, 1966; Stevenson, 1964; Stuckless and Birch, 1966; Vernon and Kohl, 1970). During the same period, observations were accumulating that even in school programs where signs were vigorously repressed, in both the United States and Europe, deaf children would resort to signs in person-to-person communication both within and outside of school (Kohl, 1966; Lenneberg, 1967; Tervoort and Verbeck, 1967).

A final factor was the influence of reports of success from the Soviet Union, which had abandoned the oral method and replaced it with a combined oral-manual system, which utilized speech and fingerspelling but not sign language. Soviet educators reported that the use of fingerspelling in preschool enhanced the speech and language development of deaf children, and endorsed a combined oral-fingerspelling system that was entitled Neo-Oralism (Moores, 1972; Morkovin, 1960; Rau, 1960; Zukov, 1962).

In the last several years there has been a dramatic shift in the methods used in classrooms with deaf children. Jordan, Gustason, and Rosen (1976) reported that by 1975 total communication was used in a majority of programs for the deaf at all levels—preschool, elementary, junior high school, and senior high school. Total communication is a term used to describe reliance on all modes of communication: speech, speechreading, residual hearing, fingerspelling and signs. Jordan, et al., present fascinating data on the number of programs reporting changes in classroom methods from 1968 to 1975. During that period a total 302 programs have changed from the oral-only method and only five have changed to it. Conversely, 333 programs changed to total communication and only eight discontinued its use (p. 530). Clearly, a revolution in methodology took place during this period.

Research on Manual Communication in the Classroom

The revolutionary change to total communication has not been due to any demonstration of its superiority in the classroom. Rather, as previously mentioned, the impetus has come from demonstrated ineffectiveness of oral-only programs at preschool, elementary, and secondary levels and the demonstrated superiority of deaf children of deaf parents. If decisions were made previously on the basis of research findings, programs would have switched from oral-only techniques to the Rochester Method, which like Russian Neo-Oralism combines speech and fingerspelling, but not signs.

Quigley (1969) compared preschool children taught through the Rochester Method to children taught by an oral-only approach. His results were similar to those reported by the Russians and showed that those taught by the Rochester Method were superior in speedreading, academic achievement, and written language. He also compared junior and senior high school students at three schools who were changed from oral-only instruction to the Rochester Method, with students at three other schools who changed from oral-only instruction to the simultaneous method (now known as total communication). Over a period of five years the students instructed in the Rochester Method established significant superiority over those using the simultaneous method in all measures of academic achievement and in grammatical functioning.

In the previously noted long-term evaluation of seven preschool programs for the deaf from 1970 to 1975, Moores, Weiss, and Goodwin (1978) reported a change from predominantly oral-only to predominantly total

Courtesy of the Lexington School for the Deaf.

communication instruction. At the end of the evaluation, only one program used oral-only methods and one used the Rochester Method. The other five used total communication. Academic achievement for children in the Rochester Method program was significantly higher than that of children in the oral-only programs. Scores of children in each of the five total communication programs were intermediate between those in the Rochester Method and the oral-only programs.

Given the evidence to date, it is surprising to note that Jordan, et al., (1976) report that only ten of 627 preschool programs and six of 353 senior high school programs utilize the Rochester Method. The impact of research on practice in education of the deaf appears to be somewhat limited.

ECONOMIC STATUS

As in so many other areas of education, vocational training in the United States was pioneered by educators of the deaf. As early as 1822 the American School for the Deaf had initiated a vocational training program for its students (Jones, 1918). Throughout the nineteenth century the economic condition of deaf Americans appeared to be equivalent to that of hearing Americans. Williams (1886) conducted an extensive survey of graduates of the American School for the Deaf and reported that the wages of deaf men and women were equivalent to general wages in New England. Most common occupations were farmers, mill operators, mechanics, carpenters, and teachers. Among the graduates were the founder of an insurance company, a patent lawyer, an artist, and three clergymen.

It was only after the United States had shifted to a predominantly industrial society that the economic position of deaf individuals dropped relative to that of the hearing. As more and more of a premium was placed on communication ability and postsecondary training, opportunities for the deaf became more and more restricted.

In a follow-up of graduates of schools for the deaf in New England, Boatner, Stuckless, and Moores (1964) reported that young deaf adults suffered high rates of unemployment, received lower wages for equivalent work, and had limited chances for advancement. For those who did not attend Gallaudet College there were very few postsecondary opportunities. In spite of all the difficulties facing them, deaf people were rated superior workers by their supervisors. A replication of the study in New England was conducted in South-central and Southwestern states by Kroneberg and Blake (1965) with similar results. In the middle of the 1960s, the status of the deaf working population could be described in terms of unemployment, underemployment, lack of postsecondary training opportunities, and limited prospects for advancement. The move to expansion of postsecondary programs at that time has been described in a previous section. Results to date suggest a relative improvement in the economic status of the deaf. In an evaluation of the federally funded vocational-technical programs for the deaf in Seattle, St. Paul, and New Orleans, it was reported by Moores, Fisher, and Harlow (1975) that significant gains had been made in the training and placement of deaf workers with an observable upward movement. However, communication problems continue to present obstacles and choice of occupations remains limited, with females still orienting to such occupations as general office practices and males to printing.

CONCLUSION

The education of hearing-impaired individuals has undergone some dramatic changes in recent times, most of them obviously beneficial. Improvements have been made in early identification and provision of services. More children are now being served, including those with mild handicaps and those who are severely multiply handicapped. For most deaf individuals, more and better educational alternatives are available. Major breakthroughs have been made at the postsecondary level in vocational, technical, and academic opportunities. Irrational prejudice against manual communication is on the decline.

The author believes that a number of issues related to human rights and personal needs will assume major importance in the years to come.

There will be a move to perceive the deaf child not in isolation but as a part of a larger family unit. Much more attention will be paid to family dynamics. It will be necessary to provide better opportunities to deaf professionals within the educational setting; at present their unique skills are ignored or underutilized. Much more attention must be devoted to provision of adequate and appropriate services to children and their families from ethnic and racial minority groups.

Finally, no major breakthroughs have been made in helping deaf children develop adequate speech and English skills. Progress is dishearteningly slow. Many of the problems which faced Ponce de Leon in the sixteenth century, Bonet in the seventeenth century, de l'Epée in the eighteenth century, and Gallaudet in the nineteenth century still plague us today. With luck we may make the task somewhat easier for our successors in the twenty-first century.

REFERENCES

Anderson, G., and Bowe, F. Racism within the deaf community. *American Annals of the Deaf,* 1972, *117,* 617–619.

Ayers, J. Home education for the deaf and dumb. *American Annals of the Deaf,* 1849, *2,* 177–187.

Babbidge, H. Education of the deaf in the United States. *Report of the Advisory Committee on Education of the Deaf.* Washington, DC: U. S. Government Printing Office, 1965.

Bartlett, D. Family education for young deaf-mute children. *American Annals of the Deaf,* 1852, *5,* 32–35.

Bell, A. G. Visible speech as a means of communicating articulation to deaf mutes. *American Annals of the Deaf,* 1872, *17,* 1–21.

————. *Memoir Upon the Formation of a Deaf Variety of the Human Race.* Washington, DC: National Academy of Science, 1883.

————. Upon a method of teaching language to a very young congenitally deaf child. *American Annals of the Deaf,* 1883, *28,* 124–139.

Bemiss, S. *Report on the Influence of Marriages of Consanguinity.* Philadelphia: Collins, 1858.

Berger, K. *The Hearing Aid: Its Operation and Development.* Detroit, MI: National Hearing Aid Society, 1970.

Best, H. *Deafness and the Deaf in the United States.* New York: The Macmillan Company, 1943.

Biklen, D. Deaf children vs. the board of education. *American Annals of the Deaf,* 1975, *120,* 382–386.

Birch, J. *Hearing Impaired Pupils in the Mainstream of Education.* Reston, VA: Council for Exceptional Children, 1975.

Boatner, E., Stuckless, E., and Moores, D. *Occupational Status of the Young Deaf Adults of New England and the Need and Demand for a*

Regional Technical Vocational Training Center. West Hartford, Conn.: American School for the Deaf, 1964.

Boatner, M. *Edward Minor Gallaudet: The Voice of the Deaf.* Washington, DC: Public Affairs Press, 1959.

Bordley, J., Brookhauser, P., Hardy, J., and Hardy, W. Observations of the effect of prenatal rubella on hearing. In F. McConnell & P. Ward (ed.), *Deafness in Childhood.* Nashville: Vanderbilt University Press, 1967, 123–141.

Brill, R. Mainstreaming: Format or quality? *American Annals of the Deaf,* 1975, *120,* 377–381.

Buxton, D. *An Inquiry into the Causes of Deaf-dumbness, Congenital and Acquired.* Liverpool, Eng: Brakell, 1858.

Calvert, D., and Silverman, R. *Speech and Deafness.* Washington, DC: Alexander Graham Bell Association, 1975.

Carhart, R. *Human Communication and Its Disorders,* Bethesda, Maryland: National Institutes of Health, Public Health Service, 1969.

Chaves, T., and Solar, J. Pedro Ponce de Leon, first teacher of the deaf. *Sign Language Studies,* 1974, *5,* 48–63.

Chenoweth, A. Planning for a mass attack on Rubella. *Children,* 1969, *16,* 94–95.

Craig, W. Effects of preschool training on the development of reading and lipreading skills of deaf children. *American Annals of the Deaf,* 1964, *109,* 280–296.

Craig, W., and Craig, H. Directory of Services. *American Annals of the Deaf,* 1977, *122.*

———, ———, and DiJohnson, A. Preschool verbotonal instruction for deaf children. *Volta Review,* 1972, *74,* 236–246.

Crouter, A. Preliminary home training. *American Annals of the Deaf,* 1885, *30,* 226–228.

Dalgarno, G. *Didascopholus; or the Deaf and Dumb Man's Tutor.* Oxford, Eng.: Timothy Halton, 1680. (Reprinted in *American Annals of the Deaf,* 1857, *9,* 14–64).

Doctor, P. Directory of services. *American Annals of the Deaf,* 1962, *107.*

Durant, J., and Lovronic, J. *Bases of Hearing Science.* Baltimore: Williams & Wilkins, 1977.

Fay, E., *Marriages of the Deaf in America.* Washington, DC: Volta Bureau, Gibson Brothers, 1898.

———. What did Luecetius say? *American Annals of the Deaf,* 1912, *57,* 213.

Frisina, R. (Chairman) *Report of the Committee to Redefine Deaf and Hard of Hearing.* Washington, DC: Conference of Executives of American Schools for the Deaf, 1974.

Furfey, P. and Harte, T. *Interaction of Deaf and Hearing in Frederick County, Maryland.* Washington, DC: Catholic University, 1964.

Gallagher, J., and Martin, E. *Windows on Russia.* Reston, VA.: Council for Exceptional Children, 1974.

Garnett, C. *The Exchange of Letters between Samuel Heinicke and Abbé*

Charles Michel de l'Epée. New York: Vantage Press, Inc., 1968.

Gentile, A., and McCarthy, B. *Additional Handicapping Conditions among Hearing Impaired Students, United States, 1971–1972.* Washington, DC: Gallaudet College Office of Demographic Studies, Ser. D., No. 14, 1973.

Gordon, J. Hints to parents. *American Annals of the Deaf,* 1885, *30,* 241–250. (a).

———. Deaf-mutes and the public schools from 1815 to the present day. *American Annals of the Deaf,* 1885, *30,* 121–143. (b).

Greenberger, D. The natural method. *American Annals of the Deaf,* 1879, *24,* 33–38.

Hester, M. Manual communication. Paper presented at International Conference on Education of the Deaf, Washington, DC, June 1963.

Hirsch, D. Advice to parents. *American Annals of the Deaf,* 1877, *22,* 93–103.

Hudgins, R. Causes of deafness among students of the Clarke School for the Deaf. *Clarke School for the Deaf, 106th Annual Report.* Northampton, MA.: Clarke School for the Deaf, 1973, 59–60.

Jones, J. One hundred years of history in the education of the deaf in America and its present status. *American Annals of the Deaf,* 1918, *63,* 1–47.

Jones, R. The Northridge plan. *American Annals of the Deaf,* 1972, *117,* 612–616.

Jordan, I., Gustason, G., and Rosen, R. Current communication trends at programs for the deaf. *American Annals of the Deaf,* 1976, *121,* 527–531.

Kanner, L. *A History of the Care and Study of the Mentally Retarded.* Springfield, IL.: Charles C Thomas, Publisher, 1967.

Kennedy, J. *Preliminary Report on the Eighth Census.* Washington, DC: U. S. Government Printing Office, 1862.

———. *Population of the United States in 1860. Eighth Census, U. S. Census Office.* Washington, DC: U. S. Government Printing Office, 1864.

Kohl, J. *Language and Education of the Deaf.* New York: Center for Urban Studies, 1966.

Kroneberg, H., and Blake, G. *Young Deaf Adults: An Occupational Survey.* Hot Springs: Arkansas Rehabilitation Service, 1966.

Ladefoged, D. *Elements of Acoustic Phonetics.* Chicago: University of Chicago Press, 1962.

Lenneberg, E. *Biological Foundations of Language.* New York: John Wiley & Sons, Inc., 1967.

Levinson, R. (ed.). *A Plato Reader.* Boston: Houghton Mifflin Company, 1967.

Lunde, A., and Bigman, S. *Occupational Conditions among the Deaf.* Washington, DC: Gallaudet College, 1959.

Maestas y Moores, J., and Moores, D. Spanish-surnamed hearing-impaired children: An analysis of social and educational needs. (In preparation).

Mallery, G. *Introduction to the Study of Sign Language among the North American Indians as Illustrating the Gesture Speech of Mankind.* Washington, DC: Smithsonian Institution Bureau of Ethnology, 1880.

McConnell, F., and Horton, K. *A Hometeaching Program for Parents of*

Very Young Deaf Children. Nashville, TN: Vanderbilt University, 1970.

McCroskey, R. Early education of infants with severe auditory impairments. *Proceedings of International Conference on Oral Education of the Deaf*. Washington, DC: A. G. Bell Association, 1967, 1891–1905.

Meadow, K. The effect of early manual communication and family climate on the deaf child's development. Unpublished doctoral dissertation, University of California, Berkeley, 1966.

Moores, D. Psycholinguistics and deafness. *American Annals of the Deaf*, 1970, *115*, 37–48.

———. Neo-oralism and education of the deaf in the Soviet Union. *Exceptional Children*, 1972, *38*, 377–384.

———. *Education of the Deaf: Psychology, Principles & Practices*. Boston: Houghton Mifflin Company, 1978.

———, Fisher, S., and Harlow, M. *Post Secondary Programs for the Deaf: Monograph VI: Summary and Guidelines*. University of Minnesota Research, Development and Demonstration Center in Education of Handicapped Children. Research Report No. 80, 1974.

———, and Oden, C. Educational needs of black deaf children. *American Annals of the Deaf*, 1977, *122*, 313–318.

———, Weiss, K., and Goodwin, M. Early intervention programs for hearing impaired children: A longitudinal evaluation. *ASHA Monographs*, 1978.

———, ———, and———. *Recommended Policies and Procedures: Preschool Programs for Hearing Impaired Children*. University of Minnesota Research Development and Demonstration Center in Education of Handicapped Children: Research Report 104, 1976.

Morkovin, B. Experiment in teaching deaf preschool children in the Soviet Union. *Volta Review*, 1960, *62*, 260–268.

Morris, O. Cansanguineous marriages, and their results in respect to deaf-dumbness. *American Annals of the Deaf*, 1861, *13*, 29–34.

Nance, J. *The Gentle Tasaday*. New York: Harcourt Brace Jovanovich, 1975.

Nelson, M. The evolutionary progress of teaching language to the deaf. *American Annals of the Deaf*, 1949, *95*, 230–294, 354–396, 491–511.

Nickerson, R. *Speech Training and Speech Reception Aids for the Deaf*. Cambridge, MA.: Bolt, Beranek, & Newman, Report No. 2890, 1975.

Northern, J. (ed.). *Hearing Disorders*. Boston: Little, Brown and Company, 1976.

Peet, D. The remote and proximate causes of deafness. *American Annals of the Deaf*, 1856, *8*, 129–158.

Peet, H. Memoir on origin and early history of the art of instructing the deaf and dumb. *American Annals of the Deaf*, 1851, *3*, 129–161.

———. *Thirty-fifth Annual Report of the New York Institution for the Instruction of the Deaf and Dumb*. New York, 1854.

———. Family instruction. *American Annals of the Deaf*, 1886, *31*, 260–271.

Pettengill, B. Home education for deaf mutes. *American Annals of the Deaf*, 1874, *19*, 1–10.

Phillips, W. Influence of preschool training on language arts, arithmetic concepts and socialization of young deaf children. Unpublished doctoral dissertation, Columbia University, 1963.

Quigley, S. *The Influence of Fingerspelling on the Development of Language, Communication and Educational Achievement of Deaf Children.* Urbana: University of Illinois, 1969.

——, Jenne, W., and Phillips, S. *Deaf Students in Colleges and Universities.* Washington, DC: Alexander Graham Bell Association, 1968.

Rau, F. *Teaching Pronunciation to the Deaf.* Moscow: Institute of Defectology, 1960.

Rawlings, B., Trybus, R., Delgado, G., and Stuckless, E. (ed.). *A Guide to College/Career Programs for Deaf Students: Revised 1975 edition.* Washington, DC: Gallaudet College; and Rochester, NY: National Technical Institute for the Deaf, 1975.

Ray, L. Family education for young deaf mute children. *American Annals of the Deaf,* 1852, *5,* 32–35.

Ries, P. *Reported Causes of Hearing Loss for Hearing Impaired Students: 1970–1971.* Annual Survey of Hearing Impaired Children and Youth. Gallaudet College Office of Demographic Studies, Series D, No. 11, 1973.

Sank, D., and Kallman, F. The role of heredity in early total deafness. *Volta Review,* 1963, *65,* 461–476.

Schein, J., and Delk, M. *The Deaf Population of the United States.* Silver Spring, MD: National Association of the Deaf, 1974.

Seguin, E. *Idiocy and its Treatment by the Physiological Method.* New York: William Wood and Company, 1866. Reprinted New York: August M. Kelley, 1971.

Simmons, A. Home demonstration teaching for parents and infants in Central Institute for the Deaf. *Proceedings of International Conference on Oral Education of the Deaf.* Washington, DC: Alexander Graham Bell Association, 1967, 1862–1873.

Stevenson, E. A study of the educational achievement of deaf children of deaf parents. *California News,* 1964, *80,* 143.

Stuckless, E., and Birch, J. The influence of early manual communication on the linguistic development of deaf children. *American Annals of the Deaf,* 1966, *111,* 452–460, 499–504.

——, and Delgado, G. *A Guide to College Career Programs for Deaf Students.* Rochester, NY: National Technical Institute for the Deaf; and Washington, DC: Gallaudet College, 1973.

Tervoort, B., and Verbeck, A. *Analysis of Communicative Structure Patterns in Deaf Children.* Groningen, The Netherlands: Z. W. O. Onderzock, N. R.: 583–615, 1967.

Turner, W. Causes of deafness. *American Annals of the Deaf.* 1848, *1,* 25–32.

Vernon, M., and Kohl, S. Effects of manual communication of deaf children's educational achievement, linguistic competence, oral skills, and psychological development. *American Annals of the Deaf,* 1970 *115,*

527–536.

———, and Prickett, H. Mainstreaming, past and present: Some issues and a model plan. *Audiology and Hearing Education,* 1976.

Waldo, M. Early home instruction. *American Annals of the Deaf,* 1859, *11,* 170–192.

Wever, E. *Theory of Hearing.* New York: Dover Publications, Inc., 1949.

Williams, J. *Seventieth Annual Report: American Asylum for the Deaf.* Hartford, CT, 1886.

Yale, C. *Formation and Development of Elementary English Sounds.* Northampton, MA: Clarke School for the Deaf, 1939.

Zemlin, W. *Speech and Hearing Science, Anatomy and Psysiology.* Englewood Cliffs, NJ: Prentice-Hall, Inc., 1968.

Zukov, S. *Textbook for Deaf Children.* Moscow: Institute of Defectology, 1962.

CHAPTER **10**

CHILDREN WITH VISUAL IMPAIRMENTS

MARJORIE E. WARD

Children with visual impairments make up a comparatively small group among the almost eight million youngsters with special educational needs in the United States today. The United States Office of Education (USOE) estimates the number of children who have little or no vision between the ages of birth and nineteen to be 66,000 (Ernst, 1977).

This chapter will focus on identifying these children and their educational needs, and on describing factors that must be carefully considered in order to determine appropriate special education services for them. The discussion opens with some consideration of attitudes, turns to the eye and how it functions, and then moves on to examine terminology describing impaired vision and children with impaired vision in school. It will examine some implications for education and instruction, and review the kinds of educational services presently available for visually handicapped children. There will be a brief look at multiply handicapped children with limited vision and a survey of current issues in their special education in view of general issues identified earlier in chapter 2.

IMPORTANCE OF ATTITUDES

If surveyed, those who read this chapter would more than likely reveal a wide band of sensitivity and a variety of feelings to the constructs of "blind," "blindness," and "partial vision." Present levels of knowledge, past experiences, and future goals would help to form the reactions readers might express to the reality of visual impairment in children or adults whom they might encounter casually, formally, or professionally.

Historically, reactions to blindness have ranged from fear, pity, and contempt to awe, loving acceptance, and profound respect. Lowenfeld (1973, 1975), shows this shift in public attitudes and practices in his history of the social status of visually handicapped people from prehistoric times until the present. According to Lowenfeld attitudes have progressed from separation, expressed at times as annihilation and at other times as veneration, to protection, with persons holding ward status, to self-emancipation for some, followed gradually by the move toward integration. He defines integration as: "mutual acceptance based on equality of opportunity and before the law, between and among groups and individuals who differ in some important characteristic, may it be racial, religious, physical, economic, or otherwise" (Lowenfeld, 1975, p. 85).

Certainly this full integration is not yet reality. However, if current changes in public opinion as expressed in litigation, state and federal legislation, negotiated contracts and agreements, and levels of financial authorization and appropriations are harbingers of what is to come, integration is today within sight of more people of all ages with special needs than it has been previously.

Even though the general emotional climate in United States society may be changing, attitudes still must be mentioned in any discussion with those in or contemplating entrance into the field of special education, particularly education of children with impaired vision. In the preface to her book *Visual Handicaps and Learning*, which provides a base for many of the ideas to be expressed later in this chapter, Barraga (1976) describes the present state of affairs:

> Misconceptions and distortions have hindered educators in their attempts to present more realistic ideas about children with visual impairments. Acceptance and integration into educational settings on the same terms as any children who have physical or other differences is an ideal toward which parents and educators are still striving (p. 2).

The effort is essential. Children learn much about themselves from the way significant others in their lives react to them. Parents are their children's first teachers of feelings, as well as of language and mobility. Imamura (1965) compared the behavior of preschool blind and sighted children with their mothers to determine what relationship, if any, existed between the children's behavior and that of their mothers. Imamura concluded, among other things, that "it is not so much the lack of sight itself, but the differential social treatment the blind receive from others that make them more dependent" (1965, p. 54).

Scott, a decade ago, wrote a thought-provoking book called *The Mak-*

ing of Blind Men (1969) which stimulated much discussion and self-evaluation among professionals providing services to persons with impaired vision. His information for the book came from interviews with blind adults and professionals in agencies for the blind, as well as a review of records and research literature. Scott expressed rather clearly the idea that an individual's knowledge of himself comes largely from the way he is treated by those around him:

> A self-concept is not given to a man when he is born; rather, it is something he acquires as he is socialized. Inherent in self-concept is the ability to take self as an object of its own perception; to do this, in turn, a person must learn to view himself from the point of view of other people. The child who plays at the role of parent and thereby learns to see and respond to himself as his parents do, and the adult who takes the perspective of the group or the community at large in order to imagine how "they" are likely to react to his anticipated behavior, are both involved in getting outside themselves and looking back at their own behavior. Self-image cannot develop without taking the role of another vis-à-vis oneself. Because of this, the substance of a man's self-image largely consists of his perceptions of the evaluations that others make of him, and particularly those others whose opinions he values most highly (p. 15).

Scott emphasizes that blindness is a social role:

> Thus, there is nothing inherent in the conditions of blindness that requires a person to be docile, dependent, melancholy, or helpless; nor is there anything about it that should lead him to become independent or assertive. Blind men are made, and by the same processes of socialization that have made us all (p. 14).

In chapter 2, advantages and disadvantages of using labels were presented. Lowenfeld (1975) has given three reasons, one of which is particularly pertinent to this discussion, why blind people are viewed as a group. Blind persons, as Lowenfold says in the vernacular, "have something wrong with their eyes; they are held together by common attitudes toward them; and they need specific means and techniques to overcome the effects of their visual handicap." The "common attitudes" toward and characteristics attributed to persons with varying degrees of visual deficit serve to create a group that has become known as "the blind." The label is a stigma, a special kind of relationship between an attribute viewed as discrediting and the stereotyped idea of the way people with that attribute behave, or "ought" to behave (Goffman, 1963).

The point to be emphasized in this consideration of attitudes of sighted persons toward persons with impaired vision is that people are influenced by those around them both in the ways they think about themselves and how they regard themselves in relation to other people. Teachers and others who work with children can, by their attitudes, facilitate (or impede) the development of abilities and positive feelings among children who have impaired vision. With that in mind, we will now turn to the topic of the eye and how we see.

THE PROCESS OF SEEING

If an incubated hen's egg is carefully opened, and if the portion of the developing chick that is destined to become an eye is detached and properly cared for, the rudimentary eye-bud can be kept alive and growing. The various eye parts will appear and the light-sensitive chemicals will form, although the small eye is no longer attached to a chick. We would be able to look at the eye and recognize it, but it could not look at us and recognize us (Mann and Pirie, 1962). Although the eye is necessary, it is not sufficient; sight as we know it requires the existence of something in addition to an eye. The process of seeing calls for a brain and the presence of light as well as an eye (Gibson, 1950).

The eye is an intricate, complex, finely-tuned structure designed to transmit messages about the environment to the brain. Light rays entering the eye are focused on the retina where surface retinal cells are stimulated, thus causing a photochemical response. The deeper rod and cone cells of the retina which are activated by the photochemical changes carry impulses back to the optic nerve. The optic nerve pathways direct them to the brain where interpretation takes place.

This simplified description of the process of seeing should suggest that the process can be interrupted (1) if sufficient light is not present or does not pass into the eye, (2) if the structures of the eye do not permit clear passage and focus on the retina, or the necessary photochemical changes do not occur, (3) if the optic nerve does not carry the impulses to the brain, and/or (4) if the brain does not accurately receive and/or interpret the messages coming to it from the optic nerve (Harley and Lawrence, 1977).

To satisfy readers who are intrigued by the structure and function of human organs as they relate to the rest of the human body, attention will now turn to the eye as organ of sight.

The eyeball or globe rests in a boney cavity or orbit surrounded by fat and connective tissue. Six muscles arise from within the orbit and are attached to the eyeball. (See Figure 10-1) These muscles act in concert with their counterpart muscles in the second eye to enable the eyeballs to move in a coordinated fashion, thus altering direction of gaze and focus. The orbit provides protection for the eyeball, as do the eye brow, lashes, and lids. These outer protective structures offer a cushion for the eye from bumps and blows, a screen against dust and perspiration, and a shield from brilliant light. Tears, with their source in the lacrimal gland situated in the upper outer portion of the orbit, lubricate the outer surface of the eyeball as they are spread by the eyelids (Newell and Ernest, 1974; Harley and Lawrence, 1977).

The eyeball is made up of three layers each with its own parts and functions. Structure of the eyeball is presented in Figure 10-2.

1. The outer layer or sclerotic coat consists of the white, opaque sclera and the transparent, oval-shaped cornea. The sclera, which makes up the posterior five-sixths of the eyeball, gives protection against injury and ex-

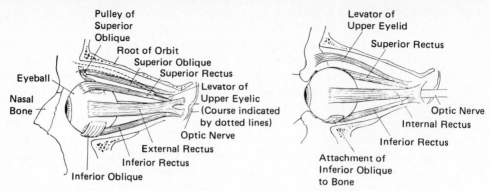

FIG. 10–1   External muscles of the eye. From W. Hathaway: *Education and Health of the Partially Seeing Child,* 4th edition, New York: Columbia University Press, 1959, by permission of the publisher.

cessive light because of its dense elastic quality. The cornea, extremely sensitive to touch, permits entrance of light into the eye. Because of its convex surface, the cornea serves as the major refractive medium of the eye and bends rays of light as they pass through to stimulate the cells on the surface of the retina. Covering the sclera, cornea, and the inner surfaces of the eyelids is the transparent conjunctiva, a thin mucous membrane that can stretch and contract to allow easy movement of the lids and eyeball.

2. The middle layer of the globe, the uveal tract, includes the iris, the ciliary body, and the choroid. This layer is a vascular structure and carries nutrients to adjacent structures, particularly the retina. The iris surrounds

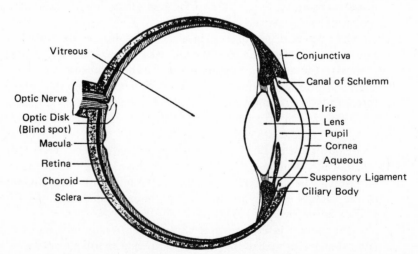

FIG. 10–2   Horizontal section of right eyeball. From W. Hathaway. *Education and Health of the Partially Seeing Child,* 4th edition, New York: Columbia University Press, 1959, by permission of the publisher.

the pupil, the round opening through which light rays pass after they leave the cornea. The muscles of the iris contract and relax to widen or narrow the size of the pupil, thus controlling the amount of light entering the eye much the way a diaphragm regulates the amount of light entering a camera. These iris muscles also enable the eye to accommodate for near and distance vision by adjusting pupil size.

The ciliary body forms a ring continuous with the posterior surface of the iris. From it extend suspensory ligaments that hold the crystalline lens in place behind the pupil. The contraction and relaxation of muscles in the ciliary body permit the curvature of the lens to vary and bring rays of light to a fine focus on the retina. The thicker the lens, the stronger its power of refraction. The ability of the lens to alter its curvature and bring about fine resolution of detail is an important characteristic that enables us to see our surroundings clearly and distinctly. The ciliary body secretes a liquid called aqueous humor, which circulates in the chambers in the anterior portion of the eye in front of the lens. The constant flow and drainage of aqueous help maintain intraocular pressure.

The choroid makes up the posterior portion of the uveal tract and extends from the ciliary body around to the optic nerve. Its rich vascular system supplies nourishment to the outer portion of the retina.

3. The inner layer of the eyeball, the retina, contains approximately 126 million photosensitive cells, 120 million rods for detecting light and dark and motion in peripheral vision, and 6 million cones concentrated in the macular area for discriminating color and form. The optic nerve picks up impulses from nerve fibers stimulated by the rods and cones and transmits the impulses to the occipital lobe of the brain at the back of the head.

In the space between the posterior surface of the lens and the retinal layer lies the vitreous. The vitreous is a transparent, gelatinous, colorless mass that helps give shape and inner support to the eyeball.

The preceding explanation of the structure of the eye is not meant to be taken as complete. Volumes have been written about the eye and its functions in anatomy, physiology, courting, and romance. The purpose here is merely to provide a basic overview sufficient to aid in understanding the process of seeing when normal vision is not present.

VISUAL IMPAIRMENT AMONG SCHOOL CHILDREN

An impairment signifies some type of tissue damage or structural defect. A visual impairment is a clinically observable deviation, which can be detected either with the naked eye or with appropriate techniques available to eye specialists. Not always is the cause of the damage discernible, as in some cases of congenital glaucoma, but the resulting defective function, structure, or organization is.

Known causes of visual impairment can be classified by the site or location of the damage (lens, retina, cornea, and so on) or by the type of cause (disease, injury, poison, and so on). To ease the task of categorizing eye conditions, The National Society for the Prevention of Blindness (NSPB) has prepared an index of diagnostic terms ranging from "abiotrophy" to "zosterophthalmicus" (*Manual*, 1966). For purposes of this discussion, causes are presented by type rather than by site.

In Table 10–1 major causes are listed for three groups of school-age blind children based on an NSPB study of reports contributed by residential schools, state departments of education, local school systems, and state agencies for the blind (Hatfield, 1975). The 3,885 children who made up the three groups represented 19.2 percent of the 20,216 blind children registered with the American Printing House for the Blind as of January 1969. During that year there were approximately 51 million children enrolled in elementary and secondary school. Of those, about 39.3 per 100,000 or 1 in 2,500 were identified as blind. This rate indicates an increase when compared to results obtained during a similar NSPB study of

Table 10–1   Percent Distribution of Blind Schoolchildren by Etiology According to Age: 1968–1969 Sample

ETIOLOGY	5–9	10–14	15–19	N.R.	TOTAL
Infectious diseases	4.1	3.2	1.6	1.9	2.8
Rubella	3.1	1.4	0.2	—	1.3
Toxoplasmosis	0.4	0.9	0.7	1.9	0.7
Other	0.6	0.9	0.6	—	0.7
Injuries and poisonings	5.1	5.9	11.7	1.9	7.9
Excessive oxygen (RLF)	3.2	4.0	9.3	1.9	5.8
Other	1.9	1.9	2.4	—	2.1
Neoplasms	3.8	4.5	2.9	1.9	3.7
General diseases	2.1	1.2	1.2	—	1.4
Central nervous system	1.1	1.0	0.7	—	0.9
Other	1.0	0.3	0.5	—	0.5
Prenatal influence	61.7	54.9	38.2	35.8	49.9
Hereditary	51.7	46.2	31.1	32.1	41.5
Other congenital	9.9	8.7	7.1	3.8	8.3
Unknown to science	0.7	1.0	0.7	—	0.8
Not reported	22.5	29.3	43.7	58.5	33.6
RLF (use of oxygen unknown)	5.2	12.8	31.4	3.8	18.0
Other	17.3	16.5	12.3	54.7	15.6
Total	100.0	100.0	100.0	100.0	100.0

Hatfield, Elizabeth M. "Why are they Blind?" *Sight-Saving Review*, vol. 45, no. 1 (Spring 1975), p. 10.

children in the 1958–59 registration. The increase may actually be real, or it may be a reflection of better reporting and case finding, increased availability of services, and greater public awareness of services for school children who are blind. Nothing so far has been said about what definition for the word "blind" was used in this study; terms chosen to describe amount of vision for various purposes, such as to determine prevalence, will be dealt with in a later section of this chapter.

Table 10–1 shows that *prenatal influences* account for the largest number of blind children in all age groups.* Cataracts, albinism, and glaucoma lead the list and account for 41.5 percent of the total 49.9 percent of cases reported as hereditary in nature.

Injuries and poisonings are the second major cause of blindness across ages. Counted in this category are children with retrolental fibroplasia (RLF), poisoning from high concentrations of oxygen over time leading to overgrowth of blood vessels from the retina into the vitreous behind the lens. A large number of children with RLF, 18 percent, were assigned to the "not reported" class since their records did not actually specify the use of oxygen with severe retinal damage in infants of low birth weight. RLF has not entirely been eliminated; however, as Hatfield has stated in her report for the NSPB, "the risk of a severe vision impairment must sometimes be weighed against the need for high oxygen in order to save a life" (p. 12).

The small number of cases of blindness attributed to *injuries* may be misleading, because frequently the injury only affects one eye. The 1976 annual report of the NSPB reports that an estimated 1,000 eye injuries occur during every working day in the United States and that in 1975 approximately 167,000 school students received eye injuries, three out of four during unsupervised activities. Although not all the injuries led to blindness in either one or both eyes, the fact is that many might have been prevented if proper protective eye covering had been used or potentially dangerous toys recognized. Thus, these figures should be enough to make persons working with children more observant and alert to possible dangers.

Tumors rank as the third leading cause of blindness among school-age children. Most tumors reported were retinoblastomas, brain tumors, or tumors of the pituitary gland.

Infectious diseases, which include maternal rubella or German measles, appear as the fourth major cause of school-age blindness. The

---

*Since this is not a technical medical text, only very brief descriptions of eye conditions are given. Readers who wish a more detailed discussion of diseases and conditions of the eye from an educator's perspective are encouraged to consult Harley and Lawrence's volume entitled *Visual Impairment in the Schools*, published by Charles C Thomas, 1977.

cataract—cloudiness of the lens of the eye.

albinism—absence of pigment in the cells of the uveal tract.

glaucoma—increased pressure within the eye; can occur secondary to other conditions and result in loss of vision starting at the peripheral field.

rubella epidemic of the early 1960s left its mark in particular on those children who were age five to nine years in the 1968–1969 sample. Mass immunization programs and clinics have provided a means for many children to be inoculated against rubella. Although such immunizations will not have any effect on the eyesight of those children inoculated, they will decrease the transmission of the disease and lessen the risk of pregnant women developing the disease and having babies with associated congenital defects.

General systemic diseases account for a very small percentage of blind children. Among those that do occur are multiple sclerosis and other diseases of the central nervous system that can affect vision.

The *not determined or not specified* category is large, partly because of the number of RLF cases included and partly because of incomplete eye examination reports for the children in the sample.

Figure 10–3 depicts the estimated blindness prevalence rates by causes as they have fluctuated during selected years since 1933–34. Careful attention in the way of research, education, and prevention should continue in an effort to bring down the blindness rate among schoolchildren; of particular concern are the great many cases of blindness due to prenatal influence. The National Society for the Prevention of Blindness recommends that, among others, the following preventive measures be initiated or, in some cases, continued:

1. An eye examination at birth and periodically thereafter for every child.
2. Control of infectious diseases.
3. Immunization of all children against rubella.
4. Prompt treatment of eye injuries.
5. Reduction of hereditary defects through genetic counseling, professional education, and research.
6. Legislation to control the use of hazardous articles such as toy weapons, BB guns, and fireworks.
7. Use of protective eyewear in all school shops, labs, and industrial art classes.

SIGNIFICANCE OF VISUAL IMPAIRMENT

Discussion of eye structures and a catalogue of causes of blindness still cannot reveal an accurate picture of the significance of impaired vision to an individual. A particular eye condition does not translate precisely into a particular level of visual functioning, or automatically determine how persons will use whatever vision they have. Visual impairment may affect visual functioning in several major ways with varying degrees of severity. Let us turn our attention to some ways in which visual function can be affected by visual impairment.

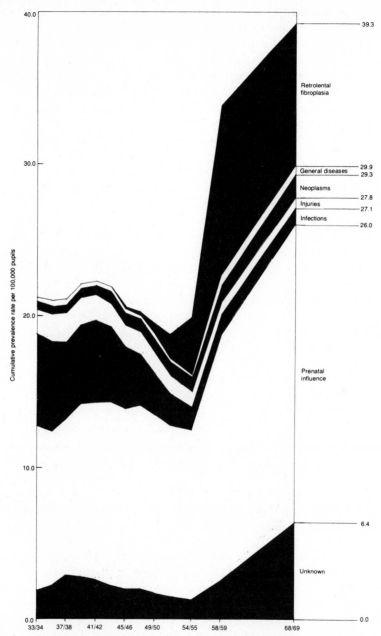

FIG. 10–3   Estimated blindness prevalence rates in schoolchildren by cause, school years 1933–1934 to 1968–1969.

Hatfield, Elizabeth M. "Why are they Blind?" *Sight-Saving Review,* vol. 45, no. 1 (Spring 1975), 18. Reprinted by permission of the National Society for the Prevention of Blindness.

REDUCED VISUAL ACUITY.   Visual acuity refers to the sharpness or clearness of central vision, that which we use to discover details of form and shape either at a distance or near to us. Refractive errors are common causes of reduced visual acuity and can result from structural defects, develop during the growth period, be secondary to disease or injury, or be related to the aging process. Most serious errors of refraction leading to blindness among schoolchildren are attributed to prenatal causes.

Sometimes light rays entering the eye are focused at a point in front of the retina because the eyeball is too long on the anterior-posterior axis, the curvature of the cornea is more convex than is necessary, or the refractive (bending) power of the lens is excessive (Harley and Lawrence, 1977). The result is myopia or nearsightedness, what our Australian neighbors would call shortsightedness. Objects nearby may be identified, but distant objects are fuzzy and blurry. In extreme cases, nothing beyond the extended fingertips can be seen clearly even with corrective lenses.

Another cause of reduced visual acuity is hyperopia or farsightedness. The light rays are brought to a theoretical point of focus behind the retina because the diameter of the eyeball is small, the curvature of the cornea is flatter than normal, or the refractive power of the lens is insufficient. With hyperopia, a person can see distant objects better than objects nearby, although in some persons both near and distance visual acuities are decreased. Young children generally have sufficient accommodative power in the lenses to adapt for close work. However, as schoolwork demands extended periods of time devoted to use of near vision, blurry pages, fatigue, and headaches may make reading tasks and other close work a difficult chore (Barraga, 1973). Special techniques can be used to detect those children whose accommodative powers are compensating for significant degrees of hyperopia.

A third refractive error known as astigmatism is generally the result of irregular curvature of the cornea. Light rays are diffused instead of focused at a point on the retina, and both near and distance vision can be blurred or distorted (Harley and Lawrence, 1977). Astigmatism can occur alone or in conjunction with myopia and hyperopia.

Presbyopia, a fourth type of refractive error, develops naturally with age. The tissues of the eye lose elasticity in time, and the ability of the lens to expand and contract to focus light rays precisely on the retina decreases. A person past the age of forty to forty-five may require corrective lenses to increase reading comfort and clarity of nearpoint vision.

Refractive errors frequently can be corrected with lenses. Lenses, like prisms, are pieces of glass or other transparent substance which, because of the relative position of their opposite surfaces, can bend light rays which pass through them. Concave lenses diverge or spread the light rays before they enter the myopic eye, convex lenses converge or bring together the light rays for the hyperopic eye, and cylindrical lenses neutralize the varying degrees of refractive power on the meridians of the cornea in the astigmatic eye.

DEFECTIVE COLOR VISION. The retinal cone cells, concentrated in the fovea or area of sharpest vision in the macula, absorb electromagnetic energy from the light rays focused on the retina and transmit information about color to the brain. Approximately 7 percent of men and 0.5 percent of women experience some degree of color vision abnormality, the most common type for both sexes being difficulty with red-green discriminations (Newell & Ernest, 1974).

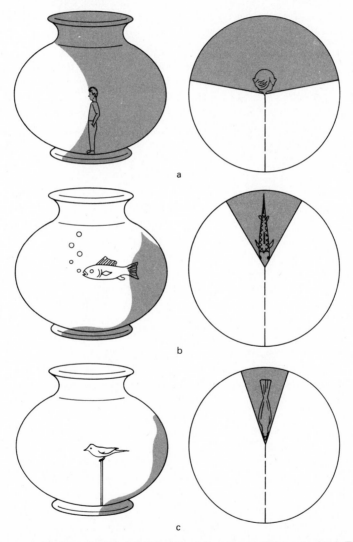

FIG. 10–4   Diagrams illustrating the field of vision of a man, a fish and a bird. The creatures are represented inside glass bowls; the portion of the bowl which is darkened is invisible. The circular diagrams show the angle of the field of vision if the observer is above the bowls: a—man; b—fish; c—bird. (From Mann & Pirie, 1952, p. 36.)

REDUCED FIELD OF VISION.   The normal visual field extends about 180 degrees laterally and 150 degrees vertically, giving us a fairly good view of what is in front of us. Figure 10–4 illustrates how the human field of vision compares with that of fish and birds whose life styles and habitat make a larger view of the world a definite advantage.

Disturbances in the visual field may occur in central vision, in the peripheral areas, or in both. For some people, then, vision for detail and color may be diminished, while others may have blank areas or blind spots in one or more quadrants of the visual field. Those with an extremely restricted field are said to have tunnel vision.

DEFECTIVE DARK/LIGHT ADAPTATION.   Quickly switching from an area of high illumination to one of a lower level may require a longer recovery period for persons with poor dark/light adaptation. The speed of adaptation decreases with age in the normal eye, but for some people, other conditions can affect the ability to adapt easily to changes in levels of illumination.

PHOTOPHOBIA.   All normal eyes are sensitive to light; light is one of the requirements for the process of seeing to occur. People vary quite a bit, however, in their reactions to both natural and artificial bright light. In some cases high levels of illumination and glare can cause painful ill effects. The glare from snow or water, the brilliant flash of a camera flashbulb, and the blue-white flames of a torch are all samples of light that can disturb the comfort of the normal eye. Much lower intensities of light can cause discomfort to persons who are extremely light sensitive.

Taken singly or in combination, these major disturbances in vision can have a great effect on how and what people see in their surroundings. When a person is a student in school, the effects can have serious consequences in three main areas: acquisition of knowledge, access to printed materials, and mobility within environment (Scholl, 1968). Fortunately, other channels besides vision can gather and carry information to the brain to enable individuals to learn and move about within their surroundings.

INFORMATION PROCESSING MODEL.   Figure 10–5 shows a diagram of the information processing model, which has been suggested to clarify the relationship of sensory input to activity attributed to the brain, and to observable vocal and motor responses (Cartwright & Cartwright, 1972). Visual, auditory and tactile input channels, sometimes acting alone but usually collecting information simultaneously, are considered the most important input channels for instructional purposes; however, gustatory and olfactory input add much flavor and aroma to the quality of the surroundings and can assume great importance for children with little or no vision.

The visual channel when functioning normally controls and coordinates most of our movements and activities. Vision enables people to monitor their behavior to see what nonverbal reactions others express

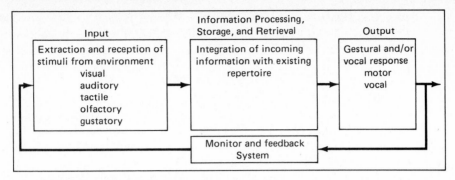

Input	Information Processing, Storage, and Retrieval	Output
Extraction and reception of stimuli from environment visual auditory tactile olfactory gustatory	Integration of incoming information with existing repertoire	Gestural and/or vocal response motor vocal

Monitor and feedback System

FIG. 10–5 Educational information processing model. Adapted from Cartwright & Cartwright, 1972, p. 28, and Smith, 1969, p. 50.

toward them; to process and store auditory and tactile input; to confirm accuracy of data received from other channels; and generally to take note of the environment, thus increasing the possibilities of being stimulated by further exploration and movement.

At the time of birth there is considerable organization of visual behavior. The newborn is immediately sensitive to light (Brazelton, 1966; Dayton, 1964). Gesell has noted that fixation responses at that time involve the whole body. Optimal regard or fixation includes open mouth, decreasing motor activity and wider eye slits (Gesell, 1967). From his observation of infants and children, Gesell concluded that the primary function of vision is the direction of movements. By the eighth week the baby's eyes begin to converge. The ability to vary and adjust posture is acquired. The eyes seem to "take hold" of the physical world before the hands reach out to grasp it. (Gesell, 1967).

Eye-hand coordination normally develops gradually and in orderly fashion during the first year of life. Harley and Lawrence (1977) have selected samples of behavior from Gesell's developmental schedules which reveal the progressive development, complexity, and integration of eye and hand movements.

EYE-HAND COORDINATION
First 28 Weeks

4 Weeks Stares vacantly at surroundings.
        Quiets when gazing toward light of window or bright moving object.
        Fixes object brought into visual scope.
        Eye and head movements not synchronized.
8 Weeks Eyes more mobile, but range of movement still limited.
        Direct regard and facial response to person's face.
        Eyes follow moving person and near object beyond midplane.
        Seeks light areas.
12 Weeks Eyes follow dangling ring 180 degrees with blinking or jerky eye movements.

Regards own hand spontaneously.

Channelizes regard for person, light, or object.

Demands focalized light.

16 Weeks Eyes move in active inspection: regards own hand, toy, surroundings.

Gives immediate regard for a suspended toy, and can retain a toy in hand with occasional regard.

20 Weeks Maintains attention within area close to body.

Lying on back, pursues dangling ring with good fixation for 180 degrees.

24 Weeks Regards object when bringing it to mouth, and then releases regard and looks out into space.

Quickly glances at person or object, and rolls eyes easily to extreme right or left.

28 Weeks Makes direct approach on pellet, but hand comes within vicinity of pellet, and rakes. This activity results in contact.

Regards handle of cup, and may approach it but not prehend it.

Piaget (1963) also links the environment very intimately with early motor and mental development and describes it as a source of stimulation for an infant. Stimulation calls for adaptation or adjustment on the infant's part to reestablish a balance between what has already been assimilated and that which is newly received. As a result, new patterns of behavior develop. For Piaget, intelligence is defined as this adaptation to the environment and is implied from behavior; new patterns of behavior indicate a more complex integration of previously acquired information which has been assimilated into mental structures. Although vision may have begun as a sensory experience that is interesting and entertaining in its own right, it assumes a richer purpose beyond pleasure and "is no longer an end in itself but an instrument at the service of vaster assimilations" (p. 75) as the infant integrates the new with the existing data that have been stored and processed.

Adelson and Fraiberg (1974) have reported that both congenitally blind and sighted children will consistently begin to move toward a sound stimulus alone during the last quarter of the first year. Of course, sighted children for months prior to that time have had visual stimuli to entice them to grope, stretch, and finally move toward interesting objects. As young as two months, as Gesell's schedules indicate, a sighted baby will typically begin to seek out visually the source of a sound. The bond between a sound and a reach for the object that makes that sound apparently becomes fixed later for both sighted and visually handicapped babies than does the bond between the visual picture of the object and a reach to attain and grasp the object for sighted babies. For children with little or no vision, the appearance of ear-hand coordination or the integration of auditory and tactile input assumes added importance, and should suggest some instructional strategies that will be examined in a later section.

Two major points must be made in this discussion of the information **processing model:**

Sonicguide—a mobility aid for the blind. Courtesy of Telesensory Systems, Inc.

1. Vision when present seems to play an important role in the stimulation of behavior and in the coordination and integration of auditory and tactile stimuli.
2. When vision is impaired, other channels exist which can still function to carry information to the brain; learning can still occur in the absence of vision.

With this background information about the eye, the process of seeing, and the significance of visual impairment, the focus will now turn to children who have visual impairments and how they are described for educational purposes.

DEFINITIONS AND TERMS

"More people have been blinded by definition than by any other cause," wrote a totally blind World War II veteran during the period he served as the first Executive Director of the Blinded Veterans Association (Schloss, 1963). Prior to and since that time, terms used to describe children as well as adults with visual impairment have generated much confusion and consternation.

Various definitions have been adopted for various purposes, and many have overlooked the fact that very few people called blind actually have no useful vision. For example, each January all local and residential schools providing programs for visually handicapped school-age children report the number of "blind" children to the American Printing House for the Blind (APH). Under the Act of 1879 "To Promote the Education of the Blind," Congress appropriates money to APH for preparation of textbooks for blind schoolchildren for the next fiscal year, based on the January registration figure. But annual surveys of mode of reading of the children registered indicate that many of the "blind" children actually use printed materials for reading. The latest annual report summarized in Table 10–2 shows that well over 40 percent of the children registered in 1976 used large type or both large type and braille; yet they were registered as "blind."

Table 10-2   **Distribution of January 5, 1976 Quota Registrations by Mode of Reading**

Location	MODE OF READING				
	Braille	Large Type	Both	Neither	Totals
Schools for Blind	3,284	2,739	403	2,296	8,722
State Departments of Education	2,916	9,687	701	6,969	20,273
Totals	6,200	12,426	1,104	9,265	28,995

Taken from annual report of the American Printing House for the Blind, Louisville, Kentucky, 1976.

Present-day terminology stems primarily from definitions the American Medical Association (AMA) approved in 1934, which referred to economic blindness as the absence of the ability to do any kind of work for which sight was necessary. Vocational blindness meant an impairment serious enough to prevent a return to the work previously done to earn a living. Educational blindness indicated an impairment that made it "difficult, dangerous, or impossible to learn by the methods that are commonly used in schools" (Schloss, 1963, p. 112). The next year the Social Security Board for its purposes modified the definition of economic blindness to specify a visual acuity of 20/200* or less in the better eye after correction or a visual field limit of 20 degrees or less (tunnel vision). It is apparent that these definitions emphasize the disability; the result is a separation of those with limited vision from the rest of the population. At that time in our history, the Great Depression left many perfectly healthy sighted persons out of work. Also, eye specialists then felt that with use, any remaining vision might further decrease. These reasons probably influenced the acceptance of definitions which overlook other abilities a person might have and which seem to ignore how a person might function visually in spite of restricted distance visual acuity or field of vision.

*A 20/200 distance visual acuity means a person is able to read the symbols or letters on a chart at a distance of 20 feet which the person with normal vision could read at a distance of 200 feet.

For many legal purposes today, the old economic definition of blindness with the word "economic" omitted still stands:

> The legally blind are defined as those with a central visual acuity for distance of 20/200 or less in the better eye with correction or, if greater than 20/200, a field of vision no greater than 20 degrees in the widest diameter (Hatfield, 1975, p. 4).

The NSPB summary of causes of blindness shown earlier in Table 10–1 and the APH report of mode of reading given Table 10–2 used this definition of blindness. Partial vision has been defined as visual acuity between 20/70 and 20/200 in the better eye after all medical and optical care are provided (Hathaway, 1959). Both definitions tend to emphasize a dysfunction within the person.

In time came the realization on the part of educators that many children labeled blind actually had useful vision. Eye specialists* also recognized that remaining vision could rarely be further decreased if the eyes were used. The trend moved away from "sight conservation" and toward "sight utilization."

Some educators suggested schoolchildren should be called blind or partially seeing depending upon whether they read braille or printed materials. An examination of the mode of reading of blind children who had better than the ability to distinguish light and dark and who were reported in 1960 to the American Printing House, found that more children in local schools were listed as primarily print readers whereas, in residential schools for the blind, more students were listed as primarily braille readers. The study concluded: "It would seem that many children reading by means of braille have as much visual acuity as many others who use print as the primary mode of reading" (Jones, 1962, p. 118).

Interest and research activity continued to turn to sight utilization and the possibilities of stimulating the use of very low vision. Hoover (1963) defined visual efficiency as "a complex of measurable visual characteristics which, when combined with other sensory and physical characteristics, provide an opportunity to utilize sight." He outlined the major characteristics of good visual efficiency as:

1. visual acuity for both near and distant vision;
2. visual versatility which includes such abilities as accommodation for near and distant objects, light/dark adaptation, color vision, and binocularity; and

*Eye specialists include: (1) ophthalmologists or oculists who are medical doctors specializing in diagnosis and treatment of defects and diseases of the eye, performing surgery when necessary or prescribing other types of treatment, including lenses; (2) optometrists who are licensed, nonmedical practitioners trained to measure refractive errors and eye muscle disturbances and prescribe lenses; and (3) opticians who grind lenses, fit them into frames, and adjust the frames to the wearer (U.S. Dept. of Health, Education and Welfare Health Information Series, No. 64).

3. visual capacity, meaning the amount or visual load a person can take in or handle for specified periods of time. (pp. 117–118)

Reflection on these components of visual efficiency should suggest, as Hoover pointed out, that visual efficiency might fluctuate widely depending upon the physical and mental state of the person at a particular time.

Barraga (1964) demonstrated that children with very low visual acuities could in fact learn to use what vision they did have more effectively and efficiently. She developed training materials and lessons designed to improve the visual behavior in children with low vision.

And so, today, a new terminology has emerged that stresses functional vision for educational purposes. While for administrative purposes the definitions of blind and partially seeing based on visual acuity may remain, for instructional planning Barraga has suggested the generic term "visually handicapped" which includes blind, low vision, and visually limited. These terms are defined as follows:

> *Visually handicapped*—this generic term refers to "the total group of children who require special educational provisions because of visual problems" (Barraga, 1976, p. 13). A visually handicapped child is "one whose visual impairment interferes with his optimal learning and achievement, unless adaptations are made in the methods of presenting learning experiences, the nature of the materials used, and/or in the learning environment" (Barraga, 1976, p. 16).
>
> *Blind* refers to those visually handicapped children who have only light perception without light projection or those who have no sense of vision whatsoever.
>
> *Low vision* indicates those children who may have very little distance vision, but who with adequate lighting and careful selection of materials are able to see objects and materials held from several inches to a few feet away from the eyes. Many will rely heavily on tactile materials but others will use vision for many tasks. These children "will always need to be made aware of what they are able to see and given assistance and encouragement in looking at educational materials and objects" (Barraga, 1976, p. 14).
>
> *Visually limited* includes visually handicapped children who have useful vision under "average circumstances. They may need special lighting, prescription lenses and/or optical aids such as magnifiers, enlarged materials, or shorter distance from eye to object. Visually limited children will be considered for all educational purposes and under all circumstances as seeing children" (Barraga, 1976, p. 14).

The term visual perception warrants clarification because of its frequent mention in connection with children who exhibit learning problems. Visual perception refers to the ability to integrate incoming visual data with what has previously been received, processed, and stored. It is a cerebral activity; impulses from the retinal cells are dispatched along the optic pathway to the brain where the signals are given meaning. The organ of sight may be intact, but perception may be poor; on the other hand, visual data may be distorted, ambiguous, or missing but interpretation may still be quite accurate. "Visual perception is a decision process that is related more to the child's learning capabilities than to the condition of his eyes" (Barraga, 1976, p. 15).

EDUCATIONAL PROGRAMS FOR VISUALLY HANDICAPPED CHILDREN

The passage of PL 94–142 has given added strength to the trend already well established in the United States today for visually handicapped children to attend public school programs. The first schools for blind children in the United States were opened in the 1830s. The New England Asylum for the Blind in Massachusetts (now Perkins School for the Blind), the New York Institution for the Blind in New York City, and the Pennsylvania Institution for the Instruction of the Blind (now Overbrook School for the Blind) were all private institutions. The Ohio State School for the Blind in Columbus opened in 1837 under state support, and other state residential schools quickly followed. Chicago opened the first regular public school class for blind children in 1900 and Cincinnati followed five years later. Unlike Chicago, where the children attended classes whenever possible with sighted children, in Cincinnati the blind children were segregated in a special building. In 1913 Cincinnati switched to Chicago's cooperative plan.

The first public school class for partially seeing children was formed in Boston in 1913. In 1938 an itinerant teaching program was initiated in Oakland, California, for children who could function in regular classes with the assistance of a traveling teacher.

Public school programs grew slowly; in 1949, 90 percent of the blind children in the United States were still attending residential schools (Koestler, 1976). In just a few years, however, the situation had changed, primarily because of the enormous increase in the number of babies blinded due to RLF. The increase came at the time of the "baby boom" after World War II, and as the children approached school age more public school programs began. By 1976 approximately 70 percent of the legally blind children were attending public day school programs, according to the American Printing House annual report. The fascinating story of the development of school programs for visually handicapped children is recorded in Lowenfeld's *The Changing Status of the Blind* (1975) and in Koestler's *The Unseen Minority* (1976).

Currently, a continuum of services is available for visually handicapped children of school age (Jones, 1966; Barraga, 1977):

1. Regular class placement with no assistance provided unless student shows a need;

2. Regular class placement with a consultant teacher providing materials and help to the classroom teacher and others working with the student;

3. Itinerant teacher program in which the child remains in the regular classroom but receives tutoring in special subjects or skills from a traveling teacher who serves several schools;

4. Resource room program where the children remain with their classmates except for instruction or assistance in specific subjects from a resource teacher in a specially equipped room, with the regular class teacher keeping major responsibility for the child's instructional program;

5. Cooperative or part-time special class program in which the child is registered in a special class for visually handicapped children but attends classes with children in the regular class as much as is feasible given specific instructional needs;

6. Full-time special class or self-contained classroom in which the child is enrolled for all of his instruction; and

7. Residential school in which students live at the school and attend classes on school campus, with some students participating in local public or private school programs in the surrounding community.

Over the years controversies have arisen concerning the merits of the various programs, but to date no research is available which clearly reveals that one type of program stands above the others.

Although the literature is replete with opinions of the advantages of one administrative pattern over others, usually by persons with limited experience in the others, there has been little substantiation of these assertions in the research findings. The practical approach, therefore, suggests a continuing study of the child and his total situation together with a careful evaluation of the facilities available to him (Taylor, 1973, p. 173).

Factors to consider when selecting the appropriate program for a child include:

1. Ophthalmological examination with reports of both near and distance visual acuity;

2. Physical examination to detect any additional physical problems which might be remedied;

3. Psychological evaluation and observations of qualified teachers;

4. Previous school history and present level of academic functioning;

5. Social history; and

6. Wishes of the parents (Scholl, 1968). Parents must be informed of their rights to due process procedures in the event honest and serious differences of opinions arise concerning an appropriate program for a particular child.

Program and placement decisions should be made by a team of professionals who are well informed about the child and the services available, and who do not regard placement decisions at any one time as final. Placement decisions must be reviewed at least annually and should be altered when a more appropriate placement can better meet the current needs of the particular child.

EDUCATIONAL IMPLICATIONS OF VISUAL IMPAIRMENT

Quay (1973) has distinguished three basic educational viewpoints in regard to the nature of educational handicaps. One viewpoint locates the disability within the child and focuses on some physical, mental, or sensory dysfunction. Another viewpoint emphasizes the contribution environmental factors can make in shaping children's behavior and influencing what and how they learn. If the environment is not rich and supportive or does not provide the right emotional climate for learning, the child may have experience defects that would have to be undone, or for which compensation should be provided in order to foster normal development. The third viewpoint acknowledges that a child's educational handicap may exist due to limited experiences or experience deficits. *Quantity* of input may be deficient. Quay proceeded to formulate a fourth viewpoint, an interactive approach, which recognizes the effects all three—dysfunction, defect, and deficit—may have in the same individual. For him, the interactive approach carries the greatest potential for instructional planning.

To a great extent the interactive approach presents a convenient structure within which to consider educational implications of visual impairments for schoolchildren. If a visual impairment inhibits or distorts the passage of visual stimuli to the brain, then information from the environment may be faulty, incomplete, inadequate, or deficient in quantity unless appropriate instructional plans are developed and implemented. A key factor in both planning and implementation becomes one of careful assessment to determine how best to provide sufficient meaningful experiences, with appropriate materials to enrich the sensory data transmitted to the brain. A strong prevention program geared to stimulate public awareness and sensitivity to causes and signs of eye problems follows as a logical complement.

Lowenfeld (1971, 1975) has identified three major areas as particularly vulnerable when vision is impaired: (1) range and variety of experiences, which can affect cognitive development; (2) mobility, which includes both orientation to one's immediate surroundings and locomotion safely and efficiently within one's surroundings; and (3) interaction with the environment. Casual and incidental acquisition of information from the immediate locale will be limited to the degree functional vision is limited, and social interactions may be fewer in number. In those interactions that do occur, the visually handicapped child may miss much of the subtle feedback sighted persons pick up from nonverbal gestures, shifts in posture, or changes in facial expression.

The Optacon, a tactile reading system for the blind, provides independent access to print to many who cannot read visually. Courtesy of Telesensory Systems, Inc.

Educational programs that aim to prepare visually handicapped children to function as competent and productive members of society must reflect appropriate assessment to uncover each child's areas of strength and weakness. Careful selection of instructional objectives and materials must be made to enhance strengths and ameliorate weaknesses. Certain curricular areas will assume greater importance for children whose vision is impaired, as will instruction in the use of special equipment and aids that have proven beneficial to those with limited vision.

ASSESSMENT

The word "assess" comes to us from the Latin *assidere*, meaning to sit beside or to assist in the office of a judge. The literal translation offers good counsel to one who would make judgments about the performance of a visually handicapped child; valuable information can be collected when sitting beside and observing how closely the child works at each task. The purpose for the assessment must be clear so the results can contain pertinent information for judgments to be made. Ysseldyke (1974) has described five main reasons for making assessments of individuals:

1. Screening—to sort out those who deviate significantly from the normal expectation along a particular dimension.
2. Classification—to identify or certify persons as members of a particular group.
3. Program planning—to gather information helpful in designing educational strategies to remediate difficulties.
4. Program evaluation—to judge the overall effectiveness of a particular treatment or strategy.
5. Assessment of individual pupil progress—to determine one pupil's progress or change.

Of these five, screening and individual assessment play a major role in educational programs for visually handicapped children. Vision screening programs to identify children who need professional eye examinations are crucial in order to reduce the number of children who pass through school with unnoticed vision problems. Many times children do not realize they are missing anything since they have never had "normal" vision. They may have difficulty seeing the chalkboard, reading duplicated worksheets, concentrating on close eye work for extended periods of time, or following written illustrations and directions because of some unrecognized impairment. Others may discover vision in one eye is poor after injury to the better eye. The National Society for the Prevention of Blindness in 1972 introduced a Home Eye Test for Preschoolers that parents, nursery school teachers, or other caregivers can use with preschool youngsters to find those who need professional eye examinations. In the five years since the kits have been available, over five million have been distributed. A total of 23,699 children have been referred to preschool eye examinations from among the 446,453 children screened in special projects completed by June 1976 (NSPB Report, 1977).

In many states periodic school vision screening programs are required at regular intervals. Screening tests should be simple, short, and inexpensive (Harley and Lawrence, 1977). Most frequently used are procedures based on the Snellen chart developed by a Dutch opthalmologist, Hermann Snellen, in 1862. Both a letter chart and an **E** symbol chart are available (see Figures 10–6 and 10–7), the latter being particularly well suited for young children. Both charts are constructed so that each letter subtends an angle of five minutes of arc and each space between letter parts takes up one minute of arc at the distance specified. Visual acuity measured with the Snellen chart is usually checked at a distance of twenty feet, and the acuity is written in the form of a fraction. The top numeral records the test distance, and the bottom numeral records the distance at which the smallest letters or symbols seen should be read by the normal eye. A 20/200 distance visual acuity indicates a person was able to read the symbol or letter at a distance of 20 feet which the normal eye could read at a distance of 200 feet.

With children of school age, teachers, school nurses, school psycholo-

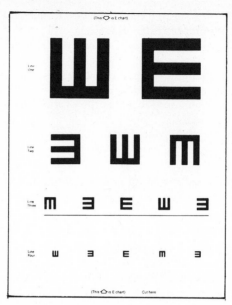

FIG. 10–6 Snellen Symbol E Chart. Courtesy of the National Society for the Prevention of Blindness, Inc., New York.

gists, and counselors are usually in the best position to spot student behavior, appearances, and complaints which could indicate troubles. The presence of one or even several of the signs does not necessarily mean a visual impairment exists, but any student who frequently shows the signs in Table 10–3 should be referred for further evaluation.

Assessment to classify children as members of a particular group has already been dealt with in the discussions of attitudes and definitions. To deny that visual impairment has any effect on the routine of daily living,

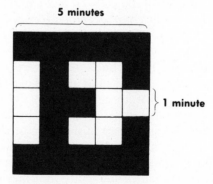

FIG. 10–7 Construction of the Snellen letter to subtend an angle of 5 minutes, with each part subtending an angle of 1 minute. Letters constructed without serifs are recommended by nearly all investigators. From Newell, Frank W.: *Ophthalmology*, ed. 4, St. Louis, 1978, The C. V. Mosby Co.

Table 10-3	**Signs of Eye Trouble in Children***

Behavior
Rubs eyes excessively.
Shuts or covers one eye, tilts head or thrusts head forward.
Has difficulty in reading or in other work requiring close use of the eyes.
Blinks more than usual or is irritable when doing close work.
Stumbles over small objects.
Holds books close to eyes.
Is unable to see distant things clearly.
Squints eyelids together or frowns.

Appearance
Crossed eyes.
Red-rimmed, encrusted, or swollen eyelids.
Inflamed or watery eyes.
Recurring sties.

Complaints
Eyes itch, burn or feel scratchy.
Cannot see well.
Dizziness
Headaches   following close eye work
Nausea
Blurred or double vision.

*"Signs of Eye Trouble in Children," National Society for the Prevention of Blindness, Inc., New York, NY.

gathering of information from the environment, and moving about and among other people is to deny reality. But to dwell on disability at the expense of capabilities or to overlook alternatives and supplements to visual learning because of labels which focus on dysfunction or defect shuts out reality also. Thus, assessment to classify may meet administrative needs but will offer little help for instructional planning.

Assessment for planning programs and determining services needed is helpful, as is assessment at the completion of sequences of instruction to determine overall effectiveness. The most productive information for instructional planning, however, comes from the assessment of individual pupil progress. The teacher as well as the psychologist who is a skilled observer will find much of value in both informal and formal assessment of performance to determine progress.

Selection of appropriate assessment instruments and administrative procedures is essential if results are to carry much meaning. Spungin and Swallow (1975) have offered advice to psychologists who plan to assess visually handicapped individuals, and their suggestions are appropriate for teachers as well:

Skilled psychologists will also probe for teaching strategies and modifications by adjusting task difficulty. What happens when the examiner points to aid visual search? What happens when the visual array is restricted by construction paper boundaries? Does it help if a stimulus card is raised to eye level? Can a slant board be employed? Does a heavy black felt-tip pen outline aid in task completion? The variety of adaptations and modifications is endless, dependent only upon the perceptibility of the psychologist. Obviously, this represents non-standardized assessment (p. 74).

Scholl and Schnur (1976), in their resource manual for professionals seeking appropriate measures of psychological, vocational, and educational functioning of visually limited persons, list alternatives to the traditional assessment procedures:

1. Observations in the home, school, or other familiar settings;
2. Observations and formal assessment in unfamiliar settings to determine adaptive behavior and coping skills;
3. Trial placements in settings being considered;
4. Behaviorally oriented assessments to chart rate and frequency of specific responses; and
5. Case material or anecdotal records.

Unless the assessment leads to action to prepare, identify, or remediate difficulties, it degenerates into "mere exercise" (Chase, 1975, p. 314).

Instruction

The similarities between visually handicapped children and so-called normal children outweigh the differences. The basic needs of both groups in school are the same. While there is nothing inherent in visual impairment that directly affects growth and development except in certain areas of cognitive development and mobility (Lowenfeld, 1971; Scholl, 1968), there are some indirect effects that must be kept in mind when specifying instructional objectives, selecting materials, and arranging the instructional environment.

In the area of *cognitive development* the restricted opportunities to interact with other people, to explore visually, to acquire concepts of color and perspective, and to move about freely can have impact on concept formation, language development, and vocabulary. Parents and teachers need to arrange experiences and structure situations for each visually handicapped child to have direct, hands-on opportunities to learn by doing. This will create a basis in the children's own repertoire of experiences for the words they use and the thoughts they express. The age of onset of visual impairment assumes great importance in connection with cognitive development as does the existence of any degree of useful vision. Stimulation of low vision, one of the components of the special or "plus" curriculum for visually handicapped children to be discussed later, is essential in the attempt to reduce the effect limited vision might have on cognitive development.

Although *motor development* basically follows the normal sequence, the rate of progression is frequently slower (Scholl, 1968, 1973). Earlier the role of vision as a coordinator of activity and stimulus for additional action and exploration was described. Hearing can assume the role of coordinator and activator, but this appears to occur at a later stage in development than for sight (Fraiberg, Siegel, and Gibson, 1966; Adelson and Fraiberg, 1974). Early opportunities for developing gross motor and fine motor coordination may therefore be limited. Structured experiences to stimulate physical activity, to encourage exploration, and to improve coordination are essential to help the visually handicapped children locate themselves in space and give meaning to their world.

Coordination and motor control are important for mobility. Kay (1974) has identified three primary factors which determine the degree to which a person may be mobile: "motive power and body control, skills in the use of motor control, and knowledge of the structure of the environment in a way that is not unlike understanding and using a language." Good posture, muscle control, physical endurance, and strength are all necessary ingredients for efficient mobility. A physical education program to build strength, endurance, balance, coordination, agility, and stamina is an important component of every visually handicapped child's educational program. Unfortunately, some children have in the past been excluded from participation in physical education programs and contact games and sports when actually they could learn much from active involvement with other students, a fact most educators recognize today. Halliday and Kurzhals (1976) have stressed the value of camping and out-of-door activities as additional means of enriching the repertoire of experiences from which visually handicapped children can draw in order to reduce the impact of limited vision on motor development.

The *emotional development* of visually handicapped children to some extent reflects the attitudes of significant persons in their lives and the way they have been treated during interactions with others. Concerns and needs that sighted children have can be intensified when vision is limited, particularly for adolescents. Needs for independence, for respect and understanding, for mobility, for privacy, for feelings of accomplishment may seem at first more difficult to meet in the face of limited vision. Concerns about the future, vocational decisions, and questions about marriage and family are no different in kind for visually handicapped than for sighted students; but the degree of concern may appear greater among those with visual impairment (Scholl, 1968, 1973).

Social development, closely intertwined with emotional development, is also subject to the influence of attitudes others express. Acceptance, encouragement, and opportunities for experiences with others, coupled with realistic expectations for school personnel, should help visually handicapped children develop socially and emotionally into mature, responsible adults who can take their places in society.

Instructional Materials

Selection of instructional materials for use with visually impaired students requires detailed knowledge of the requirements of the instructional task, and the student's present level of academic functioning and sensory functioning. In some cases the teacher may find it necessary to adapt materials other students use or to create special materials. For blind students, appropriate verbal descriptions of pictures and diagrams may occasionally suffice, but concrete experience with time to examine and manipulate real objects can better aid understanding and concept formation (Dorward and Barraga, 1968). Three-dimensional illustrations and relief or tactile maps can also be used to make ideas clear in certain areas. Studies have indicated that blind students need and can profit from instruction in map-reading skills and use of tactile aids (Franks and Nolan, 1971; Berlá and Butterfield, 1975). Many tangible aids are available from the American Printing House for the Blind.

For low vision and visually limited students, criteria for selection of visual materials include those used for selecting any instructional materials, with some special attention to visual complexity and layout. Among the important factors are:

overall size
size of items in illustrations
color variety and mix
texture
durability
safety
adaptability to other purposes
complexity in design, operation and/or detail
relative cost
results reported by others regarding effectiveness

For printed materials, of special concern are the type size and style, the amount of space or leading between lines of print, the length of the printed lines, the layout on the page and the amount of clutter in background detail, color contrast, and paper weight and finish to diminish show-through and glare.

Not all students with visual impairment will need special materials. Occasionally, some students who do are reluctant to use what might help them because of a fear that teachers and students will devalue their use. It is important to view special materials for what they are—aids to foster learning—and to provide an atmosphere and the instruction necessary for their effective use.

Instructional Environment

Closely tied to appropriate instructional materials are proper classroom working conditions. *Lighting* is critical; there must be enough to illuminate the working area without causing any direct or reflected glare. Desk tops, floors, chalkboards, glossy table tops and window sills are all possible sources of glare. *Contrast* between the materials and the working surface can ease the visual task. For example, darkening the lines on writing paper with a felt-tip pen may enable a student to write more legibly, or placing a sheet of construction paper of contrasting color on the desk surface on which a child is sorting blocks might make the discrimination task easier. Light should come from a source over the left shoulder for right-handed students to avoid shadows in the writing or working area, and over the right shoulder for left-handed students. Sometimes a high-intensity lamp can be helpful to highlight the working area.

In addition to control of light, control of *noise level* in the instructional setting can increase the ease and comfort. The size of the room, the task in progress, and the number of students and others present all are factors that help determine the level of tolerable noise. *Space* in the working area must be sufficient for the task, for moving about, and for convenient storage of supplies. *Furniture* of the right size for the students should be selected and ideally should be adjustable and movable.

Special Curriculum

In addition to the regular curriculum offered sighted students, special attention must go to the added or "plus" curriculum (Abel, 1959; Taylor, 1959). Heading this list are *vision stimulation and utilization of low vision* for those students who have at least light perception. Even very low vision may be useful for mobility if instruction is provided to enable the student to interpret the visual information received. Materials are available from the American Printing House for the Blind and various lesson guides have been developed to help teachers and parents encourage use of residual vision (Barraga, 1964; O'Brien, Hoffman, and Howard, 1971).

Listening skills are important for study as well as mobility purposes. They include identification of sounds in the environment which can provide orientation to the surroundings, "reading" by listening to recorded texts, following instructions, remembering details, and recalling information. Some students learn to listen to compressed or speeded speech to cut down the listening time. Adapted playback units with variable speed control are available from the American Printing House for the Blind and from the Library of Congress, Division for the Blind and Physically Handicapped.

Good listening skills as an aid to mobility can provide clues to location of self in relation to the surroundings and can help a person determine the content of the surroundings. First must come awareness of sound, the differentiation among sounds, identification of specific sounds, and finally location of speed and direction of moving sounds.

Typing instruction is generally started in third or fourth grade when a child has sufficient fine motor control to profit from instruction and when there is a reason to use the skill. Typing assignments may lighten the work load of students for whom handwriting is difficult and permit the blind student to prepare assignments independently to turn in to the teacher.

Basic *mobility skills* can be started early, well before entrance into school. Body awareness, muscle control, orientation to the environment, and discrimination of various terrains and textures can facilitate development of independent travel. These skills really have their origins in infancy when the baby begins to respond to sounds and move about without supervision.

Various techniques and mobility aids are available, one of which is use of a sighted guide. A sighted guide can pass on information and alert the blind person to changes in pace, direction, or position in order to enter doors, move up or down stairs, or maneuver in congested areas. Holding the guide's arm just above the elbow, the blind person is positioned approximately a half step behind and is thus able to respond in time to changes in the guide's position or movement. Use of a sighted guide can begin when a child is quite young.

Among the devices that allow a blind person to travel without the aid of another person are a long cane, a guide dog, and several electronic devices. Dr. Richard Hoover, while working with blinded veterans at Valley Forge Army Hospital in the early 1940s, developed a method of cane travel which requires instruction and supervision during the learning phase by a qualified, well-trained mobility instructor. By using the cane as a probe and by combining auditory and other sensory data (odors, heat from the sun, surface slope, and texture), a blind person can acquire proficiency, confidence, and grace in independent travel (Suterko, 1973). The Hoover or long-cane technique is taught in most school programs providing mobility training for visually handicapped children.

Dogs can be trained to follow the instructions of the adult blind person and to respond with intelligent disobedience if following instructions were to place the blind person in danger. The blind person must possess good hearing, be willing to assume responsibility for the care and continued training of the dog, have generally good health and emotional stability to manage the dog and to keep up with its pace, and of course have reason to travel.

Some electronic devices for mobility are head-borne while others are adaptations of the long cane. Some emit audible sounds to indicate the distance from overhanging structures or obstacles in the path and others feed back information tactually. Most devices are experimental, and are not commercially available at present.

The final selection of any mobility device should remain the individual's decision; it will, however, depend in part upon age, competence, orientation and locomotion skills, as well as reason and desire for independence in travel.

For students who have no useful vision, *braille skills* are essential. Originally developed in 1829 by Louis Braille who was himself blind, braille is a system for reading and writing based on combinations of six dots within a

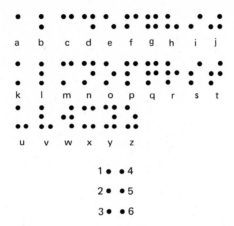

FIG. 10–8   Braille cell and Braille alphabet.

cell two dots wide and three dots high (see Figure 10–8). With the sixty-three possible dot patterns, literary, music, scientific, and mathematical materials can be embossed to give the blind student a means of writing and reading the same printed materials as his sighted peers. As is the case in other areas of the curriculum, auditory and tactual discrimination, language development, cognitive development, and breadth of experience are important readiness factors in preparation for braille reading (Lowenfeld, Abel, and Hatlen, 1969). The process of recognizing words written in braille "is a sequential integrative one in which word recognition is the result of the accumulation of information over a temporal interval from sensing the braille characters" (Nolan and Kederis, 1969, pp. 43–44). Grade 1 braille is letter-for-letter transcription into the equivalent braille character. Grade 2 braille makes use of almost two hundred contractions and shortened word forms, which add to the complexity of braille reading but also cut down the number of pages required to transcribe printed material. Although braille can be written with a slate and stylus, the easiest and fastest device is the braillewriter. Most braille textbooks for schoolchildren are produced at the American Printing House for the Blind, although volunteers produce thousands of braille pages each year for students in elementary and secondary schools, as well as in colleges across the nation, which require materials not available from any other source.

Special Equipment and Aids

Among the many instructional aids that can offer assistance to visually handicapped students are those listed below.

1. Slate and stylus—Braille characters can be embossed by punching

Courtesy of Telesensory Systems, Inc.

the braille dots with a pointed stylus into braille paper held in position by a metal or plastic slate containing a series of depressions that corresponds to the six dots of the braille cell. Each dot in each braille character must be punched individually. The slate and stylus provide a braille equivalent to writing with pencil and paper.

2. Braillewriters—The most widely used braillewriter is the Perkins Brailler developed by Howe Press in 1950 at Perkins School for the Blind. It has six keys, three on each side of a space bar, which represent the six dots of the braille cell. As the keys are depressed, an embossing head moves across the paper from left to right and produces the braille characters.

3. Large type materials—Enlarged materials, generally in 18- to 24-point type, can be helpful to some (but not all) low vision and visually limited students. No one type size seems to prove better than any other for visually limited students, and the wise procedure is to try several to determine which is best (Peabody and Birch, 1967).

4. Tape and cassette players for playback of recorded texts, tests, and pleasure reading—Tape recorders can also be used to take notes, and to answer test questions in some cases.

5. Talking Book machines and record players for recorded texts, magazines, and pleasure reading—Talking Book machines are distributed free through the Library of Congress and its system of regional libraries to children and adults who come under the legal definition of blindness or who are physically handicapped.

6. Optical aids including hand-held magnifiers, special clip-on lenses for close work, and distance or telescopic magnifiers to facilitate independent travel—Magnification is of assistance for some low vision and visually limited students, but the critical lens-to-object distance that must be maintained, the restricted field of view through the lens, and occasionally the need for supplementary lighting may hinder acceptance as well as usefulness.

7. Optacon—The Optacon is an optical-to-tactile conversion device con-

sisting of a camera, an electronic section, and a grid of 144 vibrating rods. As the user guides the camera across the line of print, one letter at a time is converted into a vibration pattern that can be detected by the index finger of the left hand as it rests lightly on the tactile grid. The optacon permits those who are trained in its use to read, by touch, materials in their original form. To date over 3,000 optacons have been distributed to users in the United States and other countries. Attachments enable use with typewriters, computer terminals, and calculators (Bliss and Moore, 1974).

The Kurzweil Reading Machine, another promising device that is computer based, converts printed materials directly into spoken English at approximately 150 words per minute. The machine is currently being field-tested with students in public and residential schools.

8. Arithmetic aids and calculators—These include the Cranmer abacus (small enough to fit into a pocket and adapted so the counting beads do not slip out of place) and the Speech Plus talking calculator with a 24-word vocabulary (available now in English, German, and Arabic).

9. Closed circuit television systems—A number of closed circuit television systems for reading and writing have been developed. These generally contain provisions for variable magnification, reverse image, and lighting control. The units usually include a camera, lens system, monitor for viewing, and table or platform for positioning material to be read or paper on which to write.

10. Miscellaneous math shapes, relief maps and globes, audible goal locators, book stands, and simple machine models.

Many of these items are available from the American Printing House for the Blind in Louisville, Kentucky, which is the official United States printery of educational materials for blind students. Other sources of special materials, aids, and equipment can be located by requesting information from local instructional materials centers serving special education programs.

Designing Instructional Programs

In closing this discussion of educational implications of visual impairment, it seems appropriate to remind readers of some general principles that should guide the design of instructional programs and the selection of materials for visually handicapped students. Lowenfeld (1952) has identified five such principles, which he describes in the context of instruction for blind children, but which might be applied to teaching all children:

1. Individualization—consideration for the fact that children exhibit a wide range of inter- and intraindividual differences and require careful assessment so programs can be designed to meet individual needs.
2. Concreteness—opportunities to touch, explore tactually, and manipulate real objects to discover shape, size, weight, hardness, surface quality, pliability, and temperature.

3. Unified instruction—careful regard for sequencing, showing relationships, and providing overall structure to a series of activities.
4. Additional stimulation—conscious and systematic planning of experiences to increase the store of information children gather on their own and to broaden awareness of surroundings—room, school, community, and beyond.
5. Self-activity—opportunities for independent activity, self-initiated exploration, curiosity, and discovery.

VISUALLY HANDICAPPED CHILDREN WITH ADDITIONAL IMPAIRMENTS

No discussion of those with impaired vision would be complete without some attention given to the children who have problems in addition to visual impairment. These multihandicapped children are described as those "with two or more disabilities so severe that it is difficult or impossible for them to profit satisfactorily from an educational program established for any one of the disabilities" (Wolf, 1967, p. 6). Although estimates place the number of multihandicapped children anywhere from approximately 18,000 to 30,000 (Dantona, 1976), exact figures are elusive because of difficulties in predicting life expectancy, in anticipating severity of rubella epidemics like those that have swept the country in the past, and in compensating for under-reporting when trying to collect data (Graham, 1968). In a survey completed in 1966, Graham found that among the 8,887 multihandicapped blind children for whom information was reported, mental retardation was the most frequently occurring condition accompanying blindiness for 80.2 percent of the children. In a survey of forty-eight residential schools for the blind just a year prior to Graham's study, Wolf (1967) found that only 25 percent of the 6,696 students were regarded as mentally retarded. Graham, in commenting on the marked disparity, stressed that the problems associated with accurate reporting, as well as the questionable validity of IQ scores and subjective evaluation of observed performance, make any figures suspect and "merely reflect the confusion in the field" (p. 13). Wolf concluded that use of IQ tests to determine mental retardation in blind children may "only reflect the blind child's reduced opportunity to interact with his environment prior to enrollment in school." Mental retardation may provide a convenient term to apply to children who "baffle educators and defy accurate diagnosis" (Hatlen, 1973, p. 238).

Visually handicapped children with other handicapping conditions include those with hearing loss, cerebral palsy, behavior problems, orthopedic problems, epilepsy, and other conditions singly or in combination. Causes include maternal rubella, complications related to premature birth, use of drugs, accidents, irradiation, genetic defects, and conditions secondary to other diseases such as encephalitis and meningitis.

As might be expected, the needs of these children and their families are great in terms of both understanding and service (Gruber, 1963). Careful assessment procedures to determine sensory input channels available, reward systems, and current levels of function are critical to adequate program planning for these children, and these are demanding tasks (Hart, 1974; Jones, 1975). Appropriate placements for service cover a range from residential to home-based, and can involve community and private agencies as well as educational and vocational rehabilitation programs. The federally sponsored network of ten regional deaf-blind centers established in 1969 has located over 5,000 deaf-blind children who are provided medical diagnosis, counseling for their families, and initial educational evaluation and reassessment when necessary.

Although the combination of various severely handicapping conditions would seem to be rather overwhelming, such children can and do learn, develop, and mature when educational intervention strategies are carefully planned and implemented.

ISSUES IN EDUCATION OF VISUALLY HANDICAPPED

Some of the major current issues in the field of special education for children with impaired vision center on assessment, curriculum, instructional materials and equipment, and the role of parents.

ASSESSMENT. In a previous discussion a point was made that assessment conducted in the absence of clear purpose degenerated into "mere exercise." Assessment should be an integral part of the diagnostic teaching process and should lead to the determination of long- and short-range goals.

In addition to assessing the child, time might profitably be spent assessing the value of the child's overall program. It is one thing to analyze a task into subtasks and component parts, but it is another to analyze the worth of teaching that task in light of all the tasks a child must master to develop any potential to its fullest. Program assessment becomes particularly important for multihandicapped visually handicapped children.

CURRICULUM. Hatlen (1976), in his discussion of priorities in programs for the visually handicapped children, urged teachers of visually handicapped to look at the children emerging from their programs and then to ask some questions about the priorities for specialized instruction in basic skills. In addition to orientation and mobility, he showed a need for emphasis on concept development and reasoning, listening skills, motor development, career education, human sexuality, and basic living skills.

Of considerable concern at present is career education. Bauman (1975) has written: "Informed vocation choice is impossible unless the individual and those who counsel him have information about jobs and about the individual's abilities, interests, and those personal and personality qualities which so much affect job success and job happiness" (p. 354).

In an age when new jobs are created almost overnight as technological advances appear, and old jobs are taken over by machines or become obsolete, career choices for no one can be approached casually or made in the vacuum of ignorance. Even more so is this true for visually handicapped youngsters. Programs for the visually handicapped should assess their appropriateness for the children they serve by examining their philosophies, policies, and service delivery systems for career education.

INSTRUCTIONAL MATERIALS AND EQUIPMENT. With the relatively recent and rapid appearance of sophisticated instructional aids for visually handicapped students, there is need for a pause to regain perspective and put into focus the role of instructional materials in the learning process. Mere availability of materials does not guarantee proper use. Programs providing service to visually handicapped children need to coordinate efforts in curriculum planning for effective dissemination and instruction in the use of materials and equipment.

ROLE OF PARENTS. Parents of visually handicapped children are rich sources of information about their sons and daughters and how they behave before and after school hours. However, educators have not always recognized this parental wealth nor have they consistently collected and refined parental information for the benefit of educational and instructional planning. As a result of recent litigation and legislation outlined earlier in this book, parents today can become much more involved in making decisions about educational programs for their children. To what extent they will, though, and just how productive their involvement will be, depends upon the attitudes teachers and others who meet them express, as well as the ways in which parental information and cooperation are elicited during the early parent-school interactions.

In a recently published annotated bibliography of literature for parents of handicapped children, the idea is expressed that "when viewed as a partnership between equals, the relationship between parent and professional has the potential to produce the most suitable educational environment" (*Help for Parents of Handicapped Children*, p. 5). Hatlen (1976) has also suggested that parents of visually handicapped children can play a vital role in the development of their children's specialized skills if they work together with teachers as partners. The burden for development of the partnership falls on the shoulders of the teachers, but as the partnership strengthens, the burden should lessen as a result of the benefits derived.

How does this partnership develop? First, professionals need to recognize parental attitudes and concerns about their children. Lowenfeld, writing at a time when many children were blinded as a result of RLF, points out:

> People who find themselves as parents of a child who is blind cannot help but feel shocked and confused when they are brought to realize this fact. We have

all heard so much about blindness and its assumed effects—all negative, if not openly, so at least by implication—that no one can help feeling this way. We hear people talk about someone as being helpless as if he were blind; we remember the blind person with the tin cup; we think of the blind person groping his way; and we have heard all our lives about "blind" in connection with fury, hatred, alley, and chance. No wonder that parents are shocked when they meet blindness as a reality in their child. (1956, pp. 5–6)

Lowenfeld's observations hold true today, and educators need to sort out their own reactions to the ideas of visual limitations and blindness, as well as their reactions to the reality of blindness in a given child.

Next, professionals working with parents need to provide information about how their children behave in school and solicit from the parents details of behavior at home. With young children, instructional programs initiated while a child is at school can be carried over into the home with the cooperation of informed parents. A two-way communication path between home and school is essential so that instructional strategies remain consistent, performance and progress are noted in various settings, and activities are changed as objectives are met and behaviors are strengthened. Mutual respect, open communication, exchange of information based on close observations of behavior, joint planning and selection of goals—these phrases should characterize the contacts of professionals with parents of visually handicapped children. Researchers need to explore strategies to enhance this cooperation and to encourage parental involvement in planning beyond that called for by laws and the courts.

CONCLUSION

From the opening discussion of attitudes toward the visually impaired to the closing look at broad issues in the field of education of visually handicapped children, the overriding concern has been the child's potential for growth and development. Persons who focus on this concern, and who choose to develop the necessary skills and serve in the field of special education for the visually handicapped should help make the future brighter for these children with special needs because of visual impairment.

REFERENCES

Abel, G. L. Problems and trends in the education of blind children and youth. In G. L. Abel (ed.), *Concerning the Education of Blind Children*. New York: American Foundation for the Blind, 1959 (Educational Series No. 12).

Adelson, E., and Fraiberg, S. Gross motor development in infants blind from birth. *Child Development,* 1974, *45,* 114–126.

Barraga, N. C. *Increased Visual Behavior in Low-Vision Children.* New York: American Foundation for the Blind, 1964.

———. Utilization of sensory-perceptive abilities. In B. Lowenfeld (ed.), *The Visually Handicapped Child in School.* New York: The John Day Company, Inc., 1973.

———. *Visual Handicaps and Learning: A Developmental Approach.* Belmont, CA: Wadsworth Publishing Company, 1976.

Bauman, M. K. Guided vocational choice. *New Outlook for the Blind,* 1975, *69,* 354–360.

Berlá, E. P., and Butterfield, L. H., Jr. Teachers' views on tactile maps for blind students: Problems and needs. *Education of the Visually Handicapped,* 1975, *7,* 116–118.

Bliss, J. C., and Moore, M. W. The Optacon reading system. *Education of the Visually Handicapped,* 1974, *6,* 98–102.

Brazelton, T. B. Visual responses in the newborn. *Pediatrics,* 1966, *37,* 284–290.

Cartwright, G. P., and Cartwright, C. A. *Computer Assisted Remedial Education: Early Identification of Handicapped Children.* University Park, PA: CAI Laboratory, The Pennsylvania State University, 1972.

Chase, J. B. Developmental assessment of handicapped infants and young children: With special attention to the visually impaired. *New Outlook for the Blind,* 1975, *69,* 341–349.

Dantona, R. Services for deaf-blind children. *Exceptional Children,* 1976, *43,* 172–174.

Dayton, G. O., Jones, M. H., Aiu, P., Rawson, R. A., Steele, B., and Rose, M. Developmental study of coordinated eye movements in the human infant: I. Visual acuity in the newborn human: A study based on induced opto-kinetic nystagmus recorded by electro-oculography. *Archives of Ophthalmology,* 1964, *71,* 865–869.

———, Jones, M. H., Steele, B., and Rose, M. Developmental study of coordinated eye movements in the human infant: II. An electro-oculographic study of the fixation reflex in the newborn. *Archives of Ophthalmology,* 1964, *71,* 871–875.

Dorward, B., and Barraga, N. *Teaching Aids for Blind and Visually Limited Children.* New York: American Foundation for the Blind, 1968.

Ernst, M. *NAVA Special Report: Education of the Handicapped.* Fairfax, VA: National Audio-Visual Association, 1977.

Fraiberg, S., Siegel, B. L., and Gibson, R. The role of sound in the search behavior of a blind infant. *Psychoanalytic Study of the Child,* 1966, *21,* 327–357.

Franks, F. L., and Nolan, C. Y. Measuring geographical concept attainment in visually handicapped students. *Education of the Visually Handicapped,* 1971, *3,* 11–17.

Gesell, A., Ilg, F. L., and Bullis, G. E. *Vision: Its Development in Infant and Child.* New York: Hafner Publishing Co., Inc., 1967.

Gibson, J. J. *The Perception of the Visual World.* Boston, MA: Houghton Mifflin Company, 1950.

Goffman, E. *Stigma: Notes on the Management of Spoiled Identity.* Englewood Cliffs, NJ: Prentice-Hall, Inc., 1963.

Graham, M. D. *Multiply-Impaired Blind Children: A National Problem.* New York: American Foundation for the Blind, 1968.

Gruber, K. F., and Moor, P. M. (ed.) *No Place to Go: A Symposium.* New York: American Foundation for the Blind, 1963.

Halliday, C., and Kurzhals, I. W. *Stimulating Environments for Children who are Visually Impaired.* Springfield, IL: Charles C Thomas, Publisher, 1976.

Harley, R. K., and Lawrence, G. A. *Visual Impairment in the Schools.* Springfield, IL: Charles C Thomas Publisher, 1977.

Hart, V. *Beginning with the Handicapped.* Springfield, IL: Charles C Thomas Publisher, 1974.

Hatfield, E. M. Why are they blind? *Sight-Saving Review,* 1975, *45,* 3–22.

Hathaway, W. *Education and Health of the Partially Seeing Child.* (4th ed.) New York: Columbia University Press, 1959.

Hatlen, P. H. Priorities in educational programs. *DVH Newsletter,* 1976, *20,* (3), 8–11.

———. Visually handicapped children with additional problems. In B. Lowenfeld (ed.), *The Visually Handicapped Child in School.* New York: The John Day Company, Inc. 1973.

Helps for Parents of Handicapped Children: An Annotated Bibliography. King of Prussia, PA: Eastern Pa. Regional Resource Center for Special Education and Pa. Resources and Information Center for Special Education, n.d.

Hoover, R. E. Visual efficiency as a criterion of service needs. In *Research Bulletin No. 3.* New York: American Foundation for the Blind, 1963, 116–119.

Imamura, S. *Mother and Blind Child.* New York: American Foundation for the Blind, 1965 (Research Series No. 14).

Jones, J. W. Problems in defining and classifying blindness. *New Outlook for the Blind,* 1962, *56,* 115–121.

———. *The Visually Handicapped Child at Home and School.* Washington, DC: United States Department of Health, Education and Welfare, 1966.

Jones, T. W., Jr. *Manual for Language Development: A Handbook of Strategies for Teaching Children Whose Communicative Skills Range from Non-Responsiveness to Use of Academic Language.* Bronx, NY: Mid-Atlantic-North and Caribbean Regional Center for Services to Deaf-Blind Children, 1975.

Kay, L. *Toward Objective Mobility Evaluation: Some Thoughts on a Theory.* New York: American Foundation for the Blind, 1974.

Koestler, F. A. *The Unseen Minority.* New York: David McKay Co., Inc., 1976.

Lowenfeld, B. The child who is blind. *Exceptional Children,* 1952, *19,* 96–102.

———. *Our Blind Children: Growing and Learning with Them.* Springfield, IL: Charles C Thomas, Publisher, 1956.

———. Psychological problems of children with impaired vision. In W. M. Cruickshank (ed.), *Psychology of Exceptional Children and Youth.* Englewood Cliffs, N.J.: Prentice-Hall, Inc., 1971.

———. (ed.) *The Visually Handicapped Child in School.* New York: The John Day Company, Inc., 1973.

———. *The Changing Status of the Blind.* Springfield, IL: Charles C Thomas, Publisher, 1975.

———, Abel, G. L., and Hatlen, P. H. *Blind Children Learn to Read.* Springfield, IL: Charles C Thomas, Publisher, 1969.

Mann, I., and Pirie, A. *The Science of Seeing.* Perth, Western Australia: Paterson Press, 1962.

Manual on Use of the NSPB Standard Classification of Causes of Severe Vision Impairment and Blindness: Part II, Index of Diagnostic Terms. New York: National Society for the Prevention of Blindness, 1966.

National Society for the Prevention of Blindness Report for the Year Ending March 31, 1976. New York: National Society for the Prevention of Blindness, 1976.

National Society for the Prevention of Blindness Report for the Year ending March 31, 1977. New York: National Society for the Prevention of Blindness, 1977.

Newell, F. W., and Ernest, J. T. *Ophthalmology: Principles and Concepts.* St. Louis, MO: The C. V. Mosby Company, 1974.

Nolan, C. Y., and Kederis, C. J. *Perceptual Factors in Braille Word Recognition.* New York: American Foundation for the Blind, 1969 (Research Series No. 20).

O'Brien, R., Hoffman, S., and Howard, R. *Vision Stimulation: A Program of Instruction Designed to Stimulate the Use of Residual Vision in Children with Low Vision.* Rockville, MD: Board of Education of Montgomery County, 1971 (Bulletin No. 227).

Peabody, R. L., and Birch, J. W. Educational implications of partial vision: New findings from a national study. *Sight-Saving Review,* 1967, *37,* 92–96.

Piaget, J. *The Origins of Intelligence in Children.* Translated by M. Cook. New York: W. W. Norton & Company, Inc., 1963.

Quay, H. C. Special education: Assumptions, techniques, and evaluative criteria. *Exceptional Children,* 1973, *40,* 165–170.

Schloss, I. P. Implications of altering the definition of blindness. In *Research Bulletin No. 3.* New York: American Foundation for the Blind, 1963, 111–116.

Scholl, G. T. *The Principal Works with the Visually Impaired.* Reston, VA: Council for Exceptional Children, 1968.

————. Understanding and meeting developmental needs. In B. Lowenfeld (ed.) *The Visually Handicapped Child in School.* New York: The John Day Company, 1973.

————, and Schnur, R. *Measures of Psychological, Vocational and Educational Functioning in the Blind and Visually Handicapped.* New York: American Foundation for the Blind, 1976.

Scott, R. A. *The Making of Blind Men: A Study of Adult Socialization.* New York: Russell Sage Foundation, 1969.

Signs of Eye Trouble in Children. New York: National Society for the Prevention of Blindness, 1964.

Smith, R. M. *Teacher Diagnosis of Educational Difficulties.* Columbus, OH: Charles E. Merrill Publishing Co., 1969.

Spungin, S. J., and Swallow, R. Psychoeducational assessment: Role of psychologist to teacher of the visually handicapped. *Education of the Visually Handicapped,* 1975, 7, 67–76.

Suterko, S. Life adjustment. In B. Lowenfeld (ed.), *The Visually Handicapped Child in School.* New York: The John Day Company, 1973.

Taylor, J. L. The itinerant teaching program for blind children. In G. L. Abel (ed.), *Concerning the Education of Blind Children.* New York: American Foundation for the Blind, 1959.

————. Educational programs. In B. Lowenfeld (ed.), *The Visually Handicapped Child in School.* New York: The John Day Company, 1973.

Wolf, J. M. *The Blind Child with Concommitant Disabilities.* New York: American Foundation for the Blind, 1967 (Research Series No. 16).

Ysseldyke, J. E. *Recent Advances in the Assessment of the Severely Retarded and Multiply Handicapped.* Paper presented at the Region IX meeting of the American Association of Mental Deficiency, Silver Spring, MD, November 1974.

CHAPTER **11**

UNUSUAL GIFTS AND TALENTS

DOROTHY SISK

THE GIFTED AND TALENTED: WHO ARE THEY?

In times of crisis, armed forces call forth their finest officers; the flagging basketball team, their best player; a floundering industry or business, their most creative consultant or executive; and a country, in time of war or financial crisis, its most outstanding leaders. Society depends on its great men and women, its gifted. However, in many ways these gifted individuals are often the most neglected group of exceptional children in schools. The schools are social institutions and consequently responsive to cultural attitudes that are prevalent in society, and in the United States the gifted enjoy a "love-hate" relationship. Part of this love-hate relationship is due to confidence in the average individual and championing the underdog, as well as fear and mistrust of the so-called "egghead" and "scientist." Also, in education, there is much enthusiasm for participation and effort, and in fact, in many schools participation and effort have become confused with accomplishment. Conditions such as those listed above contribute to what Margaret Mead called "pressures for keeping on all fours with one's classmates, neighbors, and business associates" (Mead, 1954, p. 211).

Recognition that these pressures are robbing the world of total benefits from the gifted and talented has led to increased emphasis on development of educational programs for gifted children. At the federal level, an Office of Gifted and Talented was formed in the Bureau of Education for the Handicapped in 1972. In then-Commissioner of Education Sidney Marland's 1972 report to Congress, it was stated that less than 4 percent of the gifted and talented are receiving education adequate to their needs and abilities.

There are many differing definitions of gifted in our society; however, most definitions at a local or state educational level are included in the national definition in the Congressional report, *Education of the Gifted* (Marland, 1972). The national definition is responsive to the awareness of most educators that giftedness has many dimensions.

> Gifted and talented children are those identified by professionally qualified persons who by virtue of outstanding abilities are capable of high performance. These are children who require differentiated educational programs and services beyond those normally provided by the regular school program in order to realize their contribution to self and society.
>
> Children capable of high performance include those with demonstrated achievement and/or potential ability in any of the following areas:

> 1. General intellectual ability
> 2. Specific academic aptitude
> 3. Creative or productive thinking
> 4. Leadership ability
> 5. Visual and performing arts
> 6. Psychomotor ability (p. 10)

IDENTIFICATION OF GIFTED CHILDREN

The pioneer efforts of Lewis Terman must be examined to truly understand the history of gifted and talented education. Terman became interested in ability differences while he was a student at Indiana and Clark Universities. His doctoral thesis compared learning patterns of seven "bright" students and seven "dull" students. As he worked on his thesis, Terman became intrigued with the thinking patterns of the gifted. After completing his thesis in 1907, he conducted a study of bright children in San Francisco. In this study, he carefully noted the characteristics of gifted and found that many of the stereotypes commonly held by society concerning the gifted were untrue. He found that they were healthy and well adjusted, rather than delicate and antisocial. The 1913 study led Terman to a more comprehensive work with 124 gifted children. This study laid the ground work for his lifetime investigation known as the *Stanford Studies of Genius*. The Stanford studies were started in 1921 with a grant Terman secured from the Commonwealth Foundation. Terman augmented the Commonwealth funds with university funds from Stanford and other grants. His longitudinal study consisted of 1,500 children with IQ's of 140 or above, drawn from California schools. Seventy-seven percent of the children were identified by teacher ratings, 12 percent were selected because they had good test records, and 7 percent were first recommended by community members. Terman compiled volumes of data on his 1,500 subjects and greatly contributed to our current concept of giftedness (Seagoe, 1975).

Terman found that the gifted were above average in size, in health, and in health habits. He also found that significantly large numbers of them were first children. He found that they grew taller, heavier, and stronger than their age mates. They were longer in pubescense and earlier in sexual development than other children. In summary, he found that rapid physical development in gifted children was a correlative with the development of intellectual interests and giftedness as we know it. The average age that the Stanford group entered school was six and a quarter, and 85 percent of the group were accelerated at some time in their school years. The majority of the parents noted early indications of superior ability, as listed in Table 11–1.

Further follow-up studies were conducted with the 1,500 children in 1927–1928, 1939–1940 and 1951–1952. A summary of the findings on the general characteristics of the group according to Terman and Oden (1951) is as follows:

1. The average member of our group is a slightly better physical specimen than the average child...

2. For the fields of subject matter covered in our tests, the superiority of gifted over unselected children was greater in reading, language usage, arithmetical reasoning, science, literature, and the arts. In arithmetical computa-

Table 11-1   **Early Indications of Superior Ability Noted by Parents**

GENERAL INTELLIGENCE	N-282 BOYS	N-237 GIRLS
grasps and understands new ideas quickly	50	40
desire for knowledge	31	31
retentive memory	21	21
intelligent conversation	20	15
rapid progress at school	16	16
keen general interests	22	9
range of general information	15	12
reasoning ability	13	13
early speech	11	14
asking intelligent questions	14	11
ability in accomplishing difficult things	14	11
keen observation	13	10
unusual vocabulary	8	12
originality	3	12
miscellaneous	4	6
positive report, without explanation	27	14

Terman, 1925, p. 280.

tion, spelling, and factual information about history and civics, the superiority of the gifted was somewhat less marked...

3. The interests of gifted children are many-sided and spontaneous. They learn to read easily and read more and better books than the average child. At the same time, they make numerous collections, cultivate many kinds of hobbies, and acquire far more knowledge of plays and games than the average child...

4. As compared with unselected children, they are less inclined to boast or to overstate their knowledge, they are more trustworthy when under temptation to cheat; their character preferences and social attitudes are more wholesome, and they score higher in a test of emotional stability...

5. The deviation of the gifted subjects from the generality is in the upward direction for nearly all traits. There is no law of compensation whereby the intellectual superiority of the gifted tends to be offset by inferiorities along non-intellectual lines (pp. 23–24).

Educators of the gifted reaped many advantages from Terman's lifelong study, not only through determination of the characteristics of young gifted children that can be utilized in understanding the psychology of the gifted, but also because of the rich data that conclusively show that gifted children become gifted adults. Terman found that the group at later testing scored consistently higher than at their first testing. Contrary to popular notion, early giftedness did not burn itself out, but continued to grow and develop.

With the broadened definition of gifted and talented, coupled with the information gathered from Terman's longitudinal study, the obvious comment by any casual observer would be: "What's the fuss, surely you can identify these gifted!" However, that is not the case, even though many gifted children identify themselves through outstanding achievement and aptitude or demonstrated talent. Many gifted children go unidentified and unchallenged, literally languishing away their talent through twelve miserable years in school. Many are referred to other special education programs such as those for the behavior disordered, for manifesting characteristics that are perceived by teachers as being deviant rather than gifted. Recently the state consultant for gifted in Pennsylvania cross-referenced the data in her state on educationally handicapped programs and found that 50 percent of the children being referred to the emotionally disturbed program qualified for the gifted program as well. The question immediately to be asked is what do teachers perceive as gifted? And what is being used to identify gifted students?

The Marland report found that in states where there were well-developed programs, several methods of identification were being used. Table 11–2 illustrates the percentage of educators utilizing a certain identification procedure, and also the percentage of education experts recommending the technique in the Illinois program for the gifted.

It is obvious from Table 11–2 that the education experts felt that individual intelligence test scores were the most desired factor in identifying

Table 11–2   **Major Procedures Used and Recommended in the Identification of Gifted and Talented Students**

Major Identification Procedure	Percent Used	Percent Recommendation
teacher observation and nomination	93	75
group school achievement test scores	87	74
group intelligence test scores	87	65
previously demonstrated accomplishments (including school grades)	56	78
individual intelligence test scores	23	90
scores on tests of creativity	14	74

Source: S. P. Marland, *Education of the gifted and talented.* Washington, DC: U.S. Office of Education, 1972, p. 261.

gifted children, and yet the actuality of practice in the field was that teacher observation and nomination were being used most, with less than one quarter of the children being identified by use of individual intelligence tests. It is also notable that the experts ranked group intelligence scores as least efficient in identifying gifted (Marland, 1972).

In actual practice, most gifted programs use a combination of identification procedures, often beginning with teacher nomination and use of readily available scores such as achievement, group intelligence, and grades. These are then supplemented by tests of individual intelligence, creativity, and in some cases self-concept and interest inventories. Following the gathering of these data, a case conference is called with the teacher, special teacher of the gifted, psychologist, parent, principal, and other personnel to plan a program for the child and to certify the giftedness of the child. This particular practice is in concert with the recent activity started in the schools as a result of Public Law 94–142, which calls for a conference or staffing of the exceptional child and the planning of an individualized education program (IEP).

CHARACTERISTICS OF GIFTED

Barbara "gobbles up" learning. She shifts a stack of papers from the floor beside her cluttered desk, riffles through them for her outlines and then dashes to the school library, for one more source. She keeps a "to do" list of what she wants to accomplish, "just like Ben Franklin," she says. As a sixth grader, Barbara is president of her elementary school's student body, editor of the school yearbook, and a champion swimmer.

Barbara is also a compulsive reader. "I read at least one book every two to three days—there is so much to read, I just can't waste time." She smiles, and then chuckles, "It's like a big thirst; I'm thirsty for knowledge." Barbara was reading before she was four and was adding simple sums at age three. "She knows she is bright and accepts it as a responsibility," comments her mother.

Todd is black, thirteen and physically mature. He looks eighteen. He wants to be a scientist. Each assignment in his biology class is meticulously done with his notebook filled with detailed drawings of dissections. Humming as he gingerly pins the legs of a giant grasshopper onto the cardboard, he freely interacts with his biology classroom teacher, indicating a genuine interest and enjoyment in science. In his other classes, he often daydreams and is sullen. He keeps to himself and doesn't have many friends. His best friend is Mark. "He likes biology, too," says Todd. His teachers are sympathetic with his interest in biology, but concerned that he not neglect the rest of his schooling.

Luisa is small for her nine years of age. She sits quietly kneading her clay into gently flaring flowers to place around the top of a pot. "Her work is far advanced for her age," states the director of the inner-city center. "She comes here every night after school and creates something. This class is for young adults, but we let her come because she has nowhere else to go, and she has a talent."

Luisa's parents both work at night and her older sister spends very little time at home. Luisa's mind is quick and she loves reading, especially adventure stories. She wants to write stories of her own. Luisa's parents don't take much interest in her school work. "She's a good girl," states her father. Their life is hard and they are thankful she is no extra bother. Luisa's teachers are concerned that she overcome a disadvantaged background and reach her potential.

Dale is eight. He has curly hair, freckles, and twinkly blue eyes. He has the part of Puck in the school production of *A Midsummer Night's Dream*. His mother states that he is good-natured at home and that his sense of humor is matched by his sensitivity. He helps part time with a neighborhood veterinarian. Last week, he helped remove porcupine quills from a dog's muzzle. "He vaccilates between wanting to be an actor and a veterinarian," says his father. "He knows he's smart, but uses it to help others."

Tom is a gifted musician and composes his own music. He is ten years old and lives in a small southern mountain town. For the first few years of school, Tom spent most school days in the principal's office. "He asked too many questions and kept taking up too much of the class time," said the principal.

Now, with the help of a nearby university professor, Tom plans his own independent projects and hopes to be an astronaut. "He is serious and a loner," states the professor, "and he does a lot of deep thinking, not just free rambling like most kids his age."

All of these youngsters are bright and talented and measure up to the label "gifted" defined by Paul Witty (1958) "as consistently remarkable performance in worthwhile lines of endeavor" (p. 48). Barbara, Tom, Dale, and Todd would be identified as intellectually gifted on the criterion of IQ alone. Using a broader definition as suggested by the United States Office of Gifted and Talented, and measures other than intelligence, Todd would qualify on specific aptitude. Luisa, Tom, and Barbara would be located on creativity measures, and Barbara would qualify on scales of leadership, as well as demonstrated kinesthetic giftedness with her champion swimming. Joe would be identified through demonstrated giftedness in performing arts, as would Dale with his dramatic talent.

Today most educators involved in gifted programs acknowledge an expanded view of giftedness. The majority of the fifty state consultants in gifted education use a state definition of gifted that includes from 2 to 10 percent of the total kindergarten through twelfth-grade school population. This would mean that the prevalence figure for gifted in the United States is approximately two million to five million gifted and talented youngsters.

The state definitions of gifted most often include the intellectual, the creative, and the leader. Several states, such as Pennsylvania, North Carolina, and Virginia have special programs in the performing arts for gifted and talented, as well as regular school-based programs for gifted and talented in other areas. The least often served of the six types of giftedness, as evidenced by 1977 state service reports to the United States Office of Gifted and Talented, are the kinesthetically gifted, the visual and performing arts, and children with unusual leadership ability, in that order. The most frequently served are the intellectually gifted, the creative, and those with specific aptitudes.

ISSUES IN IDENTIFICATION

The particular talents or skills that are rewarded by a society reflect the values of a given society. At various times in history, different talents have been encouraged. Different cultures and social classes also place different values on skills and talents, and consequently produce measurable differences in attitudes toward giftedness. A young man from the inner city has a very difficult time in pursuing a career in ballet, demonstrating his kinesthetic giftedness, as does a young girl from a rural area in pursuing a career in science or mathematics, utilizing her specific aptitude.

Recently, a local coordinator in a rural midwestern state reported that parents were reluctant to enroll their daughters in gifted programs, but would freely enroll sons. Their reason, "...girls don't need all that education," they said with aplomb. In many cases, the aptitude of young gifted children is never developed, as early attitudinal positions are conveyed that move them in anti-intellectual pursuits and more culturally accepted roles. One young gifted girl whose parents were migrant workers stated that "...returning home after a summer of enrichment activities at the University of South Florida's Upward Bound program was like joining a barrel of crabs being slowly pulled back down into the barrel, when I've almost reached the top." Or in the words of an eight-year-old boy enrolled in a part-time enrichment program in Garden Grove, California, "...I can't act too interested in school; my friends will think I'm queer!"

The social pressures on gifted and talented children often cause them either not to develop their talents or to conceal them. The average child cannot act gifted, but the gifted child can and does act average. Through underachievement, discipline problems and apathy, many gifted go unrecognized.

Gifted programs that define giftedness as outstanding aptitude or demonstrated achievement often use two standard deviations above the mean as the entrance criterion. This type of program calls for top achievers and also demands that the administrative arrangement for services make provisions for accelerated learning and teaching. A gifted student who does not demonstrate outstanding achievement would be excluded from such a program. In the early 1960s, California was requiring identification of the gifted to be accomplished at the elementary level through individual IQ tests, and permitting identification at the secondary level through demonstrated achievement in mathematics and/or science and language arts at the 98th percentile. Using this identification system, it was not uncommon for youngsters to be identified at the elementary level as intellectually gifted, i.e., two standard deviations above the mean on an individually administered IQ test, and then be dropped from the secondary program because they were not achieving at the 98th percentile level. And, conversely, it was not uncommon to find a youngster who was not identified as intellectually gifted at the elementary level, but who did indeed achieve at the 98th percentile in the secondary program. These kinds of differences in definition and in policy or philosophy make it difficult for large school systems to plan comprehensive programs for gifted and talented.

Philosophical differences among educators are also evident in that many administrators exclude gifted underachievers from programs for the gifted "...because they need more time with the basic program." At the same time, other administrators state, "I choose the gifted who are not achieving; they need the extra help. Why should a student who is achieving be in the gifted program; he is already getting A's and telling me he doesn't need a program."

Problems in identification of the gifted are not new in education. As early as 1950, the Educational Policy Commission was stating the following:

> A considerable proportion of the potential abilities of gifted individuals is at present lost to society through underdevelopment, underuse or misuse. Some of this waste is attributable to economic barriers to educational and vocational opportunities. Some is caused by social attitudes that tend to lower both incentive and opportunity for gifted children of families with low socioeconomic status. Some loss results from emotional maladjustment. And some human talent is wasted because the schools fail to identify, to challenge, to hold, or to educate adequately some of their gifted students (pp. 85–86).

This strong statement issued in the 1950s is still true today, three decades later.

Issues in Diagnosis and Assessment

Closely aligned to the issues in identification are issues in diagnosis and assessment. How can the culture bias of the usual IQ test be overcome? Much work was conducted in the 1950s with culture-free or culture-fair tests such as the Davis-Eells games (1952), and more recently Bernal and Reyna (1974) have designed prototype indentification instruments for use with Mexican-American children. Yet, in actual practice, most school districts at the local level are utilizing existing test data and supplementing this information with observation scales such as the Renzulli-Hartman (1971) *Behavioral Characteristic Checklist for Superior Students.* This scale lists characteristics in the areas of learning, motivation, creativity and leadership, and requires the teacher to rank a youngster on a scale of one to four. Children who score high are then observed in the classroom for further evidence of giftedness in any of the areas. These observations are then pooled with the various test scores available on the children for diagnosis and assessment.

It is rare that educators planning a gifted program will decide that intelligence tests alone will do the entire job of assessment, particularly if the program is to be built upon the strengths and weaknesses of the gifted youngsters.

In selecting a test for either individuals or groups, one needs to decide upon the necessity for one score or several scores. If all that is needed is a general prediction, then a single score such as that given by the Stanford-Binet is sufficient. However, if subscores would be useful for diagnosis and prediction, the Wechsler scales would be preferable. Individual IQ tests are most often used when group IQ scores indicate that there is a discrepancy between test scores, school achievement, or performance as indicated by behavior checklists and observations.

In general, one problem that must be taken into consideration with standardized testing is its inability to identify critical and creative thinking abilities which are characteristics of gifted children and adults. Consequently, if only one test is used, many gifted who are creative may go unrecognized. On one popular standardized intelligence test there is a question that calls for logical reasoning in which the individual is asked to respond to a given situation in a logical fashion. The answer as predicted is a man hanging from a tree. In one testing situation, a highly imaginative six-year-old youngster smiled and stated, "A white baboon swinging from a limb." This was indeed a highly creative response, but incorrect. The logical sequence called for a response that was predictable, not his divergent one, and in this case, his creativity penalized his overall score.

Group intelligence paper-and-pencil tests penalize the slow, the unmotivated, and the poor reader. Recently there has been keen interest in gifted youngsters who may also have learning problems. These "learning disabled" gifted children, as well as other handicapped youngsters who may be gifted, go unrecognized and unserved. It is only recently that attention is being called to the gifted handicapped, as witnessed by the development of model early childhood gifted handicapped programs under the sponsorship of the Bureau of Education for the Handicapped. The existence of gifted handicapped populations was documented by Alan White at the 1976 Conference on Handicapped Gifted held in New Orleans, Louisiana. White (1976) points out that the same percentage of gifted (2 to 5 percent) are being located in the handicapped population as in the general population. These types of data raise the issue of searching among the handicapped for giftedness, concentrating on the gift rather than the handicap.

Another issue in assessment of the gifted is that introduced by E. Paul Torrance in his work with disadvantaged students. Torrance (1971) suggests that educators should concentrate on the positive skills of the disadvantaged rather than the negatives or weaknesses, such as verbal and semantic skills. Some of the positives that Torrance (1971) suggests are as follows:

1. high nonverbal fluency and originality
2. high creative productivity in small groups
3. adeptness in visual art activities
4. high creativity in movement, dance and other physical activities
5. high motivation by games, music, sport, humor, and concrete objects
6. language rich in imagery (p. 75)

These "creative positives" as Torrance calls them give direction for the types of administrative arrangements, interest areas and teaching techniques that can be used as motivating departure points with disadvantaged gifted youngsters. Small group work capitalizing on active involvement and product orientation would be advantageous with these students.

Taba and Elkins (1966) sum up the challenge of the disadvantaged gifted quite well as follows:

... for culturally deprived children, school must first supplement and counteract their social learning if they are to have an equal opportunity to learn. School must also fill the gaps left by inadequate social learning at home and bridge the conflicts between the culture of the home and that of the school (p. 16).

One such forward-thinking program is being run in New Haven, Connecticut, where theater techniques are used to identify and program for disadvantaged gifted middle-school youngsters, many of whom would be overlooked if test scores were used as primary identification procedures. The program is holding "hands on" workshops to help classroom teachers learn (1) how to observe for giftedness through indices other than intellectual tests, and (2) how to plan educational interventions once students are identified (Council for Exceptional Children, 1977).

PATTERNS OF EDUCATIONAL INTERVENTION

If biographies of isolated gifted individuals are examined, it is not un-common to find that their education involved intensive stimulation and activity on the part of one parent or both. Wehrner Von Braun, who was born in Germany, showed a precocious interest in rocketry after receiving a toy rocket as a gift from his mother. At the age of twelve, he managed to construct a rocket-powered wagon and by the time he was twenty-one, he had outlined the design for a moon rocket.

Another highly gifted individual was John Stuart Mill, whose IQ was calculated by Cox (1926) as six standard deviations above the mean (ap-proximately 200). Mill's father engineered a very strict, rapid, and some-what rigid education for his young son. Young Mill was studying Greek at the age of three, pondering Plato at seven, and mastering Latin at the age of eight. At the age of nine, he was reading classics such as the *Odyssey*, and classical authors such as Theocritus, Pindar, and Livy. His father also did not want to neglect his logical thinking in mathematics and science, and he prepared lessons for the nine-year-old John in conic sections,

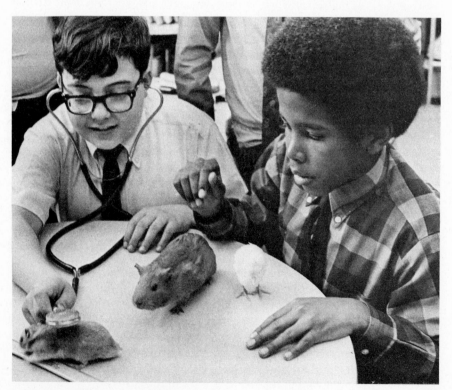

Courtesy of The Ford Foundation.

spherics, geometry, and algebra. At ten, John was studying astronomy and physics. Logic and philosophy were introduced at age twelve.

John's father used a modified Oxonian scholar method with his young son, with John preparing daily papers and debating with his father on his thoughts and conclusions. He was a very creative youngster as evidenced by a history of Rome that he completed at age six and a half. At age eleven, he constructed a synoptic table of Aristotle's rhetoric. His relationship with his father was one of deep and intense admiration. At seventeen, John published letters in defense of his father's liberal political views. John would have been identified by his outstanding intellectual ability as well as his specific aptitude, academic achievement, and creativity in writing.

During his childhood, John's mother tried unsuccessfully to intervene with his father and introduce a lighter side to the boy's education such as music and art. This was denied by the father, and John later described himself as a "reasoning machine." At twenty, the young man suffered a complete nervous breakdown, but was able to analyze his own problem and place himself on a therapy consisting of the music and poetry that his father had denied him.

John's education is an example of extreme acceleration in that the father accelerated not only his learning, but also his social and emotional development through intense involvement with the father and his male friends.

In his later adult life, John Stuart Mill typified the characteristics of gifted that involve a humane interest in "serving" and a sensitivity toward others. He dedicated himself to championing democracy and reforming a society that he felt was exploiting mankind. He worked all his life for causes such as women's rights, universal education, free speech, and right to representation.

This biographical sketch of Mill and other gifted men make up one of the most fascinating books on giftedness by Catherine Cox (1926) entitled *The Early Mental Traits of Three Hundred Geniuses: Genetic Studies of Genius.* Cox's scholarly work is part of the Stanford Series (volume 2) and outlines the lives of 282 men. As one examines the volume, it becomes clear that giftedness is related to the time and culture in which one lives. In Cox's sample, 33 percent are writers, 15 percent are statesmen and politicians, 8 percent are religious leaders, 8 percent are philosophers, and 12 percent are characterized by unusual abilities of expression and are artists, musicians, or revolutionary statesmen.

The fascinating point about studying and reading of these highly gifted individuals throughout history is to note what educational interventions were used to help ensure the use of their potential. Although many of them received intense one-on-one instruction and were successful in their studies, many others, such as Thomas Edison, Winston Churchill, and Albert Einstein, were classic cases of underachievement and failure until they were motivated in areas of interest. And furthermore, according to Cox (1926), if rigid IQ scores of two standard deviations above the mean were adhered to for identification, the giftedness of Oliver Goldsmith, Captain Cook, and Andrew Jackson would have been denied.

The earliest effort at gifted education was probably that of Plato in which he proposed that promising young men be singled out through testing and be channeled into a rigorous study of science, philosophy, and metaphysics, capitalizing on their leadership. His identification procedure was to be primarily one of teacher observation, identifying high ability in logical reasoning and noting discrepancies. Identification was to be done by placing the young men in trial-and-error situations and through discussion.

Another classic example of a gifted program was that of the Turkish empire in which the most gifted youth of the Christian population were located and given intensive education in the Mohammedan faith, history and methods of war, science, religion, and art. These highly gifted young people, who were slaves to Suleiman the Magnificent, were developed into highly prized assets for building the Ottoman Empire.

In the United States one of the first gifted programs, according to Heck (1953), was begun in the St. Louis public schools in 1868, where promotion periods were shortened to half year, quarter year, and then five-week sessions. Another early plan for gifted was in Elizabeth, New Jersey, where students were allowed to advance at their own pace.

Needless to say, there have been acceleration and special grouping types of gifted programs that have sporadically developed and then been discontinued throughout the early 1900s. The oldest and only continuous program for gifted is that developed in Cleveland, Ohio under the direction and guidance of Dorothy Norris until her death in 1977. These Cleveland Major Work Classes represent a classic example of enrichment in a special grouping setting. The classes are subject-matter classification similar to regular programs, but differentiate in the depth of examination and range of supportive activities.

Administrative Arrangements for Service

As programs for gifted are examined, they basically fall into the classic descriptive patterns of acceleration or special grouping. Enrichment, which is often listed as a third type of administrative arrangement, should be included in all types of gifted programs whether they are acceleration or special grouping. Enrichment is often defined as individual work, or differentiated assignments based on the gifted student's strengths, weaknesses, and interests. Enrichment can be "horizontal" and extend the subject matter into related areas of study, or "vertical" and involve acceleration, which crosses grade levels.

Gallagher (1975) states that there are three possible adaptations that can be utilized in adapting programs for gifted students through administrative changes: adaptations of curriculum, learning style and learning environment. In order to effect an educational intervention with gifted that will mobilize the use of their potential, teaching strategies must be identified that are particularly suitable to working with the gifted.

Acceleration

Acceleration methods vary widely and the results clearly point to success. In fact, there is no research available that clearly indicates that acceleration is detrimental to the students involved. Yet the practice of acceleration is probably the least used administrative arrangement for providing services for the gifted. Gallagher (1975) points out that a gifted student who anticipates being a professional can expect to be in school at least until the age of twenty-nine. He further suggests that anything that can be done to reduce the extended period of study benefits not only gifted students, but also society which reaps the benefit of their talent.

Acceleration can take the form of early entrance to school, and several states have early entrance laws coupled with examination requirements. One such state is Florida, where the state consultant reports that early entrance does help many gifted children who are capable of functioning in school prior to regular age requirements for school entry.

The early intervention issue, which in gifted translates to early entrance or special grouping and identification, is fraught with problems similar to the entire problem of acceleration, that of reticence of educators to deal with the giftedness of young children. According to 1977 Office of Education reports on the status of programs for gifted, most programs begin at fourth-grade level. Many educators are reluctant to identify gifted children in kindergarten for fear of misidentification or missing children who may not be as mature or verbal as they will be after several years of schooling. To not identify and serve gifted children who are demonstrating giftedness for fear of not serving and identifying "all gifted" is like not giving water to a thirsty member of a group because they don't all look thirsty. "The issue is not the same," one might say, "the gifted won't suffer." That is not so, however; they do suffer. Many lose interest in school and never regain the enthusiasm and excitement for learning that they manifest when they first enter school.

Braga (1969) investigated the effects of early admission on sixty-three gifted children in the first, third and fifth grades. He studied their academic achievement and their social and emotional development. Braga compared the early admissions to normally admitted and late admitted students and matched his subjects on IQ and sex. Results showed that there were no significant differences between the early admitted and their regular admitted peers. The parent and teacher questionnaires showed that teachers were opposed to the idea, parents of early admission students were in favor, and parents of regular admission students were not.

Braga's study substantiates the classic study of Worcester (1956) involving 4,275 pupils in Nebraska. Early entrants were found to be superior in health, achievement, coordination, acceptance by others, leadership, attitudes toward school, and emotional development.

Again the main obstacles to early entrance are indicated by teachers and parents who do not agree on emotional grounds with early intervention. The data, however, are unequivocal. A young gifted child who is ready for school is better served by early intervention through early entrance. The evidence does not indicate that the gifted will be better served to wait and join the age group when their mental age will be far above their peers.

Another form of acceleration is that of completing three years of school in two. This is most often seen at the junior high level where grades seven, eight, and nine can be covered in two years. A variation of acceleration is the upgraded primary where grades one to three or four to six can be completed in two years, or a gifted child could complete grades one to six in four years. By having "family grouping," such as the gifted program in Garden Grove, California, a group of gifted children can remain with one teacher for the given period and develop at their own pace.

At the senior high level, acceleration most often takes the form of extra courses, seminars taken with college credit, and early entrance into college.

Acceleration, to be successfully used with gifted students, demands administrators who are thoroughly aware of the individual student's ability, achievement, social and emotional maturity, as well as totally sympathetic receiving teachers, administrators, and parents. It appears that the major reason for acceleration not being used more often is the unspoken anxiety that parents and educators have toward acceleration and our cultural desire to keep students "children" as long as possible.

Where these anxieties are identified and the aims, functions, and benefits of acceleration are explained, there appears to be little problem with acceleration. In the words of a physician and state legislator who was accelerated to a university setting at age fourteen, "The only problem I had was locating a junior high nearby so I could find a date."

The most outspoken proponent of acceleration is Julian Stanley at Johns Hopkins University. In an interview with a highly gifted student concerning his views on acceleration, Stanley (1977) reports that the young man stated:

> ...At the time I made my decision, my reasons for resisting acceleration seemed cogent. I was secure (sheltered is closer to the truth) at the top of my class and liked it that way. The thought of starting in a group at least two years older than I frightened me. I had been at the same school for eight years (since the first grade). In a word, I was "accepted."

This young man brings another point of view than the Florida legislator, again underscoring the need for decision making on each individual case of acceleration.

Stanley (1976), at a recent World Conference on Gifted suggested the following factors for successful acceleration: (1) a well-prepared fast pacing instructor, (2) homogeneous grouping according to mathematical and verbal reasoning ability, (3) high expectations, and (4) concurrent and future opportunities in which the successful students can be encouraged to skip school grades, take college courses for credit while in high school, work for advanced placement, enter college full time early, and try mathematics competitions.

Stanley and his associates have formed the Study of Mathematically Precocious Youth (SMPY), directed by Stanley and funded by the Spencer Foundation. SMPY sponsors an annual talent search for high mathematics ability youngsters. Once these students are identified, the SMPY's interest in them is continuous, at least over the years they are identified until they complete graduate school and are employed. SMPY affords that intensive and caring consultation that is most necessary for acceleration to succeed.

The advantages of acceleration are reduction in the time spent in school in order to enter a professional career, and savings in cost of education of the gifted that would accrue to schools.

Special Grouping

Special grouping has most recently come under fire with the concept of "mainstreaming" exceptional children and the least restrictive environment being utilized to serve the special needs and interests of exceptional children. In states where there have been no special programs for gifted outside of enrichment in the regular classroom, the concept of least restrictive placement proves no problem. However, many "pull-out" or special grouping programs for the gifted are beginning to reevaluate their plans. Special grouping can vary widely. On one end of the continuum is full-time separation, such as the special public school for the gifted in Sarasota, Florida, started as an experimental project in the 1960s and continued as a result of public demand. On the other end of the service continuum are (1) a one-day resource room enrichment model as provided by *Project Clue* in Memphis, Tennessee, another project started under Title III and continued by a local school district, and (2) an itinerant program such as Charleston, West Virginia, where the teacher of the gifted serves children in more than one school.

Few educators of the gifted deny the position that gifted and talented youngsters need to be with other gifted and talented youngsters for at least part of the day to learn at their own pace and to motivate and stimulate one another. The advantages of special grouping to classroom teachers include the opportunity to cover extra subject matter and even extra subjects. One candid young man, speaking of his special class in Orange County, California, said, "I can't get by with my usual laziness in here, and I have to work much harder, but I'm doing better in fifth grade than fourth grade last year." His special class caused an honest self-appraisal that helped him produce better work habits and be more motivated in school.

Special School

The Bronx High School of Science in New York City is an example of a special school which is available to gifted secondary students who are identified through special aptitude. The students who enroll must qualify at the 98th percentile on achievement measures in science to enroll. In 1976 the Bronx High School of Science was awarded a three-year grant to become a model program at the secondary level for the nation. As a result of this grant, workshops have been held for teachers and model curricula have been designed for dissemination throughout the United States.

Galasso (1977) states that the students come from all economic levels to the Bronx High School of Science and participate in an enriched curriculum. Science is taught with a great deal of laboratory work and the students present scholarly papers and compete quite successfully in a variety of scientific competitions. A mathematics sequence of four years is available and a regular high school program as well. Enrichment is provided both within the class and in extra-class activities.

Pine View School in Sarasota, Florida, is an elementary, junior high, and senior high school (four to twelve) in one complex. Students are identified primarily as intellectually gifted, achieving an IQ at least two standard deviations above the mean. A case study approach is utilized for admission purposes. The staff views the past school record, achievement scores, anecdotal records on emotional and social development, and interviews both the students and their parents before admission.

The classes are small and many extra subjects and special enrichment classes are available through flexible scheduling. As at the Bronx High School of Science, enrichment is provided within classes and in extra-class activities

Special Classes

A prime example of special classes for gifted children was started in Cleveland in the 1920s. It is known as the Cleveland Major Work Classes. Here the students follow the same curriculum as that in the regular classroom, but the curriculum is differentiated in terms of depth of examination and the wide range of supporting activities such as foreign language, debate, music, and art. When one visits the Cleveland Major Work Classes, the most striking difference is the purposeful and intense activity that is going on within the classes, and oftentimes in adjoining hallways. The MWC classes, as they are called, can be found in other areas of the country such as Garden Grove, California, and Orlando, Florida, as well as in other countries such as Saskatoon, Saskatchewan, in Canada, and Tel Aviv, Israel. In Israel, the MWC is used particularly with disadvantaged students in an attempt to build a total environment which affects the learning environment, curriculum, and learning style of the gifted, as suggested by Gallagher (1975).

In-Class Grouping

The best example of in-class grouping of the gifted is where the principal or administrative central office has decided to use "cluster grouping." Cluster grouping is the placing of at least ten gifted students with ten above-average students and ten average students. In this type of administrative arrangement, the classroom teacher can group the gifted for some activities, and vary the grouping according to interest and achievement. In an exemplary cluster group, the teacher reports that five of the gifted, three of the above average, and two of the average are in the top spelling group; whereas three gifted, two above average, and four average are in the special interest group on marine biology. In this arrangement, the children receive many common learning experiences and yet the rate of progress and difficulty of material can be varied.

Special-Grouping in Resource Rooms

Many programs throughout the United States utilize a resource room for gifted. The 1977 Office of Gifted and Talented performance reports indicate that this is the most popular model for serving the gifted. In many cases the children attend a resource room in their own school where the teacher of the gifted meets with them in small groups. In other cases, the children travel to a central school where the teacher of the gifted has a resource room. By and large, these programs utilize an enrichment model, with the teacher emphasizing the development of creative and critical thinking, as well as independent learning skills.

The biggest drawback to the resource room, according to regular classroom teachers, is that they often are not kept aware of the current goals, objectives, and material in the special program. Communication and team planning by the regular program and the resource room teacher is crucially important for a successful program for the gifted. One particularly skillful teacher, who works as an itinerant teacher in Westchester County, New York, reports great success with her international days, as she involves parents, the regular classroom teacher, and the children in planning their enrichment. Enthusiasm runs high and the special days are completed with interest reports, food, dances, music, and art work to celebrate the various international days.

Resource Centers

The center approach calls for a larger space and more teachers of the gifted, but centers also serve larger numbers of students. The Learning Center for Gifted in Hillsborough County, Tampa, Florida, was started in 1969 through the efforts of a parent association led by a local businessman and father of two gifted children. The Hillsborough Association for Gifted Education (HAGE) petitioned the City Council to give the Tampa public schools an abandoned public library in the inner city as a learning center for gifted. The city council agreed and the program began in the summer of 1969 with approximately one hundred youngsters, one employee of the school system as a director, and graduate trainees in gifted education as teachers from the University of South Florida in Tampa. Since then, the program has grown to serve well over a thousand gifted children yearly. The students are bussed from their home schools throughout the county to the center.

Another example of a resource center is the New Orleans Center for Creative Arts, which affords gifted children in visual and performing arts in the New Orleans school system opportunities to work in their chosen areas of art, dance, and music with highly qualified artists as teachers.

Enrichment

All of the administrative arrangements discussed in this section, whether they include acceleration or special grouping of any kind, should involve enrichment. However, there is much discussion among leaders in gifted education as to both the meaning and value of enrichment. In some cases, as aptly described by Stanley (1976), the following is true:

> Well-meaning teachers try one of three types of "enrichment:" so-called busy work, irrelevant material (such as drama class for boys whose major interests are mathematics and science), or really effective procedures that leave the student even more bored in later grades (such as a splendid modern mathematics program in grades K-7 that leads only to conventional algebra in grade 8). Clearly, we believe that a considerable amount of acceleration in subject matter and/or grade placement must accompany enrichment or be employed in lieu of it.

The issue that administrators must resolve is whether enrichment is: (1) a somewhat unrelated series of explorations in variety with no precision and intensive work for the gifted; or (2) a viable experience in learning providing opportunities for in-depth learning of an accelerated nature and a wide range of supportive activities. The interpretation of enrichment as indepth experiences is more often favored by individuals such as Stanley (1976), who emphasize the academic purposes of education. However, in discussions with administrators in planning sessions at leadership-training institutes, the author has observed that administrators have favored enrichment without acceleration. Most teachers also favor enrichment without acceleration, as reported by Plowman and Rice (1967) in a study of acceleration in California. Much of this opposition to enrichment with acceleration may be due to a wish to avoid segregation of students. The danger to gifted programs, however, is that the programs become sporadic delights that happen once a week with no strands of continuity with the regular program or with what happens next week in the gifted program. In one such program, the teacher of the gifted proudly stated that last week the gifted class had visited a veterinarian and watched a hysterectomy performed on a dog, and next week they were going to watch a kayak race. No doubt the children were baffled, enthralled, and entertained, but is that what a gifted program is all about? Principles need to be set to establish just what enrichment is to accomplish and administrators need to closely examine the benefits of various administrative arrangements to the gifted children in their schools.

TEACHING STRATEGIES FOR WORKING WITH GIFTED CHILDREN

Self-Awareness Activities: Boundary Breakers

The importance of self-awareness to gifted education cannot be overlooked. The gifted, in order to utilize their potential, must be keenly aware of their frame of reference, which includes their basic beliefs, attitudes, and values. Through this self-awareness, they can become more aware of others (Sisk, 1976).

Much of the curriculum and life experiences of the gifted require that they deal with theoretical questions and issues as if the decision making about these questions and issues did not involve a frame of reference. Yet, the decision making involved in a differentiated curriculum calls for open, honest discussion, and this does not happen overnight. One way to encourage self-awareness and the awareness of others is through a step-by-step sequence of awareness activities such as boundary breaking and encounter lessons. The use of boundary-breaking activities helps to develop intuitive expression, listening skills, and most important, relating to others and self-awareness.

The procedure for using boundary-breaking questions is simple. The group should contain no more than about twenty and the chairs should be arranged in a circle. The leader begins with a question and proceeds around the circle with each child responding intuitively. If anyone needs more time to think or does not want to respond, they may so indicate by saying "pass." The leader and group's role is to listen and to accept the response. No questioning or justification for one's stand is involved. However, adults and children often will seek out a member following a boundary-breaking session to ask for further clarification or just to talk. Boundary breaking must include psychological safety and acceptance as discussed by Rogers (1969) to be effective.

The leader of a boundary-breaking group models keen interest and listening as well as acceptance. If there are side comments, the leader should wait patiently and then gently move on to the next person. After several sessions, the side comments, which are often prompted by the gifted children being ill at ease in this new situation, dwindle to a minimum. Quickly groups begin to enjoy the wonder of one another. One spillover value to boundary breaking is the visual imagery that develops as each person responds. Examples of boundary breakers that were listed by a group of teachers involved in a leadership-training institute for the gifted in Hawaii (1977) are as follows:

1. If you could be any plant, which would you choose?
2. If you could be reincarnated as one of our ancient gods, which one would you choose?
3. If your plant could live anywhere, where would you choose to live?
4. A legend tells of Mele Poko who survived with two items. If you were stranded on an island, which two would you want with you?
5. If we were making a record of beauty, what sound would you put on the record?
6. When you think of food at your favorite luau, what do you think of?
7. What is your favorite time of day?
8. What color is laughter?
9. What do you see yourself doing in another life?
10. Think of proud and what do you recall?

These Hawaii questions, which were constructed by both elementary and secondary teachers, are similar to a list of questions compiled by any group of teachers, and yet the flavor of the islands comes through. The questions range from simple, almost fun questions, to responses which require more thought. The leader should vary the questions, giving the group a chance to relax and flow with the warmth that comes from sharing.

Boundary breaking is particularly good for the gifted, since often gifted children in regular classrooms do not feel like other children. They often feel isolated and different. Boundary breaking demonstrates to a group of gifted students that they are different, but also that they are alike in many ways. One gifted child who was experiencing boundary breaking for the first time candidly said, "I like finding out that I'm not so different, others are different, too." And another, "I like boundary breaking 'cause I can be me." The children particularly appreciate the psychological safety that comes from total acceptance by the leader. Three or four boundary-breaking questions will warm up a group to go on to other awareness activities such as encounter lessons.

Encounter Lessons

Encounter lessons were developed at the University of South Florida (Sisk, 1975). They are activities that can be utilized with any age group, just as boundary breaking accommodates to all age groups. The maturity of the children and their backgrounds of information will cause them to naturally vary responses. The double play on words that high school students do with overtones of subtle social meanings, elementary children will do with much less frequency. Encounter lessons encourage the gifted to build their inner strengths and their perceptions of those inner strengths. Encounter lessons are based on four psychological principles which can be expressed in terms of teacher behavior (Rogers, 1969).

The teacher will:
1. Help the student think about who he is and what he can and ought to be.
2. Help the student to feel vauable and worthwhile.
3. Help the student to see learning as relevant to his individual needs.
4. Help the student to develop and maintain a learning atmosphere that reflects psychological safety and freedom.

Encounter lessons are short lessons, lasting usually fifteen to twenty minutes. They are active lessons involving the senses. The object is to truly encounter others and their ideas. The activities are quite open-ended and are particularly suited to the gifted because of their need to have free rein for their creativity and liking for new and unusual activities. Encounter lessons work best with small groups of eight to ten and can be utilized with any subject matter.

The following encounter lesson was developed by Phyllis Sturms, a teacher of the gifted in West Virginia (Sisk, 1976):

CHAIRS FANTASY

Objective: to foster creavity to identify with something and become that something.
Setting the Stage: Imagine that you are all chairs arranged around a dining-room table.
Leading Questions:
1. What is your position at the table?
2. What famous person would you like to sit upon you?
3. How would you feel if a 300-pound man sat upon you?
4. What was your most important moment as a dining-room chair?
5. What type of family would you like to belong to?
6. If you could change yourself, how would you do so?
Evaluation Questions:
1. Study various styles of furniture and their history.
2. Design and needlepoint a chair seat.
3. Refinish an old chair as a class project.
4. Conduct an independent study on the building of chairs.

In this encounter lesson, the teacher would use the interest, motivation, and curiosity aroused by the encounter to extend to other academic pursuits. In this way the encounters are clearly tied to the curriculum and are not just silly appendages or moments of creativity to be followed by "real work."

Gifted children love these student-directed encounters and begin to anticipate them. Teachers of the gifted say that they make the difference between drudgery, traditional techniques and assignments and "come alive classrooms" where fantasy has a place and gives a lift to learning.

However, there is also a need for structured teacher-directed activities and these activities follow and build upon the excitement of the student-directed activities. One way to ensure meeting the many levels of thinking can be accomplished by working from theoretical models of learning and intellectual functioning.

Use of Models in Building Differentiated Curriculum for Gifted

The use of various theoretical models has proven to be expedient in helping build curriculum for new programs for the gifted. Different models of learning and intellectual functioning can supplement and complement one another by providing opportunities for gifted students to experience cognitive and affective growth.

One such model is that of Benjamin Bloom (1956), dealing with taxonomies of educational objectives in the affective and cognitive domains. In the affective domain, Bloom lists: receiving, responding, valuing, organization, and characterization. Receiving is defined as the direction of attention, responding as behavior accompanied by feeling of satisfaction, valuing as the ascribing of worth or emotional acceptance to a situation, organization as the ordered relationship of complex values, and characterization as acquiring of generalized sets of values which are consistent with the total philosophy of beliefs.

The teacher of the gifted who wants to plan lessons utilizing both affective and cognitive experiences could use the Bloom taxonomy for the affective domain, and supplement intellectual operations as defined by J. P. Guilford (1967, 1977) in his model of the Structure of Intellect (SOI). The ideas basic to the Structure of Intellect theory were formulated in the late 1950s, and were successfully refined until the present model was formulated. The model is a three-way classification of intellectual abilities designed to encompass and organize intellectual-aptitude factors. It has also served to predict the existence of undiscovered factors.

The three dimensions of the model presented in Figure 11-1, specify (a) the operation, (b) the content, and (c) the product of a given intellectual act. Guilford defines cognition as understanding, discovery, rediscovery, awareness, and comprehension. Memory is the retention and recall of knowledge. Convergent thinking is the reorganization of information and divergent thinking is imaginative, spontaneous, and fluent self-expression. Lastly, evaluation is judging, assessing and evaluating.

An example of how a lesson for gifted could be planned and utilized according to Bloom's and Guilford's models is as follows:

> For a group of eighth-grade gifted students in English, the short story "The Interlopers" by H. H. Munro (Saki) could be distributed and time given for silent reading. In this story by Saki, two men, who are mortal enemies, Gradwitz and Znayem, experience a terrifying situation, and out of this experience is born a new relationship and insight into life. Following the silent

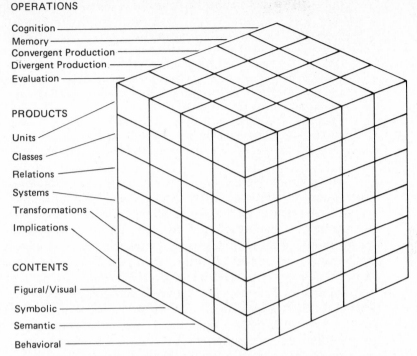

OPERATIONS

Cognition
Memory
Convergent Production
Divergent Production
Evaluation

PRODUCTS

Units
Classes
Relations
Systems
Transformations
Implications

CONTENTS

Figural/Visual
Symbolic
Semantic
Behavioral

FIG. 11–1 Guilford's Structure of Intellect. From Guilford, J.P. *The Nature of Human Intelligence,* New York: McGraw-Hill, 1967, 1977.

reading, the teacher could utilize questions from the cognitive domain following the operations component of Guilford's SOI model such as the following:

Cognition—For what were Gradwitz and his men hunting? Why?

Memory—During what time of the year did the story take place?

Convergent—What made these two men enemies? What brought about the sudden change of emotions between the two men?

Divergent—What do you think might have happened if one of the men had been killed by the fallen limb? What would you have done if you were one of the men after having spied the wolves?

Evaluation—Do you think Gradwitz's attitude was appropriate toward Znayem? Why or why not?

Through planning questions to cover all levels of the Guilford intellectual operations, the teacher will consciously lead the students from the lowest level of thinking—that of cognition—to the higher and more challenging levels of evaluative thinking. This type of lesson planning is extremely important for gifted students as these higher levels of creative thinking and evaluative thinking are characteristics of being gifted. When the regular classroom does not make allowances for these levels of thinking, the gifted student becomes bored or disruptive, or makes valiant attempts to lead the class in the direction of higher levels by what many teachers call "wild goose questions or responses."

The affective domain can be tapped through questions based on Bloom, such as:

Receiving—Did you find the story interesting?

Responding—What part of the story touched you the most emotionally?

Valuing—Do you feel there was any worthwhile moral to this story?

Organization—Does this moral have present day applications? How?

Characterization—Can you relate this story to any feelings you have about events in your own life?

Again, with the guidance of a theoretical model such as Bloom's, the teacher of the gifted can plan, in an organized fashion, to explore the values, insights and attitudes of the students in a deliberate manner.

Most classroom periods are a complex mixture of thinking at any one time; however, observation of teachers of gifted in action who have planned lessons around the SOI or Bloom models indicates that the levels of thinking exhibited by gifted children is commensurate with the types of questions and activities planned by the teacher. Mary Meeker has formed the Structure of Intellect Institute at Loyola University in California to provide examples of how to translate a given skill from the SOI to curriculum suggestions. Recently, Meeker (1977) has also published tests for each level of the SOI, along with curriculum strategies. With theoretical models such as those provided by Bloom and Guilford as guides, specific and direct instructional techniques can be devised to maximize the use of classroom time at the higher levels of thinking for gifted students.

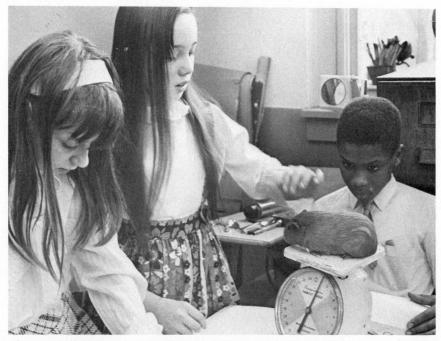

Courtesy of The Ford Foundation.

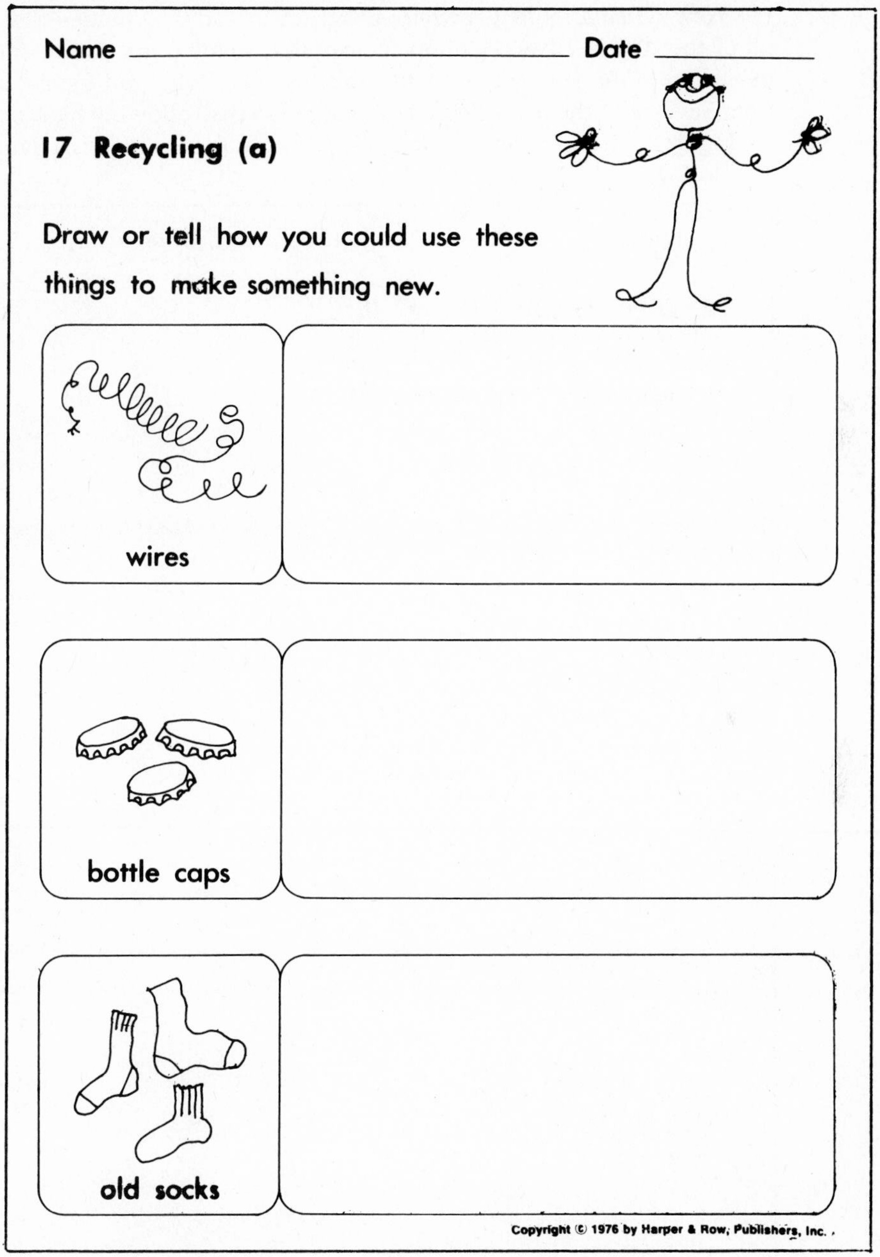
Name ____________________ Date __________

17 Recycling (a)

Draw or tell how you could use these things to make something new.

wires

bottle caps

old socks

Copyright © 1976 by Harper & Row, Publishers, Inc.

FIG. 11–2 Recycling. *New Directions in Creativity—Mark A* by Joseph S. Renzulli. Copyright© 1973 by Harper & Row, Publishers, New York.

Renzulli (1973) has developed a program that deals mainly with the divergent production operation of the Structure of the Intellect Model. His *New Directions in Creativity* program includes activities that sample all of the divergent production factors that involve the use of semantics, as well as some selected activities that use symbolic and figural information. Several of the activities are presented in the following figures.

Figure 11–2 shows an activity called "Recycling," which is a figural elab-

Name _____   Date _____

12 What do you think of? (b)

Rainy days make me think of . . .

FIG. 11–3 What Do You Think Of? *New Directions in Creativity—Mark A* by Joseph S. Renzulli. Copyright© 1973 by Harper & Row, Publishers, New York.

Name _____ Date _____

23 Make a creature (b)

Can you make some new creatures?

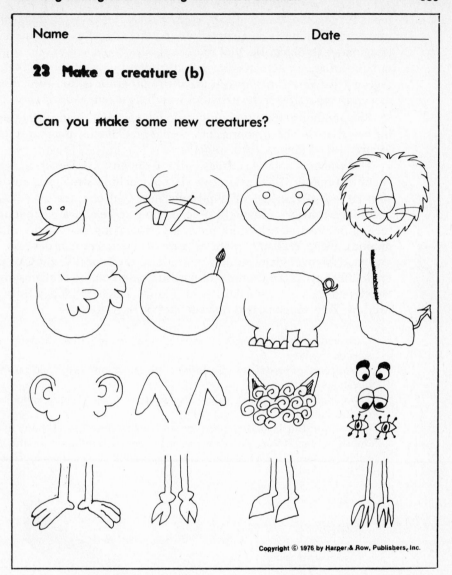

FIG 11–4   Make a New Creature. *New Directions in Creativity—Mark A* by Joseph S. Renzulli. Copyright© 1973 by Harper & Row, Publishers, New York.

oration exercise. It focuses on developing the gifted child's ability to think of alternative uses and the ability to combine given elements into a new whole. Figure 11–3 is a semantic and figural activity. It has as its major objective developing verbal fluency and flexibility. It also helps the gifted child to develop the understanding that given information may have different meanings to different individuals.

Figure 11–4 (figural systems) has as its primary objective the development of the ability to create an original character by combining given figural information. It is planned to further develop the gifted child's imaginative thinking. Each of these activities could serve as introductions or supplementary activities for gifted students. One of the distinct advantages to the *New Directions in Creativity* program is that the gifted child can carry out many of the activities with little teacher supervision.

Still another helpful theoretical model, particularly in further developing creativity in gifted youngsters, is that of Williams' plank, presented in Figure 11–5 (Williams, 1970, p. 203).

The Williams' model consists of three dimensions. Dimension one (D1) is subject matter, Dimension two (D2) is teaching strategies, and Dimension three (D3) consists of pupil behaviors that one can expect, such as cognitive behaviors, (fluent, flexible, original and elaborative thinking) and feeling, or affective behaviors, (curiosity, risk taking, complexity, and imagination). Using Williams' plant as a model, teachers can develop lessons designed to cover given subject matter and elicit specific levels or types of student behavior. An example of a lesson based on the Williams' model as developed by a group of Lakeland, Florida teachers (Peggy Burr, Carole Marlow, Tony Hughes, and Sharon Shelton) is as follows:

> *Objectives:* To encourage original and imaginative thinking through science.
> *Strategies:* Process of invention, visualization skill and provocative questions
> *Materials:* Pencil, paper, rulers, blue print, compass, T-square, books on mechanical machines, gears, and pulleys
> *Activities:* Display a blue print for students to view. List as many things you think this machine can do as you can. What are some unique ways this machine could be powered? List as many as you can think of. List the materials needed

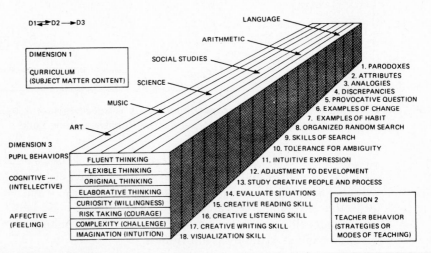

FIG. 11–5 Williams' Plank.

to build this machine. From your list, choose the best way to use the machine. Name it. If you could change this machine, how would you improve it? Draw your own blueprint. Give a description of what your machine could do.

Follow-up: Make a model of your machine.

Through combining and using the theoretical models presented above, teachers of the gifted are engineering many exciting experiences in the classroom. Education of gifted students highlights the necessity of working from theoretical models of learning and behavior, since gifted students must be continually challenged along many dimensions of learning and levels of intellectual pursuit.

Independent Study

Independent study is one of the most promising areas for developing curriculum for the gifted, since it builds upon the gifted student's desire for self-initiated learning. Through independent study, the gifted student can experience responding to environment. The teacher's role in independent study becomes that of a director, encouraging the gifted to initiate projects of their own. These projects can be used successfully in special groupings and enrichment plans.

Through independent study, gifted students can acquire motivations and skills that will help them to continue learning throughout life. A simple format that can be used with gifted elementary children is the following: (Sisk, 1976)

My Independent Study

WHAT I WANT TO STUDY ABOUT	HOW I WILL GO ABOUT IT	WHAT I WILL DO WITH MY KNOWLEDGE
1. I want to learn about math, algebra, geometry, and fractions.	1. Ask an expert in the field of math or a teacher.	1. Help other kids with their math in the room.
2. I want to learn more about word problems.	2. Consult different math books.	2. Be a math tutor for other grades.
	3. Find books in the library about math.	3. Set up math corner in the pod for others.

This independent study was mapped out for a fourth-grade gifted student who would be an example of a gifted child with a specific aptitude. His math achievement was 8.6, or eighth grade and six months. Yet he was small in stature and accelerating him would have been detrimental to his social and emotional development, as he was also somewhat immature for a nine-year-old. However, his enrichment needed to be accelerated and as the independent study indicates, it was.

For older gifted students, a format such as that listed below can be utilized:

Independent Study Worksheet

CONTENT TO BE STUDIED	RESOURCES	LEARNING PROCESS/PRODUCT
1. Russia	1. Books on Russia	1. Final written report
2. History of the various dynasties	2. Interview with professor in Russian language	2. Article for school newspaper
3. Geography of the country and its resources	3. Interview with Russian Orthodox priest.	3. Oral report for Phi Delta Kappa
4. Political leaders and history	4. Travel bureau for recent visitors to Russia to communicate with by letter or interview	
5. Educational system, particulary the university system		

The above independent study was planned for a thirteen-year-old junior high student in a core language arts/social studies gifted program in Los Angeles County, who became so involved in his study that he talked his mother and father into taking a tour to Russia over the Christmas holidays. He was a veritable guide from his interest and work in the project.

Many teachers are fearful of self-initiated learning because they are used to having all their students study the same subject matter. Fears about these differences in content can be reduced by giving the students broad topics. Under the umbrella topic, teachers can permit students to design their own projects. The above project was part of a study on history. Each student chose a country and the underlying strand was how natural resources, historical background, religion, education, and political framework help to form a nation. The teacher reported that the discussion following the various reports was fascinating and the insightful predictions concerning the futures of the countries was even more meaningful since the basic work was done by the gifted students.

Simulation

Another technique that is uniquely appropriate for the gifted is simulation. It has high motivational value because the students see an immediately useful reason to learn—to succeed and win a simulation game. Simulation also affords gifted children opportunities to do high-level thinking. Students demonstrate critical thinking, creative thinking, and logical thinking. But the most important value for the gifted in using simulation as a tool is the teaching of social values. Gifted children are quite competitive and in simulation games competition is experienced, but co-operation is also utilized to experience a common goal. In simulation, gifted children act and interact. They become involved in the facts, the process, and the key concepts to be learned in the game. Powerful and deep learning takes place while the gifted are engaged in exciting and satisfying play.

Simulation games can involve complex topics such as foreign policy or political processes, or very young gifted children can have fun with a simple simulation such as the following:

CALCULATOR

...Each child plays the role of a number. The ten digits of the decimal system are placed on large cards which can then be pinned to the shirts of the students. The teacher or student leader calls out problems, such as what is the product of 3 and 4. The first children to arrange themselves to show the answer win a point.

Avis Reid has developed an excellent format for constructing simulation games. Reid suggests that teachers use a problem base for simulation (Sisk, 1976). For example, decide on a concise statement of the problem, such as: a communicable disease has broken out in a community. Then decide on the objectives of the game: the students will experience group dynamics such as reaching a concensus; the students will develop insight into their own personal value system and that of others; the students will explore various methods of decision making.

Following the decision on objectives, then a scenario or scenes should be written that could include background information, the present time and setting, and conditions that will affect the game. For example, the community is multi-ethnic and comparatively isolated, it is midwinter, and the decision on the communicable disease must be made within twenty-four hours.

Characters and their goals must then be identified: doctors, nurses, parents, teachers, principals, and students are involved. When deciding on the brief description, physical characteristics and personalities of characters, the teacher may call upon role playing as a help. The final decision may be made such as the following: the doctor is the only one who knows how the cure must be utilized; he is to be assisted by a panel of citizens which includes two nurses who are against the serum's use. Each role or some of the roles can be spelled out, thus leaving either no leeway or considerable leeway for the gifted students to "flesh out" the roles with their own ideas and values.

Following the establishment of the characters and their goals, Reid suggests that an exact point in time be given when the game begins. She also suggests listing the resources to be used for the game. Whether they be physical, social, economic, political, or personal, the resources can be included to give the game greater complexity.

Rules and their administration are the last to be included. These rules should govern (1) the players, (2) the game patterns, (3) the scoring, and (4) how all of these are to be implemented. In the case of our communicable disease game, perhaps fifteen people have been exposed and there is serum for eight. How can decisions be made to save eight people and sacrifice the lives of seven others? Each person could be given a role on the advisory panel and a certain number of points. A consensus could be required to make decisions and a time constraint of one hour could be added for timing purposes.

The last area to be considered in devising a game is the evaluation and feedback. During this time, the teacher of the gifted can lead the students to examine how decisions were made and how they felt about the decisions. Here the teacher can reinforce positive social attitudes that have been observed and begin to arrange other experiences for information gathering to help the students build better understanding. Analogies can be made to the present and past situations from observations that the teacher and the gifted students have made. The debriefing is extremely important and should be allotted a quarter of the playing time on any given day. That is, if a sixty-minute playing period is experienced, fifteen minutes should be allowed for debriefing.

Simulation helps make learning as exciting as it should be for gifted students and involves the total intellect. Once gifted children learn the format for simulation games, they will be busy making their own for the entire class to experience.

Inquiry

Another useful technique for gifted is that of inquiry. The heart of inquiry is direct comprehension of nature coming from a rich exposure to first hand experiences.

In inquiry, the teacher of the gifted acts as a guide or consultant. The teacher provides situations or materials that create questions in the minds of the students. The teacher may utilize a systematic answering system of "yes" or "no" in encouraging the students to observe and then do mental experiments, formulating hypotheses, and testing theories. This type of discussion or inquiry can be an electrifying and stimulating experience for gifted students. Suchman (1965) is an excellent source to utilize in setting up inquiry sessions for gifted. He has devised a series of experiments that are on film, and on records for use by classroom teachers. Inquiry is particularly good for the gifted because of their natural inquisitiveness and curiosity, as well as high reasoning ability.

In working with gifted students, it is imperative that the teacher observe the students for their learning style, interests, and particular needs and characteristics, as many other strategies will become clearly called for to maximize the gifted student's learning. It also goes without saying that many of the strategies used with gifted students will be strategies that are useful and important for all children. The difference will be the pace or rapidity with which the gifted learn and respond, and the product which is often two to three years above their chronological age mates.

ADULT PROBLEMS/INTERVENTION

Terman fought to dispel the idea that gifted individuals are plagued by insanity and unhappiness at adulthood. In his follow-up studies in 1950 with his subjects as adults, he found that they suffered fewer nervous breakdowns, were hospitalized less, had lower suicide rates than the average population's projection figures, had better marriage rates, and in general demonstrated wider interests than the population at large. In the 1959 data, the rate of hospital admissions for men continued just below average, but for women it was slightly above average. These admission statistics may be due to economic success and insight into one's needs that encourages gifted women to seek help before serious damage is done; however, it does appear that serious emotional problems are more common among gifted women than average women in later life. At the 1972 Terman symposiums, one of the Terman women related, "I wish I had had my own career, although I loved my husband and my children—now I wish I had a career. I know I was as bright as any of the men here." Perhaps part of the problem with the bright women is not having used their talent, and reaching a point in life at which a lack of personal fulfillment is felt.

To combat midlife loss of talent, a program for midcareer gifted individuals has been developed at George Washington University. This program selects outstanding men and women who want to switch careers to work with other gifted young people in some capacity. These men and women are then placed in internship experiences to gain on-the-job training with administrators or decision makers in the field of gifted, such as state consultants for the gifted, regional offices of education, and national organizations such as the National Association of Secondary School Principals. The interns have varied from Ph.D's in education to museum curators to creative women with B.A. degrees who have never worked and now want to do so.

A crucial need in gifted education is more long-term studies of adults who have been enrolled in gifted programs and those who have not been involved in gifted programs to ascertain the effects of special programs. Also, more information is needed on whether gifted adults utilize their ability to its maximum in order that we might intervene and make available help to ensure that society benefits from this most precious and irretrievable resource—its gifted and talented people.

REFERENCES

Bernal, E. M., and Reyna, J. *Analysis of Giftedness in Mexican American Children and Design of a Prototype Identification Instrument.* Austin, TX: Southwest Educational Development Laboratory, 1974.

Bloom, B. (ed.) *Taxonomy of Educational Objectives: Handbook I. Cognitive Domain.* New York: David McKay Co., Inc., 1956.

Braga, J. Early admission: Opinion vs evidence. *Elementary School Journal,* 1972, 72, 35–46.

Cox, C. M. *The Early Mental Traits of Three Hundred Geniuses, Genetic Studies of Genius, Vol. II.* Sanford, CA: Stanford University Press, 1926.

Davis, A., and Eells, K. *Davis-Eells Games.* Chicago: World Book Company, 1952.

Educational Policies Commission. *Education of the Gifted.* Washington, DC: National Educational Association, 1950.

Gallagher, J. *Teaching the Gifted Child.* Boston: Allyn and Bacon, Inc., 1975.

Galasso, V. *Model Project for the Creatively Gifted and Talented in Science, Final Report.* Washington, DC: U. S. Office of Education, 1977.

Guilford, J. P. *Way Beyond the IQ.* New York: Creative Education Foundation, Inc., and Creative Synergetic Associates, 1977.

————. *The Nature of Human Intelligence.* New York: McGraw-Hill, 1977.

Heck, A. *The Education of Exceptional Children.* New York: McGraw-Hill, Inc., 1953.

Krathwohl, D. R., et al. *Taxonomy of Educational Objectives—Handbook II—the Affective Domain.* New York: David McKay Co., Inc., 1964.

Marland, S. P. *Education of the Gifted and Talented.* Washington, DC: U. S. Office of Education, 1972.

Mead, M. The gifted child in the American culture of today. *Journal of Teacher Education,* 1954, 3, 211.

Meeker, M. *The Structure of Intellect: Its Interpretation and Uses.* Columbus, OH: Charles E. Merrill Publishing Co., 1969.

————. *SOI Learning Abilities Test.* El Segundo, CA: SOI Institute, 1977.

Plowman, P. and Rice, J. *California Project Talent: Final Report.* Sacramento: California State Department of Education, 1967.

Renzulli, J., and Hartman, R. Scale for rating behavioral characteristics of superior students. *Exceptional Children,* 1971, 38, 243–248.

————. *New Directions in Creativity.* New York: Harper & Row, Publishers, 1973.

Rogers, C. *Freedom to Learn.* Columbus, OH: Charles E. Merrill Publishing Co., 1969.

Seagoe, M. *Terman and the Gifted.* Los Altos, CA: Wm. Kaufman, Inc., 1975.

Sisk, D. Encounter lessons: activities to stimulate creativity and positive feelings of worth. *Gifted Child Quarterly,* 1975, 19, 346–349.

————. *Teaching Gifted Children.* Columbia, SC: South Carolina State Department of Education, 1976.

Stanley, J. "Educated Non-Acceleration: An International Tragedy," Proceedings from the Second World Conference on Gifted, San Francisco, 1976.

———. Some thoughts on not having accelerated. *Intellectually Talented Youth Bulletin, vol. 3*, #7, 1977.

Suchman, R. Inquiry and education no! In, J. Gallagher (ed.), *Teaching Gifted Students: A Book of Readings*. Boston: Allyn and Bacon, Inc., 1965.

Taba, H., and Elkins, D. *Teaching Strategies for the Culturally Disadvanted*. Skokie, IL: Rand McNally & Company, 1966.

Terman, L., et al. *Mental and Physical Traits of a Thousand Gifted Children: Genetic Studies of Genius, vol. 1*. Stanford, CA: Stanford University Press, 1925.

———, and Oden, M. The Stanford Studies of Genius. In P. Witty (ed.), *The Gifted Child*. Lexington, MA: D.C. Heath & Company, 1951.

Torrance, E. P. Are the Torrance tests of creative thinking biased against or in favor of disadvantaged groups? *Gifted Child Quarterly*, 1971, *15*, 75–80.

White, A. Gifted among the handicapped. Proceedings from the 2nd Annual Conference on the Handicapped Gifted, New Orleans, The Association for the Gifted, TAG, 1976.

Williams, F. *Classroom Ideas for Encouraging Thinking and Feeling*. Buffalo, NY: Dissemination of Knowledge Publishers, 1970.

Witty, P. Who are the gifted? *Education for the Gifted, Fifty-Seventh Yearbook of the National Society for the Study of Education, Pt. II*. Chicago: National Society for the Study of Education, 1958.

Worcester, D. A. *The Education of Children of Above Average Mental Ability*. Lincoln: University of Nebraska Press, 1956.

CHAPTER 12

ORGANIZATIONAL ISSUES IN SPECIAL EDUCATION

M. STEPHEN LILLY

The information presented in the preceding chapters provides an orientation to major programmatic trends in special education, as well as a knowledge base in all areas of that field. This final chapter is devoted to a discussion of two topics which pervade all serious discussions of not only special education, but education in general. These critical factors are: (1) provision of adequate financial resources for program development and maintenance; and (2) availability of adequately trained and highly skilled special education teachers, administrators, and support personnel. Without money and people, the system doesn't run.

These topics are important because of their direct bearing on many of the major issues facing the field. For example, it can be argued that while most special educators ignore the area of school finance and make little or no attempt to understand special education funding systems, those same funding systems constitute the chief factor prolonging the use of traditional special education categories. Likewise, while needed changes in special education programs have been outlined in this book and elsewhere, these changes can occur only through systematic personnel development activities in school districts, as well as in colleges and universities. It is important for all who are involved in special education to be aware of the forces which shape their environment, and to attempt to influence policy decisions whenever possible. It is hoped the basic information presented here will help to "professionalize" readers beyond their own classrooms or administrative offices.

SPECIAL EDUCATION FINANCE

Special education is an expensive undertaking, not only in some absolute sense, but also in comparison to standard education programs. In comparison to regular education, special education class size and caseloads are smaller, resulting in comparatively higher costs for personnel, facilities, equipment, transportation, and administrative services. Local school districts cannot be expected to bear the total cost of special education services, since total local responsibility would place an unbearable strain on local resources and taxing capabilities. In addition, it can be argued that when education programs are supported solely (or even primarily) from local funds, economic inequity results because of relative wealth and taxing capabilities of neighboring school districts. Thus, two children might receive vastly unequal educational opportunities due to circumstances of birth, economic condition, and/or place of residence. Some special education funding systems attempt to redress these inequities, while other funding structures actually contribute to unequal educational opportunity for children in special education.

Funds for providing special education services to children with special needs come from three primary sources: federal, state, and local tax dollars. Most local tax dollars for education come from personal and business property taxes, while state education funds derive primarily from sales and income taxes. Federal taxation mechanisms are more varied, with income taxes being the primary source of funds used for education.

It has long been accepted by both state and federal governments that local school districts should not bear the total cost of education, not to mention the excess costs associated with special education services. The amount and type of state support varies widely, however, and only recently has the federal government provided money directly to local school districts for basic support of special education services.

Local Funding of Special Education

It can safely be said that in most states, local school districts currently provide the majority of funds to support special education. In essence, it is the responsibility of each local district to provide special education to residents who qualify for services, and while states have delegated this responsibility to the local districts, no further delegation is possible. In the famous words of Harry Truman, "the buck stops here" in terms of providing and funding special education services.

Not all local school districts can provide adequate special education services, often due to the limited number of students in the district. If a school district has less than forty students in need of special education, it is hardly efficient for that district to hire a director of special education, program consultants, and a full range of support personnel necessary to offer a quality special education program. Furthermore, the district might have one deaf child, one blind child, and two severely or profoundly handicapped children. In this case, inappropriate grouping of children for special education could practically be assured.

The problem outlined above is not an isolated situation. In Illinois, for example, there were over 1,000 legally constituted school districts in 1978, many of which served very small numbers of children. In states that have large numbers of school districts, a common pattern of organization has involved formation of special education "cooperatives." In this arrangement, several school districts enter into an agreement to cooperate in offering special education services, usually hiring one director and supportive service staff. The cooperative becomes a single administrative unit serving more than one school district, and answerable to the boards of education in each cooperating district.

In terms of funding, it can generally be said that school districts provide all the funds for special education that are not provided by the state or federal governments. This statement assumes that all school-age children are being provided a free, appropriate public education, an assump-

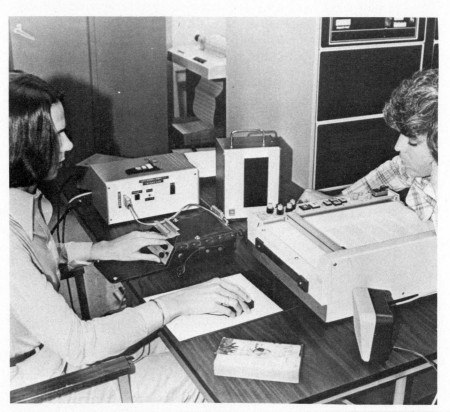

Courtesy of Telesensory Systems, Inc.

tion which is presently closer than ever to reality but, nonetheless, not totally true. The point to be made, however, is that special education programming requires something of a "blank check" financing policy by school districts. If a state law promises a certain dollar amount for special education to a local district, and the state legislature fails to appropriate enough money to meet that dollar commitment, then the state contribution is "prorated," or reduced a proportional amount. The same is true for federal funding. If state and federal funds are prorated, the local district is required to produce the funds from local revenues.

This situation naturally leads many local school districts to be very cautious in starting new special education programs, or even adequately funding existing programs. Ironically, school districts which offer high quality special education services are often most affected by this funding structure. It is not at all unusual to find parents with handicapped children who have moved to another community because of the reputation of a particular special education program in that community. The armed forces routinely grant "sympathetic reassignment" to servicemen with handicapped children, so that they will be near high quality special education programs. Thus, many school districts are faced with the dilemma that if they continue to develop excellent special education programs, they will also continue to attract increasing numbers of new families requiring such programs, with each new family representing an increase in the local school budget.

In reaction to the situation just described, Weintraub, Abeson, and Braddock (1975) have proposed that special education funding systems should be developed so as not to penalize school districts that offer high quality programs. Specifically, they suggest that each school district be required to spend the same amount of money on each child, whether or not the child is in special education, and that additional costs associated with provision of special education services (commonly called excess costs) be borne by the state and federal governments. Thus, if a school district spends $1,350 per year to educate a normal child, the school district obligation for children in special education would also be $1,350 per child, with additional costs being reimbursed to the school district from state and federal sources.

One additional problem associated with local funding involves determining which school district should pay for educating a student who lives away from home, in a residential setting. It is hardly fair to ask school districts to pay for special education for children from other communities, merely because they are the location of a state or private residential facility. Many court cases have focused on "place of residence" as it relates to special education funding. By and large, judicial decrees have supported the concept that the "local school district" for funding purposes is the district of residence for the child's parents, not the district in which the child resides. Thus, if parents in Corvallis, Oregon, place a child in a residential home in Portland, it can generally be assumed that Corvallis, not Portland, is responsible for paying the local share of the cost of educating the child.

State Funding of Special Education

Next to local governments, the largest source of funds for special education is state government. State funding patterns vary greatly, and the manner in which states reimburse local school districts can affect not only the quantity of special education services, but the organization and quality of those services as well (Weintraub et al., 1975). For example, some state funding systems actually encourage labeling of children, while others minimize the necessity of labels. Likewise, some state funding mechanisms are conducive to development of teacher consultation services—as described in chapter 4—while others encourage development of special class services.

There are two basic dimensions on which state funding systems can be classified: (1) some provide funds for each child served, others fund "units of service" such as classrooms or teachers, and still others fund "excess costs," and (2) some systems provide funds on a "straight sum" basis, while others weigh the reimbursement according to predetermined factors. Various types of state funding systems will be presented below, grouped according to the first breakdown just presented. Specific state systems will not be described, due to the regularity with which such systems are modified, thus rendering current descriptions obsolete. This is intended to be only an overview of state funding systems; the interested reader is referred to Thomas (1973), Marinelli (1975), Weintraub, Abeson, and Braddock (1975), and Bernstein, Hartman, and Marshall (1976) for more detailed information.

Per Child Reimbursement Systems

State reimbursement systems that provide funds to school districts based on the number of children served are of two types: flat grant and weighted formula. *Flat grant* systems are very straightforward, in that school districts receive a specified dollar amount for each child served. Often, the dollar amount varies for different handicapping conditions, so that a school district might receive $200 for a student receiving speech services, and $400 for a visually impaired student. The flat grant system is easy to administer, and requires a minimum of red tape. However, flat grant systems suffer from the following inadequacies:

1. School districts are encouraged to label children in ways that will generate more state money;
2. Since the size of the grants often bears no relationship to the actual cost of special education services at the local level, districts are encouraged to cut corners and develop inexpensive programs;
3. Since each child within a given category generates the same amount of

money, school districts are encouraged to develop the largest possible class size or caseloads, since large classes ease the burden on local budgets; and

4. Flat grant systems assume that all children within a given category have the same needs, and allow for little flexibility or individualized programs within categories.

Systems for state funding based on *weighted formulas* attempt to quantify the differential costs associated with educating various types of handicapped children. As a part of the National Education Finance Project, Rossmiller (1971) studied twenty-four school districts in five states, to determine actual differential costs of providing quality special education services. These costs are stated in terms of "weights," which relate costs of educating normal children with various special education costs. For example, if a weight for a given special education category is 2.0, this would indicate that it costs twice as much to educate a child in that category as a typical child in the school district. Similarly, a weight of 3.0 would signify three times the typical cost for a normal child. Based on his study, Rossmiller posits the following weights for costing special education services:

Category	Weight (related to regular education)
Educable mentally retarded	1.87 × normal cost
Trainable mentally retarded	2.10 × normal cost
Auditorially handicapped	2.99 × normal cost
Visually handicapped	2.97 × normal cost
Speech handicapped	1.18 × normal cost
Physically handicapped	3.64 × normal cost
Learning disabled	2.16 × normal cost
Emotionally disturbed	2.83 × normal cost
Multiply handicapped	2.73 × normal cost
Homebound	1.42 × normal cost

The Rossmiller data must be treated with caution, since they were collected in the late 1960s when special education services were substantially different from today. For example, a major category in any such study today would be severely and profoundly handicapped, a category which did not appear in the Rossmiller study.

Weighted formula systems for state reimbursement for special education were quite popular for several years, and a number of states have adopted such systems. Weighted formula systems have an advantage over flat grant systems in that the weights are often based on actual study of special education costs in a given state. On the negative side, weighted systems are highly categorical and demand labeling of children as a precondition of state funding. Marinelli (1975), in an analysis of Florida's weighted formula for reimbursement reports that the system resulted in a move away from resource services to special classes, an increase in the size of special classes, a trend toward hiring less expensive teachers, and pressure to identify more students as handicapped to earn more state money. In general, weighted systems suffer from the same drawbacks stated earlier for flat grant systems.

Per Unit Reinbursement Systems

Many states have reimbursement formulas which use as the basis for computation units of instruction rather than individual children. Such systems have the potential of being less categorical and offering more flexibility to school districts in planning special education programs, although these are merely *potential* benefits. Unit reimbursement systems can be, and sometimes are, as categorical and inflexible as child reimbursement systems.

One form of unit reimbursement is the *flat grant* system, in which a school district is given a flat dollar amount for each unit of instruction. A unit of instruction is usually defined as a certain number of children identified as needing special education. For example, a school district might receive $800 for every ten students identified as needing a certain type of special education service. Sometimes "administrative units" are awarded to school districts according to the number of instructional units in the district, so that part of the cost of administering special education programs is covered by the state. Flat grant systems of unit reimbursement are an improvement over child-based systems in that school districts are not necessarily encouraged to "pack" classes to generate maximum state reimbursement. Further, they have the potential of offering greater flexibility to school districts in terms of labeling students and organizing services. However, as with per child flat grants, the amount of the grant often bears no resemblance to the actual amount of money spent by the school district in providing the service.

A second form of unit reimbursement, in use in several states, is known as "personnel reimbursement." Personnel reimbursement systems provide specified amounts of state money for qualified special education teachers, aides, administrators, and support personnel hired by the school district. This support might be a flat dollar figure, such as $6,000 for teachers, administrators, and support personnel and $2,500 for aides, or it might be a percentage, such as 60 percent of personnel costs. Often, states reimburse a percent of personnel costs with a maximum amount to be paid for any individual (for example, 70 percent of a teacher's salary not to exceed $7,500). Personnel reimbursement systems offer substantial flexibility to school districts in organizing services, and address the major item of expense in special education. However, personnel reimbursement systems encourage large class sizes or caseloads, since the district receives the same amount of money, no matter how many children are served by an individual teacher. A further disadvantage is that personnel reimbursement systems generally fall far short of covering actual excess costs incurred by school districts in offering special education programs.

Excess Cost Reimbursement Systems

A third type of state reimbursement system attempts to establish actual excess costs incurred by school districts and use these cost figures as the basis for state funding. Excess costs generally include expenditures for such items as personnel, administration, support services, transportation, facilities, materials, special equipment, and sometimes inservice training. Some states have laws which call for funding only a percentage (e.g., 70 percent) of excess costs incurred by local districts, while other state laws call for state funding of all excess costs. It is obvious that full state and federal funding of excess costs has the greatest potential for reducing reliance on categorical labels, and offering school districts flexibility in organizing services. The Council for Exceptional Children (1972) has gone on record as supporting full state and federal funding of excess costs. In addition, as a part of compliance with P. L. 94–142, states and local districts are required to present excess cost figures in order to qualify for federal funds. However, several problems must be taken into account in establishing excess cost funding systems at the state level.

1. Without safeguards, an excess cost system can be a "blank check" for school districts to develop overly elaborate programs and charge the bill to the state. This problem is generally solved by establishing upper limits on the amount of money that can be claimed for any given type of service.

2. Somewhat in contrast to the prior point, an excess cost system is meaningless if state legislatures never appropriate enough funds to fully support the system. A partially funded excess cost system, in which local districts receive only a percentage of the actual legitimate claim, provides the same disincentives for quality programs as delineated above for other systems of funding.

3. Formulas for figuring excess cost are often so complicated that they create the necessity of additional administrative staff just to complete the paperwork necessary for receiving funds. Excess cost formulas must be straightforward and incorporate only essential information.

4. In administering excess cost formulas, state education agencies must assure that the local school district spends the same amount of local funds on children in special education and children not receiving special education. School districts cannot be allowed to "make money" by placing children in special education.

5. As with all funding systems outlined herein, the state must assure that funds are expended on *quality* special education programs. This requires monitoring systems apart from those dealing primarily with fiscal matters. Due process procedures are necessary but not sufficient for maintaining quality in special education programs; it is the state's responsibility to evaluate on a regular basis all special education programs receiving state funds.

Special Reimbursements

In addition to the basic reimbursement patterns outlined above, many states have special systems for funding specific activities. For example, in many states, transportation is funded separately rather than as a part of the basic reimbursement system. School districts make claims for transportation costs and are reimbursed, usually on a percentage basis. Likewise, many states have separate systems for financing construction projects, and for such activities as research, inservice training, instructional materials, and assessment. All special reimbursement patterns exist alongside one of the basic systems outlined above. Excess cost systems usually figure all categories of expenditure into the basic allotment, and have no special reimbursement provision.

Summary

This section has provided only a brief overview of state funding systems. It is highly recommended that everyone involved with special education in the schools—teachers, supportive service personnel, parents and others—learn as much as possible about the system of funding in the state in which they live or work. As mentioned earlier, a year does not pass in which some states do not change their reimbursement patterns, and the shape of the funding system can have a direct effect on the rules governing provision of services in local school districts. Furthermore, each state has a set of rules and regulations governing special education. These rules cover not only reimbursement, but other important topics such as limitations on class size or caseload, assessment requirements, instructional planning requirements, and due process procedures. In order to be truly "professional" educators, we must go beyond the confines of our own work situations and attempt to know and understand as much as possible about the total context in which we work. For teachers who are knowledgeable concerning such topics as funding and rules/regulations governing special education, opportunities for involvement in important policy decisions will arise. Often teachers assume that their only job is to affect the children with whom they interact daily. It is sometimes possible, however, to improve those daily interactions by affecting the total system in which they occur. Furthermore, while teachers have been the primary example used here, the same can be said concerning the general advocacy function of parents and administrators.

Federal Funding of Special Education

This section will *not* review all sources of federal funding for special education; some information of this nature is contained in chapter 2 and the remainder is beyond the purview of this book. Rather, what is presented here is a summary of the direct federal support for special education services at the local level, as embodied in Public Law 94–142.

Until the passage of P.L. 94–142, the only federal government funding of direct services to children was in the form of grants for research and demonstration with exemplary programs. Some of these grants were made directly from the federal level, while others were funded through state education agencies using federal monies given to the states on a "formula" basis. P.L. 94–142 introduced a new type of federal funds for special education, in which funds are channeled through state education agencies to local school districts, to be used in providing services to children with special needs. These funds are distributed based on how many children received special education in a given school district during the prior school year, and are intended to be used for *basic service delivery*.

P.L. 94–142 funding is determined according to a formula, which is based on the *national average per pupil expenditure* (NAPPE) in a given year. Basically, each state is entitled to an amount of money for each student served in special education, and this amount of money is determined by taking a percentage of the national average per pupil expenditure in that year, as follows:

FISCAL YEAR	PERCENTAGE OF NAPPE USED IN FIGURING STATE ENTITLEMENT
1979	10
1980	20
1981	30
1982 and thereafter	40

Thus if a mythical (and small) state were to serve 10,000 children in special education in the 1980–1981 school year, and the national average per pupil expenditure that year were $1,650, the state's P.L. 94–142 allotment would be figured as follows:

1. Twenty percent of $1,650 is $330 per student.
2. Ten thousand students at $330 apiece results in a state allotment of $3,300,000.

Of the $3,300,000, 25 percent would remain at the state level and 75 percent would flow directly to school districts within the state, based on the number of students receiving special education in each district.

It should be noted that in 1982, if the same state were still serving ten thousand children in special education and the NAPPE remained the same, the state would be entitled to twice as much P.L. 94–142 money, since the allotment would be based on 40 percent of the NAPPE, as compared to 20 percent in 1980. Thus, the potential dollars for local school districts from P.L. 94–142 will reach significant new levels within the next decade, since not only does the percentage figure used for allotments increase to 40 percent, but the number of students served and the NAPPE can be expected to rise annually as well.

One note of caution regarding this rosy economic picture deserves mention. The figures presented above represent *allotments* to which states and local school districts are *entitled* under P.L. 94–142. The actual amount of money received will depend on annual appropriation of funds by Congress, and the funds actually distributed will be prorated according to how much money is made available annually by Congress. Thus, in any given year, a state and its local districts may receive only a percentage of the funds to which they are entitled. One of the most interesting political developments to watch in the next decade will be the extent to which Congress lives up to its promised levels of financial support in P.L. 94–142.

This section has provided only a summary of the major points regarding funding of direct special education services through P.L. 94–142. For more detailed information, the reader is directed to the current rules and regulations governing P.L. 94–142, distributed by the U.S. Office of Education, Department of Health, Education, and Welfare.

PERSONNEL PREPARATION IN SPECIAL EDUCATION

In all of the funding systems outlined above, a basic prerequisite for special education reimbursement from the state or federal level is employment of an adequate number of qualified special education personnel. These personnel include administrators, supervisors, teachers, aides, social workers, assessment specialists, physical therapists, occupational therapists, and others. Generally, a "qualified" teacher is one who has completed an approved and recognized teacher education program, resulting in a certificate to teach in a given state. Certification also is the criterion by which administrators and the other support personnel listed above are deemed to be "qualified" for their jobs. The only job classification listed above in which certification is not the standard for qualification is the aide, or paraprofessional, for whom no established standards of training have been set. For teachers and other special education personnel, teacher certification standards vary widely from state to state, and a limited number of states still do not have separate standards for special education certification.

Teacher education has long been a topic of concern in special education. Wallin (1914) reported that as early as 1897 the University of Pennsylvania offered a three-course sequence in education of the mentally retarded. Burke (1976) has pointed out that personnel preparation programs have undergone a tremendous expansion in recent years, with fewer than forty colleges and universities offering special education programs in 1958, as opposed to over four hundred such programs in 1976.

Without question, the single most influential factor contributing to the growth of special education teacher preparation programs has been federal government support for such programs. In 1958, P.L. 85–926 was enacted by Congress, authorizing grants for preparation of teachers and leadership personnel in the area of mental retardation. This authorization was expanded in 1963, through P.L. 88–164, to include all areas of special education (Burke, 1976). Federal support for teacher preparation in special education has grown to the point that in 1978, the Division of Personnel Preparation in the Bureau of Education for the Handicapped (BEH) awarded approximately $45 million to colleges and universities, state education agencies, local school districts, and other agencies involved in teacher education.

Early BEH support for teacher education was strongly categorical in its orientation. Each category of exceptionality had its own budget, and BEH received proposals for federal funds targeted specifically to the category. Thus, if a university offered teacher preparation in five categories of exceptionality, five separate (and often independent) proposals were submitted to BEH. The categories that were funded separately included mental retardation, speech and hearing, visually handicapped, crippled and other health impaired, early childhood, learning disabilities, multiple handicaps, and emotional disturbance (Burke, 1976). Teacher preparation grants provided funds for student support, faculty salaries, and other basic support services. Many early teacher education programs in colleges and universities were begun with total funding from BEH, and gradually built state program support funds over a period of years.

In the early 1970s, BEH initiated (based on clearly observable trends in special education nationwide) a series of changes in funding procedures for teacher education programs, changes that have contributed to a quiet revolution in special education teacher preparation over the last decade. First, the Bureau encouraged proposals for "interrelated" teacher education programs that cut across traditional categorical boundaries. Second, the proposal format was changed so that Departments of Special Education in colleges and universities were to submit only one proposal containing all program components, thus encouraging cross-categorical cooperation among college faculty in special education. Third, BEH guidelines for preparation of proposals began to stress a listing of program competencies to be learned by trainees. As various categorical programs began to compare lists of training competencies, it became clear that most categorical training programs were more alike than different. "Core" courses were often developed to reflect common program content. Fourth, BEH began to award increasing amounts of training funds to state education agencies and local school districts, with a corresponding increase of emphasis on in-service education of practicing teachers. In 1978, approximately 45 percent of all BEH training funds were spent for in-service education. And fifth, BEH began to use a priority system in funding programs of teacher education, focusing increasing amounts of money on emerging priorities such as severely and profoundly handicapped, vocational education of the handicapped, and special education training for regular educators.

While it is accurate to assert that the BEH actions listed above were in reaction to professional developments in special education nationally, it is also clear that these actions have helped to bring about major changes in teacher education programs. Cross-categorical and noncategorical teacher preparation programs are now the rule rather than the exception. In-service education for employed teachers and other professionals is now a national priority. Preparation of regular educators to deal with learning and behavior problems in the classroom is a growing concern of both school districts and institutions of higher education. An increasing number of teacher preparation programs are organizing around statements of specific skills to be learned by program trainees, as opposed to traditional lists of courses with vague titles and inconsistent content.

Control of Teacher Education

An emerging controversy in general teacher education, which is having its impact on special education as well, concerns the extent to which colleges and universities are seen as isolated entities in planning and carrying out teacher education programs. The Council for Exceptional Children (1976) has published guidelines to be used in developing teacher education programs, and one of these guidelines states:

> The planning and implementation of special education preparation programs should include opportunities at all levels for input from all constituent groups, including the consumer, affected by the planning (p. 17).

The consumers of teacher preparation programs include directors of special education, parents of students in special education, and the trainees themselves. While parents have not been consistently vocal in demanding input into teacher preparation programs, the same cannot be said of directors of special education. Roger Reger, a special education director in New York State, has decried the lack of cooperation between institutions of higher education and school administrators. Reger (1974) says that some special education trainees are poorly trained, while others are trained for roles that do not fit the realities of special education in the public schools. Reger calls for establishment of elected advisory boards, similar to boards of education in local school districts, to serve as policymaking boards for programs of teacher preparation in colleges and universities. Another local director of special education, Paul Irvine (1974), has gone even further in suggesting that the schools take over complete responsibility for the last year of teacher preparation. Many institutions of higher education have established advisory committees to provide input on special education teacher preparation programs, a trend that will surely accelerate in the future.

One further development must be mentioned if the topic of control of teacher education is to be adequately summarized: the unmistakable surge toward control of teacher certification and licensing by professional teacher organizations. The National Education Association and American Federation of Teachers are gaining increasing responsibility in matters of certification and licensing, and in many states, a specified number of seats on State Teacher Certification Boards are designated as slots to be filled by representatives of the formal teacher organizations. It is unclear exactly what effect this trend will have on special education teacher preparation, but it is apparent that the balance of power is shifting in teacher education as a whole.

Competency-Based Teacher Education

Perhaps the most clearly distinguishable trend in special education teacher preparation is toward what has loosely been termed "competency-based teacher education" (Connor, 1976). Essentially, competency-based teacher education, or CBTE, refers to teacher education programs "in which performance goals for trainees are specified in rigorous detail and agreed to in advance of instruction." (Semmel and Semmel, 1976, p. 69). CBTE programs have stated objectives, and more or less conform to the behavioral model of instruction presented in chapter 4.

Largely because the BEH guidelines for development of personnel preparation proposals require specification of training program competencies, nearly all special education programs have specified lists of skills to be learned by all trainees. This does not mean, however, that all of these programs are "competency-based." The author has pointed out that "competency-based training has been used in some cases to offer a traditional training program in a traditional way, with a new set of labels attached to it" (Lilly, 1976, p. 106).

Competency-based teacher education has generated a good deal of controversy, with some special educators refusing to jump on the bandwagon (Blatt, 1976). The special education literature is replete, however, with reports on competency-based training programs at institutions such as the University of Washington (Edgar and Neel, 1976), Wayne State University (Hanninen, Coleman and Parres, 1977), the University of Kentucky (Berdine and Kelly, 1977; Cegelka and Tawney, 1975), the University of Missouri (Altman and Meyen, 1974), Florida State University (Schwartz and Oseroff, 1975), and Peabody College (Wiegerink, 1973).

Competency-based teacher education (CBTE) is controversial because it has not, as some had hoped it would, made a science of teacher education. Public specification of intended outcomes of teacher preparation programs has not always been followed by objective evaluation of achievement of training objectives by program trainees. Indeed, such precise measurement of learning outcomes is seldom possible in teacher education. What is often overlooked, however, is the fact that making training program objectives public is a worthwhile activity in and of itself. In traditional special education teacher preparation programs, it is not particu-

Courtesy of the Institute for the Crippled and Disabled.

larly helpful to be able to say that one has had a "methods course in learning disabilities," since the course may cover completely different material in two universities, or in the same university when offered by two different instructors. If CBTE leads us to focus on the course content rather than on nebulous course titles, it is well worth the change in orientation.

This section has barely scratched the surface of the controversy concerning competency-based teacher education. Many readers of this book will be enrolled in teacher preparation programs which are competency-based at one or another level of sophistication. Trainees in such programs should not expect their preparation to be easier, or even more valid, because it is called competency-based. In our continual quest to be more systematic, we must not be seduced into believing that teaching and learning, at any level, is an exact and predictable science. If, however, we accept the inherent limitations of CBTE, it can serve as a most effective communication tool concerning what we are trying to teach. This type of communication is essential among college instructors, as well as between institutions of higher education and those who hire and work with graduates of teacher preparation programs. Readers desiring more detailed information on CBTE are referred to Semmel and Semmel (1976), Elam (1971), and Houston (1974).

Generic Special Education Training

One outgrowth of the CBTE movement in special education has been increasing communication among college faculty concerning course content, since listings of skills taught in various courses will inevitably be compared. As colleges and universities began to develop "interrelated" special education training programs, it became clear that the overlap between various categorical training programs was phenomenal. As one teacher educator was heard to remark, "When you examine methods courses in EMR, LD, and BD, you're always meeting yourself coming around the corner."

The BEH call for interrelated training programs in the early 1970s resulted largely from the expressed frustration of many colleges and universities in trying to develop noncategorical training emphases while still conforming to the then-categorical guidelines for BEH funding. The past decade has seen significant expansion of noncategorical teacher training programs in special education, particularly in the areas of educable mental retardation, learning disabilities, and behavior disorders. Categorical programs continue to prevail in areas such as visual impairment, hearing impairment, and deaf-blind, in which it is clear that teachers need specialized skills specific to a category of exceptionality in order to meet the educational needs of children with given disabilities.

Several states have moved to combine the areas of EMR, LD, and BD into a single category for certification of special education teachers, thus helping to assure broad training for special educators of children with learning and behavior problems. While most states are just now beginning to consider certification of teachers of severely and profoundly handicapped children, there are indications that this area of certification will tend to be generic as well, including an emphasis on mental retardation, emotional disturbance, and crippling conditions.

In summary, it can be said that there is a noticeable trend toward less categorical certification patterns and teacher preparation programs in the areas of special education covered in chapters 3, 4, 5, 6, and 7 of this book. At the same time, the categories of exceptionality covered in chapters 8 through 11 remain more or less separate entities for the purpose of teacher education and certification. While there continue to be university training programs in all areas of exceptionality, the "interrelatedness" of the categories continues to be a growing concern for all special educators involved in teacher preparation.

In-Service Education

One of the most awesome responsibilities facing education today is the need for retraining of regular and special educators called for in P.L. 94–142. There has long been an interest in lifelong education for teachers and other school personnel, as evidenced by the fact that in many states, teaching certificates must be occasionally renewed based on evidence of teacher involvement in programs of continuing education. While the schools have always expressed interest in lifelong learning for school personnel, there has generally been neither the demand nor the financial resources to make universal in-service education a reality.

Public Law 94–142 has changed this situation by creating both the demand and a potential source of funds for massive in-service education efforts. Essentially, P.L. 94–142 requires that within a reasonable period of time, all regular and special educators receive in-service education aimed at upgrading their teaching skills. Also, it is possible under certain conditions to use P.L. 94–142 funds to pay for such in-service efforts.

While most special educators see the in-service education demands of P.L. 94–142 as a tremendous opportunity, there is also concern over the fact that very little is known about how to mount high-quality, large-scale in-service education programs. Many special educators are convinced that short-term workshops offered to large numbers of teachers result in very little change in actual classroom teaching behavior. On the other hand, models of in-service education which involve on-going contact with teachers in their own classrooms are very time-consuming and expensive to implement. Many teacher educators, both in universities and in the public schools, are hoping that a forced choice does not develop, with one choice being to meet the demands of the law for universal in-service education, and the other choice being quality in-service efforts at a more deliberate pace. It is hoped that such a dilemma need never be faced.

One point that should be made concerns formats for in-service education. Most often, in-service education is seen as gathering a group of educators in a central place for a "workshop" or similar learning experience. However, this limited view of in-service education ignores the fact that learning can be a continuous process, and can occur anywhere. For example, the "teacher consultation" approach to special education services described in chapter 4 is a perfect example of ongoing in-service education coordinated by members of the school staff, and occurring in teachers' own classrooms. Shaw and Shaw (1972) have described an "in-service experience plan" for teachers, focused on specific problems in the classroom which are the subject of teacher referrals. In-service education need not take place in a special room at a special time; it can be a part of the basic support services offered to teachers in helping them cope with day-to-day problems in the classroom.

Special Education for Regular Educators

One of the fastest growing areas of special education is preparation of "regular educators" to deal with problems of academic learning and social behavior in the regular classroom. The previous section discussed this process from an in-service education point of view. The present section will describe efforts to provide such training for teachers-in-preparation in university training programs in elementary, secondary, and vocational-technical education.

Since the inception of the "mainstreaming" movement described earlier in the book, a constant concern of both special and regular educators has been the readiness of mainstream teachers to deal successfully with special education-related problems. As a mechanism for encouraging colleges and universities to infuse special education training into standard teacher education curricula, the Bureau of Education for the Handicapped has established and funded "Deans' Grants." The "Deans' Grants" are so-called because in the early stages of the program, BEH required that the project director be the dean of the college of education which received the grant. This was done to help assure that the project was a total college effort, not a "pet project" of a few people in the college. Eventually, the requirement that deans direct all "Deans' Grant" projects was relaxed, although college-level coordination is still a prerequisite for receiving funds.

The purpose of a Deans' Grant is to fundamentally alter teacher education curricula so that teachers are prepared to deal with a broader range of problems within the regular classroom. In some cases, new courses are added to the curriculum, while in other cases existing courses undergo substantial modification. Many colleges and universities have accomplished such curriculum revision without the aid of a Deans' Grant, and with or without federal funding, such projects have met with mixed success. Perhaps the most positive outcome of Deans' Grant activities in general is that college faculty from different fields are talking together concerning problems of special education. In many cases, special educators have learned as much about regular education as regular educators have learned about special education. In summary, the emphasis on special education training for regular educators, as embodied in Deans' Grants and other similar activities, has contributed to increased interaction among college faculty from various fields, a situation which can only be seen as positive.

One final trend must be mentioned. Some states are beginning to adopt legislation requiring that regular educators must have one or more courses in special education before a teaching certificate will be issued or renewed. While the intent behind such laws is admirable, a word of caution is in order. Mandates tied to teacher certification are binding, and the needs created by such mandates are pressing. Sometimes, the needs are so pressing that quality is sacrificed in the rush to meet the mandate. This author was told of one state that passed such a legislative requirement, in which 5,000 teachers were gathered in a large auditorium and given a survey course in special education. While the state mandate for regular educators to receive special education training was met, it is hard to believe that the process met the intent of the original legislation. We must be concerned that the goals we set for ourselves are both challenging and achievable, and that quality is not sacrificed in the rush to accomplish quickly things that should be done thoroughly.

CONCLUSION

Teacher education is one of the most exciting areas of special education. Every reader of this book will be directly affected by one or more of the trends discussed in the last few pages. It is hoped that as educators we will always be inquisitive, searching, and open to new ideas. No one has a single answer to the problems facing education in general, and special education specifically. As long as we continue to search for alternatives to maximize the value of our students' school experiences, we're making progress and performing our professional duties. Complacency has no place in the lives of educators. An astute observer of life once said, "Life is not the goal, it's the trip." It is my hope that this book has contributed to the reader's fascination with the profession of education in general, and special education in particular. It is fitting that the last section of the book covers teacher education, since it serves to fix our focus on the ever-changing nature of our knowledge base and professional responsibilities. The trip is well worth it, and we might just accomplish some goals along the way.

REFERENCES

Altman, R., and Meyen, E. L. Some observations on competency based instruction. *Exceptional Children*, 1974, *40*, 260–265.

Berdine, W. H., and Kelly, D. Certification programs in trainable mentally handicapped. *Exceptional Children*, 1977, *43*, 455–457.

Bernstein, C. D., Hartman, W. T., and Marshall, R. S. Major policy issues in financing special education. *Journal of Educational Finance*, 1976, *1*, 299–317.

Blatt, B. On competencies and incompetencies, instruction and destruction, individualization and depersonalization: Reflections on the now-movement. *Behavioral Disorders*, 1976, *1*, 89–96.

Bullock, L. M., Dykes, M. K., and Kelly, T. J. Competency based teacher preparation in behavior disorders. *Exceptional Children*, 1974, *41*, 192–194.

Burke, P. J. Personnel preparation: Historical perspectives. *Exceptional Children*, 1976, *43*, 144–147.

Cegelka, P. T., and Tawney, J. W. Decreasing the discrepancy: A case study in teacher reeducation. *Exceptional Children*, 1975, *41*, 268–269.

Connor, F. P. The past is prologue: Teacher preparation in special education. *Exceptional Children*, 1976, *42*, 366–378.

Council for Exceptional Children. *Basic Commitments and Responsibilities to Exceptional Children and Policy Statement on Governmental Affairs.* Reston, VA: Council for Exceptional Children, 1972.

Council for Exceptional Children. *Guidelines for Personnel in the Education of Exceptional Children.* Reston, VA: Council for Exceptional Children, 1976.

Edgar, E., and Neel, R. S. Results of a competency based teacher training program. *Exceptional Children,* 1976, *43,* 33–35.

Elam, S. *Performance-Based Teacher Education.* Washington, DC: American Association of Colleges for Teacher Education, 1971.

Hanninen, K. A., Coleman, T. W., and Parres, R. M. Anatomy of change: Curriculum revision in special education teacher training. *Exceptional Children,* 1977, *43,* 311–312.

Houston, W. R. (ed.) *Exploring Competency-Based Education.* Berkeley: McCutchan Publishing Corp., 1974.

Irvine, P. Should the schools teach the teachers or train the trainers? *Journal of Special Education,* 1974, *8,* 39–41.

Lilly, M. S. Competency-based teacher education: A personal perspective. *Behavioral Disorders,* 1976, *1,* 105–111.

Marinelli, J. Critical issues in the financing of education for the handicapped. *Journal of Educational Finance,* 1975, *1,* 246–269.

Reger, R. How can we influence teacher-training programs? *Journal of Special Education,* 1974, *8,* 7–13.

Rossmiller, R. A. Resource configurations and costs in educational programs for exceptional children. In R. L. Johns, K. Alexander, and K. R. Jordan (ed.), *Planning to Finance Education.* Gainesville, FL: National Education Finance Project, 1971.

Schwartz, L., and Oseroff, A. *The Clinical Teacher for Special Education— Final Report.* Washington, DC: U. S. Office of Education, 1975.

Semmel, M. I., and Semmel, D. S. Competency-based teacher education: An overview. *Behavioral Disorders,* 1976, *1,* 69–82.

Shaw, S. F. and Shaw, W. K. The in-service experience plan, or changing the bath without losing the baby. *Journal of Special Education,* 1972, *6,* 121–126.

Thomas, M. A. Finance: Without which there is no special education. *Exceptional Children,* 1973, *39,* 475–480.

Wallin, J. E. W. *The Mental Health of the School Child.* New Haven, CT: Yale University Press, 1914.

Weintraub, F., Abeson, A. R. and Braddock, D. L. *State Law and Education of Handicapped Children: Issues and Recommendations.* Reston, VA: Council for Exceptional Children, 1975.

Wiegerink, R. An organizational model for preparing future special educators. *Journal of Special Education,* 1973, *7,* 205–216.

NAME INDEX

SUBJECT INDEX